America and the Germans

America
and the Germans

AN ASSESSMENT OF
A THREE-HUNDRED-YEAR HISTORY

Frank Trommler
and Joseph McVeigh, EDITORS

VOLUME ONE

Immigration, Language, Ethnicity

upp

University of Pennsylvania Press
PHILADELPHIA

Copyright © 1985 by the University of Pennsylvania Press
First paperback printing 1990
All rights reserved

Library of Congress Cataloging in Publication Data

Main entry under title:

America and the Germans.

  Rev. versions of papers presented at the Tricentennial
Conference of German-American History, Politics,
and Culture, held at the University of Pennsylvania,
Philadelphia, Oct. 3–6, 1983.
  Includes indexes.
  Contents: v. 1. Immigration, language, ethnicity—
v. 2. The relationship in the twentieth century.
    1. German Americans—History—Congresses.
2. United States—Foreign relations—Germany—Congresses.
3. Germany—Foreign relations—United States—Congresses.
I. Trommler, Frank, 1939–   II. McVeigh, Joseph.
III. Tricentennial of German-American History, Politics,
and Culture (1983 : University of Pennsylvania,
Philadelphia)
E184.G3A39   1985   973'.0431   85-1063
ISBN 0-8122-1350-5 (v. 1)
ISBN 0-8122-1351-3 (v. 2)
ISBN 0-8122-1425-2 (set)

Printed in the United States of America

Contents

Preface

THE ESSAYS IN THIS BOOK, together with those in the second volume, *The Relationship in the Twentieth Century*, are the revised versions of papers delivered at the Tricentennial Conference of German-American History, Politics and Culture at the University of Pennsylvania, Philadelphia, on October 3–6, 1983. The conference, part of the German-American Tricentennial celebrations in Philadelphia, was made possible through generous grants from institutions in the United States and the Federal Republic of Germany. The contributions of the William Penn Foundation, Philadelphia, the Fritz Thyssen Stiftung, Cologne, the United States Information Agency, Washington, D.C., the German Marshall Fund of the United States, Washington, D.C., and the Ford Foundation, New York, are gratefully acknowledged. The editors would like to express their special appreciation to the Max Kade Foundation, New York, the William Penn Foundation, Philadelphia, and the American Association of Teachers of German for making this publication possible.

Many friends and colleagues helped in preparing the conference and provided valuable advice concerning its composition and program. We would particularly like to thank Erich Angermann, James Bergquist, Thomas Childers, Ernst-Otto Czempiel, Horst Daemmrich, Peter Demetz, Reinhard Doerries, Richard Dunn, Hans Gatzke, Ira Glazier, Wolfram Hanrieder, Theodore Hershberg, Walter Hinderer, Peter Uwe Hohendahl, Carl-Ludwig Holtfrerich, Martin Jay, John Jentz, Walter Kamphoefner, Hartmut Keil, Anna Kuhn, Bruce Kuklick, Vernon Lidtke, Albert Lloyd, John McCarthy, Günter Moltmann, William Parsons, Eric Rentschler, George Romoser, Scott Swank, Hans Trefousse, Hermann Wellenreuther, and Don Yoder.

Introduction

IN 1883, at the Bicentennial of the founding of Germantown as the first German settlement in North America, the German community rode a wave of pro-German sentiment which no one would have believed a few decades earlier and no one wanted to believe a few decades later. Neither in 1917 nor in 1945, when the stock of everything German had sunk to its lowest point ever in American history, could the possibility have seemed more remote that the Tricentennial of German-American immigration in 1983 would become a significant and even lively affair, highlighted by a state dinner of the American and German presidents in the White House. The United States Senate officially recognized the event by designating the year 1983 as the Tricentennial Anniversary Year of German Settlement in America and, in a joint resolution, celebrated "the immeasurable human, economic, political, social, and cultural contributions to this country by millions of German immigrants over the last three centuries."

Historians have talked about the invention of ethnic groups as social and cultural entities in the nineteenth century. The term *invention* is appropriate here because it indicates the intentions of a group to win acceptance in American society as a particular entity, even though the existence of this entity does not extend much beyond celebratory speeches at anniversary banquets. This might well have been the case with the German-Americans in 1883. The heritage of those celebrations is the misguided notion that has pervaded many homespun histories of the German-Americans: that this ethnic group, obviously the largest besides the British contingent, was once a unified group with considerable self-confidence and a strong commitment to the German language. This was, in fact, never the case. This group shares with the German-speaking areas of Europe divisiveness, regionalism, and dissension, as well as the tendency to overburden the concepts of unity and community with a variety of airy redeeming qualities.

It is this vague but influential connection with a country more than three thousand miles away that makes the Bicentennial of 1883 still interesting in 1983. Without the unification of Germany by Bismark in 1871, the invention of a notion of ethnic unity among German-Americans would not have become such an issue in American politics. And without this political notion of ethnic self-understanding the outcry of millions of Americans against their German-American compatriots in 1917 cannot be fully understood as an almost irrational reaction at a time when most Americans, as H. L. Mencken emphasized in his harsh critique of the German-Americans in *Die neue Rundschau* in 1928, were convinced of their basic decency and virtuousness as citizens. Although most of the specific issues have become history, the influence of developments in the homeland on the self-definition of this ethnic group had clearly left its mark on the Bicentennial of 1883.

In light of this tradition, which can easily be traced through the twentieth century, the considerable political dimension of the Tricentennial celebrations in 1983 hardly comes as a surprise. In the Senate resolution, the salute to the German-Americans is immediately followed by an equally strong celebration of the friendship of the United States and the Federal Republic of Germany, "based on the common values of democracy, guaranteed individual liberties, tolerance of personal differences, and opposition to totalitarianism." No anniversary of comparable significance in German-American history has ever had such a strong political component. Was it, then, as some observers said, just an ethnically veiled political demonstration of friendship at a time of grave concerns about the state of the Atlantic alliance? Or, from another perspective, did a newly awakened ethnic consciousness give way to diplomatic platitudes and tourist-sponsored symbolism?

The case is more complex than could be expressed in an either-or answer. There can be little doubt that the ethnic revival, which has been noted since the mid-1960s not only in America but all over the world, also gave the ethnic self-identification of numerous German-Americans a boost. Taking language as an indicator of ethnic loyalties, one can discern an impressive upswing of those who claim German as their mother tongue between 1960 and 1970. In this volume Joshua Fishman points to an increase of 93 percent, which, according to the census figures, puts the number of claimants of German tongue at 6,093,054 in 1970. Of course, as Fishman says, one swallow does not make a summer and one index does not make a revival. What his statistics confirm, however, is a substantial growth in ethnic consciousness in the last decades without which the considerable interest of

German-Americans in the Tricentennial would not have been possible. By the same token, the influence of the state of affairs in Germany on German-American ethnic consciousness cannot be denied. Fishman's statistics strongly prove this correspondence, and his optimistic prediction for the state of the German language in 2083, the year of the Quatricentennial, ascribe considerable weight to the political relationship.

The celebrations of 1983 seem to have been shaped by both factors, a renewed ethnic orientation which directs itself toward symbolic events as well as a strong interest of the American and the West German governments in shaping these symbolic events according to their concerns. Although the American government made no attempt to conceal its desire to counter the mounting criticism of its nuclear policy in West Germany, the government of the Federal Republic tried to build goodwill in the United States at a time of obvious conflicts of interest in the political and economic spheres. These moves received critical attention in the national press of both countries. They became the focus of political demonstrations in Philadelphia and other American cities and—during Vice-President George Bush's official visit—also in Krefeld, the German city which, as the home of the first immigrant families, received much attention in celebrating the anniversary of their departure in June of 1683.

The ethnic character of thousands of commemorative events from New England to the Midwest and from Texas to California cannot be overlooked. It expressed itself in an explicitly local and regional orientation, thus reconfirming that it is hard to locate the German-Americans beyond politics, statistics, and symbolism. Those who celebrated did so as Pennsylvania Germans and Maryland Germans, Texas Germans and Wisconsin Germans, Ohio Germans and Missouri Germans, and within other regional groups to whom many immigrants from other German-speaking areas in Europe have to be added, for instance the Danube Swabians and Volga Germans. The landing of the *Concord* on October 6, 1683, with the first thirteen families from Krefeld provided the common historical reference, but the focus concentrated on local traditions. So strong are these traditions that the showing of the much acclaimed exhibition, "The Pennsylvania Germans: A Celebration of Their Arts, 1683–1850," in Houston raised eyebrows among Texas Germans who questioned the appropriateness of such a venture in their midst—and nevertheless attended in droves. The exhibition, a joint venture of the Philadelphia Art Museum and the Winterthur Museum, opened the celebrations in Philadelphia in the fall of 1982 and traveled to Houston, San Francisco, and Chicago in 1983.

Needless to say, the common starting point of German-American history, the founding of Germantown under the guidance of Francis Daniel Pastorius, was again, as in 1883, an "invented" date for all groups outside of Pennsylvania. In 1983 the visual representation of the anniversary focused even more on the origins of German immigration to America, which the Anglo-Americans had so successfully developed with respect to their own American origins in the late nineteenth century. As a derivation from an answer to the story of the *Mayflower*, the German-American heritage was promoted with the image of a ship, the *Concord*, crossing the Atlantic, which appeared on bumperstickers, stamps, and posters. After the American Bicentennial in 1976 had stimulated the search for a unifying symbolic concept and provided a German publishing house with a head start for its design, the battle for an official symbol was fought with much official station-

Parade badges from the German-American Bicentennial celebration of 1883. The badge on the left shows the insignia of Germantown, incorporated into the City of Philadelphia in the nineteenth century. The founding of Germantown in 1683 was celebrated as the starting point of the German presence in America. October 6 was designated "German Day" and was commemorated in many American cities with speeches and parades as the landing date of the first settlers from Krefeld. (Roughwood Collection)

1683 ～ 1983

Insignias of the German-American Tricentennial of 1983. The story of the *Mayflower* and the first English immigrants to America provided a model for a similar tale of "German Pilgrims" from Krefeld and their ship, the *Concord*, which soon became an important part of German-American ethnic identity. (Tricentennial Committee; Heinz Moos Verlag, Munich)

ery, several unsuccessful diplomatic interventions, and thousands of letters to Washington from German-Americans. It was not until a last-minute surprise move that this battle for a square inch of American public attention was decided, and the Tricentennial became official in the form of a twenty-cent commemorative stamp. Designed by a German-American, it depicts the *Concord* and was issued along with other stamps honoring the accomplishments of famous German-Americans: John Augustus Roebling's Brooklyn Bridge, the nineteenth-century politician Carl Schurz, and the legendary baseball player Babe Ruth. In addition, the Presidential Commission for the German-American Tricentennial, looking for suitable expressions of current American-German friendship, came up with the idea of a friendship garden lo-

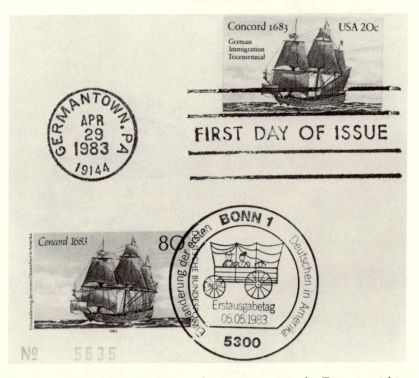

American and German stamps issued to commemorate the Tricentennial in 1983 had similar designs in order to highlight the common history of Germans and Americans celebrated on this occasion. These stamps were officially unveiled at ceremonies in Germantown and Bonn.

cated between the White House and the Jefferson Monument, "one of America's most treasured sites." As the official brochure reads: "Its prominent location in Washington may inspire communities in both countries to create similar friendship gardens to be enjoyed by citizens and visitors alike." Like a picture from a nineteenth-century family album, it carries an idyllic symbolic message: a garden needs constant maintenance or it will go to waste.

On a less symbolic and more critical level, the Tricentennial Conference of German-American History, Politics and Culture offered a forum for the analysis of the ethnic and political aspects of this relationship as part of the commemoration. As numerous academic events all over the United States illuminated various components of the Tricentennial, this conference at the University of Pennsylvania in Philadelphia on October 3–6, 1983, focused particularly on the interplay of

The American Postal Service honored the accomplishments of German-Americans with a number of special issues in 1983: John Augustus Roebling's Brooklyn Bridge, the legendary baseball star Babe Ruth, and the statesman Carl Schurz. The 500th anniversary of Martin Luther's birth in 1983 provided an additional reminder of the significance of America's German heritage.

the history of the Germans in America and American-German relations. It would probably be too much to say that the eighty speakers, commentators, and chairpersons of the seventeen panels arrived at a new understanding of this complex relationship. But there has rarely been a symposium with more renowned American, German, and Swiss scholars from such different disciplines as political science, literature, ethnic and immigration history, *Amerikanistik*, linguistics, film, history, and anthropology joining forces in a critical assessment of German-American affairs. Panel discussions dealt with the state of the German language in America, the contemporary German film and its reception in the United States, and the impact of three hundred years of German-American history on present-day politics. On October 6 the conference concluded with an address by the president of the Federal Republic of Germany, Karl Carstens. In cooperation with the Tricentennial Conference, the Henry Francis du Pont Winterthur Museum in Delaware held a parallel conference on German-American Art and Culture on October 3 and 4, 1983, which featured the visual arts and material culture of German-Americans from 1750 to 1900, focusing on folk, popular, and cosmopolitan culture.

The Tricentennial Conference was intended to open doors between the disciplines and to carry the interest of scholars and nonscholars in German-American affairs beyond the confines of traditional ethnic understanding, thus encouraging new ventures in the field. Although the high attendance and the lively participation of the audience during the four days could be cited as a sign of widespread interest, the proof lies in the scholarly contributions. The speakers adhered to the suggestion of formulating concise and critical assessments of important areas, to expand on their current research, and to facilitate an informed discussion. The editors certainly regret that limitations on the size of these two volumes do not allow for the inclusion of the videotaped discussions of the conference. The only liberty they have taken besides a certain amount of editorial coordination is to encourage the authors to retain the quality of spoken language as much as possible in the revised version. Each paper was inspired and limited by its nature as a critical assessment at the Tricentennial in 1983. Several important areas, especially religion, the press, and the military, are missing from the program; their inclusion in special panels would have made the conference unmanageable.

The essays in this volume are grouped in general chapters. After pointing to Joshua Fishman's sanguine views concerning the current state of the German language in America, other perspectives might be of special interest. Jürgen Eichhoff and Marion Huffines state the case less optimistically. Nonetheless, as John McCarthy notes in his summary of the lively panel discussion among college and high school teachers, much work is currently being done to break out of the language ghetto in the educational sphere. The problems are formidable, but there are ways to improve the situation, as the seven points suggested in John McCarthy's paper would indicate.

The traditional identification of the German language with ethnicity by many German-Americans has both helped and hindered its revival. Several speakers admirably demonstrate the new ways in which ethnic studies have to be pursued in order to avoid what could be called the contributionists' fallacy. Kathleen Conzen and Willi Paul Adams give first insights into their current project on "man-made" German ethnicity in the nineteenth century; Hartmut Keil, speaking for the Chicago Projekt on the social history of German workers in Chicago between 1850 and 1914, shows, as Carol Poore does in regard to the Centennial celebration in 1876, the "other" ethnicity of social protest within the German groups. Again, little remains of the "unity" theme that accompanied the German-American Bicentennial. Hans Trefousse, biographer of Carl Schurz, disproves the view that the new German Reich drew only positive comments from German-Americans. Frederick Luebke widens the perspective toward a comparison with the ethnic politics of the Germans in Brazil.

Much work still needs to be done in the realm of German-American literature, as several speakers point out. Harold Jantz and Christoph Schweitzer assess the situation from a personal point of view, and Patricia Herminghouse adds the perspective of social history and gives initial insights into literary forms that have long been neglected by scholars, although once popular among readers: the serial novel as the most successful example of mass literature in the nineteenth century. Analyzing novels of such women authors as Therese Robinson, Mathilde Anneke, and Fernande Richter, Martha K. Wallach provides another look at the literary and social history of the nineteenth century, and Maria Wagner examines the journalistic reporting on American political developments from 1830 to 1865 in German newspapers. Although the study of German-American literature is being enlivened by the new interest in social and political history, few attempts have been made so far to draw on the new scholarship concerning ethnicity and ethnic history. The topic also calls for comparative studies in the context of other minority literatures in America as well as other German minority literatures in different countries. Alexander Ritter, a scholar of minority literature in the German language, offers some general perspectives for the study of present-day German-American literature.

By comparison, the field of immigration studies is well established thanks to recent endeavors such as the Hamburg Projekt on German immigration, directed by Günter Moltmann. New research is providing a comprehensive view of the developments since the *Concord* crossed the Atlantic in 1683. Although limited space allows only a condensed version of recent studies, it is interesting to observe that some of the immigration patterns which for so long had been attributed to the nineteenth century already existed in the eighteenth century. Marianne Wokeck presents considerable material on the eighteenth century. Günter Moltmann and Agnes Bretting summarize their extensive research on the organization and flow of German migration to North America in the nineteenth century.

Central to a conference at an institution that carries the name University of Pennsylvania and was founded by Benjamin Franklin in 1740 is, of course, the history of the Pennsylvania Germans. Although a great body of scholarship already exists in this area, the 1983 celebration inspired new ventures, as the contributions of Don Yoder, Stephanie Wolf, Hermann Wellenreuther, John Hostetler, and Leo Schelbert document in an impressive manner. The anniversary also resurrected the old controversy concerning the nationality of the first settlers from Krefeld. The *New York Times* focused on the contrary perceptions of Stephanie Wolf and Don Yoder as to whether the first families were German or Dutch or half-German or half-Dutch, but both scholars made it clear at the conference that this question does not occupy the center of current discussions. Don Yoder, himself a Pennsylvania German, gives a particularly informed and moving assessment of the history of this ethnic group. His contribution is more than a scholarly piece by a historian. It is also ethnic politics, a fascinating plea for a new look at the present state of ethnicity, thus bridging the gap between the past and the present.

The two poles of historical and contemporary issues between which the conference attempted to build new bridges are clearly marked by the division of the conference papers into two volumes. The study of the German heritage in America—to which this volume is devoted—and the discussion of American-German relations in the twentieth century—which fills the second volume—have long been viewed as distinctly separate areas of interest which attract different clienteles. It is hoped that the recognition of their interrelationship was not just a passing phenomenon of the anniversary of 1983 but continues to be seen and explored more closely. In this connection, the much discussed keynote address by Steven Muller, President of the Johns Hopkins University, is exemplary in its comprehensive approach to the topic "America and the Germans." Steven Muller, German-born and American-trained, an excellent intermediator between America and Germany, not only gives a convincing introduction to a fascinating and troublesome relationship, but, more importantly, sets the tone for the critical assessment of German-American history, politics, and culture presented in both volumes of this work.

Frank Trommler and Joseph McVeigh

After Three Hundred Years:
A Keynote Address in 1983

STEVEN MULLER

MR. CHAIRMAN, distinguished colleagues, ladies and gentlemen:

With deep appreciation and humility, I recognize that I was selected to make these opening remarks primarily because I happen so conveniently to symbolize part of what this occasion is about. It is my good fortune to serve as president of Johns Hopkins, whose founding was so intimately rooted in German origin; and I am also one of those many Americans born in Germany whose United States citizenship is based on naturalization. Let me try, therefore, to respect this symbolism with some comments about the German influence on American higher education. A keynote address should not trespass on the learned papers we are about to hear. But the German influence on the modern American university does not appear specifically on the program and may be worthy of mention before this conference of scholars.

Only two countries contributed fundamentally to the development of higher education in America: Great Britain and Germany. The British legacy of course came first. In the American colonies of England, colleges were very soon founded that were patterned on what then existed in Great Britain. Harvard College was founded in the Massachusetts Bay Colony as early as 1636, and the College of William and Mary in Virginia in 1693. By the time of the American Revolution, numerous such colleges had been founded, and many others were established as American settlement spread westward across the continent. These colleges were sometimes called universities, but they were far from that in the modern sense.

They were designed for the higher education of young men of

privilege, to prepare them primarily for two professions, the ministry and the law. Physicians at first learned their profession in proprietary schools run by established doctors, and teachers were ministers, sometimes lawyers, or not trained at the college level. These were liberal arts colleges that taught a rigid, narrow curriculum over four years. Almost all of them operated under the auspices of a particular religious denomination. They differed from British experience in that in the United States there were so many different denominations, that their funding therefore came from religious communities and wealthy individuals to a far greater extent than from public funds, and that no community of such colleges ever came together to form the type of British university represented by Oxford or Cambridge.

By the early nineteenth century there was increasing dissatisfaction with the American colleges. It was charged that their learning was dull, restrictive, and of low quality. Their tradition ran counter to spreading democracy and to the loosening of religious orthodoxies. Above all, they produced no practical education in a new nation that had begun a mighty process of industrial development. The following comments from Henry P. Tappan, later president of the University of Michigan, summarize the dissatisfaction with the collegiate system of American higher education by 1851 :

The Colleges of America are plainly copied from the Colleges of the English Universities. The course of studies, the President and Tutors, the number of years occupied by the course, are all copied from the English model. We have seen that in the English Institutions, the name of University alone remained, while the collegial or tutorial system absorbed all the educational functions. In America, while Colleges were professedly established, they soon assumed a mixed character. Professors were appointed, but they discharged only the duty of tutors in the higher grades of study; so that the tutors were really assistant professors or the professors only tutors of the first rank. Our Colleges also have from the beginning conferred degrees in all the faculties, which in England belongs only to the University. . . .

We inspire no general desire for high education, and fail to collect students, because we promise and do not perform. Hence we fall into disrepute, and young men of ability contrive to prepare themselves for active life without our aid. In connection with this the commercial spirit of our country and the many avenues to wealth which are opened before enterprise create a distaste for study deeply inimical to education. The manufacturer, the merchant, the gold-digger, will not pause in their career to gain intellectual accomplishments. While gaining knowledge, they are losing the opportunities to gain money. The political condition of our country, too, is such, that a high education and a high order of talent do not generally form the sure guarantees of success. The tact of the demagogue triumphs over the accomplishments of the scholar and the man of genius.

Put these causes together, and the phenomena we witness and lament are explained. Our colleges are complacently neglected when they neither afford the satisfaction and distinction of a thorough and lofty education, and yield no advantages in gaining wealth and political eminence.[1]

A new start was needed, and for this purpose American eyes turned to the German university. This did not happen primarily because there was reluctance to turn back once more to Britain, nor merely because there was general respect for the state of German learning. It occurred primarily because of the extraordinary reforms in the German universities that Wilhelm von Humboldt had achieved, beginning with the foundation of the University of Berlin in 1809, and rapidly thereafter throughout the German universities. The key to Humboldt's reforms was the famous statement that the principles which ought to permeate and dominate establishments of true scholarship were "solitude and freedom." By solitude, Humboldt meant the protection of the scholar from the pressure of practical needs and demands, permitting a total individual commitment to scholarly investigation without regard to utilitarian factors. By freedom, Humboldt did not mean the autonomy of universities, but freedom of teaching and freedom of learning: a professor should be free to teach what he wanted to teach, and a student should be free to attend whatever lectures interested him. These ideals put into practice meant a university committed to research, and research for its own sake, carried on by professors free to investigate as they chose, and by students free to study what and with whom they chose. This was the ideal of the new university which Wilhelm von Humboldt founded in Berlin.

It is not proper here to attempt a history of the development of the German university in the nineteenth century, but two practical effects of the spread of Humboldt's ideas must be mentioned. The first was the elevation of the faculty of philosophy—which earlier had prepared students for work in the three higher professional faculties of theology, medicine, and law—to the same level as the other three. This raising of the status of the philosophical faculty had the crucial effect that the various disciplines gathered together in this faculty were at last free to develop along their own lines. The second was the added impetus which the commitment to research gave to the seminar system of instruction. The seminar meant not only a limited research project undertaken by a small, carefully selected group of students under the direction of a professor, but also a separate room or a number of separate rooms where the meetings are held and in which special libraries and other teaching resources are placed.

What American eyes found most appealing of all in the German university in mid-nineteenth century was the leading position which Germany had achieved in the natural sciences. Here there is irony. Wilhelm von Humboldt himself had been antagonistic to the pursuit of knowledge for practical purposes or utilitarian reasons, but in the German universities reformed by his ideas the natural sciences, so closely linked to industrialization, gained prominence. This was largely because of the encouragement and financial support given to the development of the natural sciences by the Prussian and other German governments and also because the basic idea of the Humboldtian university—the stress on pure research and the seminar system—ideally fitted the interests of the natural scientists. And it was Wilhelm's brother, Alexander von Humboldt, who used his own great influence in the Prussian court to promote the development of the natural sciences within the reformed philosophical faculties of the universities.

Shortly after the 1850s Americans saw in the contemporary German research university with its vigorous work in the natural sciences the inspiration for the reform of American higher education. It was not Humboldt's humanism per se that inspired Americans. It was that the university model that had evolved from his ideas was able to offer disciplined training for practical, utilitarian tasks and was free of the domination of religious orthodoxy. Few Americans were troubled by, if indeed they were even aware of, the fact that Humboldt would have despised their concern for education in the mechanical, industrial, and commercial arts and sciences and that he would probably have failed to understand the restraints that religious orthodoxy had placed on the early American colleges. For a quick appreciation of how the German university looked to American eyes in 1851 we may again turn to Tappan, for a summary of what many other leading American educators saw and thought:

We have spoken of the German Universities as model institutions. Their excellence consists in two things: first, they are purely Universities, without any admixture of collegial tuition. Secondly, they are complete as Universities, providing libraries and all other material of learning, and having professors of eminence to lecture on theology, law, and medicine, the philosophical, mathematical, natural, philological, and political Sciences, on history and geography, on the history and principles of Art, *in fine*, upon every branch of human knowledge. The professors are so numerous that a proper division of labor takes place, and every subject is thoroughly discussed. At the University every student selects the courses he is to attend. He is thrown upon his own responsibility and diligence. He is left free to pursue his studies; but, if he wishes to become a clergyman, a physician, a lawyer, a statesman, a professor, or a teacher in any superior school, he must go through the most rigid examinations, both oral and written.

Collegial tuition in the German Universities does not exist, because wholly unnecessary, the student being fully prepared at the Gymnasium before he is permitted to enter the University. Without the Gymnasium, the University would be worth little.[2]

Thus in the period after the American Civil War the idea of the research university and the prominence of the natural sciences was introduced from Germany into American higher education. The impact was widespread. From the first decade of the nineteenth century Americans had begun to study at German universities. An astonishing total of more than ten thousand Americans attended German universities during the century. Leading American educational reformers traveled to Germany for inspiration. In 1868, Cornell University was founded to provide a nonsectarian and practical education, with emphasis on the mechanical and agricultural arts. The first president was Andrew D. White, who had matriculated at the University of Berlin in 1855, had served at Michigan with Tappan, and drew heavily on his German experience in building Cornell. Charles William Eliot, who in his forty years as president beginning in 1869 remade Harvard into a university, spent most of 1863 at Marburg and drew from there most of his ideas for the reform of Harvard.

The importation of German university ideas often met resistance, particularly when religious orthodoxy was offended. At Amherst in 1877 a German-trained professor of biology was removed for teaching biology as a science and not "as an absolutely dependent product of an absolutely independent spiritual creator."[3] There were public protests in several places against "Germanism," which led to the establishment of German-style beer parlors on the edge of campus. Tappan, whom I quoted earlier, made a vigorous effort as President of Michigan to reform that university along German lines but was ousted by the faculty after a decade largely because of his "Germanic pretensions," which included the "intemperate" habit of drinking wine with meals.

The single most direct, dramatic, and far-reaching translation of the German university idea to the United States occurred in 1876 with the opening of The Johns Hopkins University in Baltimore. The founding president was Daniel Coit Gilman, who had studied at Berlin in

1854 and 1855. Gilman returned to Germany in 1875 in preparation for the founding of the new university and visited a number of German universities, most notably Strassburg, Freiburg, Göttingen, and Berlin. The Johns Hopkins University under Gilman was the first new American university explicitly founded as an institution committed to advanced study and research along German lines. Many of the early faculty at Johns Hopkins had been students at German universities, including Ira Remsen, the first professor of chemistry and second president of the university, who studied at Munich, took his doctorate at Göttingen in 1870, and taught at Tübingen; William E. Story, professor of mathematics, who took his doctorate at Leipzig in 1875; Basil L. Gildersleeve, the first professor of classics, who studied at Berlin and Bonn and took his doctorate at Göttingen in 1853; and Henry A. Rowland, the first professor of physics, who studied in Berlin. The Johns Hopkins University was nicknamed "Göttingen in Baltimore" and was the first American university to offer systematic study for the doctorate degree in various disciplines.

Despite its nickname, however, The Johns Hopkins University was not a German university. Gilman had stated, "We did not undertake to establish a German university, nor an English university, but an American university, based upon and applied to the existing institutions of this country."[4] In the simplest terms, what happened in American higher education was that the collegiate sector remained but that there was superimposed upon it research-oriented instruction at the graduate and professional levels, which is postbaccalaureate in that it follows the college years, rather than replacing them. The collegiate pattern still shows evidence of its British roots, but university graduate and professional patterns owe most to the nineteenth-century German university as Americans saw it. The German experience was also used to liberate the American university from religious influence, ever since Cornell, Johns Hopkins, Chicago, and the great state-owned universities were explicitly established as nonsectarian institutions.

With this look backward at the German influence on the evolution of the American university, let us now return to the present and look ahead. As a personal symbol of recent German emigration to the United States, let me say that my complete Americanization and my absolute commitment to the United States do not prevent me from maintaining a special and continuing interest in German affairs. Natural as that may be, such an interest in the German present and future is largely shared by most Americans who recognize the pivotal position occupied by German-speaking peoples in the heart of Europe. This conference thus seems to me to be of double importance because its focus is wide enough to include German-American relationships not only as they were in the past but as they are today and will continue into the future. Three hundred years are an unfinished and ongoing story. And in my opinion the division of Europe that has existed since the 1940s is not permanently stable, and new questions are likely to arise in the future context of German-American relations.

The present division of Europe denies a lot of history and economic geography. Some of the legacy of a shared past and a common culture still spills across the boundaries between east and west, as does a considerably larger flow of commerce. But although history and the configurations of nature are not negligible forces, they are probably less powerful today than they might have been in the past. Modern technology—in economics, transportation, communications, and the employment of synthetic substances—makes the shape of nature less relevant. And the unprecedented fear of nuclear annihilation may be more than sufficient to choke off any emotion based merely on the historical past. The fact that the division of Europe is ahistorical and unnatural may therefore be a bit awkward, but alone it probably poses no serious threat to the status quo.

It is of greater concern that the stability of the status quo depends so much on everyone's ability to look only backward, never forward. Whenever we in the West are troubled in our resolve to preserve the status quo we appeal to the past. Our leaders invoke on our behalf the names of Marshall, Churchill, Truman, or Adenauer and recall the resolve in the founding of NATO or the Berlin airlift. It is, of course, natural that immobility is hard to bear. To go forward is too risky. To go backward is not possible either, but there is psychological relief in going back in spirit to where it all started and then marching forward mentally to where we already are. This may work less well with repetition. And it may become more awkward to accomplish when it involves a future generation, which is asked to rally around a past it did not experience and therefore cannot remember. It is not surprising that those most committed to the status quo are deeply worried about the successor generation, to whom the constant need to look backward may be less appealing and satisfying. Young people have a natural tendency to look forward and even to seek change. It is therefore a bit frustrating for them and for their elders to have to insist that things must stay the same and to compel them to fix their vision as firmly as possible on the past.

When one is wholly committed to the status quo, the past is not only prologue but epilogue as well. That tends to make the present somewhat stale. Thus if one can look forward only to a lifetime of fearful deadlock across the middle of Europe, one may have to be content to find mobility and change within the confines of one's nation-state. In the postwar days, when the status quo of the division of Europe came into being, nationalism had a bad name. Today this is much less true. I believe that the renaissance of nationalism in Europe is linked to the preservation of Europe's division. It is of deep concern to me that the preservation of the status quo so harshly inhibits any hopeful, changing vision of the future. That in itself is difficult to sustain—unstable, if you like—and ever more so for a new generation. But the revival of nationalism worries me even more.

Why should this be so, and am I even right about nationalism? One of the more popular slogans in the United States in the very recent past has been "Let Poland be Poland." Polish nationalism, at least, is still explicitly celebrated. Please do not misunderstand me; I do not fail to sympathize with the fate of the Polish people. But it is a fact that the status quo of the division of Europe rests on the division of Germany or, more properly said, the existence of two German states. Are the Poles alone in their nationalism? What about the British? The French? And how do you like the sound of "Let Germany be Germany"?

It may be bad taste to say that. But—alas—silence is not always golden. Truth can indeed be hard to face at times, but there may nevertheless be more virtue in confronting it than not. It is difficult to believe that, if nationalism really is once again popular and evident in so many other European states, Germans should remain indefinitely immune to it. To reach such a conclusion it is not necessary to make any reference to German nationalism in the past two centuries. Quite the reverse: the simpler assumption that Germans in many ways are apt to behave rather like their neighbors would argue that nationalism among their neighbors is likely to foster nationalism among Germans. But if that belief is true, then one must appraise the special problems attached to contemporary German nationalism.

Of course, there are two German states today, with social systems that are not only very different but indeed are vigorously opposed to each other. The most obvious assumption therefore would be that both may be nationalist in their own way and that this will pose no special problems for anyone else. But should one believe that this most obvious assumption is also the most likely? Several factors make such a belief at least questionable. It is already acknowledged that the relationship between the two German states is unique and in certain ways differs from relations between other states that share a common border. It is also beyond argument that the situation of Berlin is unique and unusual. Also, it seems to me that Germans in the Federal Republic—especially younger citizens—may not look back at the origins of the Western alliance in the same way as others do, when the appeal is made to reaffirm the founding of the status quo. After all, one should perhaps not wholly ignore the fact that for Germans the aftermath of World War II involved national defeat rather than victory. It appears that special efforts have been made in the German Federal Republic to deemphasize nationalism as much as possible. If that is true, it may be justifiable and even admirable, but it may have an unintended reverse effect. If an effort to repress nationalism induces frustration, frustrated nationalism may in the long run become even stronger than vigorous nationalism freely and openly expressed. That does seem to be precisely true in the case of Poland, which has claimed so much of our attention and sympathy recently.

I hope it is evident that I am making an effort to tread gently on tender ground. Even so, I reach an unavoidable conclusion: that the preservation of the status quo, of the division of Europe without much foreseeable prospect of change, poses special difficulties for Germans: that the revival of nationalism throughout Europe implies that these special difficulties are more likely to increase in the future rather than to lessen, and that the key position of Germans in Europe makes it likely that any added difficulties they experience will also pose additional difficulties for their neighbors. As gently as possible but firmly I would therefore argue that the existence of two German states remains as much a problem as it represents a solution and that this will be at least as much the situation in future years as it is today—perhaps even more so.

There is, then, reason to believe that American-German relations in days to come will retain intensity and deep mutual interest, while at the same time these relations may not necessarily be easy. That is in part why—while this conference is in progress—some associates and I will formally establish a new American Institute for Contemporary German Studies. No such national resource has until now existed in the United States. In founding such an institute, in Washington, D.C., and in affiliation with The Johns Hopkins University, we expect to create an institutional base for those particularly concerned with contemporary German affairs and with contemporary American-German relations—to conduct studies; present informational programs; promote improved mutual understanding and interrelationships; and assemble a current and complete library and other relevant materials. As the title of the institute proclaims, our concern will not be with the German language or the past but with the contemporary, and we hope to include within the contemporary not only scholarship in many fields but also journalism, statesmanship, and cultural achievement.

The same concern that leads to the creation of the American Institute for Contemporary German Studies lends special importance to this Tricentennial Conference of German-American History, Politics and Culture. As we shed light on three centuries of fateful German-American interaction, we shall see not only the past but also the present more clearly and be better prepared for the future.

Notes

1. Henry Tappan, *University Education* (New York: Arno Press, 1969), 45.
2. Ibid., 43.
3. Frederick Rudolph, *The American College and University: A History* (New York: Knopf, 1962), 247.
4. Daniel Coit Gilman, *The Launching of a University and Other Papers: A Sheaf of Remembrances* (New York: Dodd, Mead and Co., 1906), 49.

PART I:

Immigration

1.

German Immigration
to Colonial America:
Prototype of a Transatlantic
Mass Migration

MARIANNE WOKECK

IN 1981 WE OBSERVED the granting of the charter of Pennsylvania; last year we celebrated the arrival of William Penn in the Delaware Valley; and this year is the tercentenary of the landing of the first group of immigrants from Germany and the founding of Germantown. These three historical events that cause us to commemorate the rich heritage of our past were intricately connected and of the utmost importance for the relocation of about one hundred thousand German-speaking immigrants to the American colonies. The forces that shaped this first large-scale, voluntary influx of non-British aliens are the focus of this essay.[1]

William Penn was instrumental in creating conditions that helped set the transatlantic flow of Continental Protestants in motion. His influence was twofold: he launched a colony according to a plan that consciously included settlers drawn from outside the dominions of the English crown; and his personal connections and beliefs were crucial in attracting the first pathfinding and trend-setting group from Krefeld and one member of the Frankfort Company—Francis Daniel Pastorius.

Three characteristics of this early migration were especially important as they combined to generate further immigration from the Rhinelands, a gathering tide that crested in the middle of the eighteenth century. First, this vanguard of settlers and investors in Penn's colony came from a region along the Rhine in which many of the residents had only recently established their homes and among whom the tradition to migrate in response to political upheaval, economic instability, and religious persecution was strong. Second, the Germantown pioneers were people of dissenting religious convictions, which caused them to leave their intolerant hometowns, and yet they were also sufficiently independent economically to finance the move to the New World. Moreover, a variety of ties connecting coreligionists with their families, friends, and former neighbors was essential to lure more immigrants later, after trustworthy reports of religious toleration, a good, quiet government, and ample opportunity to make a decent living in the Delaware Valley had singled out Pennsylvania as the preferred overseas destination for Germans willing or pressed to leave their homelands.

The Germantown settlers had links with those sympathetic to their endeavor, including contacts with prominent Friends and Mennonites in Rotterdam and Amsterdam as well as their partners in London and Philadelphia. These points of mediation between settlers in Pennsylvania and Germans subjected to religious intolerance were of far-reaching consequence. In particular, the dual role of Benjamin Furly, Penn's Continental agent, as leader of the Rotterdam Quaker community and as an influential merchant with wide-ranging business interests and connections led to the emergence of Rotterdam as the principal port of embarkation for German immigrants to the American colonies. This commercial aspect of the pioneering migration from Germany resulted in the development of a transatlantic transportation system for emigrants as a regular business. What had begun as an occasional service mostly for coreligionists grew into a highly specialized trading activity conducted by a relatively small number of English merchants in Rotterdam whose interest in profit-making superseded considerations rooted in shared religious beliefs.

The three basic factors coming into play in the transatlantic move of the Germantown pioneers were also responsible for the dynamics that shaped the German migration to colonial Pennsylvania as a whole. Continental Protestants responded to a variety of oppressive conditions at home that made relocation seem desirable. Meanwhile, potential emigrants in Germany were alternately attracted or discouraged as news reached them of improving or worsening conditions in the Delaware Valley and elsewhere. But these forces of "push" and "pull" were separated by three thousand miles of dangerous ocean and by weeks of difficult and expensive travel to reach the seacoast in the first place. Thus the third essential force in determining how the migration first flowed and then ebbed, who came and when, and what expectations and resources they brought to the New World was the trade organized by merchants who found profit in the business of moving large numbers of people from Europe to America.

To understand better the complex relationship between the different factors that combined to initiate and maintain the German immigration to colonial Pennsylvania, it is useful to bear in mind the basic shape and characteristics of the immigrant flow. After the initial settlement of the Germantown pioneers in 1683, only occasionally did groups of German immigrants—often traveling together in families or congregations—land in Philadelphia before 1727.[2] From this point, with emigration from the Rhinelands to the colonies established, large numbers began to come regularly. Thereafter the German immigration continued to swell more or less gradually until an immense wave of migrants (about thirty-seven thousand) reached Philadelphia during the years 1749–54. In this rising stream of German newcomers the proportion of families at first continued to be high, but increasingly heads of households were younger and proportionally more single people landed on the Delaware. Though transatlantic relocation resumed in 1763 after the French and Indian War, the renewed flow of arrivals from Continental Europe was now but a retreating ebb (about twelve thousand) in the twelve years before the Revolution. Among those who undertook the voyage in the years 1763 to 1776, the proportion of single men was large, and many of the immigrants were poor. In the following discussion it is important to remember this characteristic pattern of rise, peak, and decline.

The "push factors" for emigration from Germany were many and intricately related. Recurrent agrarian crises and war, high taxes and oppressive regulations of all spheres of life affected particularly farmers, artisans, and laborers with limited resources in their efforts to make a "decent living"—conditions that had prompted many inhabitants of the Rhinelands (including the German-speaking cantons of Switzerland and Alsace-Lorraine) to move temporarily or permanently well before the migration to North America began from this part of Europe. Given political and economic instability, and religious intolerance throughout southwestern Germany, migration was familiar to many people in this region because they themselves had either relocated previously or knew others who had done so. Historians of other, later transatlantic migrations have found that the combination of a strong tradition to migrate with any one or more other push factors (ranging from the pursuit of personal happiness to principled political opposition) nearly always resulted in substantial levels of emigration.

Apparently, this was also the case in the eighteenth-century Rhine-lands. It is intriguing to note that the Swiss and Palatines, for example, speak proverbially and typically of *Wanderlust* as an ethnic character trait, thereby creating a positive concept when describing the motivation of people whom adverse circumstances offered little choice but to leave their homelands in search of a better livelihood elsewhere.[3]

In offering attractions to new settlers, the American colonies, and especially Pennsylvania, compared very well with other colonizing opportunities in Europe. As one Württemberger put it after he arrived in Philadelphia in 1754:

Those who do not know hunger and need cannot comprehend why thousands of people undertake the voyage. The complaints about the government are legion! Work is no longer of any help in making a living—in a situation like this people become truely desperate. . . . We are told that those who want to go to Prussia will get travel money and land as in America, but what is a free man compared to a slave or serf? How much fun can a man have in a country where he has to work himself to death for his lord and where his sons are never protected from the miseries of a soldier's life?

There are indeed great differences between America and Europe.[4]

In the eyes of many German emigrants, Pennsylvania seemed to be granted "special blessings."[5] The lasting attraction first of the Delaware region and, later, of the vastly expanding backcountry of the more southern colonies was composed of a variety of ingredients. The opportunities open to newcomers determined not only what immigrants were most likely to be attracted to a place but also their chances of being successfully integrated into a new life. When in the 1720s Germans first began to arrive in Pennsylvania in significant numbers, toleration for Protestants of different backgrounds and lifestyles generally existed, land could be obtained at relatively low cost, wages as well as prices for the products of one's work were considered high; but the cost of relocation had to be paid in cash, largely in advance. Given these circumstances, Pennsylvania particularly attracted settlers who arrived with some starting capital (mostly in the form of European goods brought over for resale) and could avoid the costs for labor by bringing family members and even servants along with them. These conditions early in the history of the migration also favored immigrants who could sell skills and labor profitably to acquire the means to purchase a farm or set up shop after a few years.

As such favorable opportunities became more widely known in

Germany, Pennsylvania lured relatives, friends, and neighbors of those already settled in the colony, who were often willing and able to help others make the transition. At a time when newspapers were just beginning to appear regularly in the largest cities and when postal service was practically unavailable to common men and women, networks of personal communication—letters delivered by trustworthy messengers or occasionally even visits by relatives or friends—were immensely important in conveying news about opportunities far away. Families and congregations therefore often sent one or several of their members as "scouts" before the majority of them made the hazardous move. Conversely, when former emigrants who had left independently gave word of their success—frequently after long years and initial struggle—or returned for a visit, they acted as a catalyst in persuading relatives and friends to follow their examples. After the attractive reputation of the Delaware Valley had been established, however, the rapidly accelerating rate of immigration could be sustained only through the initiative of enterprising merchants who provided transatlantic passage on credit, thereby expanding the pool of potential emigrants considerably, reaching even those who did not have substantial resources or relatives to help them move.[6] The role of the businessmen, who furthered emigration independently so they could profit from the transportation of migrants, distinguished the activities and interests of merchants with transatlantic shipping from those of private or government land developers in search of colonists. The combined effect of the persuasive recruiting of new settlers by former migrants, so-called newlanders, and credit extended by merchants to expand their profits produced the brief but massive inflow of Germans to the colonies in the late 1740s and early 1750s. (Even though the figure of thirty-seven thousand immigrants in six years may sound unimpressive to our twentieth-century ears, the influx of an average of six thousand newcomers each fall must have seemed extraordinary to the citizens of Philadelphia—a city of about seventeen thousand inhabitants, including Southwark and the Northern Liberties in 1756.)

The development of the German passenger trade reveals much about how the merchants tried to capitalize on the changing flow and composition of the migration. In the late 1720s, when embarkation for German emigrants to colonial Pennsylvania in Rotterdam first became regular, all passages had to be paid in advance. Once the merchants involved in the trade were assured profits from rapidly increasing demands for transatlantic transportation, however, they relaxed their policy of requiring advance payment. First they extended credit to young, single men and women in expectation of selling their labor to purchasers in Pennsylvania—a practice analogous to the long-established English custom of servant transportation. Yet they went further and innovatively adapted that practice to the outstanding group characteristic of the German immigration, the large proportion of families. Confident that children could be bound out profitably, merchants accepted a down payment on the family fare with the balance of the credit payable in Philadelphia. At the height of the German immigration in the early 1750s, the custom of placing a substantial portion of passage money on credit had become well established. To feel sure of a return on their investment, merchants required only that about half the ship's freight charges be paid in advance. This more liberal credit policy allowed immigrants to delay paying all or part of their fare until arrival in Philadelphia, thereby subsidizing many less well-to-do Germans for whom initial relocation costs were otherwise prohibitive.

The security upon which merchants extended such credit in Europe could be an explicit invitation from relatives or friends already settled in the colonies who offered to help defray costs, a well-stocked chest of goods that could be sold or a promise to work for the unpaid portion of the fares as indentured servants. This last alternative was a financial guarantee often shouldered by a family's teenage children. As the German immigration declined in the two decades preceding the Revolution, however, financially independent newcomers, those able to provide adequate security to receive credit, decreased continuously as a proportion of the total transatlantic flow. Because the custom of putting fares on credit was by then so firmly established as to be virtually irreversible, merchants found new ways to counteract dwindling profits as advance payments diminished and passage debts became riskier investments. They did this by including anticipated losses in the fare price charged in Philadelphia, and they exploited to the fullest the indenture system as a guarantee for a return on their outlay. In these ways, merchants adjusted their credit policies to changes in the migration flow.

The astute business sense with which some merchants seized the opportunity of providing transportation for large numbers of Germans led to a highly specialized transatlantic trading activity which had far-reaching consequences for both passengers and promoters. This mercantile specialization to exploit a voluntary transatlantic population movement for profit distinguishes the German flow to colonial America from all migrations that preceded it. The colonial servant and eighteenth-century Irish passenger trade were largely handled as part of the regular commodities trade between the British Isles and America. The outfitting and provisioning of slave ships also bore little resemblance to the immigrant trade because the profits in the slave trade were in the resale of slaves, not in the demand for transportation of free people. This specialization in passenger trade, furthermore, foreshadowed the ways in which merchants at later times again and again profited from offering passage at reasonable terms to satisfy the demand of large numbers of people with limited means from many different parts of Europe willing or pressed to migrate to the United States. By the nineteenth century, however, transatlantic fares were relatively cheaper, thus eliminating the need for indentured servitude as a way to finance the relocation. Sending prepaid tickets had replaced the custom of redemption upon arrival by relatives and friends. And vastly improved international communication and banking facilities had made the mediating role of the newlander obsolete.

It is difficult to overestimate the importance of the development of the full-fledged business in transporting German immigrants for establishing a dependable link between principal areas of outmigration in southwestern Germany and Pennsylvania, which for a long time was either the "best poor man's country" or the beginning of an easy path down the great valley to where such opportunity was. Yet it took the growth of a specific immigrant trade to enable this transatlantic migration to expand fully until its tide crested around 1750. Any durable success of merchants with regular and long-term interests in this trade, furthermore, depended on their recognizing that both the size and the composition of the emigration changed over time. And it was cooperation among partners in London, Rotterdam, and Philadelphia which enabled these merchants to monitor, though not control, who left the Rhinelands, and in what numbers, and to relate these to conditions in the colonies that encouraged the importation of new settlers and servants. With such knowledge the businessmen involved in the immigrant trade could adjust their operations to deal with variations in demand and could tailor their pricing policies according to the circumstances of their passengers and the situation of the Pennsylvania labor market.

Crossing the Atlantic Ocean in eighteenth-century sailing vessels was a difficult and hazardous endeavor even under the best of circumstances. The practice of crowding passengers—often accompanied by thin provisioning—occurred in individual peak years but became particularly prevalent at the height of the German immigration, 1749–54. It greatly increased the risks to the health of the immigrants. In addition, the vulnerability of passengers was compounded by considerable property losses during the voyage (largely pilfered or stolen chests and embezzled travel funds), the threat of which was magnified during the peak years when large numbers of inadequately prepared emigrants were most easily exploited.

The extraordinary circumstances of the peak period of the immigration, when several thousand Germans landed within a few weeks each fall, had already brought to light some of the problems that became fully apparent after the migration resumed in 1764. Unchecked, these abuses in the trade reduced the financial resources and flexibility of many newcomers. Those who received no assistance from close friends to overcome such difficulties were not only likely to default on their credit payments but were also seriously and permanently impaired in their efforts to make a better life for themselves in the New World. The plight of those unfortunate Germans—highlighted by their large absolute numbers during the peak immigration years—mobilized a variety of Philadelphians who either felt threatened by the often obviously contagious presence of these more unfortunate immigrants or were moved charitably to prevent by legal means the causes of such destitution. After only partial successes around midcentury, the German Society of Pennsylvania eventually became effective in alleviating the need of many poor, newly arrived Germans and in supporting their just claims at law, thereby filling much of the role that immediate relatives and friends had played at an earlier date when more immigrants were likely to have connections in the colony.

In the later years, bound service became a more frequent solution to the economic problems of immigrants. Irrespective of the reasons that induced recently landed Germans to indenture themselves, in the majority of cases the indenture system guaranteed fast initiation into the new society and determined to a large extent the way in which the immigrants could be integrated into local society. Most of the servants bound in exchange for payment of their passage debts by a stranger (after arrival in Philadelphia) were young and therefore receptive to the new ways of their masters in shop or house or on the farm. How well they fared depended mainly on "their masters' disposition, situation, and rank in society" and to some extent on the servants' age and familial circumstances.[7] Before indentured servitude became a widely used means of financing all or most of the passages in the 1750s, as the number of German immigrants grew and their character changed, young adults and teenage children—many of them from families coming together to settle somewhere in the province—bound themselves out for the financial and educational advantages and opportunities the system offered toward a later, independent start as farmer or artisan. During the peak of the immigration, however, when many passengers depended on finding purchasers willing to pay their freight, diverse newcomers sought indenture, and the masters who employed them represented a broad socioeconomic group. Ironically, when after the 1750s on the average at least half of all immigrants had to rely on the indenture system as the only realistic option open for defraying their passage debts, the range of prospective employers for newly arrived Germans became more limited and discriminating as supplies of labor changed—immigrants of different ethnic background, slaves, and (increasingly) free wage workers made up the bulk of the labor market in Pennsylvania.

In summary, the importance of successful settlement efforts of relatively few, moderately affluent pioneering immigrants who drew followers to America, either from among their coreligionists or their former neighbors in Europe, merits emphasis. Built on personal connections, the recommendations of former migrants broadened the subsequent stream of newcomers and quickened its flow. As a consequence, the immediate return on promises of cheap farms and high wages became more elusive. Land was taken up at a rapid rate, forcing settlers to go farther out from Philadelphia and even leave Pennsylvania in search of farms that were affordable. In this movement they were soon encouraged by land speculators of colonies to the south. At the same time, growing financial dependence of later migrants on the merchants who channeled the emigration flow to Philadelphia decreased the options for newly arrived settlers who had to compete in ever larger numbers to pay off their passage debts and to accumulate enough capital to start out on their own. News of serious troubles with the Indians in 1754 further undermined Pennsylvania's already waning reputation. Thereafter the declining inflow of German settlers that has been observed—largely a result of the combined effect of government restriction on emigration to the American colonies and the appeal of new settlement projects in eastern Europe promoted and highly subsidized by Prussia, Russia, and Austria—was mostly composed of immigrants with personal ties to those already established in the province and newcomers of limited means who had reached the Delaware by way of long-standing lines of communication, shipping, and credit among merchants involved in the transatlantic transportation of German passengers. Particularly evident in this later period were single, probably young, men oriented to the Philadelphia area labor market rather than desiring to settle on farms in southeastern Pennsylvania and beyond. The onset of the American Revolution virtually ended substantial German immigration to Pennsylvania. Not only was Pennsylvania comparatively less attractive for German immigrants by the time of the war; changes taking place in Europe also drew heavy numbers of settlers to the east. The combination of American warfare (first for independence and then with European powers) and East European redevelopment practically stopped German immigration to the newly formed republic. When, years later, the migration to America resumed, Pennsylvania received only a small portion of it.

The characteristic pattern of the history of the eighteenth-century German immigration to colonial Pennsylvania reflected an intricate web of many different forces that combined in changing ways over time first to generate, then to sustain, and finally to reduce the tide of about one hundred thousand newcomers from the Rhinelands who came to the American colonies from 1683 to 1776. Inhabitants of southwestern Germany, where the tradition to migrate in reaction to adversities at home and opportunity elsewhere was strong, were drawn by the promise of political and personal freedom, religious toleration, and plenty of land and work in colonial America, even though the relocation was difficult and the costs were substantial. Lured by the potential of profits in providing large numbers of emigrants with transportation to Philadelphia, merchants devised a system that enabled emigrants of limited means to undertake the voyage. As a consequence of the successful broadening of the pool from which immigrants to the American colonies were recruited, opportunities in the Delaware Valley region declined as land was taken up and the labor force expanded. These changes in turn reduced the emigration from Germany.

This pattern of rise, peak, and decline, first in family groups, then increasingly as younger, single persons, that characterized the wave of German immigration coming into and through Philadelphia in the eighteenth century was repeated again and again later when people from different parts of Europe tried to take advantage of settlement and employment opportunities that opened in the United States in the nineteenth century. The German immigration to colonial America, then, has shown how the development of a trade specializing in mass transportation that linked the will of free Europeans to find a better life with opportunities and the need for people in the New World worked in ways that became the prototype of Atlantic migrations.

Notes

1. The literature on the German immigration to colonial America is vast, scattered, and uneven. This essay is based on my dissertation, "A Tide of Alien Tongues: The Flow and Ebb of the German Immigration to Pennsylvania, 1683–1776" (Temple University, 1983), which contains extensive documentation and a bibliography.

2. For more detail see Marianne Wokeck, "The Flow and the Composition of German Immigration to Philadelphia, 1727–1775," *Pennsylvania Magazine of History and Biography* 105 (1981): 249–78.

3. The first part of the compound *Wanderlust* is to be understood here not in the narrow sense of "hiking"—a relatively modern usage—but as in "Auswanderung" (emigration) and "Einwanderung" (immigration).

4. *Pennsylvanische Berichte*, December 1, 1754.

5. Ibid.

6. For more detail see Marianne S. Wokeck, "Passengers and Promoters," in *The World of William Penn*, ed. Richard Dunn and Mary Dunn (Philadelphia: University of Pennsylvania Press, forthcoming).

7. Heinrich Melchior Muhlenberg, *Nachrichten von den vereinigten Deutschen Evangelisch-Lutherischen Gemeinden in Nord-Amerika*, 2 vols. (Halle: Waisenhaus, 1787; rpt. with intro. by Johann Ludwig Schulze, Allentown, Pa.: Brobst, Diehl and Co., 1886 and 1895), 2:461.

2.

The Pattern of German Emigration to the United States in the Nineteenth Century

GÜNTER MOLTMANN

THE HISTORICAL PROCESS OF GERMAN EMIGRATION to North America can generally be divided into three periods: (1) from its beginning in the seventeenth century until 1815, that is, for the entire colonial period and the four following decades during which Europe was torn by changes and emigration decreased drastically; (2) the century from 1815 until 1914, that is, from the Congress of Vienna to the outbreak of World War I; and (3) from World War I to the present day.

Statistics reveal that during the colonial period some sixty-five to seventy thousand or perhaps as many as one hundred thousand Germans emigrated to British North America; during the subsequent forty years the number of German emigrants cannot be precisely ascertained, but it was not very high. During the mass emigration period from 1816 to 1914 approximately 5.5 million Germans went to the United States. Since World War I German emigrants to America number some 1.5 million. All in all, more than 7 million Germans exchanged their "fatherland" for a home in North America.

According to conventional historiography, these periods had the following characteristics. During the first phase the emigrants were mostly groups of religious dissidents who did not wish to suffer any longer in Germany and sought a better and more secure world across the ocean. During the second phase they left because of social and political pressures; they were liberals who protested against the reactionary system, who wished to escape military service, and who saw in America a land of freedom and progress. The third period was represented by the hopeless emigrants, who after two lost wars saw no chance for a career and personal success. The large group that suffered persecution under the Nazi regime and emigrated should perhaps not be considered along with the other emigrants.

This conventional division with relatively simple underlying differences has been criticized for some time by emigration researchers. It has been argued—and correctly so—that in addition to idealistic motivations, economic and social motivations were important, perhaps more important than any others. The number of religious and political dissidents was limited, and the flight from military service has been overemphasized. In retrospect, the motives of emigrants were overly idealized.

In view of the similarity between the emigration curve and the agricultural and industrial economic cycles, great significance can be attached to socioeconomic grounds, at least with regard to the nineteenth century. Even in the first phase, the emigration era of Quakers, Mennonites, Labadists and Rosenkreuzers, Tunkers, Schwenkfelders, Salzburgers, Moravian Brethren, and Rappites, economic reasons played a major role in one's decision to migrate to the New World. A look at the causes of the large emigration from the Palatinate to America in 1709 proves this fact. The aftermath of war, severe winters, poor harvests, and starvation sent thousands on their way; the forcible return to Catholicism imposed by the electors was not as significant in the history of emigration as has been thought. It should be stressed that Catholics also left for America.[1]

If one disregards the religious dissidents for a moment, an examination of German-Americans of Lutheran and Reformed faiths in British North America reveals their lax attitude toward the church; the efforts of a Heinrich Melchior Muhlenberg and a Michael Schlatter were necessary to bring many lost sheep back into the church. One can thus conclude that religious motivation was not strong among many early emigrants.

Likewise, a glance at the nineteenth century shows complex reasons for emigration. During this period not only were emigrants motivated by economic and social grounds but also dissident religious groups wished to escape the pressures of the authorities in Germany, as for example the Zoarists (1817), the Amanites (1843), the Old Lutherans (after 1838), and the Catholics at the time of Bismarck's *Kulturkampf*. Furthermore, one can find that peculiarities usually associated with the nineteenth century were not limited to it. Mass emigration, chain migration, certain organizational patterns of emigration, and emigration as a business existed not only in the second phase but had already been apparent in the first. The question therefore arises as to what actually were the characteristics of German emigration in the nineteenth century. Can it be distinguished from that of the eighteenth century? Did changes occur after 1815 in the appearance and structure of the exodus?

A series of important innovations after 1815 greatly altered the structure of German emigration to America in spite of proven continuities. These changes occurred in migration financing, the mobility and transportation system, the range of the origins and destinations of the emigrants and their composition, and with respect to their ideas about America and their reactions to the new environment.

Of greatest importance was the disappearance of the redemptionist system in the 1820s. During the previous one hundred years this system had given emigrants the opportunity to obtain free passage to America in return for services to a master for several years without pay. In return the master paid the ship captain's cost of the passage and thus freed the emigrant from debt. This system was sometimes termed "white slavery," but this designation is not accurate. Besides the disadvantage of a year-long loss of personal freedom, it offered to the redemptioner the chance to migrate, the opportunity to learn the English language, and material security to start with.

The proportion of redemptioners in the German emigration to America in the eighteenth century is estimated to have been between 50 and 60 percent.[2] More than half of the Germans were at first under obligation to serve as workers (on farms, as artisans and tradesmen, and in families). Only in this manner was it possible for thousands of poor farmers, craftsmen, and agricultural workers to gather together the sum needed for such a journey. As late as 1816–17, the poor masses from southern Germany who emigrated to America could afford this adventure only because they could work off the debt of the ship's passage later.

After the large migration wave of 1816–17 this system disappeared and with it the opportunity to obtain a cheap passage. A new law governing ship passage, which stipulated the maximum space on board to be provided for each passenger, meant that ships could no longer be overfilled and thereby helped end the big business of mass transport with payment after the journey.[3] Other factors were also at work. New economic structures that developed in the nineteenth century introduced flexible wages instead of long-lasting contracts. Furthermore, during the era of Jacksonian Democracy, strong demands for personal equality and freedom were raised. The indenture system had become outdated.

For Germans the end of the indenture system meant that poor people longing to emigrate could no longer travel to America. They lacked the money to purchase a ticket before sailing. There remained only two possible ways in which poor Germans could undertake the trip: either the travel costs were paid in advance by other family members or friends already in America (this had also been done in the eighteenth century), or the costs were paid in Germany by the family, friends, community, or, in special instances, the state.

During difficult times in Württemberg, Baden, and Hesse, the state sponsored transport of the poor, giving travel costs plus an "An-

Immigrants landing at Castle Garden, New York. Engraving in *Harper's Weekly* by A. B. Shults, 1880. European immigrants identifiable by their dress include (from left) immigrants from the British Isles in derby and plaid vest, the Eastern European Jew with Torah, the Mediterranean immigrant with cloak and cap, and the German student in traditional uniform. Note on the right the well-dressed Americans apparently awaiting the arrival of new servants. (*Harper's Weekly*)

fangsgroschen" to emigrants to enable them to make a new start in America. Through such a onetime financing, it was thought that money would be saved that otherwise would have been spent supporting the poor over a period of years from the community funds designated for that purpose. A secondary motivation was that undesirables could be gotten rid of, such as troublemakers and potential revolutionaries.[4]

As a rule, however, in the nineteenth century the very poor did not migrate to America; only those who had enough money (or through sale of their property obtained the sum needed) were able to cross the Atlantic and start a new existence. In spite of the need to finance one's journey oneself, the volume of migration exceeded that of the eighteenth century. Specific social developments gave emigrants a high motivation. From the latter part of the eighteenth century the population in Germany increased greatly. More people than ever sought work, bread, and a roof over their heads. The livelihood that was difficult to find in Germany was easy to come by in North America. The United States was expanding rapidly westward, cheap land was available, and workers were sorely needed.

Furthermore, there were changes in the family and career structure: the autarkic family in farming, crafts, and businesses loosened; factories and industry introduced the division of labor. The place of occupation, the hometown, and plans for the future became more variable, thereby increasing the mobility of people. Freedom of movement became less restricted and was finally granted without limits.

The great mobility was supported by changes in the transportation system. After the American Revolution, shipping between Europe and the New World was open to international competition. Technical innovations during the Industrial Revolution led to an increased and more diversified conveyance system. Transportation to the interior was improved for travelers through the employment of steamships on rivers and canals and the construction of railways. Ocean traffic was greatly improved by the change from the tramp system to the package lines and by the introduction of the steamship. Distances shrank accordingly. Travel time shortened. The communications system improved. International press coverage became more detailed. The postal services became more efficient.

Closely associated with these changes is the second characteristic of the migration movement in the nineteenth century, the rationalization and organization of the transportation of large numbers of migrants in accordance with demand. A prerequisite for this mobility was the disappearance of English control on traffic to North America. Thus the way was free for the entry of new transportation operators who could do big business and, at the same time, meet the wishes and interests of the emigrants and serve them accordingly.

Ships that sailed from America to Europe carried primarily such staples as tobacco, cotton, rice, and whale oil and needed the storage space for them. On the western route they were laden with tools, linen, glassware, wine, and other items that required less room. To use the spare space, emigrants were offered passage to America in steerage. The freight route from west to east became the passenger route from east to west.

Since "human" wares could not be "stored" at harbors as easily as staples, ship owners turned to package lines to handle the people with the care they needed. Thus migration became easier to organize. Set departure times and travel routes helped make advanced planning possible. Agents who made contracts with prospective emigrants would now announce when a ship would sail to America. This system, introduced in Germany in the 1830s, made it easier to decide to emigrate, shortened the trip, and lowered its cost.[5]

More aids to the rationalization and organization of migration traffic came about through the construction of railways and the introduction of the steamship. For a while shipping firms offered special railway rates to migrants in order to fill their vessels. In times of heavy migrant traffic, special trains were run. The steamship shortened the transatlantic voyage on the average from seven weeks to eighteen to twenty days. Near the close of the nineteenth century faster steamers were built, shortening the trip to ten to twelve days. At the same time comfort increased. Individual emigrants, however, were only a very small part of the great numbers transported. The large ships built for emigration at the turn of the nineteenth century to the twentieth century held fifteen to twenty-four hundred passengers in steerage.

A third trait of the migration movement in the nineteenth century is related to the improved organization of emigration: the regional enlargement of the area from which the emigrants came and the regional growth of the area to which they went. In the eighteenth century the home territory of the migrants to America can be clearly defined—emigrants came mainly, though not exclusively, from southwestern Germany. In the nineteenth century the desire to migrate spread to other parts of Germany. The Northwest, Hannover, Saxony, Thuringia, and Bavaria all contributed migrants by the middle of the century. The area north and east of the Elbe River followed in the second half of the

The Immigrant's Progress. Caricature cards published by George Topp in 1882. The top, left card shows the "green" newcomer Hans Schloppenberg in his native costume and pipe. The top, right card depicts him two years later, working as a waiter in a local taproom. In the bottom, left card, five years have passed and he owns the taproom. The bottom, right card portrays him ten years after his arrival as the proud and respected owner of the Schloppenberg Brewery. (Roughwood Collection)

century. Emigration to America became a concern for people in all parts of Germany. In times of crises the emigration potential grew accordingly. The emigration peaks of 1854 and 1882, both numbering about a quarter of a million, could not have been reached without this wide reservoir.[6]

The principal destination of German settlement in the United States during the eighteenth century was the Middle Atlantic colonies, particularly Pennsylvania. The nineteenth century brought a noticeable broadening of settlements to the Old Northwest and further. The so-called "German Belt" spread from Connecticut, New York, New Jersey, Delaware, and Maryland through Pennsylvania to Ohio, Indiana, Illinois, and Wisconsin, branching further out into Michigan, Minnesota, Iowa, South Dakota, Nebraska, Kansas, Missouri, and Arkansas. In addition, there were heavy settlements in Louisiana, Texas, Colorado, California, and Washington. By the beginning of the twentieth century Germans were to be found in all the states of the Union.[7]

The great mobility of people in the nineteenth century and the different backgrounds of the migrants were reflected in the wide spectrum of people who took part in the settling of America. This is the fourth characteristic of this period of emigration. Although even in the eighteenth century emigrants were not only small farmers and craftsmen, the greatest number of German-Americans practiced these occupations. The colorful picture of the emigrants of the nineteenth century is depicted, for example, in a description by Friedrich Gerstaecker in the foreword to his popular book *Nach Amerika!* (To America):

"To America," cries the madcap gaily and audaciously, defiant against the first sad hour which will put his strength to the test . . . —"to America," whispers the desperate man who here on the margin of ruin was being pulled, slowly but surely, toward the abyss—"to America," says the poor man, softly and resolutely, who again and again had struggled with manly strength, put futilely against the power of circumstances . . . —"to America," laughs the criminal after his successfully perpetrated robbery . . . —"to America," exults the idealist, spurning the real world . . . hoping for a world over there across the ocean which matches the one produced in his own frantic brain.[8]

This characterization of emigrants of the nineteenth century could be extended. Political refugees went to America to flee the reactionary politics of the Metternich system, the persecution following the 1848–49 revolution, and the effects of Bismarck's antisocialist law. Academics, the so-called Latin farmers, experimented with agriculture in

America. In the middle of the century, Germans joined in the throngs of goldseekers from around the world to try their luck in California. Toward the end of the century, domestic servants and factory workers emigrated to the New World. Not to be overlooked are large numbers of young people with their own motives for emigrating, independent souls who did not feel comfortable in their home society for personal reasons and believed that they could live better in America.

Could one live better? The image of America in the nineteenth century differed from that of the eighteenth century. This, too, distinguishes the second phase of emigration from the first. During the colonial period, the New World offered opportunities and freedom of thought and belief. With the American Revolution, the United States became the land of political freedom. In the nineteenth century America appeared to many Germans as the "land of unlimited opportunity," which was the title of a book appearing in 1903, written by Ludwig Max Goldberger.[9]

In the nineteenth century information reaching Germany about America became much more complex, replacing the simple stereotypes of a century earlier. But too much information could also distort the picture. Any emigrant could pick out that information which best suited or served him. Only after his arrival in the United States did he become aware that opportunity in America had limitations. Integration into American society often proved long and difficult.

The last characteristic that should be mentioned here is the assistance given to the immigrants by German neighborhood societies. Close adherence to such groups and principles of self-help greatly eased the immigrants' early adjustments. Closed German communities with their own churches and schools existed in the colonial period, particularly in Pennsylvania. Now other institutions were added to help bridge the difficulties. The first German societies to help immigrants get a start in their new home were founded in the late eighteenth century. In the nineteenth century an active club life developed. In addition to the immigrant aid societies, there were savings and insurance groups, lodges, societies for self-help, militias, shooting clubs, fire brigades, gymnastics clubs, choirs, theater groups, and other diverse organizations.

These institutions functioned as a bridge between German tradition and American society exactly as German schools and churches had done in colonial times. They offered the members security in an accustomed atmosphere and prepared them for the newness with which they would have to cope. In the larger cities there sprang up in the 1830s and 1840s the well-known Little Germanies, areas in which German-Americans lived, where German stores and beer halls, German clubhouses and theaters were to be found, and where the German language could be heard and read everywhere. These Little Germanies functioned mainly as a buffer zone. They protected the immigrant at first from the dangers and difficulties of living in entirely new foreign surroundings and helped speed up the process of integration once the immigrant had established himself.[10]

Thus the Little Germanies had a limited life. They too became Americanized. The decrease in German cultural life in the United States was accelerated by World War I, but it was already noticeable in the first decade of the twentieth century as the great flood of immigrants vanished. German quarters in American cities after the war were not as lively as they had been in the nineteenth century.

German immigration to America in the twentieth century was different in many ways. The number of migrants receded drastically. Industrialization in Germany was able to absorb larger numbers of the excess population, and the introduction of quotas in the United States checked the influx of unlimited numbers of immigrants. The mobility of people increased and modern transportation made traveling easier. But emigration lost part of its appeal as more opportunities for advancement became available in Europe. Only with the renewed deprivations in parts of Europe after two world wars did migration again increase.

Each of the three phases of migration delineated here has in turn become history. In current migration research the rough periodization between the centuries can still be regarded as useful, but the differences between them can be clearly recognized. The nineteenth century was the era of the great German-American symbiosis, which may have led to an affinity between the two nations that is apparent today. It is sometimes good to look at the past and to observe that the German-American relationship rests not only on common interests but also on demographic ties that reached their peak during the last century.

Notes

1. See Fritz Trautz, *Die Pfälzische Auswanderung nach Nordamerika im 18. Jahrhundert*, Heidelberger Veröffentlichungen zur Landesgeschichte und Landeskunde, no. 4 (Heidelberg: Carl Winter, 1959), 17–21; for a discussion of eighteenth-century emigration motives in Württemberg see Wolfgang von Hippel, *Auswanderung aus Südwestdeutschland: Studien zur württembergischen Auswanderung und Auswanderungspolitik im 18. and 19. Jahrhundert* (Stuttgart: Klett-Cotta, 1984), 58–94.

2. Abbott Emerson Smith, *Colonists in Bondage: White Servitude and Convict Labor in America, 1607–1776* (Chapel Hill: University of North Carolina Press, 1947), 336.

3. "An Act Regulating Passenger Ships and Vessels," March 2, 1819, in *Immigration Legislation*, Reports of the Immigration Commission, 61st Cong., 3d sess., Senate Document 758, 41 vols. (Washington, D.C.: U.S. Government Printing Office, 1911), 39: 395–96.

4. See Christine Hansen, "Die deutsche Auswanderung im 19. Jahrhundert—ein Mittel zur Lösung sozialer und sozialpolitischer Probleme?" in Günter Moltmann, ed., *Deutsche Amerikaauswanderung im 19. Jahrhundert: Sozialgeschichtliche Beiträge* (Stuttgart: Metzler, 1976), 9–61; Günter Moltmann, "Nordamerikanische 'Frontier' und deutsche Auswanderung—soziale Sicherheitsventile im 19. Jahrhundert?" in Dirk Stegmann et al., eds., *Industrielle Gesellschaft und politisches System: Beiträge zur politischen Sozialgeschichte* (Bonn: Neue Gesellschaft, 1978), 279–96.

5. See Hermann Wätjen, *Aus der Frühzeit des Nordatlantikverkehrs: Studien zur Geschichte der deutschen Schiffahrt und deutschen Auswanderung nach den Vereinigten Staaten bis zum Ende des amerikanischen Bürgerkrieges* (Leipzig: Felix Meiner, 1932), 21–23.

6. See Peter Marschalck, *Deutsche Überseewanderung im 19. Jahrhundert: Ein Beitrag zur soziologischen Theorie der Bevölkerung* (Stuttgart: Klett, 1973), 38–39.

7. See map "Distribution of Natives of Germany in 1900," Twelfth Census of the United States, in Albert Bernhardt Faust, *The German Element in the United States with Special Reference to Its Political, Moral, Social, and Educational Influence*, 2 vols. (New York: Steuben Society of America, 1927), 1: opposite p. 578.

8. Friedrich Gerstäcker, *Nach Amerika! Ein Volksbuch*, 6 vols. (Leipzig: Costenoble, 1855), 1: preface.

9. Ludwig Max Goldenberger, *Das Land der unbegrenzten Möglichkeiten: Beobachtungen über das Wirtschaftsleben der Vereinigten Staaten von Amerika* (Berlin: F. Fontane, 1903).

10. See Agnes Bretting, *Soziale Probleme deutscher Einwanderer in New York City, 1800–1860* (Wiesbaden: Steiner, 1981), esp. 81–88.

3.

Organizing German Immigration: The Role of State Authorities in Germany and the United States

AGNES BRETTING

F. C. HUBER, WHO IN 1898 analyzed the attitude of state authorities toward emigration in the German kingdom of Württemberg, compared the masses of emigrants to a school of herring being substantially diminished by their enemies, who waited for the prey en route to America.[1] This comparison is certainly impressive, but is it valid?

German emigrants have always been cheated and fleeced by emigration agents, brokers, merchants, ship owners, captains, bankers, and many others, especially during the nineteenth century, the time of mass emigration. There have always been those who made a living off the needs of the emigrants and who took advantage of the wanderers' helplessness. And it is also true that most German governments showed little interest in the suffering of those subjects who decided to leave the country for good.

In the nineteenth century, however, the rapid increase in emigration forced state authorities to enact laws designed to protect the state from the negative consequences of mass emigration. These laws had advantages for the former subjects as well. Legal control of passage contracting or regulation of the transport conditions on board ship, for instance, meant that the emigrant was not totally helpless, even though he was still prey to swindlers.

Few of the emigration and immigration laws of the nineteenth century were designed to protect emigrants. Emigration legislation on both sides of the Atlantic was a reaction, a response to evils connected with the mass movement. State authorities in most cases lacked far-

sighted planning. But the efforts to organize emigration and to remedy
the chaotic conditions of the traffic did give emigrants some protection
and safety.

Emigration laws were numerous in Germany as well as in the
United States. What is important, however, is not the number of instructions or prohibitions but the legislators' motives for enacting
those laws. To make this point, I will outline the basic characteristics
of emigration and immigration legislation, rather than describe the details of those laws.

There are other aspects that could be discussed: the effectiveness
of emigration laws as seen by the legislators, the interpretation of instructions by local authorities, or the important role transit countries
such as France, Belgium, and the Netherlands played in shaping German emigration legislation. But what I want to show is the organizing
role of state authorities in Germany and in the United States, which
was forced upon the legislators by a mass movement they could not
stop, and its positive effect for those Germans who migrated to America.

In the Old World as in the New, the cumulative experience of
the eighteenth century and earlier periods had an impact on official
attitudes toward the problem of emigration and constituted the background for legislative action in later years. Most German state authorities pursued a repressive policy against any emigration. Their attitude
in the eighteenth century was determined by the principles of mercan-
tilism. Only a few states—notably Baden and Württemberg—showed
a tendency to let people go, if possible only the poor, the helpless, and
the useless.[2] Authorities did not inquire into the causes of the emigration movement. They believed that solicitors, the so-called *Seelenverkäufer* or newlanders, were to blame for it. There were hundreds of
these solicitors at work in Germany, and there is no doubt that many of
them were unscrupulous, greedy adventurers who were not concerned
with the fate of the emigrants after they had signed and paid for their
passage contracts. But solicitors did not create the desire to leave the
country for an unknown future. Social, political, and religious conditions should have been examined by the governments to discern why
their subjects wanted to go. Instead, authorities tried to check the unwelcome phenomenon mainly by enacting antisolicitation laws, which
provided for harsh penalties and thereby indirectly discouraged potential emigrants. Those who nevertheless insisted and succeeded in leaving were completely on their own. They lost the protection of state
authorities as soon as they received consent to leave, and they could no
longer claim any rights, help, or care from their mother country.

C. F. Elwert's Exchange and Shipping Company in Philadelphia c.1880. Agencies of this kind which aided in arranging passage for German immigrants were common in many American cities in the latter half of the nineteenth century. (Roughwood Collection)

Up to 1816–17 no sovereign needed to consider emigration an urgent problem; periods of massive emigration usually were of short duration. So despite the antisolicitation laws state authorities usually followed a laissez-faire policy as long as possible. Some solicitors were even able to get official permission for their efforts to recruit emigrants. The administrative practice was, in short, subject mostly to the fiscal interests of the sovereign.[3] As long as the number of emigrants was relatively small, individuals were able to travel to the seaport cities at their own risk, contact a ship owner or captain, and bargain for the best contract for the voyage to America. But events in the years 1816–17 clearly showed that this system was not appropriate when masses of emigrants arrived in the coastal cities. When a general economic distress intensified by two years of disastrous harvests induced tens of thousands of emigrants to leave southwestern Germany, mostly to the port of Amsterdam, they had great difficulty securing space on board ship. Overcrowded vessels left for America, where many a redemptioner could not find a master and had to start his life in the New World a pauper. Hundreds of emigrants were left behind in the Netherlands absolutely destitute and had to beg their way home to a mother country that no longer wanted them.[4]

One consequence of this event was the gradual concession in Germany of the right to emigrate. During the first half of the nineteenth century, freedom of emigration was granted in almost all states, though legal guarantees were sometimes given very late. Liberal Baden and Württemberg had known this right as early as the eighteenth century and had seen only a few short-lived periods of restrictive emigration legislation.[5] Prussia granted freedom of emigration in 1818, Hesse followed in 1821, and Saxony in 1831. Bavaria was late, but her freedom of emigration act in 1868 only sanctioned what had been tolerated for the last twenty-five years. Laws controlling and organizing the emigration movement followed. Despite the time lag in taking legal action, the main features of legislation were the same in almost all German states. It is therefore justified to speak of *the* German state authorities handling mass emigration.

Emigrants in eighteenth-century Germany, one might say, had to fight their way out. On the other side of the Atlantic, however, in the British colonies and later in the United States, they could not always count on a hearty welcome. From the very beginning, settlers in America looked with mixed feelings at those who arrived after them.[6] Immigrants were needed as farmers, artisans, and laborers; up to the end of the nineteenth century, America had a great demand for laborers.

In the eighteenth century only one piece of legislation openly expressed the desire to stem the flow of incoming foreigners. But the Alien and Sedition Laws of the year 1798, which for the first time included the right to deport unwanted foreigners, contained a proviso that the laws should expire two years after passage. The passage of this law, though motivated by the imminent danger of war, expressed an underlying distrust of alien minorities, the reasons for which will have to be left open here.[7] Opposition to the act was strong; most states clung to the idea of America as an asylum for the oppressed and preferred to rely on immigration laws already enacted.

Since greater numbers meant greater economic strength and security for the colonies, the original founders and proprietors had actively recruited settlers. Germans in particular were induced to come, by promises of land grants, religious tolerance, tax exemption for a specified term of years, financial help or travel grants, and easy terms of naturalization. Some emigrants, however, were considered undesirable. Thus even in colonial days there evidently existed some hostility toward immigrants, its strength varying depending on the economic situation of the colony and the number of foreigners coming.[8]

Colonial authorities tried to select immigrants by excluding those regarded as undesirable. Legal action was taken to control or regulate the immigration movement in such a way that benefits would be saved and difficulties reduced. After the Declaration of Independence this pattern prevailed. In the 1820s the two means by which states tried to control immigration were through laws requiring written information on all incoming passengers—so called manifesting laws—and through bonding laws, which required a payment of up to $300 security for every passenger who was deemed likely to become a public charge. The bond had to be paid by the ship owner or captain. If the immigrant managed to earn his living without public assistance during the first two years, the security had to be repaid. Most states could and did go back to the manifesting and bonding laws of the colonial period. The mass movement of the nineteenth century confronted state authorities with entirely new problems, and it took quite some time until these problems were addressed by new standards of thinking and official action.

The same was true in Germany. For much of the nineteenth century legal instructions by the authorities given to the police, mayors, and other local representatives were biased against emigration. Despite a more liberal attitude toward the problem "the anti-solicitation laws had been kept on the books and brought to bear whenever it seemed advisable."[9] This attitude is particularly evident in the legislation concerning emigration agents. Their trade, which was not new, was to become an important business. By the time mass emigration started again in the 1830s, a network of emigration agencies had developed all over Germany or was rapidly coming into existence. The agent contracted for the sea voyage before the emigrant left his hometown, told him when to leave, and helped plan the trip from hometown to the seaport and then to the United States. He thus had an important role in organizing and smoothing over the difficulties connected with the journey from the Old World to the New. Of course, emigration agents were interested in promoting emigration. But they were not simply successors of the eighteenth-century *Seelenverkäufer* or newlanders. They offered greater assistance than did their predecessors.[10]

State authorities were well aware that without these agents the mass movement would lead to chaotic conditions in the transportation sector. Hundreds of emigrants would be ruined on their way and be a burden to public and private charity. Nevertheless, the profession of emigration agents was subjected to strict legal limitations, dictated by the constant fear that agents would seduce or persuade people to leave the country. Dozens of documents—such as official reports sent by mayors or district police officers to the respective Department of the Interior or instructions given to local authorities—give evidence of this constant suspicion against persons who had a professional interest in the emigration movement.

Authorities wanted the regulating influence of the agents, but they did not want to encourage potential emigrants. Therefore, for practically the entire nineteenth century, the question of propaganda by emigration agents was discussed over and over again. It was difficult to draw a clear line between seducing propaganda and necessary information, and officials were hard-pressed to do so. In 1865, the Department of the Interior of the government of Hesse ordered the confiscation of all signboards outside emigration agencies. This measure was justified because some agents had complained that their competitors were advertising illegally by using unusually elaborate and multicolored signboards.[11] Agents would often post timetables of sailing vessels going to America in public places. Could this be more than information? In 1881 the Hessian government ordered all police officers in their districts to visit the beer houses and report whether such timetables were likely to attract attention and trigger discussion among the guests. The reports by the police were negative, and no action was taken.[12]

State authorities in Germany continually attempted to keep a firm grip on emigration: agents had to be licensed, and the granting of the license was restrictive; they had to use officially approved booklets and contracts; they had to guarantee certain services to the emigrant such as financial refunding for delay in departure; they had to keep records of their business; and they had to deposit a specified sum as security with the government. Through these legal requirements authorities tried to control the role of the emigration agents. But they were well aware that legislation had a double effect. The government of the kingdom of Saxony, for instance, argued against legislative action because it was afraid that the security given to the emigrant by placing emigration agents under legal surveillance would promote the inclination toward emigration.[13] Most governments, however, welcomed this double effect. As the government of Brunswick-Lunenburg put it in 1854, legislation was "partly in the interest of the state in order to curtail illegal emigration, and partly in the interest of the emigrants themselves, who get protection from cheating and misleading information." [14]

It is not that surveillance of the agents was unnecessary. German archives contain hundreds of documents demonstrating the manifold and ingenuous ways emigration agents had invented to trick emigrants out of their money. Furthermore, during the nineteenth century illegal emigration solicitors were actively at work. They recruited for foreign military service (for instance, for Union troops during the Civil War), for states in need of settlers and laborers after the Civil War, and for strikebreakers for American industries during the 1880s. [15] But the surveillance of agents by German state authorities, though necessary, was often narrow-minded and at the local level sometimes ridiculously so. It was biased by the negative image emigration and emigration agents still had in the eyes of officials.

Nevertheless, the laws and ordinances were helpful to the agents and the emigrants. Emigrants in the 1840s and later years were able to get fairly reliable information about travel routes, prices, and the situation in the United States. They could plan their voyage in advance and thus avoid time- and money-consuming delays on the trip. Those who contracted with an officially licensed agent had some protection against fraud. That the price they had to pay included a profit for the agent was worth the expense.

The attitude of state authorities toward emigration in the nineteenth century was influenced not only by fiscal and political interests but by public opinion as well. Since the early 1840s numerous philanthropic societies advocated positive action by the state authorities in their efforts to control mass emigration. Two of the more important such groups, the Central Society for German Emigrants (founded in Berlin in 1844) and the National Society (founded in Darmstadt in 1847), considered emigration a possible safety valve for social problems. They advocated state assistance and guidance for the movement.

This more liberal attitude together with a strong national feeling—the wish that German emigrants should keep their German identity even in their new homelands—came to bear on the debates in the Frankfurt Parliament in 1848. Even though it considered other problems much more important than emigration, the National Convention adopted a paragraph for the constitution saying that "the emigration problem shall be under the active care and the protection of the Reich." The revolution failed, and nothing came of these efforts. [16] Although some governments did show more concern about the welfare of their emigrants than before, several initiatives toward a better coordination of state emigration policies failed. Except for the traditionally liberal governments of Baden and Württemberg all governments in the 1860s were content with simply controlling mass emigration. Care for emigrants within their own borders and beyond as well as attempts to organize emigration would have needed a strong, centralized political power.

Two of the German governments are exceptions insofar as they had a traditionally positive attitude toward emigration: the senates of the seaport cities of Bremen and Hamburg, which were responsible for the organization of the sea voyage. These two cities did an excellent job in making the dangerous trip across the Atlantic safer, faster, and more comfortable for the steerage passengers. From the very beginning of mass migration to America, Bremen, and a little later Hamburg, tried to increase their share of the emigrant trade. Previously the leading ports in this business were Le Havre, Antwerp, and Rotterdam. The two German cities started competition by offering better conditions to emigrants. The Bremen law of 1832 and the Hamburg law of 1836 were more than efforts in organization; they were designed to protect the emigrants.

Of course, the background for this legislation was economic interest rather than philanthropic unselfishness. In both cities many senators were merchants or ship owners. As early as the eighteenth century they had opposed or ignored strong legislation against emigration enacted by other states. Here, too, economic interests dictated the role state authorities played in emigration. But because in this case the interest was promotion of the movement and transportation of as many emigrants as possible, the organization was excellent, guidance and protection given, and emigrants cared for.[17]

In the United States, the arrival of thousands of immigrants every year confronted state authorities with enormous problems. From 1820 to 1850 almost 2.5 million immigrants were looking for jobs and homes in the New World; roughly 24 percent of them were Germans. In the second half of the century the numbers of newcomers increased. The vast majority of them were welcome, but those who were not able to find a place in the new society posed a problem. As in Germany, American authorities reacted to the new situation by reenacting or intensifying old laws. Besides quarantine regulations, which were designed to protect the country from the importation of epidemics, manifesting laws and the bonding of immigrants continued to be the two main legislative efforts to keep out the unwanted. According to Robert G.

Albion, "those two fears of pauperism and epidemic lay behind the municipal and state regulation of the [immigrant] traffic."[18]

This attitude of state authorities cannot come as a surprise. Though epidemics such as yellow fever and cholera were not brought over by immigrants, and even though the number of paupers and criminals among the thousands of immigrants was negligible, contemporaries were concerned that a high percentage of the inmates of prisons, almshouses, and other public institutions was foreign-born and that developing slums in the cities were inhabited mainly by foreigners. The seaport cities bore the brunt of these problems. In reaction, almost all coastal states, including California, passed laws to protect themselves against the burden of the immigrant poor. Massachusetts and New York took the lead in this legislation. The state most concerned was New York because from the 1840s on roughly 70 to 80 percent of all immigrants arrived in New York City.[19]

Many contemporaries considered the immigrants responsible for almost every problem. In the 1840s and 1850s, when antagonism between employers and labor unions grew violent, the newcomers, who competed for jobs with the older residents, were the scapegoat. Any form of radicalism was believed to be un-American, so it had to have been introduced by foreigners. This period was a time of social change and unrest brought about by urbanization, developing industrialization, and technical revolution. Mass immigration aggravated some of the problems, especially in the big cities. The strength of the anti-immigration feeling varied and was dependent upon the economic situation. Nativist movements gained power in times of depression, but the idea of the United States as an asylum for the oppressed always prevailed.

The federal government had left immigration almost entirely in the hands of authorities in the individual states. They dealt with the problem as they thought best for their own safety and welfare, but they did not try to stop the movement. Congress in Washington hesitated to become active in immigration legislation, mainly because of the constitutional problem of jurisdiction.[20] The first federal law was passed in 1819. By this act the government tried to protect both the immigrants and the country of immigration. The provision that no ship should carry more than two passengers per five tons was meant to improve conditions on board ship for the immigrants and thereby reduce the number of newcomers who entered the United States in a starved, sick, and wretched condition, asking for help as soon as they had landed.

Despite the heavy increase in immigration, the next federal law did not come until 1847. It was directed especially against the evil of overcrowding on board the emigrant ships. In 1855 Congress passed an even more detailed act on this subject, inspired by the report of a Senate committee, which had investigated the conditions on vessels carrying immigrants. By requiring minimum space and food provisions and at least one hot meal per day for every passenger, this act was supposed to protect the immigrants from famine and epidemic. But "in the final analysis, there was hardly any means to combat violations that took place outside the country's sovereign territory."[21]

But despite the lack of efficiency, passing these laws was important. The passage of the act of 1847 was especially the result of immense pressure from public and private charities, mainly those in New York and Massachusetts. American charities have played an important role for immigrants. Their influence in shaping the attitude of legislators toward immigration cannot be overestimated. In New York City, where merchants, dubious brokers, forwarding agents, moneychangers, landlords, land speculators, and others had made mass immigration a profitable business, several societies were formed to protect the newcomers from fraud. For the Germans, the major such group was the influential German Society of the City of New York, founded in 1784 and still in existence and active.

These private associations were not against mass immigration. Members of the German Society, for instance, many of whom were merchants—like the senators in the Hanse cities—actively promoted the movement. These societies were successful in focusing public interest on the intolerable conditions in the immigration traffic. They demanded protection of the immigrants by state and federal law, and they succeeded despite vehement protests by all those who profited from the traffic, such as shipping companies, land speculators, railroad interests, diverse boards of trade, and certain political groups.

In 1847 New York created the Commissioners of Emigration of the State of New York in an effort to make the handling of the incoming masses more effective. The commissioners were obligated to care for destitute and helpless immigrants for their first five years in the country. The appointment of the commissioners marked a turning point in New York's history of immigration and had implications for the history of immigration in the country as a whole. The federal law of 1847 concerning conditions on board emigrant ships resulted from the same lobbying and the same public sentiment as motivated the Commissioners of Emigration Act. With these two laws the attitude of the legislators "to protect the country from undesirables rather than to protect the immigrants"[22] had changed a bit in favor of the latter.

In 1864 Congress passed an act to encourage immigration. By this act immigrants could assign their wages for a year or less or encumber their land to pay for the expense of emigrating to the United States and thus contract labor was legalized. The law was inspired by a labor shortage as a consequence of the Civil War. It was repealed in 1868, when the men in the army came back to their peacetime jobs.

With the exception of this act, the motivation of protecting the country was prevalent in all federal laws. The act of 1847 contained an exact definition of unwanted immigrants and stipulated that those who offended the rules of entry be transported back to their homelands at the cost of the ship owner who had brought them. This practice had long been prevalent in New York State. What is important is that this law forced German ship owners to react to a federal law, which could not be as easily circumvented as state laws.[23] Bremen and Hamburg had to adapt their legal requirements for emigrant ships to the high standards of this American law. The government of Hesse intensified legal supervision of emigration agents so as to avoid the rejection of their subjects in America, and other German governments followed suit. This act of 1847 clearly demonstrates the interaction between state authorities on both sides of the Atlantic. Emigration and immigration were inseparable, and so were legislative efforts to organize them in Germany and in the United States.

In the United States the complete change from state to federal control became inevitable. In 1849 the Supreme Court decided that the state practice of imposing a head tax on all incoming passengers for the purpose of collecting a fund for the assistance of the poor was unconstitutional.[24] As a result of this decision, immigration was no longer a state problem; it was a national one requiring uniform legislation. Not until 1875 was a first attempt made to achieve this goal, but since no machinery was provided to enforce the law passed that year, it was of no importance. In the 1880s other acts passed by Congress marked the end of the hitherto liberal attitude toward immigration. The act of 1882 required a general head tax for immigrants and stipulated the nonadmission of certain classes such as convicts, the mentally retarded, and all those who were likely to become public charges. In 1885 a law was enacted to prohibit contract labor, and in 1887 another law provided for the deportation of offenders at the expense of the steamship companies.[25]

By this time, however, other nationalities, constituting the so-called New Immigration, occupied public opinion and the debates in Congress. Immigrants from eastern and southeastern Europe were coming to America in ever-increasing numbers. Unlike the Germans, Scandinavians, Dutch, and even the Irish, these people seemed difficult to assimilate. Their strong feeling of group consciousness, seemingly odd customs, a strange mentality, and even their striking outer appearance were attacked by nativist groups. Many Americans decided that millions of aliens could no longer be assimilated.[26] Public opinion had an impact on the legislators, and the practice of legislation became increasingly directed to exclusion and admission, which meant abandoning the protective work of the state commission.[27] In 1909 the money collected by the imposition of a head tax was taken from the special Immigration Fund and given to the general revenue.

In Germany, the establishment of the Reich in 1871 could have been the foundation for effective, forward-looking emigration legislation. But nothing was done. In 1897, almost fifty years after the National Assembly at the Paulskirche, an act was finally passed which acknowledged emigration to be a problem of federal care and administration. This law was shaped in the interest of the two leading shipping companies in Germany, the Hapag in Hamburg and the Lloyd in Bremen. It came at a time when German emigration had stopped being a mass movement. Hamburg and Bremen now handled the thousands of transitory Russians, Poles, Jews, Bohemians, Croatians, Hungarians, and others. So with the beginning of the twentieth century the American policy of unrestricted immigration had changed completely, and German emigration legislation had finally become liberal and unrestricted.[28]

German mass emigration to America in the nineteenth century confronted state authorities in Germany as well as in the United States with hitherto unknown problems to which they had to react. By trying to organize the mass movement legally they did help the individual emigrant. But they lacked farsighted planning; for many of the emigrants helpful laws came too late. In this sense Huber's metaphor of emigrants being like a school of herring is true: emigrants were prey to a variety of swindlers; the little protection they got was solely the result of their traveling in masses.

Notes

1. F. C. Huber, "Auswanderung und Auswanderungspolitik im Königreich Württemberg," in Eugen von Philippovich, ed., *Auswanderung und Auswanderungspolitik in Deutschland*, Schriften des Vereins für Socialpolitik 52 (Leipzig: Dunker und Humblot, 1892), 275.

2. See Gerhard P. Bassler, "Auswanderungsfreiheit und Auswandererfürsorge in Württemberg 1815–1855, Zur Geschichte der südwestdeutschen Massenwanderung nach Nordamerika," *Zeitschrift für Württembergische Landesgeschichte* 33 (1974): 117–60.

3. See Hans Fenske, "Die deutsche Auswanderung," *Mitteilungen des Historischen Vereins der Pfalz* 76 (1978): 213.

4. See Günter Moltmann, ed., *Aufbruch nach Amerika, Friedrich List und die Auswanderung aus Baden und Württemberg 1816/1817* (Tübingen: Wunderlich, 1979), 188–214.

5. See Wilhelm Mönckmeier, *Die deutsche überseeische Auswanderung* (Jena: Fischer, 1912), 228–30.

6. See Edward Prince Hutchinson, *Legislative History of American Immigration Policy, 1798–1965* (Philadelphia: University of Pennsylvania Press, 1981), 388.

7. A brief discussion of this act is given by Roy L. Garis, *Immigration Restrictions: A Study of the Opposition to and Regulation of Immigration into the United States* (New York: Macmillan, 1927), 32.

8. See ibid., 18.

9. Mack Walker, *Germany and the Emigration, 1816–1885* (Cambridge, Mass.: Harvard University Press, 1964), 147.

10. See Agnes Bretting, *Die Auswanderungsagenturen in Deutschland im 19. und 20. Jahrhundert. Ihre Funktion im Gesamtauswanderungsprozess* (publication forthcoming).

11. Staatsarchiv Marburg, Bestand 100, Nr. 3535, Act of April 20, 1865.

12. Hessisches Hauptstaatsarchiv Wiesbaden, Abt. 405, Nr. 2589, B1. 54–86.

13. Not before May 1853 did Saxony pass an act regulating the business of emigration agents, similar to those already in existence in the neighboring states.

14. Niedersächsisches Staatsarchiv Wolfenbüttel 129 Neu 30/387, report of the minister of state, October 18, 1854.

15. Mack Walker, "The Mercenaries," *New England Quarterly* 33 (1966): 390–98; Ingrid Schöberl, "Auswandererwerbung durch Information: Amerikanische Broschüren in Deutschland im späten 19. und frühen 20. Jahrhundert," *Amerikastudien/ American Studies* 27 (1982): 299–342; Charlotte Erickson, *American Industry and the European Immigrant, 1860–1885* (Cambridge, Mass.: Harvard University Press, 1957).

16. See Walker, *Germany*, 135–39.

17. See Birgit Gelberg, *Auswanderung nach Übersee: Soziale Probleme der Auswandererbeförderung in Hamburg und Bremen von der Mitte des 19. Jahrhunderts bis zum 1. Weltkrieg*, Beiträge zur Geschichte Hamburgs, ed. Verein für Hamburgische Geschichte, vol. 10 (Hamburg: Christians, 1973).

18. Robert G. Albion, *The Rise of New York Port, 1815–1860* (New York: Scribner, 1939), 349.

19. See Agnes Bretting, *Soziale Probleme deutscher Einwanderer in New York City, 1800–1860* (Wiesbaden: Steiner, 1981).

20. See Garis, *Immigration Restrictions*, 58.

21. Ingrid Schöberl, "Emigration Policy in Germany and Immigration Policy in the United States," in Günter Moltmann, ed., *Germans to America: 300 Years of Immigration, 1683 to 1983* (Stuttgart: Eugen Heinz, 1982), 41.

22. George M. Stephenson, *A History of American Immigration, 1820–1924* (1926; rpt. New York: Russell & Russell, 1964), 253–54.

23. See Bretting, *Soziale Probleme*, 33–34.

24. "The States attempted to devise laws acceptable under this decision, but a last attempt by New York in 1881 to find a means of collecting 'head money' was again struck down by a 1883 decision, which established in effect that . . . the regulation of immigration is the prerogative of the federal government" (Hutchinson, *Legislative History*, 403).

25. See Edith Abbott, "Federal Immigration Policies, 1864–1924," *University Journal of Business* 2 (March 1924): 141.

26. See Schöberl, "Emigration Policy," 42.

27. Abbott, "Federal Immigration Policies," 143.

28. See Schöberl, "Emigration Policy," 43.

PART II:

The Pennsylvania Germans

George Washington, as seen by the Pennsylvania German artist Durs Rudi, Jr. (1789–1850). This watercolor of Washington, who was revered as a hero by many Germans in Pennsylvania, combines military and revolutionary symbols with those of an idyllic existence. These elements are paralleled by the inscription at the top of the picture: "Freedom, equality, unity and fraternity." (Philadelphia Museum of Art: Titus C. Geesey Collection)

4.

The Pennsylvania Germans:
Three Centuries of Identity Crisis

DON YODER

OF ALL THE ETHNIC GROUPS of early Pennsylvania, the Pennsylvania Germans have been both the most vocal and the most researched.[1] Their identity has been shaped gradually over three centuries by their confrontation with the American experience, their contact with their non-German ethnic neighbors, and their wrestling with their Germanness in relation to other German emigrant groups. In this essay I will survey the major ethnicizing trends within the Pennsylvania German population, with attention to three major viewpoints around which Pennsylvania Germans have rallied in the long process of finding out who they are and where they stand in American culture.

We celebrate this year the three-hundredth anniversary of the founding of the Pennsylvania German culture with the settlement of Germantown. I believe that we can speak of "German-American studies" even though there are no "German-Americans" as such. One has to study the German emigration and its influence in America in time and space, that is, in relation to specific historical, geographical, and cultural environments. There are thus Texas Germans, Wisconsin Germans, Missouri Germans, New York Palatines, Georgia Salzburgers, and in primary focus here, the largest and earliest of all the compact German-speaking settlements of the United States, the Pennsylvania Germans.

The world of early America soon became aware that in and beyond Pennsylvania's gateway city of Philadelphia there were extensive settlements that were ethnically, culturally, and above all linguistically different from their Anglo-American neighbors. European travelers and native commentators on the Pennsylvania Germans noted their early and rapid assimilation to American ways of thinking, in politics in the eighteenth century and in religion in the nineteenth. By the twentieth century, Pennsylvania German culture was for the most part a regional variation of American culture as a whole. There was and is one significant difference, and that is that the Pennsylvania Germans expressed their very Americanized, very hybrid culture, in German and/or Pennsylvania German.

Ethnic consciousness, or ethnic identity, is an attitude toward oneself and one's cultural world, which is shaped in individuals and eventually in groups through contact with other self-conscious groups of human beings with whom one comes into regular contact.[2] Although a sense of group identification exists in most ethnic groups, it varies from individual to individual, from mildly passive consciousness of one's ethnic roots to the ardent ethnicity of activist leaders who want to "do something" to defend, protect, and advance the group and its culture. In a complex society such as the United States the identity crisis of individuals can and frequently does involve consciousness of one's own ethnic heritage, culture, and history. The intensity of ethnic consciousness can also vary over time, with latent ethnicity turning into activist ethnicity in generations like the present when we are witnessing in a sense a reethnicizing of America. The Pennsylvania Germans are a prime example of this variation in ethnic involvement over time.

With its mixture of ethnic groups from the very beginning, Pennsylvania must have been in the colonial period a fascinating place to observe the human condition. It was a veritable Babel of accents and languages—not only English and German but Swedish, Holland Dutch, French, and Indian, with all the regional accents of the British Isles added for good measure. By the time of the Revolution the Pennsylvania Germans were estimated to make up a third of the population of the colony, with the English and the Scotch-Irish (then called simply "Irish") making up the other two-thirds. German relations with the Irish were not cordial. Dutch-Irish riots were reported on many colonial election days, and as late as 1798 a Scottish schoolmaster in Bucks County wrote in a letter to his father that "the very sound of an Irishman's voice will make a Dutchman draw down his eyebrows, gather up his pockets, and shrink into himself like a tortoise."[3]

Four general and underlying problems in relation to Pennsylvania German ethnicity must be outlined at this point.

The first and central fact about Pennsylvania German ethnicity is that the Pennsylvania Germans are a composite of various ethnic strands. So many Palatines came to America in the colonial era that the very word "Palatine" became an umbrella term for all German-speaking immigrants at least until the Revolution.[4] In addition, there were other large regional German components—Swabians, Alsatians, Westphalians, Hessians, Silesians, and some Lower Rhinelanders. And one must not forget the Huguenots, Swiss, and Austrian Protestants who migrated into what is now West Germany after the Thirty Years' War.

This ethnic mixture turns out not to be so frightening or insoluble as it first appears. All of these groups spoke German by the time they (or individuals among them) arrived in Pennsylvania. The Huguenots bore French names, but these had already taken German form in the Rhineland, as for example *Girard* into *Schirra*, as witnessed in the surname of the astronaut Schirra in our time. The Swiss went through the same cultural adaptation. Most of them had stayed in Germany a generation or two and had married German wives, and their children spoke with Palatine or Swabian rather than with *Schwyzerdütsch* accents. All of these acculturated to one another further in Pennsylvania. The Swabians quickly acculturated, but they left a cultural legacy including Swabian foods like the dish my grandmother used to call *Schwowegnepp* (Swabian dumplings)—and of course we still tell ethnic jokes about the Seven Swabians—*die Siwwe Schwowe*.[5]

The preliminary ethnic disunity of the Pennsylvania German population rapidly solved itself, and by the nineteenth century most Pennsylvania Germans could speak in ethnic terms of *unser Satt Leit*— "our kind of people." In the twentieth century one of these now merged ethnic strands was artificially extracted from the mixture when a few Pennsylvania Germans in 1918—note the date—decided to become "Pennsylvania Frenchmen" and founded the Pennsylvania Huguenot Society. I have named this process selective ethnicity, a common phenomenon among "Old Americans" who for various reasons decide to extract and emphasize one ethnic strand from their mixed family background. This process involves in a sense a genealogical definition of one's identity.

To complicate Pennsylvania German identity further, there was added to this confusion of European ethnicity within Pennsylvania German society an even more complex confusion of denominational difference. Unlike the ethnic subgroups that have by now all merged into a general Pennsylvania German population, the religious groupings are still somewhat uneroded and even today form the major obstacle toward the creation of a complete Pennsylvania German cultural unity. The major division is still between the so-called "church" and "sect" groups, or, better, between the world-accepting groups and the world-denying groups. The two major denominations are still, as earlier, the Lutherans and Reformed (United Church), but although they represent the same religious practice, they have drifted apart in the last century. It used to be said that the only difference between them was that the Reformed began the Lord's Prayer with *Unser Vater* and the Lutherans with *Vater Unser*. Even in Pennsylvania it was more complex than that, but in the old days the two denominations—our Reformed Zion and our Lutheran Zion, as they affectionately called each other—formed one cultural world among the Pennsylvanians and for the most part shared union church buildings and other joint institutions.[6]

Radically opposed to the way the churches conceived Christianity were the sectarian or protest groups, the Mennonites, Amish, and Brethren. These created for themselves a religious and social microcosm, a counterculture, so to speak, away from the larger world.[7] In addition, there was an extreme form of this world-fleeing stance which created the communitarian settlements of Ephrata, Bethlehem, and Harmony. A fourth pattern of Pennsylvania German denominationalism, which I will discuss later, was the native American revival groups modeled essentially on Methodism. Because of this basic religious disunity, this radically differing way of perceiving one's role in the world, which continues to this day, the Pennsylvania Germans, unlike the French Canadians, for example, whose culture and religion have formed an ethnic unity, have never been able to agree on any single cultural question.

A third complicating factor, mostly semantic but confusing to everyone, including the Pennsylvania Germans themselves, is the scholars' war over the terms "Pennsylvania German" and "Pennsylvania Dutch." The shift of the word "Dutch" from its seventeenth-century meaning for anything from Holland to Switzerland and its present limitation to Holland confuses many Pennsylvanians. Even some Pennsylvania Germans—who should know better—have added windmills to their restaurants to attract tourists.[8]

A fourth complicating factor in Pennsylvania German identity, and a very contemporary one, is the influence of the tourist image of the culture on the culture itself. The major tourist industry that brings millions of dollars yearly to eastern Pennsylvania preserves the legitimate Americanism "Pennsylvania Dutch" but makes it synonymous with "Amish." Because of tourist focus on the Old Order Amish of Lancaster County, that area has become a major tourist area in the eastern United States. Motels, restaurants, menus, festivals, and souvenir shops all tout the Amish theme so monotonously that the unwary tourist and even the unwary non-Amish Pennsylvania Dutchman is thrown into confusion as to who and what is Pennsylvania Dutch.

To determine the stages of Pennsylvania German ethnic development, I propose to analyze three different attitudes which Pennsylvania Germans have taken toward themselves and their culture in relation to the American experience. These attitudes are rooted in the three languages of the culture—English, High German, and Pennsylvania German. The approaches, in all of which there were influences from outside the culture as well as responses from within, are (1) the Americanizing approach, (2) the Germanizing approach, and (3) the dialectizing approach.

The two basic trends have been the Americanizing and the Germanizing trends. There have been, from William Penn's time to the present, Americanizers and Germanizers—those who wished to gear the Pennsylvania Germans completely into American life, beginning with anglicizing them, and those who hoped that they would preserve distinct and intact their German language and ethnic character.[9] The original conflict arose in the eighteenth century from the fear, on the part of Anglo-Americans, that the German would wag the tail of the Pennsylvania dog, linguistically, politically, and culturally.

The linguistic adaptation of the Pennsylvania Germans continued into the nineteenth century. As knowledge of High German decayed with the coming of the public schools and the loss of the German-language parochial school system of the churches, the Pennsylvania German dialect became the target of the Americanizers. Educated European German travelers described it as "Bush-German" and "Bastard-Kauderwelsch"; to Anglo-Americans it was everything from "Kitchen-Dutch" and "Fireside-Dutch" to "Black-Dutch." Heinz Kloss, the twentieth-century historical linguist, speaks of it as only a *Halbsprache* among German tongues, a language that made it no more than half-way to literary usage.[10] He was speaking of the period before 1950, when it had not yet truly become a literary language, used for written communication, formal preaching in the churches, instruction in schools, or journalism.

As the High German institutions of eastern Pennsylvania were replaced with Anglo-American models in the pre–Civil War era, the educators of Pennsylvania, whether Yankee schoolmasters or native Pennsylvania Germans attempting to anglicize rural schoolchildren, came increasingly to point to the dialect as the culprit that retarded the progress of the German counties. This schoolmasterly approach to

Americanization was to root out the Pennsylvania Dutch dialect, scrap it, because it was an unsafe, unworthy vehicle of expression.

This radical program of Americanization in language—getting rid of both High German and the Pennsylvania German dialect—is illustrated in George F. Baer's address *The Pennsylvania Germans*, delivered at the dedication of Palatinate College at Myerstown, Pennsylvania, December 23, 1875. Baer was one of the most successful Pennsylvania Germans in the nineteenth century, a leading American financier and president of the Philadelphia and Reading Railway Company. On that occasion, his words were hardly a happy Christmas present to his own people:

The very first great lesson to be taught to our people is this: That as long as we cling to the German language, in the sense of preferring it to English, the development of our people will be retarded. It is no question of merit between two languages. The language of this country is unalterably fixed. The English is the language of the Government, of legislation, of courts, of business, of newspapers; it follows that it must be the language of the literature of the country. No other language can supplant it. No literature printed in any other language can ever reach the masses, or become known and read, as literature must be, in this age of invention and learning, by those who desire to keep pace with the onward progress of the world. To seek to ignore this fact and all that is implied in it, is simply to commit a great crime against our race. Pure German can never become a general language here. As for Pennsylvania German, it is a mere dialect, the *patois* of the Palatinate, with a sprinkling of English words. It is a mere vulgar delusion, to suppose that it can be elevated to the dignity of a language, capable of being taught, and used in writing as a medium of expressing thoughts. It can never become a written language. It has never been used except in conversation. The Pennsylvania Germans would not for one minute tolerate its use in the pulpit. Think of the German in Luther's translation of the Bible, or in those grand old chorals and hymns being changed to Pennsylvania German, and read and sung in church, that, too, in this age! It is impossible to create a literature in Pennsylvania German.[11]

These antidialect sentiments can be matched in the writings and addresses of other Pennsylvania Germans who had succeeded in the outside world and felt called upon to encourage their brethren to give up their own language.

Such messages from leading Pennsylvania Germans left a permanent legacy of defeat and disillusionment among the Dutch farming classes, which continued in some areas into the first decades of the twentieth century, creating a mass Pennsylvania German inferiority complex. So successful was this Americanizing campaign, carried on especially through the public schools and engineered in part by native teachers, that when the so-called renaissance of interest in the dialect arrived somewhat belatedly in the 1930s, it came as an unsettling surprise to the speakers of the dialect. First, they had been told that "Dutch" was bad and must be destroyed; now they were told that it was good and must be preserved.[12]

Of the key Pennsylvania German institutions the school has been least studied in its relation to ethnic identity.[13] The public school, which after the 1830s replaced the German-language parochial school, became the instrument of radical Americanization because it insisted on instruction in the English language alone. The teaching staff was for the most part home-grown. Teachers were Pennsylvania Germans, who represented both the outside, English-speaking world of their own education and the Dutch-speaking world of home and community. Most of them consciously chose the American world and rejected, at least in the school context, their own Pennsylvania German culture.

The teachers and administrators of the school system were of the opinion that a dialect accent held a child back, and they did their best to root out Dutch accents. In 1891 E. L. Kemp, the president of Palatinate College, spoke to a group of Berks County teachers as follows:

There is no shame in being Pennsylvania German or a foreigner, but we have no right to let our children be stamped as foreigners, and we should, as far as possible, put an English accent on their tongues. One of the very best means of giving our boys and girls the power to use the English language fluently and correctly is to have them read plenty of English and to speak it when opportunity offers. On the playground and at home many of the children of this county come in contact only with those who have little knowledge of the English.[14]

This drive toward English is reflected even in the publication of the first Pennsylvania German "manuals," which were compiled not to perpetuate the dialect but rather, as Horne's *Pennsylvania German Manual* put it, to "serve as a guide to the study of English, and that it may facilitate the acquisition of the language, a thorough knowledge of which is indispensable to every Pennsylvanian."[15] The author, A. R. Horne, in his schoolmasterly way, provided pages of pronunciation exercises for his students to practice so as to rid themselves of stubborn Dutch accents. My favorite example from his book is "The wolunteers fired a wolley down the walley." That certainly helps one to mind one's v's and w's, besides having a nice Civil War ring to it.

A submotif of the Americanizing stance was the religious approach: Americanize the Pennsylvania Germans by converting them to Anglo-American, Puritan, or Yankee forms of religion. This, too, has left a permanent cultural deposit in Pennsylvania German denominationalism. Massive attempts were made by the revivalist groups, headed by the very aggressive movement of Methodism, to remake the Pennsylvania Germans into religious patterns that could take part in what is called by American church historians the "Evangelical Empire" of pre–Civil War America.[16] In this drive for conversion, outside evangelists were joined by native Pennsylvania Germans. The movement was so successful that it planted Anglo-American denominations such as Methodism in all the Dutch counties and resulted in the formation of new Protestant denominations founded on American soil, combining residual Pietism from the Continental churches with the Evangelical-Methodist-revivalist theology and organization. The organizations involved were the United Brethren, the Evangelical Association, the Churches of God, and their later progeny.

In addition to this radical reworking of the denominational map of Pennsylvania, revivalism, with its choice between old and new "up-to-date" American methods of doing church work, and between high and low church forms, split the already existing Pennsylvania German groups into competing schismatic denominations. Hence the terms "Old" and "New" Lutherans, "Old" and "New" Reformed, "Old" and "New" Mennonites, and "Old Order" and "Progressive" Brethren. In some of these schisms language was also involved. General Synod Lutheranism, with its spiritual home in the Gettysburg Lutheran Seminary, for example, combined the revivalist liturgical approach with emphasis on English services, whereas the Ministerium of Pennsylvania, which eventually founded a rival seminary, followed a conservative, confessional, and German-language position.[17] Hence the curious term "English Lutheran," which one used to see on church bulletin boards in Pennsylvania.

There are dozens of quotations to illustrate the Americanizing approach via religion. Methodist circuit riders left journals describing the Pennsylvania German churches, as did Bishop Francis Asbury in 1807, as "citadels of formality—fortifications erected against the apostolic itinerancy of a more evangelical ministry."[18] William Colbert in 1810 described the Dutch villages as "influenced by wicked prejudiced Dutch priests and almost every species of wickedness."[19] But most of the Anglo-American churches looked upon Pennsylvania Germandom as missionary territory. For my principal illustration I have chosen a Presbyterian example.

James Patterson (1779–1837), a native of Bucks County who grew up in Franklin County, after graduation from Jefferson College and studying theology at Princeton, became a Presbyterian clergyman in Philadelphia. He appears to have been one of the leaders of an unsuccessful attempt to Presbyterianize the Pennsylvania Germans. His biographer describes the depth of his interest as follows:

For several years before the close of his valuable life, he took a lively interest in the spiritual improvement of the German population of Pennsylvania. In secret, he often wept over their indifference to vital piety, and wrestled before the mercy seat for the revival of pure religion among them. He hailed with inexpressible delight, every indication that the Head of the churches was about to enlist the energies of this wealthy and influential people, in bringing about the final triumph of the gospel. In his various schemes for doing good, therefore, this portion of the community was not overlooked. As one of his elders one day opened the door of his study, the tears were observed to trickle down the care worn cheeks of this man of God. Wiping them away, he addressed his friend thus: "I have been thinking what is going to become of the Germans, there seem to be very few indeed who care about their souls." [20]

Obviously the Reverend Mr. Patterson, like the Methodists, represented the nineteenth-century version of the "born-again" variety of the Protestant religion. Therefore, he judged and found wanting the traditional Lutheran and Reformed emphasis on growing up within the church rather than entering through conversion. Actually the question at issue was the conflict between two legitimate but different interpretations of Protestantism. One was more aggressive than the other and attempted to retread Pennsylvania German religion into the American version of British Evangelicalism, with American Puritan morality thrown into the bargain.

Also in this evangelical "package deal" that came with revivalism were such new institutions (new, that is, to Pennsylvania Germans) as the Sunday school, the missionary society, the tract society, religious journalism, theological seminary education, and the reform movements (including temperance) of activist Protestantism in the pre–Civil War era. After some generations of confusion and indecision, all of the Pennsylvania German denominations except the "old order" sects have by now finally accepted the larger part of this complex of new evangelistic methods of church work. In the twentieth century all the refined "joinery" of Anglo-American Protestantism—from Cradle Rollers to Golden Agers—was added to the Pennsylvania German parish organization, so that the average American Lutheran or Reformed congregation diverged greatly from its current counterparts in Europe. This radical Americanization of the parish church was noted by an official visitor from the World Council of Churches in 1937. So Americanized and different did our Protestant churches seem to him that he symbolized it all with the statement that the first thing one notices about an American church is the parking lot. [21]

The Americanizers, whether we speak of them in the linguistic or the ecclesiastical sense, had on their side first, the inexorable cultural adaptation of subculture to larger culture, and second, the ingrained and continuing religious disunity that made any united front for a Pennsylvania German cultural program impossible.

To oppose the inroads of the Americanizing process, however, there arose a handful of Pennsylvania German leaders whom we can call the Germanizers. These were mostly ministers of German-speaking churches and editors of German-language newspapers, both with vested interests in the preservation of German language and German cultural loyalties. Many of these, like the public school teachers, had been educated in the Anglo-American world but took the other path and consciously chose the Germanizing approach. They attempted to unite the Pennsylvania Germans under the banner of German language and culture. Their program ranged from a campaign to spread the German language to overemphasizing German, German-American, and/or Pennsylvania German "contributions" to American life.

The Germanizing movement is partially explainable from forces within the Pennsylvania German culture. Ethnic leaders of any non-English group rally around their cultural language when that language is threatened, at the same time buttressing their program with appeals to ethnic religion and calls to preserve the ethnic virtues. One of the earliest proponents of Germanizing was Justus Heinrich Christian Helmuth (1745–1825), the leading Lutheran minister of Philadelphia in the postrevolutionary generation. [22] In 1813 Pastor Helmuth published an appeal to the Germans in America, which includes the following fantasy:

What would Philadelphia be in forty years if the Germans there were to remain German, and retain their language and customs? It would not be forty years until Philadelphia would be a German city, just as York and Lancaster are German counties. The English would be driven to the bushes if they would build no longer in the southern part of the city. What would be the result throughout Pennsylvania and northern Maryland in forty or fifty years? An entirely German state, where, as formerly in Germantown, the beautiful German language would be used in the legislative halls and the courts of justice.[23]

The Lutheran historian Henry Eyster Jacobs calls this statement "castles in the air."[24]

The Germanizing movement among Pennsylvania Germans in the middle and latter decades of the nineteenth century was heavily influenced by contacts with the nineteenth-century German immigrants and their very different sense of ethnic identity.[25] German romantic nationalism and the German unification movement left among nineteenth-century emigrant Germans in the United States a heightened self-consciousness, a sense of *Deutschtum* and destiny. Their isolated situation in America of course heightened their own sense of Germanness. To promote German ethnicity, they founded a series of German-American alliances, historical societies, and federations.[26] Their publications ranged from scientific historical monographs to pro-Vaterland propaganda.

These nineteenth-century German emigrants, particularly the Forty-eighters,[27] were the group that more than any other sharpened Pennsylvania German self-consciousness. These people puzzled the Pennsylvanians—they were Germans, they spoke the German language, but they were radically different in cultural and political outlook. The Pennsylvania Germans had several names for them—"New Germans" or "European Germans" or simply *Deitschlenner, Deutschländer* or Germany-Germans. Largely an urban phenomenon, these *Deitschlenner* settled in the Pennsylvania German cities, where they took over positions of prominence in the worlds of the church, the newspaper, and business.[28]

These new German emigrants created the *gemütlich* world of the *Biergarten*, the *Volksfest*, the *Turnverein*, the *Männerchor*, and the *Sängerfest*. While the Pennsylvania Germans filled the American fraternal orders from the Odd Fellows to the Elks, the newcomers built a world of their own, in which, as Carl Wittke has put it, the highest praise for something was that it was *gerade wie in Deutschland*. Of course, it never was, but they liked to think so with their exile mentality. These "German-Americans," as they came to call themselves, attempted in part to recreate for themselves in America a German bourgeois atmosphere in their urban neighborhoods, churches, and lodges. Whereas the Pennsylvania Germans had long ago given up interest in Europe, these new Americans tried to be "Germans in America," and they cultivated *Deutschtum* in all their institutions. And

Samuel Kistler Brobst (1822–1876), Pennsylvania German Lutheran pastor and writer, was one of the best-known proponents of the continuation of High German in Pennsylvania. The use of dialect among Pennsylvania Germans survived the decline of High German in the nineteenth and twentieth centuries. (Roughwood Collection)

after 1871 they were not lacking in praise for the new united German Empire.

The Pennsylvania Germans largely rejected the German-Americans and their world. As late as 1895, in an article in a Reformed church periodical, the following statement was made:

The Pennsylvanians now do not readily associate with the European German, and where not sufficiently numerous to form societies of their own, they prefer the society of Americans of English descent to that of their German cousins. So also the European Germans, where they can possibly do so, rather congregate with persons coming from their own country than with the Pennsylvania German.[29]

A minority of native leaders attempted to preserve the High German language,[30] but most of the Pennsylvania Germans felt they had no stake in this movement and took its gradual decline and disappearance as a matter of course. They also were not in the habit of calling themselves "German-Americans." The European traveler J. G. Kohl, who has given us one of the more sympathetic portraits of the Pennsylvania Germans by a native German, found out that they considered immigrant Germans foreigners. He made the mistake of calling two pipe-smoking Pennsylvania German women "Germans." They replied that they were "Americans." This, he found, was the usual answer in Pennsylvania.

They might, it appears to me, at least pay the Fatherland the compliment of saying a "German-American," but, on the contrary, it seemed sometimes when they were talking of the Yankees, the New Englanders, the Irish, etc., that they meant to give themselves out for Americans, *par excellence.* Even their language they denominate "Pennsylvanian." "We speak Pennsylvanian," at the utmost "Pennsylfoany-Deutsch."[31]

In the long run, then, it proved impossible to unite nineteenth-century emigrant Germans and Pennsylvania Germans. The enmity between the two elements split most of the Pennsylvania German denominations into hostile parties, and in some cases separate organizations were formed. And such emigrant organizations as the German-American Alliance found it impossible to gain Pennsylvanian support.[32] The Pennsylvanian forces organized their own Pennsylvania German Society in 1891 and in 1900 began publishing the *Pennsylvania German*, devoted to "the history, biography, genealogy, poetry, folklore and general interests of the Pennsylvania Germans and their descendants."[33]

A wave of relief seems to have passed over eastern Pennsylvania when the Pennsylvania German Society was finally founded in 1891, and many congratulatory editorials were penned at the time. A Reformed editor wrote,

It is highly gratifying to note that in Pennsylvania historical societies have been organized by which the Pennsylvanians, in studying the history of their ancestry, are made more and more conscious of the eminent services rendered our country by the German pioneers of Pennsylvania, who were by no means inferior to the Plymouth Pilgrims either in moral or in mental quality. Learning to know more of them cannot but deeply impress the Pennsylvanians with the high value of their God-given peculiarities and thus help them to be true to themselves.[34]

The third and last of the major movements around which Pennsylvania German ethnic identity has centered is the dialectizing movement, which has arisen largely from the 1930s to the present, with the so-called renaissance of Pennsylvania German dialect and culture. Obviously by this time in our history High German has, with the exception of its continuance by a few of the smaller sectarian groups, totally disappeared from the culture and English has taken its place as the major cultural vehicle. This is not to say, however, that the Americanizing party has won the day completely. The Americanizers were against both the High German language and the Pennsylvania German dialect. The dialect has survived to the present day, despite periodic predictions of its imminent disappearance. In fact it appears to be stronger in 1983 than it has been for some decades.

What has intervened is the movement that attempts to focus or continue to focus the Pennsylvania German sense of identity in the dialect. In the 1930s two institutions were initiated for promoting the dialect—the so-called *Fersammlinge*[35] and the *Grundsow Lodches*.[36] Both are all-dialect evenings, with a huge Dutch meal and plenty (or *blendi*) of dialect entertainment. They have spread across the length and breadth of the Pennsylvania German counties. Also the dialect theater has increased in the last half century,[37] and dialect programs have been presented on radio and television. Some of these programs are adaptations of American popular culture events transmuted into the dialect context, but they are exercising a positive effect in strengthening the dialect consciousness.[38]

But most important of all is the growth, since 1945, of dialect

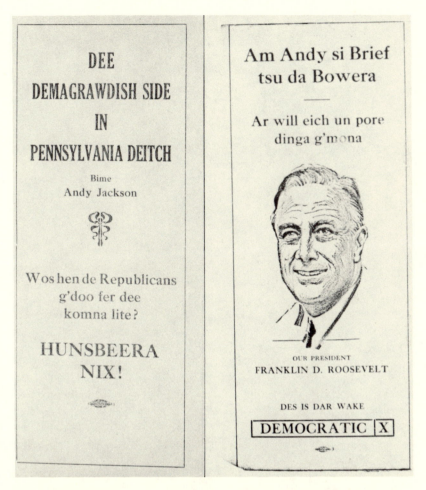

DEE
DEMAGRAWDISH SIDE
IN
PENNSYLVANIA DEITCH

Bime
Andy Jackson

Wos hen de Republicans
g'doo fer dee
komna lite?

HUNSBEERA
NIX!

Am Andy si Brief
tsu da Bowera

Ar will eich un pore
dinga g'mona

OUR PRESIDENT
FRANKLIN D. ROOSEVELT

DES IS DAR WAKE

DEMOCRATIC [X]

Election flyers for Franklin Delano Roosevelt and the Democrats in 1936 in Pennsylvania German. Left: "What have the Republicans done for the little guy? Damn little!" Right: "Andy's letter to farmers. I want to remind you of a few things." By the 1930s the use of High German in Pennsylvania German areas was all but extinct. Appeals such as these in dialect, however, went beyond language in addressing deep-seated emotions. (Roughwood Collection)

DIE ZEHET
YAIRLICH FERSOMMLUNG

GRUNDSOW LODCH NUMMER DRIE

FILDELFY   PENNSYLFAWNI

17 HARNUNG 1950

MITTEN GANG   TEMPLE UNIVERSITATE

Program of the 10th annual meeting of Groundhog-Lodge No. 3,
Temple University, Philadelphia, February 17, 1950. Since the
1930s such evenings conducted in dialect, primarily around the
time of Candlemas (February 2), have contributed to a renewal
of group identity among Pennsylvania Germans. (Roughwood
Collection)

church services, which are held in dozens of Lutheran, United Church, and other congregations, again over the length and breadth of Pennsylvania Germandom. It was only in 1935 that the last regular High German services gave way to English in our rural churches. Since only the very oldest of the parishioners remember the old favorite High German hymns and prayers, the younger generations in many congregations have since 1945 begun to hold dialect services at least once a year. Gradually a body of dialect hymn translations has been built up which can be used everywhere. The four gospels and several other New Testament books have now appeared in translation. What has developed is a grass-roots movement to preserve and use in the church context the language that is closest to the Pennsylvania German heart. As such it is parallel to the nineteenth-century movements in Germany to elevate Low German into a liturgical language and to the very recent beginnings in the Palatinate of preaching in the Palatine dialect.[39]

This dialect church service movement is potentially the most important of all dialectizing trends because it unites two major cultural networks, religion and language. If I may be permitted to quote myself, this is what I said of the significance of the movement in an article on the dialect church service which appeared in Germany:

Surely in an age when the "folk mass" and the "jazz mass" can enter the sacred atmosphere of the Catholic and Episcopal services, when liturgical dance has been rediscovered by the Christian Church, and when liturgies have been vernacularized in Catholicism and the liturgical Protestant churches, the movement for dialect services in the Pennsylvania German speaking parishes of Eastern and Central Pennsylvania can be seen for what it is—a significant effort from the grass roots to preserve and maintain the Pennsylvania German mother tongue. It is important that the Church, which was the last traditional institution in the Pennsylvania German community to preserve High German, should be the last of the older institutions in the culture to attempt to preserve Pennsylvania German.[40]

What is the situation in regard to Pennsylvania German ethnic consciousness today, in the tricentennial year of 1983? Again the key appears to be the dialect. The upswing in dialect institutionalization that began in the 1930s has continued. The Pennsylvania German Society demonstrates even more interest in the preservation of the dialect than in many decades past. The president, the Reverend Richard Druckenbrod, is a native dialect speaker, and a great many of the twenty-four-member board of directors speak, or at least understand, what they like to call *die Mudderschprooch,* the mother tongue. The quarterly periodical put out by the society is called *Der Reggeboge*—the rainbow—founded in 1967, when two rival Pennsylvania German societies merged. A recent annual volume of the society (1980) bore the dialect title, *Ebbes fer Alle-Ebber, Ebbes fer Dich*—something for everybody, something for you.

In the past two years three grammars of the dialect have been issued. First is Earl C. Haag, *Pennsylvania German Grammar and Reader* (Pennsylvania State University Press). Haag teaches courses in the dialect at the Schuylkill campus of the university. The second is Richard Druckenbrod's *Mir Lanne Deitsch* (We're learning Pennsylvania German) (1981), complete with four cassettes of lessons to enable the student to acquire the Pennsylvania German accent, to get back those accents that the school tried to drum out of the children earlier. Third is J. William Frey's *A Simple Grammar of Pennsylvania Dutch,* which first appeared in 1943 and is now available in paperback with an introduction on the work of Frey by C. Richard Beam of Millersville University. Beam also teaches courses in the dialect and writes regular dialect columns for three newspapers.

The dialect theater is flourishing. New playwrights have appeared in recent years, and several repertory groups have been formed to offer plays both new and old. In September 1983, in Lehigh County, two evenings of dialect theater offered to the public were widely attended. The program included two new plays written for the Tricentennial, Mark S. Trumbore's *Uff der Fedderscht Porch* (On the front porch) and Francis C. Laudenslager's *Alles im Kopp* (All in the head). In addition, there were several older skits and plays: *Siss weg Galaind* (It's out on loan) by Paul R. Wieand (1936), *Die Retscherei* (Gossiping) by John Birmelin (1937), *Der Asseba Grickt die Hohr G'schnitta* (Asseba gets a haircut) by Clarence R. Rahn (1944), and a selection from *Hamlet* translated in 1873 by Edward H. Rauch. The program was interspersed with dialect folk songs, and a good time was had by all.[41]

On April 4, 1983, at Kutztown State College, now Kutztown University, the Baerricks Caunty Fersammling held its forty-third annual meeting.[42] A dinner was attended by 650 people in the college dining hall—a huge Pennsylvania Dutch *Bauereschmaus*—and a dialect and musical program was given which lasted for four hours. It was an all-dialect evening, and in honor of the tricentennial I was asked to give the main address, which I called "En Gebottsdaagsgruss far die Pennsylvanisch-Deitsche" (A birthday greeting for the Pennsylvania Germans). I was touched and honored to be asked to do this for *Alt-*

Announcement of the West Berks County Versammling, a Pennsylvania German dialect organization, 1980. (Roughwood Collection)

Announcement of the 6th annual dialect Sunday School in Huff's Church, Berks County, Pennsylvania, 1973. Design by Clarence G. Reitnauer, author of a weekly dialect column in *Town and Country*. (Roughwood Collection)

Baerricks—old Berks County—where my own Swiss-born ancestor Hans Joder had settled in 1714.

In conclusion, one must say that the story of the labored travailing for ethnic identity on the part of the Pennsylvania Germans cannot be completely told until many aspects of the culture have been more thoroughly studied or restudied. It is time for a new look at all the institutions that shaped our culture—the home, the church, the school, the press, the marketing system, the urban-rural complex which related upstate Pennsylvanians to the cities. It is time also for a new look at the old-fashioned, antiquated, filiopietistic histories of the Pennsylvania Germans by nineteenth-century scholars. These can now be viewed as what they are—expressions of earlier ethnic identity crises and parallels to the ethnocentric historiography of all the other American ethnic groups. We need to move beyond them, of course, as the Pennsylvania German Society has long ago done with its long line of solid monographs on aspects of Pennsylvania German culture. Also needed are deeper looks at the European backgrounds of the culture, at the acculturation process on American soil, and at what happened to Pennsylvania German identity in the diaspora to the South, to Canada, and to the Midwest, where through most of the nineteenth and some of the twentieth centuries Pennsylvania Germans were an identifiable ethnic entity. One remembers here the statement of Governor Gustave Koerner of Illinois in the 1860s that in his opinion "a Pennsylvania German was a match for a Yankee any day."[43] Thank you, Governor Koerner.

It is time as well to take a new look at the key persons in Pennsylvania German history, the ethnic leaders, the culture determiners, the symbolic Pennsylvania Germans, whose personal attitudes toward their Pennsylvania-Germanness have influenced others. Baron Friedrich von Steuben is not one of these—Pennsylvania Germans hardly know his name. Yet he has become a symbol of the German-American movements, in which the great majority of the Pennsylvania Germans have no interest or share. Pastorius, too, who with some justification could be called the first Pennsylvania German, is forgotten. Nearer to us there are such figures as Henry Harbaugh (1817–67), the first widely known poet in the dialect.[44] Harbaugh and a group of his associates in the Reformed ministry, including William A. Helffrich, Benjamin Bausman, and Eli Keller, made major contributions to Pennsylvania German identity. Immediately after the Civil War this small group of self-conscious Pennsylvania Germans banded together in a sense of duty to "our people," as they called the Pennsylvania Germans. They founded what I consider the most important periodical of the culture, *Der Reformirte Hausfreund*, which ran from 1866 to 1903. It was in High German but dedicated to the world and outlook of the Pennsylvanians. It was edited from Reading rather than Philadelphia, to keep it out of the hands of the European Germans who controlled the other German periodicals of the Reformed denomination. It had an important effect in creating a positive Pennsylvania German self-image through the end of the nineteenth century. With this beginning in the 1860s it was easy to move on to the formation of a Pennsylvania German Society in 1891.[45]

But all the culture leaders of the Pennsylvania German world—the Americanizers, the Germanizers, and the dialectizers—need closer attention. What were the influences that led them to their positions, their stance in relation to their own ethnic identity?

And finally, the entire chronicle has to be set in a wider American setting, particularly in two important areas. Obviously the Pennsylvania German Society's beginnings in 1891 need to be seen against the centennial wave of American historiography as well as the late nineteenth-century WASP revival, with its mixed motives of anti-emigrant feeling and its pride in the Revolution and the colonial period. The so-called colonial revival was a conscious separation of the "Old Americans" to show that "we" (the WASPs) were here at the founding of the nation and "they" (the ethnics) were not. At the same time other colonial ethnic groups awakened from within to organize the Scotch-Irish Society, the St. Andrew's Society, the Holland Society, the Welcome Society, and all the other progeny of the Daughters of the American Revolution (DAR) and its deposit of general WASP institutionalization. The best treatment of this movement and its mixed motivation is still the book *Patriotism on Parade* by Wallace E. Davies; see the chapter "Blue Blood Turns Red, White, and Blue."[46] All these institutions were alike in limiting membership to descendants of early American immigrants. The Pennsylvania German Society also originally limited its "first-class membership" to descendants of German or Swiss emigrants who had arrived in America before 1808.[47] One of my colleagues once said that, like the DAR, the Pennsylvania German Society required its members to have "dated blood." Fortunately, the society has long since given up this self-imposed limitation.

Finally, we need to place the Pennsylvania German struggle for identity against the new current wave of American ethnicity.[48] All American ethnic groups, including the Pennsylvania Germans, have swung the ethnic pendulum from radical anglicizing to radical ethnicizing, from acceptance to rejection of the common American culture. Other ethnic groups have smarted under outside criticism and run the gauntlet of ethnic slur [49] and arrived at a balanced appreciation of their own distinctive culture in relation to the cultural pluralist complex that is America today. If "Black is Beautiful," and "Red is Beautiful," then "Dutch is Beautiful," too.

The leaders of the Pennsylvania German awakening of 1983, the dialectizers, in their resolve to preserve the dialect and with it as much of the Pennsylvania German traditional culture as possible, would agree with the admonition of Pastor William A. Helffrich, one of the mainstays of the Pennsylvania German ethnic awakening of the 1860s. In his German autobiography he gives the reader the advice, "Halt fescht was du hoscht"—Hold on firmly to what you have. [50]

Notes

1. For some indication of the vast extent of this literature, see Emil Meynen, comp. and ed., *Bibliography on German Settlements in Colonial North America, Especially on the Pennsylvania Germans and Their Descendants, 1683–1933* (Leipzig: Otto Harrassowitz, 1937), a 636-page, double-column work. The literature produced in the fifty-year period from 1933 to 1983 would fill an almost equally large volume.

2. For major ideas, see Philip Gleason, "American Identity and Americanization," and William Petersen, "Concepts of Ethnicity," in Stephan Thernstrom et al., eds., *Harvard Encyclopedia of American Ethnic Groups* (Cambridge, Mass.: Belknap Press of Harvard University Press, 1980), 31–58, 234–42.

3. Don Yoder, "The Irish and the Dutch," *Pennsylvania Dutchman* 2 (June 1, 1950):6. The author was Alexander Wilson, ornithologist and poet.

4. For "Palatine," see *The Oxford English Dictionary*, 7:389–90; also Don Yoder, "Palatine, Hessian, Dutchman: Three Images of the German in America," in Frederick S. Weiser, ed., *Ebbes fer Alle-Ebber, Ebbes fer Dich: Something for Everybody, Something for You* (Breinigsville: Pennsylvania German Society, 1980), 107–29.

5. See Thomas R. Brendle and William S. Troxell, comps. and eds., *Pennsylvania German Folk Tales, Legends, Once-Upon-A-Time Stories, Maxims, and Sayings Spoken in the Dialect Popularly Known as Pennsylvania Dutch* (Norristown: Pennsylvania German Society, 1944), 109–20.

6. Mark Owen Heller, "The Union Church Problem in Eastern Pennsylvania," *Lutheran Church Quarterly* 14 (1941):174–90; Don Yoder, "Lutheran and Reformed Union Proposals, 1800–1850: An American Experiment in Ecumenics," *Bulletin Theological Seminary of the Evangelical and Reformed Church in the United States* 17 (January 1946):38–77.

7. The best introduction to the history and rationale of the Mennonites and Amish is the four-volume *Mennonite Encyclopedia* (Scottdale, Pa.: Mennonite Publishing House, 1955–59). See also the many volumes on both Mennonites and Amish by the anthropologist John A. Hostetler, particularly *Amish Society*, 3d ed. (Baltimore: Johns Hopkins University Press, 1983).

8. For the shift in the meaning of the terms "Dutch" and "Dutchman," see *The Oxford English Dictionary*, 3:728–29; also my article cited in footnote 4 above, 122–29. Tourism is, of course, a worldwide problem for culture. See the symposium, "Tourismus and Kulturwandel," in *Zeitschrift für Kulturaustausch* 28 (1978).

9. Useful as theoretical framework though not exactly parallel is Milton M. Gordon's threefold categorization of Anglo-Conformity, Melting Pot, and Cultural Pluralism as emigrant reactions to the American experience in his *Assimilation in American Life: The Role of Race, Religion, and National Origins* (New York: Oxford University Press, 1964). For the language problem among all German groups in America see Heinz Kloss, "German-American Language Maintenance Efforts," in Joshua A. Fishman et al., eds., *Language Loyalty in the United States: The Maintenance and Perpetuation of Non-English Mother Tongues by American Ethnic and Religious Groups* (The Hague: Mouton, 1966), 206–52.

10. Heinz Kloss, *Die Entwicklung neuer germanischer Kultursprachen von 1800 bis 1950* (Munich: Pohl, 1952), Schriftenreihe des Goethe-Instituts, vol. 1: 119–26.

11. George F. Baer, *The Pennsylvania Germans: An Address Delivered at the Dedication of Palatinate College, Myerstown, Pa., December 23, 1875* (N.p., n.d.), reprinted from the *Mercersburg Review* 23 (1876):248–67. For Baer (1842–1914) see *Dictionary of American Biography*, 1:489–90.

12. Clyde S. Stine, "The Pennsylvania Germans and the School," in Ralph Wood, ed., *The Pennsylvania Germans* (Princeton: Princeton University Press, 1942), 103–27; and Don Yoder, "Pennsylvania German Folklore Research: A Historical Analysis," in Glenn G. Gilbert, ed., *The German Language in America: A Symposium* (Austin: University of Texas Press, 1971), 76–86, 154–56.

13. One of the few treatments of the subject is Clyde S. Stine, "The Pennsylvania Germans and the School."

14. *Twenty-Ninth Annual Session of the Berks County Teachers' Institute Held at Reading, Pa., September 21st to 25th, 1891* (Reading, 1891).

15. A. R. Horne, *Horne's Pennsylvania German Manual*. The quotation is from the preface to the second edition (Allentown: National Educator print., 1895).

16. For the impact of Methodist revivalism in particular upon the Pennsylvania Germans, see Paul H. Eller, "Revivalism and the German Churches of Pennsylvania, 1783–1816" (Ph.D. dissertation, University of Chicago, 1933); and Don Yoder, *Pennsylvania Spirituals* (Lancaster, Pa.: Pennsylvania Folklife Society, 1961).

17. Vergilius Ferm, *The Crisis in American Lutheran Theology: A Study of the Issue between American Lutheranism and Old Lutheranism* (New York: Century Co., 1927); Richard C. Wolf, "The Americanization of the German Lutherans, 1683 to 1829" (Ph.D. dissertation, Yale University, 1947); and John B. Frantz, "Revivalism in the German Reformed Church in America, with Emphasis on the Eastern Synod" (Ph.D. dissertation, University of Pennsylvania, 1961).

18. Elmer T. Clark et al., eds., *The Journal and Letters of Francis Asbury*, vol. 2: *The Journal, 1794 to 1816* (London: Epworth Press; Nashville: Abingdon Press, 1958), 550.

19. William Colbert, "A Letter to Bishop Asbury," ed. Don Yoder, *Pennsylvania Dutchman* 1 (May 12, 1949):5.

20. Robert Adair, *Memoir of Rev. James Patterson, Late Pastor of the First Presbyterian Church, N[orthern]. L[iberties]., Phila[delphia].* (Philadelphia: Henry Perkins, 1840), 199–200.

21. Adolf Keller, *Amerikanisches Christentum—Heute* (Zollikon-Zürich: Evangelischer Verlag, 1943).

22. For Helmuth's career, see *Dictionary of American Biography*, 8:515–16.

23. "Zuruf an die Deutschen in Amerika," *Evangelisches Magazin* 2 (1813):175.

24. Henry Eyster Jacobs, *A History of the Evangelical Lutheran Church in the United States*, American Church History Series, vol. 4 (New York: Christian Literature Co., 1897), 331.

25. John J. Appel, "Immigrant Historical Societies in the United States, 1880–1950" (Ph.D. dissertation, University of Pennsylvania, 1960).

26. John J. Appel, "Marion Dexter Learned and the German American Historical Society," *Pennsylvania Magazine of History and Biography* 86 (1962):287–318.

27. For the nineteenth-century emigration see Carl Wittke, *We Who Built America: The Saga of the Immigrant* (New York: Prentice-Hall, 1945), 187–261.

28. Carl Wittke, *Refugees of Revolution: The German Forty-Eighters in America* (Philadelphia: University of Pennsylvania Press, 1952).

29. H. J. Ruetenik, "The Pennsylvanians and the Foreign Germans," *Reformed Church Messenger*, September 26, 1895, p. 3.

30. Samuel Kistler Brobst (1822–76) is the best example. For his career see Ralph C. Wood, "S. K. Brobst—Our Pennsylvania Dutch Language Leader," *Pennsylvania Dutchman* 1 (August 4, 1949):7.

31. J[ohann]. G[eorg]. Kohl, *Reisen in Canada und durch die Staaten New York und Pennsylvanien* (Stuttgart: J. G. Cotta, 1856), 527–28.

32. See Appel, "Marion Dexter Learned."

33. Homer T. Rosenberger, *The Pennsylvania Germans, 1891–1965 (Frequently Known as the "Pennsylvania Dutch"): Seventy-Fifth Anniversary Volume of the Pennsylvania German Society*, The Pennsylvania German Society, vol. 63 (Gettysburg, Pa., 1966), 73–90.

34. Ruetenik, "Pennsylvania and the Foreign Germans," 3.

35. A. F. Kemp, "The Pennsylvania German Versammlinge," *Pennsylvania German Folklore Society* 9 (1944):187–218; Russell W. Gilbert, "Pennsylvania German Versammling Speeches," *Pennsylvania Speech Annual* 13 (1956):3–20.

36. Groundhog Day, February 2, was *Lichtmess* (Candlemas), a winter midpoint in the traditional Pennsylvania German calendar. At that time, according to the ancient rhyme, spinning was to be over for the winter, and half the fodder should still be in the barn (*Lichtmess, schpinn vergess, halb gfresst*). Through the Groundhog Lodges the groundhog has since the 1930s become an unofficial symbol of Pennsylvania German culture along with the distelfink, the hex sign, and the Amishman.

37. For the history of the dialect theater in Pennsylvania and examples of dialect plays, see Albert F. Buffington, ed., *The Reichard Collection of Early Pennsylvania German Dialogues and Plays* (Lancaster: Pennsylvania German Society, 1962).

38. Earlier forms of dialect literature were also Pennsylvania German adaptations of general American popular culture phenomena. For example, the *Zeitingsbrief* or newspaper letter was modeled on the humorous "letters to the editor" in the Anglo-American press. These first appeared in the period of the War of 1812 and are still the major feature of Pennsylvania German literary production.

39. Russell W. Gilbert, "Religious Services in Pennsylvania German," *Susquehanna University Studies* 5 (1956):277–89.

40. Don Yoder, "The Dialect Church Service in the Pennsylvania German Culture," in Karl Scherer, ed., *Pfälzer—Palatines: Beiträge zur pfälzischen Ein- und Aus-*

wanderung sowie zur Volkskunde und Mundartforschung der Pfalz und der Zielländer pfälzischer Auswanderer im 18. und 19. Jahrhundert (Kaiserslautern: Heimatstelle Pfalz, 1981), 349–60. For facsimiles of programs of dialect church services, see *Pennsylvania Folklife* 27 (Summer 1978):2–13.

41. *A Pennsylvania German Folk Theatre Sampler* (N.p., 1983).

42. *Die Fier un Fazichscht Pennsylfawnish Deitsch Fersammling fon Baerricks Kounty, In der Kutztown State Collitsch Ess-Schtubb in Kutztown, Der Fierd Obril om Halwer Siwwe Owets. For die wu Deitsch Schwetze Kenne* (Oley, Pa.: W. W. Wagonseller, Drucker, 1983).

43. Thomas J. McCormack, ed., *Memoirs of Gustave Koerner, 1809–1896: Life-Sketches Written at the Suggestion of His Children,* 2 vols. (Cedar Rapids, Iowa: Torch Press, 1909), 1:322.

44. See Elizabeth Clarke Kieffer, "Henry Harbaugh: Pennsylvania Dutchman, 1817–1867," *The Pennsylvania German Society Proceedings and Addresses* (Norristown: Norristown Herald, Inc., 1945), vol. 51, pt. 2:1–365.

45. Don Yoder: "The Reformed Church and Pennsylvania German Identity," *Yearbook of German-American Studies* 18 (1983):63–82.

46. Wallace E. Davies, *Patriotism on Parade: The Story of Veterans' and Hereditary Organizations in America, 1783–1900* (Cambridge, Mass.: Harvard University Press, 1955).

47. In addition, associate membership was open to those who were "of full age, good moral character, and of German descent not native to this State, or a foreign-born German naturalized and resident in this State not less than ten years." Finally, honorary membership was open to "persons who have made the history, genealogy, principles, etc., of the Pennsylvania Germans a special subject of study and research, and any other persons eminent in their profession or calling, to whatever nationality they may belong, who have shown themselves in sympathy with the Pennsylvania Germans" (Constitution of the Society, adopted April 15, 1891, *Proceedings of the Pennsylvania German Society* [Lancaster: Pennsylvania German Society, 1891], 1:85).

48. For the new ethnicity, see Thernstrom et al., eds., *Harvard Encyclopedia of American Ethnic Groups;* also Milton L. Barron, *American Minorities: A Textbook of Readings in Intergroup Relations* (New York: Alfred A. Knopf, 1957); Nathan Glazer and Daniel P. Moynihan, eds., *Ethnicity: Theory and Experience* (Cambridge, Mass.: Harvard University Press, 1975); Charles F. Marden and Gladys Meyer, *Minorities in American Society,* 3d ed. (New York: American Book Co., 1968); and Michael Novak, *The Rise of the Unmeltable Ethnics: Politics and Culture in the Seventies* (New York: Macmillan, 1973).

49. For "terms of abuse," of which "the American language boasts a large stock, chiefly directed at aliens," see H. L. Mencken, *The American Language: An Inquiry into the Development of English in the United States,* 4th ed., abridged by Raven I. McDavid, Jr. (New York: Alfred A. Knopf, 1974), 367–89.

50. William A. Helffrich, *Lebensbild aus dem pennsylvanisch-deutschen Predigerstand; Oder Wahrheit in Licht und Schatten,* ed. N. W. A. and W. U. Helffrich (Allentown: Private edition, 1906).

5.
Hyphenated America: The Creation of an Eighteenth-Century German-American Culture

STEPHANIE GRAUMAN WOLF

"SEEK AND YE SHALL FIND" the Bible advises us, and this advice has been at once watchword and spur to countless generations of researchers. Like the prophecies of the Delphic oracle, however, there is a dark side or obverse to this seemingly positivist approach all too often ignored by scholars in search of the "truth" of the past. It might be expressed as "Do not seek and ye shall not find," or, perhaps, even more dangerously, "Ye shall find only that which ye seek." Thus the philosophical preconceptions of certain disciplines and the intellectual context of their scholars create interpretations of the past limited by the ideology of the present. Anthropologists and folklorists search for continuity: they find it. Historians build models based on change: they, too, find what they expect. As social scientists we structure a hypothesis and test it, and, although the data we collect are not prejudged and may prove or disprove our hypothetical model, the answer will always be conditioned by the nature and structure of the original question.

These warnings are especially pertinent to those of us who search for an understanding of the cultural and ethnic identification of eighteenth-century colonial Americans. The problem lies not only in deciding what we mean by ethnicity but in determining what they would have meant had the term been available to them.[1] Modern models of ethnicity are so firmly built on nineteenth-century notions of nationalism that it is almost impossible to reconstruct them without consciously establishing entirely new foundations. Failure to do this results in frustrating attempts to discuss the heterogeneous nature of the colonial experience by reference to measurements of acculturation that were almost surely irrelevant to the people of the seventeenth and eighteenth centuries. Because colonial Americans knew perfectly well what they meant by such terms as "German," "Dutch," "Swedish," or "English," they rarely bothered to explain their criteria, and twentieth-century observers may easily misinterpret the labels by accepting them in the modern nationalistic or political context. Moreover, it seems likely that the environment of ethnic populations was so heavily affected in Pennsylvania by the extreme heterogeneity of the colony that the meanings themselves began to change during the period under consideration.

It would be impossible, of course, to transport an ethnic population to a different environment and to maintain its cultural integrity intact. Even its most deeply held, most idiosyncratic, and most conspicuous traits will be affected by the new context, both natural and social. The degree of deviation from the old ethnic base can be seen along a continuum in which the group disappears into a surrounding, more dominant culture (amalgamation), incorporates significant new values and patterns of behavior into the system (acculturation), or modifies its own patterns into new forms related to—but not identical with—those of its neighbors (adaptation).[2] The result of these various levels of assimilation, in all but the case of total amalgamation, is the creation of a new culture, sharing more or less in the old ethnic group norms but differing in significant ways from both the original base and the surrounding group, many of whose traits it has adopted in transmogrified form. The full scope of the transformation is more easily observable to those who view the new cultural construct from a vantage point widely separated from it in space or time and who have come to acknowledge it in the use of hyphenated designations.

Germantown, Pennsylvania, is a particularly interesting focus for a study of the creation of a new cultural entity from a variety of ethnic bits and pieces. Since the late nineteenth century, it has served as the site of an ethnic variant of our mythic national creation story and thus as a signifier of identity for millions of hyphenated Americans of German descent.[3] The unhyphenated, or Anglo version of the founding of America is familiar to all, being retold every November in story, song, and television drama: briefly summarized, it describes a cold autumn day in 1620, when a little band of Pilgrims under the spiritual and community leadership of William Bradford landed in the "howling wilderness" of the New World. Surrounded by glowering forests, threatening beasts, and pagan savages, its members created a "little common-wealth," a replica—purified—of the Christian world of seventeenth-century England.

The German-American version is less often told because American ideology usually requires that the roots of all citizens be symbolically derived from the Anglo experience. But on rare occasions when we wish to celebrate our ethnic diversity, such as on the three hundredth anniversary of German immigration to America, the founding of Germantown may be remembered as a parallel offering to the establishment of Plymouth. Sixty-three years after the Pilgrims arrived, and at the same unfriendly time of year, thirteen devout families of Krefeld linen weavers braved the same dangers and trials of a difficult ocean voyage to settle in Penn's woods. They pursued a similar mission of religious and communal purity, led by Francis Daniel Pastorius, a man of piety and learning. Both myths achieve their symbolic ends by ignoring unsuitable historic realities: that Englishmen and Germans, to say nothing of the indigenous population and a variety of other European Christians, had long been resident on the continent; that neither colony was composed of a united group of homogenous believers; and that both clearly understood the economic as well as the religious motive for migration.

The ironies of myth-making are even more notable, however, in the choice of Germantown and its founding as a central focus for the beginning of German history in America. In the prenationalistic context of seventeenth-century attitudes toward ethnicity, the cultural background of the first Krefeld settlers owes a great deal to its Dutch origins, just as the more traditional German orientation of Pastorius was noted at the time: "Pastorus, [sic] the *German* Friend, Agent for the Company at Frankford, with his *Dutch* People, are preparing to make Brick next year," wrote Penn in 1685.[4] In addition to contemporary literary evidence, the names of the Krefeld families and the use of the Dutch language in the early court records provide further confirmation of the designation.[5]

By the late nineteenth century, however, an emphasis on the identification of nationality with political boundaries, and a lack of distinction between the original families who settled in Germantown and those who soon followed them, created a historical argument that still rages between adherents of the "Germantowners-as-German" and the "Germantowners-as-Dutch" schools of thought. The deep political antagonisms of World War II fueled much of the divisive literature that appeared on the topic.[6] The most recent German scholarship has tended to reconcile the two extremes by both recognizing the Dutch orientation of the founding families and acknowledging the effect of their long period of residence in Krefeld before their arrival in America: "Most of the Krefeld emigrants doubtless had Dutch names. One can assume that they belonged to the religious refugees who had moved from Holland to the liberal town on the lower Rhine. The op de Graeff family had emigrated from the Dutch town of Aldekerk as early as 1609. The emigrants of this name who had gone to Germantown were hence already second generation descendants of Dutch refugees. . . . Nevertheless, it can be said that the founders had come from a German town and that at least some of them had lived there for a long time. . . . The story is complicated a little by the fact that the County of Moers, in which Krefeld was situated, belonged to the area ruled over by the Princes of Nassau and Orange who simultaneously were hereditary stadtholders in the Netherlands between 1600 and 1702." This synthesis of earlier conclusions tacitly makes the point that if "in our times of supra-national thinking [such designations] ought not to be considered to be of decisive importance," we share an approach with seventeenth-century folk for whom also this was not the crucial issue.[7]

There are several reasons why later generations came to regard these first arrivals as German. First, seventeenth- and eighteenth-century criteria for ethnic identification were headed by the ability to speak a given language whatever an individual's place of birth, ancestry, or former political allegiance. Susan Klepp's careful study of five census records taken by the Swedish church in Pennsylvania between 1683 and 1784 indicates that in the earliest period being a "Swede" was a matter of self-definition in a congregation that was, by modern standards, extremely heterogeneous: "A Swede was a person, of no matter what ethnic background, able to speak the Swedish language."[8] If the first Krefeld settlers, as would seem likely from their period of residence in Germany, spoke German, at least in public, as well as Dutch, some of the confusion may be accounted for.

The strong synthesis between language and ethnic identification was matched by an equally strong tie of both to religion. To belong to a church was to accept its cultural orientation along with its doctrine. For the first few years after the founding of Germantown, the only formal religious institution available to the settlers was a Quaker meeting. The Quakers were clearly identified as an English group, and it was necessary for the Krefelders to learn the language quickly so they could participate in the widespread organization of monthly meetings and charitable associations of their coreligionists. Although Mennonite gatherings began in private homes sometime before 1690, no meetinghouse was erected until 1708, by which time German immigration to the town had changed the ethnic mix of the population. Those Krefelders who remained Quaker at the time of the Keithian controversy at the turn of the century were completely amalgamated into the English culture, but those who chose to become Mennonites acquired a German identification. Since amalgamation with the English involved name anglicization, descendants of these settlers disappeared as a visible group, while the Dutch roots of the Mennonite converts were concealed by the German nature of the Pennsylvania congregations.[9]

The perception that early Germantown was, in fact, what Pastorius had named it in fancy—a German town—became fixed in historical consciousness in the middle of the nineteenth century by its first and most widely respected chronicler. By defining the parameters of its distinctive culture as "German," John Fanning Watson almost guaranteed that those who came after would seek—and find—this ethnic orientation, ignoring evidence that might point to the development of a far more complex, uniquely local cultural construct. As he wrote in 1842: "Persons now visiting Germantown, and witnessing its universal *English* population, could hardly imagine that a place so near Philadelphia could have retained its *German character*, down to the year 1793. Before that time, all the public preaching was in German; and nearly all the plays of the boys, and their conversation, was in that tongue."[10]

It is worthwhile analyzing Watson's writings briefly, if only because he was used as a reliable source for most historians writing in the nineteenth and early twentieth centuries. Indeed, his work is so filled with interesting anecdotes and bits of material that can be found nowhere else that there is sometimes an overwhelming temptation to throw in a quote, uncritically, just for color. Watson moved to Germantown in 1814 to become a clerk at the Bank of Germantown, and it is obvious that he began to gather much of his information before the 1820s, since he noted conversations with men who are known to have died by that time.[11] His *Annals* are an almost archetypal antiquarian collection, and it is clear that he was indefatigable in his collection of documents, artifacts, and oral history, whenever possible, but his concerns and level of sophistication were those of his time. Many of his "facts" (concerning documents he had not seen) are wrong. He records, for example, twenty log houses in the old style still standing in 1844 and several more which he recorded as having been recently removed. Yet fewer such dwellings appear in the tax assessments forty-five years earlier, and almost certainly none were built after that time. In relation to the use of German in the Germantown churches, close examination of the records indicates frequent use of English at a much earlier period, although no English churches were established until the 1790s.[12]

In addition, many of Watson's authorities were, like Anthony Johnson, clearly recounting incidents that took place in the middle of the eighteenth century, and a large part of his section on Germantown is devoted to anecdotes of the revolutionary war and the British occupation. Most of Watson's other informants were the sons of prominent families of German descent, active in the German churches, and solid, though not necessarily upper-income, members of the craft community. Analysis of his interviews with them indicates that, by the time of the Revolution, there was no language barrier between these children and their families, on the one hand, and the British soldiers or other English visitors who appeared in the town, on the other. Watson presents the picture of a bilingual population, perhaps using the old language in private life, although making the common public business of the town an English affair. Thus the boys whose "plays and conversation" were all in German wrote and read English in school and used it in more formal situations.

The assumption of two different cultural faces in Germantown—a public one of assimilation and a private one of ethnic tradition—may well represent a solution created by many urban eighteenth-century Pennsylvania Germans to the problem of group identification. As far as language is concerned, this was not merely a local Germantown phenomenon, for, as Benjamin Rush noted in 1798: "The intercourse of the Germans with each other is kept chiefly in their own language, but most of their men who visit the capital and trading or country towns of the state, speak the English language."[13] In Reading, Pennsylvania, easy social mingling took place in the inns and taverns, and residential patterns in neighborhoods were determined more by class than by ethnic background, but private clubs and intimate family decisions resisted amalgamation.[14]

Much more complex patterns of intercultural penetration appear to have taken place on the level of material life. Here, particularly, generations of researchers have found what they sought: distinctly different "Pennsylvania Dutch" painted furniture, stylistically and conceptually derived from German antecedents. What they have frequently failed to identify are the myriad pieces of "Pennsylvania Ger-

Decorative plate (c.1800) attributed to the Pennsylvania German artist David Spinner (1758–1811). The inscription reads: "Thou hast been a dear man to me since first I ever looked at thee." Spinner, a well-to-do farmer, justice of the peace, and tax collector in Milford Township, Bucks County, Pennsylvania, painted and inscribed some of the most beautiful plates of this kind still in existence. (Philadelphia Museum of Art: Gift of John T. Morris)

man production . . . gone English"; they also tend to characterize items made by German craftsmen in predominantly German parts of the colony as awkwardly misconstrued examples of attempts to copy Philadelphia style when, in fact, they may really represent a conscious accommodation of German taste to life in Pennsylvania among the English. The most complete blending of the two cultures is seen in an American clothes press with a row of drawers marching down the middle, integrating an English preference with an otherwise easily recognizable German furniture form. Very few pieces of furniture survive that can be directly documented to Germantown cabinetmakers, but those that do exhibit, for the most part, a similar mingling of cultural options. The end product is, in effect, the creation of a new and unified identity that has elected which of the old elements to retain, which to adapt, and which to drop. Continuity of the old occurs most frequently in method rather than form, indicating that habitual work patterns of craftsmanship dictated the retention of old construction techniques even while surface style changed to meet the new context.[15]

Even within areas rarely penetrated by cultural outsiders, acculturational distinctions seem to have been made. Artifacts created for use in the church or even in the public spaces of the home incorporated English ideas, while the purely private rooms continued to be filled with older ethnic signifiers such as chests and *schranks*.[16] An inventory study of the artifacts found in Germantown houses indicates the way in which the people of this urban, more cosmopolitan settlement created a cultural pattern all their own. The variation in the contents of Germantown estates had to do with the wealth of decedents and the numbers of goods they listed rather than with their ethnic origins. German, English, or Dutch, they presented a mixed picture of showy English forms in the public spaces and more simple German ones in family areas. One curious sidelight is that Germantowners of all ethnic backgrounds continued to prefer chests over chests of drawers for storage throughout the eighteenth century, long after the latter form had become a standard item in most colonial homes.

The development of a peculiarly local culture in Germantown was a response to the unique rhythm of demographic changes in this particular town that shaped the nature of its life, building a physical environment that replicated the variety of its mental constructs and world views. Population did not grow smoothly in Germantown, but rather in a series of incremental leaps, followed by periods of relative stagnation.[17] Increase was the product of inmigration: natural increase was uncharacteristically low for colonial America, and outmigration was high. The result was that a small group of relatively stable families remained and prospered, and a much larger group constantly shifted, moved, and eventually disappeared from the community.[18] Although the stable family groups were varied in respect to their original ethnic derivations, they eventually built the homogeneous culture of peculiarly local character that came to be identified with Germantown.

Each of the growth spurts in population involved not only a large influx of newcomers to the town but a basically different group ethnically or culturally as well, who were different from each other and different from the matrix of Germantown society at the time of their arrival. The first group of additional settlers arrived in 1685 and was the one exception to the rule of demographic difference: its members were mostly Dutch Quakers who had met William Penn on his trip through Holland and Germany in 1677 and arrived in Pennsylvania after some years of residence in the German town of Kriegsheim in the Palatinate.[19]

From then on there was a steady accretion of Germans to the town, and by 1709, when the starving time on the Continent caused mass migration, a clearly German majority in the township was permanently established.[20] The next local demographic crisis took place at midcentury during the period of the great migration to Pennsylvania, and although a heavy proportion of those who arrived were German, they were probably not the poorest of the new immigrants.[21] This increment also saw the beginning trickle of a new cultural group whose influence grew out of all proportion to its numbers: successful Philadelphians who saw Germantown as the ideal spot for country homes. After the Revolution, Germantown was "discovered" in earnest, and the trickle became a flood, but the nature of later summer visitors was somewhat different. It was composed of people who were not interested in summer establishments but merely in renting rooms or local homes for the season. They tended to return year after year and clearly had a marked effect on the life of the community, but, in general, they are not quantifiable, appearing on no tax lists or church records.[22] The final decade of the eighteenth century again saw an enormous demographic shift, the proportion of separately owned properties increasing by 67 percent and the number of properties of less then an acre rising from 83 to 221.[23] Many of the new properties can be identified as rental units, indicating the growth in real estate speculation to serve the semitransient tourist. Most of the new owners had English names not previously appearing in the records. It is impossible to know whether a significant number of these newcomers were of German background with anglicized names. For purposes of understanding cultural orientation, the point is irrelevant, however, since use of the English form of the surname (along with a typically English, rather than German, given name) is one of the strongest statements available for ethnic reidentification.

Accompanied by the opening of branches of city shops that intruded into the economic rhythm of the town, this large accretion of new residents, especially transient ones, must have had a catastrophic effect on cultural patterns that had been slowly growing throughout the century. Although Watson may have misinterpreted the *German* quality of life before that date, his perception that things were indeed different, gleaned from his interviews and his visual perception of his surroundings, has the ring of truth: "The yellow fever of 1793 brought out here all the officers of the general and state governments, and of the banks, and filled all the houses with new inmates. In the next and subsequent years, sundry families from the city became summer residents."[24]

Given the unique patterns of demographic change in Germantown—growth by accretion rather than natural increase and by cultural and numerical assault—it speaks to a strength of community identity that the population of stable families from a variety of ethnic backgrounds developed marked cultural cohesiveness. As the century wore on, old-time Germantowners of whatever ethnic derivation relied more and more on one another in the economic areas of life, weaving intricate networks of business and financial obligations. Children of these families married each other more than twice as often as they married temporary residents, and the families of summer people and year-round inhabitants were almost never joined. By the end of the century, as the outsiders began to establish their own churches, clubs, and institutions, native Germantowners continued to associate primarily with each other.

There can be no doubt that this culture involved only a part of the new community and was under continual pressure from new groups within the town. An ingenious method for measuring the cultural consensus of a population has been developed by anthropologists and rests on a close study of inventories to relate the naming of rooms within the house to the items within the rooms. The theory is that room names change uniformly within a culture in close connection with the social (as opposed to the physical) use of the space.[25] Use of these names thus becomes an indication of community agreement on the social use of space. In view of many recent studies that tend to show that only the Quakers presented a truly united front in the face of heterogeneity in colonial Pennsylvania, it is interesting to note that Chester County, which was overwhelmingly Quaker, was the only county regularly to name rooms in its inventories during this period. Although it is possible to make educated guesses about the location of objects within the Germantown houses because of the method of inventory-taking, no room names were ever used.

Perhaps the most graphic illustration of the way in which changing demographic patterns influenced the cultural patterns of eighteenth-century Germantown is to be found in a study of the built environment. Here again is an area in which the perceptions of the observer are most influenced by his background and his understanding of what he sees. Solid, material objects like houses seem to be unchanging: alterations are frequently unnoticed by later arrivals, structures that are "colonial" may be assumed to have been original when, in fact, the entire building may have been reworked so many times that nothing remains to indicate either the first form or the intent of the builder that lay behind it. The period known as the colonial revival at the beginning of the twentieth century wreaked particular havoc in Germantown: popular conceptions of colonial architecture rather than research into the actual appearance of Germantown architecture dictated the restorations made to eighteenth-century houses when the obvious nineteenth-century accretions were removed. Although Germantown Avenue boasts the greatest number of colonial and federal structures still standing in association with each other along any street in the United States, it also presents a doubly misleading aspect just because it is "real."

Comments made by outside visitors, even those closer to the time, looking at much that was "original" are also suspect. As the subsequent narrative illustrates, Germantowners began tinkering with their houses—changing, enlarging, and improving them—almost from the minute they were built. Value judgments based on the cultural milieu of the observer cast an additional veil of misinterpretation over the scene. In Germantown, the most obvious error is the assumption that the built environment represented a "German" picture rather than an adaptive response to a unique situation by a community continually in the process of creating its own patterns.

Although interpretations of the architectural history of Germantown differ, the time line for various types of construction and style is fairly well established, and not surprisingly it closely replicates the pattern of demographic change. Tradition insists that the first arrivals from Krefeld lived in "caves or crude huts" made of wood, dirt floors, and mud chimneys. No physical evidence survives of this first stage of habitation in Germantown, although Pastorius noted in his reminiscences that he occupied such a dwelling in Philadelphia when he first arrived. The only case that might be made in favor of the tradition is based on the somewhat labored reasoning that there were no carpenters among the Krefelders and that house-building was a specialized enough skill in the seventeenth century to be beyond the abilities of the average townsman.[26]

The first houses of which there is any documented evidence are simple two-room dwellings in the vernacular style of the Continent. Some of their features, such as the interior chimney and the corner fireplace, as well as the room placements, seem specifically German. Most of their other features are Continental and might be found almost anywhere in northern Europe, although they were not built in America by any of the English immigrants except the Scotch-Irish, who appear to have borrowed them from the Pennsylvania Germans. Leaving out Watson's culturally biased value judgments of the early structures still standing when he arrived in Germantown in 1814, his description of them is keen and worth quoting:

Most of the old houses in Germantown are plastered on the inside with clay and straw mixed, and over it is laid a finishing coat of thin lime plaster; some old houses seem to be made with log frames and the interstices filled with wattle, river rushes, and clay intermixed. . . . They are of but one story, so low that a man six feet high can readily touch the eaves of the roof. Their gable ends are to the street. The ground story is of stone or of logs, and they have generally one room behind the other. The roof is high and mostly hipped, forms a low bed chamber; the ends of the houses above the first story are of boards or sometimes of shingles, with a small chamber window at each end . . . the doors all divide in the middle, so as to have an upper and lower door: and in some houses the upper door folds. The windows are two doors, opening inwards, and were at first set in leaden frames with outside frames of wood.[27]

These early houses were being enlarged by the early eighteenth century or torn down and replaced by larger houses, still conceived in the European vernacular tradition but on a three-room plan, frequently of two and a half stories, often entirely of stone. The gable end still faced the road, but the roof was no longer gambrel (or "hipped," as Watson described it) but conformed to the gable roof line, which was the pattern among Pennsylvania English structures as well. These

Sketch of a house in Germantown originally built in the seventeenth century which subsequently underwent considerable renovations. All that remains of the original design in this picture are the roof line, the arched cellar windows, and possibly an interior chimney (not visible). Obvious changes: stone exterior covering; sash windows; new door, moved from gable end and given overlights and a pent roof. This sketch is by John Richard whose 1863–1889 sketchbook has captured in pen and ink many images of Germantown which have since disappeared. (Germantown Historical Society)

first two phases of Germantown building were replicated by Hans Milan, a Dutch Quaker, who settled in Germantown before 1690. His house, which later became known as Wyck, is still standing and bears evidence of its early rebuilding in the huge central chimney and three-room plan of the second phase, visible in joists, floor, and beams. When Milan's daughter married, he built a one-room house with side entry hall for her, directly in front of his own house and aligned with it along the south wall and the roof axis. This house bore no traces of Germanic plan.[28]

By midcentury a new form of house was being built in Germantown, which architectural historians have come to regard as "the" Germantown house. No doubt many were erected, especially by the more prosperous members of the community, but their number in relation to the total housing stock must have been small, for as late as 1798 very few houses in the township were anywhere near as large as these purportedly "typical" houses. Because they were among the most substan-

The Johnson house, built 1765–1768, embodies most of the characteristics of the substantial, urban Germantown dwelling that has come to be regarded as "typical," including a dressed front and rubble sides of local "glimmer" stone, pent roof, arched cellar windows, a front stoop with wooden benches, and a gable roof aligned to the street. From John Richard's sketchbook. (Germantown Historical Society)

tial buildings, because they were usually located in advantageous spots along the main road, and because the Georgian arrangement of their facades continued to be popular, they survived to make up 47 percent of all Germantown domestic architecture documented to the colonial or federal periods by the historic survey done in 1952.[29] These new structures did, however, represent what must have been considered appropriate by the community as town living quarters for those who could afford them. More than 80 percent of these houses were built by families with long Germantown histories, and most of them were located just outside the main part of town, where the land was not prohibitively expensive but the atmosphere was appropriately urban. Their incidence dropped off sharply in the more rural part of Germantown. Reuben Haines, for example, a fourth-generation member of the family at Wyck, ignored the new indigenous pattern, although he could easily have afforded it, in favor of continuing country traditions. He enlarged his farm property in 1771 by making a second-floor connec-

The Wyck house after a total remodeling by Strickland, with only a few clues to its origins and development behind the artfully integrated facade. Note the gable-end alignment to the street (at right), the irregular roof showing an amalgamation of two houses, the enclosure of an old cartway in the center, and the large central chimney in the rear house. From John Richard's sketchbook. (Germantown Historical Society)

tion between the two older houses, creating a covered cartway below.

The earliest cited example of the more urban "Germantown" dwelling dates from 1744, the latest from 1798, indicating acceptance of the form for at least fifty years. Although several of its attributes have been called "German"—such as the pent roofs, the arched cellar windows, and the double doors—these are part of the general architectural vocabulary of the time. The combination of these details with the use of local glimmer stone gives them their distinctive appearance. These structures are surely not vernacular in conception, but they are a peculiarly local variant of the academically designed houses of Philadelphia. In the twentieth century, during the colonial revival, hundreds of reproductions of these houses were built in the Germantown area, with the result that they have become ever more firmly fixed as a significant part of the Germantown scene.

During the last ten years of the eighteenth century, in response to a population explosion that demanded large additions to the available housing stock, most of the new buildings seem to have been part of the popular national style known as Federal. Much that was older remained, but many of the old houses received "face-lifts," new doorways with fanlights, taller, more elegant windows, and white front facings. The most recent inheritor of Wyck stuccoed over his joined farmhouse to give it a lighter, more imposing look.

The change in the face of Germantown from a distinctively local look to amalgamation with the broader culture was undoubtedly achieved slowly; Watson dates the transformation between 1814 and 1840. His attitude toward the transformation is interesting: he represented the new permanent resident as being of strong Anglo background, one who identified with a broad national culture. As an antiquarian, he appreciated the "olden times" enough to devote a great deal of his life to collecting its artifacts and stories, but he remained outside local patterns and values, as is clear from his description:

Those who now visit Germantown, and notice the general neatness and whiteness of the front faces of the houses, and see the elegance of some of the country seats, can have little idea how differently it looked in 1814, when the writer first became a resident in the place. Then, most of the houses were of dark, moss-grown stone, and of sombre and prison-like aspect, with little old fashioned windows, and monstrous corner chimneys, formed of stone. Now the chimneys are rebuilt of brick, and taken from the corners; and nearly all of the front walls are plastered over in imitation marble. . . . Many of the old houses, now of two stories, have been raised from one and a half stories, with high double hipped roofs.[30]

Final changes to Wyck objectify general submersion of the unique local culture that had developed in Germantown over almost 150 years. In 1820, Reuben Haines, who was living in Philadelphia, inherited the property and moved his family "to the country." He hired the famous Philadelphia architect William Strickland to redesign the building, and the result, though handsome and distinctive, spoke of Philadelphia "functional and aesthetic integration" far more than it did of the structure's ethnic and local history.[31] By the 1850s, when the coming of commuter rail service turned Germantown into a bedroom community for nearby Philadelphia, it was possible to think that all traces of its admittedly idiosyncratic version of Pennsylvania-German ethnicity had finally vanished. But deep-rooted cultural affinities die hard. Well into the twentieth century, old-timers could still remember when German was spoken by families running small shops in the less fashionable sections of town. A few small businesses along Germantown Avenue continued to be owned by the descendants of eighteenth-century craftsmen, and into the 1970s German continued to be used in the services and sermons of St. Michael's Lutheran Church even though it was understood by only a few very old parishioners, the majority of the congregation long having been black.

The question of ethnicity may, in the end, be one of self-identification and contrast. By 1800 communal life in Germantown bore no resemblance to the "Germanopolis" of Pastorius's vision or to Penn's "German Town" of Dutch weavers. It was made up of people involved in a cultural context of economic and social interchanges, shared habits of living and ideas of style and taste, and perhaps a local manner of speech, who carefully distinguished within the town itself between "themselves" and "others." Whatever they called themselves, the "others" labeled them "quaint" and "German." In time the myth became the reality, and it is likely that whatever survived of the underlying culture of colonial Germantown became more "German" during the nineteenth century as a result of acceptance of the myth by both sides.

Notes

1. Although the word "ethnic" has been in use in the English language since the fifteenth century, it carried its original Greek meaning of "pagan" or "heathen" at least through the eighteenth century (see *The Oxford English Dictionary*).

2. These categories have been derived and adapted from Milton M. Gordon's schema of assimilation indices in *Human Nature, Class, and Ethnicity* (New York: Oxford University Press, 1978), 169. Gordon develops seven assimilation variables ranging from "cultural patterns" to the "absence of value and power conflict." The main problem with this system is that it is in a linear mode: although the process may stop at #1 (cultural or behavioral assimilation), if it continues to #2 (structural assimilation) all other stages necessarily follow, and amalgamation is inevitable. Particularly in a self-conscious period of ethnic identification, however, the process may well be reversible. See William M. Newman, *American Pluralism: A Study of Minority Groups and Social Theory* (New York: Harper & Row, 1973).

3. For the retelling of this story with all of its symbolic meanings stressed, see, for example, Naamen Keyser et al., *History of Old Germantown: With a Description of Its Settlement and Some Account of Its Important Persons, Buildings and Places Connected with Its Development* (Germantown: H. F. McCann, 1907).

4. "A Further Account of the Province of Pennsylvania by William Penn," in Albert Cook Myers, ed., *Narratives of Early Pennsylvania, West New Jersey and Delaware, 1630–1707* (New York: Scribner, 1912), 271; emphasis added.

5. The original manuscript of the *Raths Buch der Germantownishen Gemeinde* is located in the Historical Society of Pennsylvania. It has never been reprinted. Sections written by Pastorius are in German; those kept by other members of the Germantown community are in Dutch.

6. See, for example, Friedrich Nieper, *Die ersten deutschen Auswanderer von*

Krefeld nach Pennsylvanien: Ein Bild aus der religiösen Ideengeschichte des 17. und 18. Jahrhunderts (Neukirchen, Kr. Moers: Buchhandlung des Erziehungsvereins, 1940), for the Pan-German expression, and Bertus Harry Wabeke, "Dutch Emigration to British America, 1664–1776," *de Halve Maen, Quarterly Magazine of the Dutch Colonial Period in America* 57 (August 1983): 1–4, reprint of an article that first appeared in 1944, for the other point of view.

7. Ingrid Schöberl, "Franz Daniel Pastorius and the Foundation of Germantown," trans. Robert W. Culverhouse, in Günter Moltmann, ed., *Germans to America: 300 Years of Immigration, 1683 to 1983* (Stuttgart: Eugen Heinz, 1982), 19.

8. Susan Klepp, "Five Early Pennsylvania Censuses," *Pennsylvania Magazine of History and Biography* 106 (October 1982): 504.

9. For a more complete analysis of this complex situation see Stephanie Grauman Wolf, *Urban Village: Population, Community and Family Structure in Germantown, Pennsylvania, 1683–1800* (Princeton: Princeton University Press, 1976), 147–50, 82.

10. John F. Watson, *Annals of Philadelphia and Pennsylvania in the Olden Time: Being a Collection of Memoirs, Anecdotes and Incidents of the City and Its Inhabitants,* 3 vols. (Philadelphia: Leary, Stuart Company, 1927), 2:63.

11. See, for example, the anecdote related by Anthony Johnson "who died in 1823, aged 78" (ibid., 35).

12. See Wolf, *Urban Village*, 35, 147.

13. Theodore E. Schmauk, "An Account of the Manners of the German Inhabitants of Pennsylvania, by Benjamin Rush," *The Pennsylvania German Society, Proceedings and Addresses* 19 (1910), pt. 21:104.

14. See Laura Becker, "Diversity and Its Significance in an Eighteenth Century Pennsylvania Town," in Michael Zuckerman, ed., *Friends and Neighbors: Group Life in America's First Plural Society* (Philadelphia: Temple University Press, 1982), 196–221.

15. Benno M. Forman, "German Influences in Pennsylvania Furniture," in Scott T. Swank et al., *Arts of the Pennsylvania Germans*, ed. Catherine E. Hutchins (New York: Norton, 1983), 102–70.

16. See, for example, Doris Devine Fanelli, "The Building and Furniture Trades in Lancaster, Pennsylvania, 1750–1800" (M.A. thesis, University of Delaware, 1979), and Charles F. Montgomery, *A History of American Pewter* (New York: Dutton, 1970).

17. For statistical details of population growth in Germantown see Wolf, *Urban Village*, 38–46 and passim.

18. Daniel Snydacker, "Kinship and Community in Rural Pennsylvania, 1749–1820," *Journal of Interdisciplinary History* 13 (1982): 58, discovered a similar pattern of outmigration and family instability among the Presbyterians, Lutherans, and Moravians in eighteenth-century York County, although not among the Quakers. Although I had not tested for ethnicity in this regard, when I did so, I found that the largest proportion of stable Germantown families (after the first settlers had moved to more rural locations) were the Quakers.

19. For a description of this meeting, see Mary Maples Dunn and Richard S. Dunn, eds., "An Account of My Journey into Holland and Germany," in *The Papers of William Penn*, vol. 1: 1644–1679 (Philadelphia: University of Pennsylvania Press, 1981), 448.

20. Margaret Tinkcom, "Germantown: Urbane Village, 1683–1850," in "Wyck: A Manual for Guides," March 1981 (typescript), 6.

21. The most recent information on the patterns of German immigration to Pennsylvania can be found in Marianne Wokeck, "The Flow and Composition of German

Immigration to Philadelphia, 1727–1775," *Pennsylvania Magazine of History and Biography* 105 (1981):249–78.

22. The one place they show up outside of the real estate advertisements and account books is in the marriage records. It was evidently popular to marry in Germantown and then spend the summer there. These records seriously bias the demographic use of the aggregate data from the churches for figuring family size. See Wolf, *Urban Village*, 151.

23. Ibid., 43, 67.

24. Watson, *Annals*, 63.

25. For a fuller explanation of the technique and its theoretical base, see Stephen Tyler, ed., *Cognitive Anthropology* (New York: Holt, Rinehart & Winston, 1969). A case study using the methodology may be found in Dell Upton, "Vernacular Domestic Architecture in Eighteenth Century Virginia," *Winterthur Portfolio* 17 (Summer–Autumn 1982):95–119.

26. David Polk and Amy Polk, "Architecture: A Brief Outline of the Architecture of Germantown as Related to the History of Wyck," "Wyck," 10. That the original Krefelders were not generalized in the rural crafts which might include carpentry might be inferred from Pastorius's comment that the Germantowners in 1684 were "mostly linen weavers and not any too skilled in agriculture" (Myers, ed., *Narratives*, 399). The craft of weaving, however, required a knowledge of carpentry for assembling and setting up the loom.

27. Watson, *Annals*, 2:18–19.

28. Polk and Polk, "Architecture," 11–13.

29. This percentage was derived from an analysis of the photographs and plans in Harry M. Tinkcom, Margaret B. Tinkcom, and Grant Miles Simon, *Historic Germantown: From the Founding to the Early Part of the Nineteenth Century. A Survey of the German Township* (Philadelphia: American Philosophical Society, 1955).

30. Watson, *Annals*, 2:49.

31. Polk and Polk, "Architecture," 14.

6.

Image and Counterimage, Tradition and Expectation: The German Immigrants in English Colonial Society in Pennsylvania, 1700–1765

HERMANN WELLENREUTHER

DESPITE CONSIDERABLE RESEARCH into German-English relations in eighteenth-century Pennsylvania, important problems remain unsolved. We know precious little about the way the Germans viewed themselves in Pennsylvania, we have virtually no information about the German image of the English in general and of America and Pennsylvania in particular, and most important, we know very little about German reactions to English grumblings concerning the German danger to the glorious British constitution.[1] Thus, profiting from the learned works of others and looking afresh at material printed in Pennsylvania between 1700 and 1765, I will concentrate on images and concepts, definitions and terminologies, which were developed in the eighteenth century in the search for clearer and more meaningful explanations of ethnic conflicts and the way they were solved in William Penn's colony.[2] In examining the contents of public images as they were expressed in books and pamphlets of the period, I will exclude private perceptions of other ethnic groups based on the daily experience of living together, sharing problems (if they did), and doing things together. I am of course aware that restricting the scope of this essay invites methodological objections as well as raises the simple question whether it is meaningful to pursue such a concept as public perception and image. Although space does not allow me to deal with the methodological issues, I am confident that the second question will be answered at the end of the chapter.

German immigrants found it easy to name those who were already living in Pennsylvania. Yet the English, if one believes the printed evidence, had problems: German immigrants are lumped together with others as "aliens" in a pamphlet published in 1725; in the same year another author referred to them as "Palatines"; an almanac writer fluctuated between "Dutch Boar" and "Goose and Turkey Palatine" in his allegoric disquisition on Pennsylvania's multiethnic society. And although German immigration had increased in the 1720s and 1730s, an author in 1735 still referred to the German immigrants only as "For-

"The German bleeds and bears the furs. . . ." Engraving by James Claypole, Jr., from 1764. This famous cartoon presents the point of view of Pennsylvanians who defended the border against Indian raids and who accused the Quakers of betraying the common defense for the sake of trade and profits. Benjamin Franklin (left) is portrayed as a clever, and not completely trustworthy, mediator (as symbolized by the fox at his feet). A procession of strange figures approaches from the right. The white man—apparently the German—who is carrying an Indian on his back is literally being led by the nose by a Quaker in a broad-brimmed hat. The Quaker figure can be identified as Israel Pemberton who controlled a significant part of the trade in Pennsylvania. The procession moves over three corpses through the countryside of Pennsylvania which is filled with burning houses and lurking Indians. (The Library Company of Philadelphia)

eigners of divers Nations." Finally, in 1747 the Germans acquired individuality in print. Hoping to enlist their support for his "Voluntary
Association," Benjamin Franklin praised the "*brave* and *steady* GER-
MANS," who had "fought well for their Tyrants and Oppressors."[3] Certainly these tidbits did not help the English settlers to understand the
numerous German immigrants arriving in their colony. They had
heard almost nothing about German political conditions, German cultural values, the state of religion, the economic situation, or the German outlook on life. The little information available reinforced the
already widespread belief that the English political system alone had
preserved ancient and glorious constitutional values and rights.[4]

If the English were unprepared for the German influx, were they
given any help by the immigrants themselves? What did the newcomers know about the English colonies in the New World and especially about Pennsylvania? What impact did published writings, letters
sent from America, and reports brought back by newlanders, semi-
professional emigration agents, have on prospective emigrants?[5] Fortunately, petitions and other material collected by German authorities
provide some valuable clues.[6] A sample of statements collected from
emigrants in 1709 will illustrate the range of knowledge: Christian
Schneider, aged twenty-five, related that he "only knew it [America] to
be a waste country which, however, could be improved by cultivation";
Adam Hartmann confessed he had been told that "one year's work
would yield a harvest sufficient to live off for two years"; another admitted his ignorance except that he thought things were better in the
new country.[7] In 1709 the level of expectation of these first participants
in a large-scale emigration movement to North America was surprisingly low. And later, when the sources of information about Pennsylvania became more numerous, the potential emigrants' expectations
as well as their image of Pennsylvania or America still remained vague.
Thus a petition from Nürtingen to the elector of Württemberg dated
May 6, 1753, simply expressed the hope "for a better livelihood." In
1762 another petition repeats this expectation; and in yet another petition two years later Franz Kuhn from Aich justified his resolution to
emigrate to Pennsylvania because of his "poverty and the times' op-
pressions and difficulties, the lack of vineyards to cultivate and the impossibility of finding sufficient nourishment."[8]

These components of the German image of America—they contained nothing about the English settlers—were reinforced by letters
received from those who had settled in the English colonies. The
letters collected by the authorities of Baden Durlach warn about the

serious hardships suffered during the crossing of the Atlantic and bemoan the expense of wine in Pennsylvania yet agree that "those who want to work will find a decent livelihood, for the land is big and not so overpopulated," as Catharina Thomen wrote from Philadelphia in October 1736. Others explicitly warned against indentured servitude.[9] Seldom did the immigrants comment on political conditions in the new country. One important exception is Johs Hayn's letter of October 15, 1752. Confessing that he had sworn allegiance to King William II [sic], he reported that in Pennsylvania "the subjects are not as oppressed by their lords and do not have to pay feudal dues. The lords are annually elected. Everything is free, all occupations and professions. It is, God be thanked, a fruitful and good country, full of plants and fruits."[10]

In sum, the image of America the immigrants brought to Pennsylvania was determined by the negative economic and social conditions in the Old World. These immigrants were bent on carving out a better living for themselves, the results of which they expected to enjoy and not share with their feudal lord. Yet their indistinct image of Pennsylvania and its English settlers did not imply that the people from southern Germany came to the New World with no expectations at all. Rather, we have to assume that they expected to be able to transfer their ways of living to Pennsylvania without undergoing a major transition: to settle together in nucleated villages, tend their fields or work in their shops, accumulate modest riches, be told by the local clergyman and magistrate what to do, but be protected against others who disagreed. For these emigrants were not averse to authority; those touching on that subject always carefully limited their remarks to feudal privileges.[11]

Viewed from both sides, then, a sizable gulf of expectations and images separated the English from those arriving in Pennsylvania from southern Germany, which must have made it difficult to work out a tolerable modus vivendi. In looking at the various stages in which the two ethnic groups developed new concepts and images, three overlapping periods stand out: an initial period ending around 1746 during which the groups underwent learning experiences and established the first patterns of political cooperation; a second period lasting until about 1758 when the English as well as the Germans searched for concepts of a multiethnic society; and finally, the years after 1758 when the experiences of common sufferings and a successful war established the foundations for a common ideological consciousness centered in a newly discovered common historical past.

Before 1746 English authors were pessimistic about the possibility of establishing a multiethnic society. In his almanac for 1726 John Hughes explicitly denounced a multiethnic society as a "monstrous Hydra." Ten years later the political implications of the German problem were discussed for the first time. Granted, "the Intent and Design of that Great Man [William Penn]" had been, as an author wrote in 1735, that justices ought to be elected by freeholders. But had he foreseen the possibility that Pennsylvania would become a "Colony numerous of Foreigners of Divers Nations, as well as English Subjects" eager to join the political decision-making process, would he have included in his Charter of Liberties and Privileges "so precarious and unprecedented a Scheme for the Administration of Justice, when possibly these Foreigners may be advanced to those Seats, and our Constitution thereby lost?" Clearly the author felt that Penn would not.[12] Six years later Conrad Weiser offered at least indirect proof for the English author's suspicions. Ignoring the partisan character of the conflict between the Quaker-dominated assembly, the governor, and the small band of proprietary supporters, Weiser interpreted German political support for Quakers under the leadership of the printer Christopher Sauer as approval of the Quakers' negative response to justified royal demands for defensive measures. Such a political attitude displayed a deplorable ingratitude toward the crown and an ignorance of secular and divine law, raised the question of German loyalty toward England, and represented a misuse of the freedom granted with naturalization and disrespect to authority rightfully constituted.[13]

It is well to recall that the Germans arriving in Pennsylvania brought with them definite notions about the function and role of governments and authority. They were used to being told what to do and when, not only in the secular but—with the exception of some sects—in the religious sphere. Yet this concept of an omnibus function of state authority which Weiser and the proprietors' followers evoked in 1741 was strangely out of place in Quaker-dominated Pennsylvania.[14] Indeed, the lack of authority in Pennsylvania irritated German immigrants and was a major obstacle in their efforts to adjust to Pennsylvania's political life. According to the anonymous author of a German pamphlet on education, for example, this deficient functioning of state authority was the cause of a sad decline in morals and religious standards; people in Pennsylvania, the author lamented, took this false freedom as license to sin.[15]

The Moravians agreed with this analysis. In 1742 their spokesman Georg Neisser suggested two reasons for the deplorable decline of public morals in the colony; the more important was "the refusal of authority to maintain honesty and public standards of behavior which ought to be its main function. This particular deficiency of the Government to support virtue as the mainstay of a public life coupled with the fact that everywhere little evils and injustices are tolerated" were to Neisser the principal causes for the "boundless outrages" committed everywhere in the colony.[16] The Lutherans, foremost among them Heinrich Melchior Muhlenberg, shared the Moravians' notion about authority. They were used to state interference in church affairs and habitually called on the government to help them deal with dissidents within their own ranks.[17]

The clearest evidence showing the persistence of this strong concept of authority among Germans in Pennsylvania comes, however, from a large handbook published by Christopher Sauer in 1751 as a guide for German settlers in learning English. This compendium contained a large section in which the English vocabulary was arranged in semantic fields. The last and smallest of these is headlined "Of Authority." It lists the following words and phrases: "All the before mentioned visible Men, Arts, Callings, Trade and Occupations are to be Submise to the Superiority—The Magistrates are ordained from God—The Emperor, King, Prince, Governor, Proprietor, Councillor, Ruler—Loyal Subjects—Awfull—Submissively—Submission, Allegiance—to be a Liege Man, a Vasal."[18] These terms betray a complete disregard for Pennsylvania's political reality. Apparently by the end of the 1740s the increasing German community in Pennsylvania had yet to learn the fundamentals of English political life.

Contrasting with their desire for a strong authority are numerous indications that Germans were anything but tame and obedient subjects. German writings published in the 1740s suggest that German settlers were an unruly lot. The energetic pastor Heinrich M. Muhlenberg stated matter-of-factly that deacons and elders were not accepted by parishioners as "authority" because they were not backed by the authority of a minister.[19] The spatial setting of the German communities probably contributed to their unruliness. In Germany communal life was intimately connected with the nucleated village, but in the New World miles separated one family from another. Muhlenberg noted: "In the rural parts the houses are not built together as are the villages in Germany, but there are some thousands of acres in one piece. . . . If one travels one continually passes through forests; only occasionally does one pass a house, some miles further on there may be another house on the road. Yet most houses are far away from the roads."[20] These different spatial conditions involved drastic changes in the community-building process. Whereas community in Germany was experienced as a daily routine, communal life in Pennsylvania was compressed into few occasions—birth, marriage, death—which brought people together from scattered plantations. Communal togetherness was an extraordinary, rare event that seems to have led to an urge to make it an intense, memorable, even jolly affair. At the same time these rare events transcended the family bounds; virtually an entire region would congregate and share in this community experience.[21]

The fractionalization of the German community ideal increased the difficulties associated with the assimilation process. At the same time, by the beginning of the 1750s the English and the proprietary group's apprehensions increased about the fate of their beloved constitution, which they saw in danger of becoming "germanized."[22] These experiences with an ever-growing different ethnic group resulted in a new consciousness about what it meant to be English—a process that peaked in the first years of the Seven Years' War—followed by programs and plans to anglicize the German settlers. This second aspect was an important part of the increasingly bitter fight between the small group of proprietary followers and the dominant Quaker party.

Up to 1747 the English in Pennsylvania were reluctant to praise the obvious, for everyone knew that English was best. The Germans, on the other hand, were not so sure. A number of German authors, including Christopher Sauer, pointedly disapproved of loose English morals. Sauer remarked on slavery as America's worst evil, yet sadly added that some Germans indulged in this barbarous habit.[23] Yet, except for some hints in Conrad Weiser's pamphlet of 1741, the fundamental problem of German loyalty in times of crises was left untouched. That was to change in 1747. In opposition to Franklin's somber plea "to all of us, whatever SECT or NATION" to unite for the preservation of their "most precious *Liberty* and *Property*," Christopher Sauer set his definition of what he considered the *summa* of a nation's raison d'être: "Only they are true patriots and friends of the fatherland, who at first have conquered their lust and greed through the blood of the lamb . . . who in denying their Self and in rejecting the world . . . march against the Lord of Darkness . . . and resist him."[24] And after English newspapers had accused Germans of lacking loyalty—the Moravians were a favorite target—Sauer attempted a secular definition of what he thought distinguished a "true Englishman." In a carefully phrased passage he spelled out his opinion that only those who "had a true English heart and mind" qualified. Englishness could only be felt; there was no possible external test; loyalty was true emotion and attachment.[25]

Sauer was answered in an anonymously published piece that accused him of spreading libel and of inciting the Germans to rebellion. The presumably English author charged Sauer "with a malicious and false heart. He is not satisfied that he and others of his Nation . . . can live under an English government as a favor as long as they behave themselves peacefully . . . yet he wants to have more, he wants, along with his followers, to participate in government and order everything according to their own liking."[26] Because there is little indication that Sauer preached participation in politics to Germans—if he pleaded with them at all to safeguard their rights[27]—this charge against him makes sense only if seen in the context of his efforts to broaden the ideological basis of Germans and Quakers. His opponent apparently leveled his charges at Sauer in an effort to drive a wedge between the Quaker party and the potentially large German voting population—for it had not yet become a substantial reality.[28] According to Sauer's critic, the Germans were tolerated "during good behavior"; by innuendo and threat the readers were reminded that German settlers had not sworn an oath of allegiance to a particular Quaker assembly but to the king and that, besides, the opposition party was as keen on maintaining Pennsylvania's liberties as were the Quakers.[29]

That loyalty in the form of what it meant to be English became an issue at all indicated the insecurity of English settlers. Yet in the context of Pennsylvania politics, the issue of loyalty was also joined with the larger issue of the proprietary-Quaker conflict, which shortly before the Seven Years' War was inseparably merged with imperial issues. In his *Sermon on Education* the leading proprietary supporter and provincial secretary, Richard Peters, pointed to the existence of "a national as well as personal Humour," adding that "as *English* People abound with this more than any other; it is the Duty of every English Man to prefer and cultivate to the utmost his native Language."[30] The young Anglican William Smith linked these general notions with the idea that the essence of education was to be the improvement of "the Spirit of Liberty and *Virtue*." To educate American youth, as Smith wrote in 1752 in *Some Thoughts on Education*, was to teach them true English values as preparation for the inescapable fact that England would sooner or later "fall into the Way of other Nations" and have "sunk back to its pristine Sloth. . . . And then America, English America, would be the last Retreat/of Arts, imperial *Liberty* and *Truth.*" Then "Empire and Liberty their radiant Wings/Expand to quit the sluggish *eastern* World;/and cross the vast *Atlantic* mediate/ . . . To this *New World.*" Clearly, America was destined to become the future seat of empire and guardian of the true English traditions and values. Thus it became all the more important to forge out of the disparate social and ethnic elements one homogeneous society.[31] It is therefore not surprising that when Smith was appointed provost of the Philadelphia Academy, he became an ardent propagator of anglicization programs for Germans. Their purpose was, he explained in 1755, "to qualify the *Germans* for all the Advantages of native *English Subjects*" and thus enable them "to judge and act entirely for themselves, without being obliged to take Things upon the Words of others whose Interest it may be to deceive and mislead them."[32]

This rediscovery of English values, education in English culture, the beauty of the English language, and, most important, a sense of mission within the British Empire increased the pressures on the German settlers between 1748 and 1755 to come to grips with their new environment. They were now faced with demands that implied major changes in their attitudes toward their own culture and way of life. Yet there are strong indications that German settlers were experiencing internal problems of some proportion, partly as a reaction to these pressures. One problem was that the composition of the German immigrants had been changing. In 1752 Sauer loudly complained about the declining moral standards of the new immigrants.[33] There are also clear signs of German disenchantment with their English neighbors. Mühlenberg reacted with outrage to the charges of an Englishman in 1751 that "we were German boors and oxen; we did not know how to live; we had not the manners to associate with *gentle* folk etc."[34] In 1758 Sauer thought that Pennsylvania was losing its good reputation in Europe as a result of numerous iniquities against poor German immigrants. "The English Nation," Sauer's son Christian wrote in the same almanac, "consists of proud and conceited people who denigrate all others, who oppress all those nations of whom they can be master."[35]

It is obvious that the pressure to learn and to acculturate was heavier on the German immigrants than on the English, and it is therefore not surprising that this pressure produced irritations. Numerous practical necessities forced the Germans to learn English customs, legal and otherwise. It is no coincidence that the first manuals of the English language were printed between 1748 and 1751; Germans were realizing the need to learn English so as to fend for themselves in this New World. Even the clannish Moravians resolved in 1754 "that learning the English languages should now be tried out and started." [36] At the same time, the pressure to acculturate created new problems. In the almanac for 1754 Sauer's "Newcomer" confessed to not knowing how to welcome another German "since the Germans are becoming half English and say 'Hau di thu.'" Learning English seems to have caused intergenerational conflicts, too. Some obviously even felt that the German language was losing too much ground against English. The editor of the *Grammatica Anglicana-Concentrata* hoped that "there may be none who would forget his German language— while learning and practicing the English language—or would even go so far as to be ashamed of speaking German." [37]

With the outbreak of the Seven Years' War the pressure on the German settlers to acculturate again focused on the problem of loyalty, broadly conceived. To people such as Benjamin Franklin, William Smith, and Richard Peters being a loyal English subject meant accepting English political values and religious attitudes and adopting the English language as the only mode of communication. Yet once again, the problem of loyalty became complicated because it was tied to the issue of Quaker pacifism as well as to the religious interpretation of the Seven Years' War. In 1755 Thomas Barton, an Anglican preacher, and William Smith emphasized what was at stake: "The Rights of *Britons* and of *Protestants*" were pitted against the powers of darkness, that is, France and popery as veritable embodiments of Antichrist. [38] Samuel Finley, a Presbyterian minister, made it clear that there was no "*Medium* between *not defending* a Post which is attacked and *surrendering* it to the *Enemy*" and that, therefore, "they who belong to a Community, and yet will not assist, in defending it when attacked, are to be esteemed as *virtual Enemies*" and not considered to "be *fit Members* of a *Community* in all Circumstances." [39] Thus at the beginning of the Seven Years' War the German settlers in Pennsylvania were not only faced with the various external and internal problems related to acculturation but also with the unqualified demand by leading English politicians to make up their minds about where their loyalties were. To make matters worse, their English political patrons, badly divided among themselves since the autumn of 1755, failed to offer them any clue as to which course to pursue; indeed, German liaison with Quakers had become a liability.

The Germans reacted to this crisis in a number of ways. Those who followed Sauer's line interpreted the struggle between England and France as the final battle before the beginning of the millennium.

Yet Sauer pursued a double course. While viewing the secular events in millennarian terms and advocating a retreat from the wicked world, as a politician he now asked his German readers actively to protect their endangered political rights.[40] Most of the German settlers accepted Sauer's second but not his first bit of advice. Even such pacifists as the Moravians and the Mennonites joined English efforts to build up the colony's defenses in 1755.[41] Thus the war brought both ethnic groups together. On January 14, 1756, Franklin spoke of Bethlehem as being "fill'd with Refugees, the Workmen's Shops, and even the Cellars being crowded with Women and Children," most of them probably of English or Irish stock. Most of the families in "the back parts" had to flee from the enemy one or more times and bemoaned loss of material goods, friends, or relatives. Marie le Roy and Barbara Leininger, who had been captured by Indians in 1756, met many English during their captivity and planned and executed their escape with two young Englishmen. In the appendix to their captivity tale published in 1759 they listed fifty-one captives held by Indians in the Ohio area, thirty-four of whom were either of English or Irish and seventeen of German origin.[42] This common experience had dramatic results. Gradually, particularly with respect to the Indians, widely divergent attitudes merged. Again the Moravians marked the way. The Disciples' Conference on May 12, 1757, adopted the resolution: "Henceforth, when speaking about our Indian brothers and sisters, we will refer to them as Indians; yet if we mean the murderers then we will call them 'die Wilden' or in English 'Sauvages.'"[43]

By the time the first English pamphlets containing a vigorous defense of Germans against William Smith's accusations appeared in print in 1758,[44] a new consensus between Germans and English was slowly emerging, giving these pleadings for German loyalty a somewhat antiquated ring. After the elder Sauer's death in 1758, his son silently dropped the apocalyptic interpretation of the war. His turnabout was completed with his inclusion of laudatory verses about the lately deceased General James Wolfe in his almanac for 1761.[45] This new consensus was broadened almost immediately by mutual German and English admiration for the Prussian king's victories. Indeed, this English admiration opened the way for German settlers to discover hitherto hidden possibilities of merging English and German historical traditions.[46]

By 1760 German periodicals began to print accounts of recent English history in unabashedly positive terms. Sauer now saw "God's benign finger that after so many undescribable sufferings, desolations and horrors England had the blessing of three successive kings given to it by the House of Braunschweig-Lüneburg who were so distinguished by their love of justice." And he quoted Nostradamus as his authority that "the accession of a German noble family to the English throne" will "last until the days of final judgment."[47] A year earlier, the German Reformed pastor Johann Conrad Steiner developed in lengthy and tedious words the image of George II as Moses leading his people out of darkness to the promised land and concluded: "The German Nation in particular cannot praise enough the happiness which it experienced under George's happy and blessed reign in this country."[48]

Thus in a curious yet perfectly understandable way English history became a bit "germanized" and was thereby saved. The English lawyer David Henderson provided a medieval historical perspective to this new consciousness. According to him, "the old English came from Germany, and I am therefore convinced that the largest majority of the successors of these German emigrants to England will now welcome their close relations with open arms in order to become one with them." Not to be left behind, the Moravian printer Henrich Miller joined Henderson in the Saxon woods by noting that not only "all the words with one syllable" were "derived from the German language," as Henderson had thought, but "most words of the English languages are of German origin."[49]

In short, since the English had had the good sense to accept a German noble family as their kings, had allowed themselves to be saved by George II of Hannover, and had judiciously taken most of their language from the German, they were, in the words of Henrich Miller, "on the whole an honest, lively, courageous and pensive people," although occasionally "tending to be hot-tempered, moody and quite often unsteady."[50] After living together for more than a third of a century the German settlers finally had put together an image of the English rich in texture although probably not totally agreeable to their English neighbors.

In the following year this new attitude effectively defused the German issue when it flared up again in the context of the bitter fight over the petition to the crown to take Pennsylvania under her immediate government. The open prejudice against Germans of earlier times was now used as a political weapon against individual English politicians. On the whole those anti-German sentiments had been viewed somewhat skeptically by the English-speaking population—although neither Franklin's nor Smith's thoughts published in the 1750s were actually far off the mark. Yet these old sayings were now resuscitated with damaging results, not for German settlers but for the political standing of Benjamin Franklin and William Smith. In the acid test of the bitterest political fight in the colonial history of Pennsylvania, the changed attitudes of Germans and English toward each other bore the first tangible fruits. A modus vivendi had been found.[51]

Notes

1. Alan Tully, "Englishmen and Germans: National-Group Contact in Colonial Pennsylvania, 1700–1755," *Pennsylvania History* 45 (1978):237–56. Two recent important monographs on Germans in colonial Pennsylvania are Dietmar Rothermund, *The Layman's Progress: Religious and Political Experience in Colonial Pennsylvania, 1740–1770* (Philadelphia: University of Pennsylvania Press, 1961), and William T. Parsons, *The Pennsylvania Dutch: A Persistent Minority* (Boston: Twayne, 1976), 17–135. The following monographs offer additional important material: Alan Tully, *William Penn's Legacy: Politics and Social Structure in Provincial Pennsylvania, 1726–1755*, Johns Hopkins University Studies in Historical and Political Science, 95th ser., no. 2 (Baltimore: Johns Hopkins University Press, 1977); James T. Lemon, *The Best Poor Man's Country: A Geographical Study of Early Southeastern Pennsylvania* (Baltimore: Johns Hopkins University Press, 1972); Stephanie Grauman Wolf, *Urban Village: Population, Community, and Family Structure in Germantown, Pennsylvania, 1683–1800* (Princeton: Princeton University Press, 1976); Jerome H. Wood, Jr., *Conestoga Crossroads: Lancaster, Pennsylvania, 1730–1790* (Harrisburg: Pennsylvania Historical and Museum Commission, 1979); David G. Williams, *The Lower Jordan Valley Pennsylvania German Settlement*, Proceedings of the Lehigh County Historical Society 18 (Allentown: H. Ray Haas, 1950); and on pacifism among Germans esp. Richard K. MacMaster, Samuel L. Horst, and Robert F. Ulle, *Conscience in Crisis: Mennonites and Other Peace Churches in America, 1739–1789, Interpretation and Documents*, Studies in Anabaptist and Mennonite History, 20 (Scottdale, Pa.: Herald Press, 1979); on the Quakers' Peace Testimony see Hermann Wellenreuther, *Glaube und Politik in Pennsylvania, 1681–1776: Die Wandlungen der Obrigkeitsdoktrin und des Peace Testimony der Quäker*, Kölner Historische Abhandlungen, 20 (Cologne: Böhlau, 1972).

2. I have not found modern concepts of ethnicity particularly helpful; see Nathan Glazer et al., eds., *Ethnicity: Theory and Experience* (Cambridge, Mass.: Harvard University Press, 1975). In the eighteenth century "ethnicity" was defined as "Heathendom, heathen, superstition" (*Oxford English Dictionary*, 3:314). Samuel Johnson defined "Ethnicks" as "Heathen; Pagan; not Jewish; not Christian" (*A Dictionary of the English Language: In Which the Words Are Deduced from Their Originals, and Illustrated in Their Different Significations by Examples from the Best Writers*, 2 vols. [London: W. Strahan, for J. and P. Knapton, 1755], vol. 1, s.v. "Ethnick"). These definitions suggest a framework in which another ethnic group could be seen as devoid of culture and civilization just as "heathens" were still considered "barbarians" and uncultured; for this concept see Diderot's *Encyclopédie, ou dictionair raisonné* (Paris: Briasson, 1751–65), 6:56, s.v. "Ethnophrones." Unfortunately, I was unable to use colonial newspapers because they are not available in Germany.

3. *A Dialogue between Mr. Robert Rich and Roger Plowman* (Philadelphia: Samuel Keimer, 1725), 3; *A Dialogue Shewing What's Therein* (Philadelphia: Samuel Keimer, 1725), 26; John Hughes, *An Ephemeris for the Year 1726* (Philadelphia: Andrew Bradford, 1725). No page citation can be given for almanacs published during the colonial period. *The Remainder of the Observations Promised in the Mercury* (Philadelphia: Andrew Bradford, 1735), 2; Leonard W. Labaree et al., eds., *The Papers of Benjamin Franklin*, 23 vols. (New Haven: Yale University Press, 1959–[1983]), 2:358; Benjamin Franklin, *Plain Truth: Or, Serious Considerations on the Present State of the City of Philadelphia and Province of Pennsylvania* (1747), rpr. in Labaree et al., eds., *Papers of Benjamin Franklin*, 3:188–204, quotation on p. 203.

4. Thomas Rymer, *Of the Antiquity, Power and Decay of Parliaments, Being a General View of Government, and Civil Policy in Europe* (London: J. Roberts, 1714); see also D. W. L. Earl, "Procrustean Feudalism: An Interpretive Dilemma in English Historical Narration, 1700–1725," *Historical Journal* 19 (1976):33–51. James Logan did not own Rymer's book; see Edwin Wolf II, *The Library of James Logan of Philadelphia, 1674–1751* (Philadelphia: Library Company of Philadelphia, 1974), yet this aspect of Rymer's findings was spread far and wide throughout the colonies by Cato's Letters; see [John Trenchard and Thomas Gordon], *Cato's Letters: Essays on Liberty, Civil and Religious, and Other Important Subjects*, 6th ed., 4 vols. (London: J. Walthoe, T. and T. Longman, 1755), 2:236–44, 257–66, 278–92; 3:64–66; 4:73–81, 225–35; and Bernard Bailyn, *The Ideological Origins of the American Revolution* (Cambridge, Mass.: Belknap Press of Harvard University Press, 1967), 79–80. The few Pennsylvanians who were able to subscribe to London periodicals were, of course, well informed about events and developments in the Holy Roman Empire.

5. Volker Meid, "Francisci, Happel und Pocahontas. Amerikanisches in der deutschen Literatur des 17. Jahrhunderts," in S. Bauschinger, H. Denkler, and W. Malsch, eds., *Amerika in der Deutschen Literatur. Neue Welt—Nordamerika—USA* (Stuttgart: Reclam, 1975), 12–27, esp. 22; Karl S. Guthke, "Edle Wilde mit Zahnausfall. Albrecht von Hallers Indianerbild," ibid., 28–44; in general Harold Jantz, "Amerika im Deutschen Dichten und Denken," in Wolfgang Stammler, ed., *Deutsche Philologie im Aufriss*, 3 vols. (Berlin: E. Schmidt, 1962), 3:310–72, and Hans Galinsky, "Deutschlands literarisches Amerikabild: Ein kritischer Bericht zu Geschichte, Stand und Aufgaben der Forschung," in Alexander Ritter, ed., *Deutschlands literarisches Amerikabild. Neuere Forschungen zur Amerikarezeption der deutschen Literatur* (Hildesheim: Olms, 1977). There is a rare complete set of the *Carlsruhe Wochenblatt oder Nachrichten* at the Generallandesarchiv Karlsruhe which I have used. The only exceptions are occasional advertisements of books relating to North America, such as issues of January 12, 19, May 18, 1757, July 29, 1761, and November 4, 1762.

6. Adolf Gerber, *Die Nassau-Dillenburger Auswanderung nach Amerika im 18. Jahrhundert. Das Verhalten der Regierungen dazu und die späteren Schicksale der Auswanderer* (Flensburg: Flensburger Nachrichten, 1930), 19–20; Otto Wiegandt, "Ulm als Stadt der Auswanderer," *Mitteilungen des Vereins für Kunst und Altertum in Ulm und Oberschwaben* 31 (1941):88–114, esp. 100–102; Hermann von Ham, "Die Stellung des Staates und der Regierungsbehörden im Rheinland zum Auswanderungsproblem im 18. und 19. Jahrhundert," *Deutsches Archiv für Landes- und Volksforschung* 6 (1942):261–309. The margrave of Baden in 1735–36 collected letters which are in GLA 74/9847, Generallandesarchiv Karlsruhe. The source value of these letters is discussed by Hansmartin Schwarzmaier, "Auswandererbriefe aus Nordamerika. Quellen im Grenzbereich von geschichtlicher Landeskunde, Wanderungsforschung und Literatursoziologie," *Zeitschrift für die Geschichte des Oberrheins* 126 (1978):303–69.

7. All this material is printed in Julius Goebel, ed., "Neue Dokumente zur Geschichte der Massenauswanderung im Jahre 1709," *Jahrbuch der deutsch-amerikanischen historischen Gesellschaft von Illinois* 13 (1913):181–201, esp. 184, 185, 186, 187, 188–92. Except otherwise noted, all translations of German texts are mine.

8. Otto Schuster, "Die Auswanderung nach Pennsylvanien 1746–1772 unter Herzog Karl," in *Unsere Heimat. Die Kirche* (Nürtingen: Henzler, 1931), 127–38, esp. 129–33. For a summary of social conditions in the middle Neckar Valley region see Paul Sauer, "Not und Armut in den Dörfern des Mittleren Neckarraumes in vorindustrieller Zeit," *Zeitschrift für Württembergische Landesgeschichte* 41 (1982):131–49.

9. Catherina Thomen quote from GLA 74/9847, fol. 19; Johann Friedrich Naschold, October 26, 1754, in Friedrich Krebs, ed., "Eine Amerikareise vor 200 Jahren," *Genealogie* 15–16 (1966–67):534–45; Johann Theobald Schramm's letter, October 20, 1769, in Krebs, ed., "Ein Auswandererbrief von 1769 aus America," *Pfälzer Heimat* 5 (1954):26.

10. Hayn's letter is printed almost in full in Gerber, *Nassau-Dillenburger Auswanderung*, 20–21. Characteristically, Gottlieb Mittelberger, *Journey to Pennsylvania*, ed. Oscar Handlin and John Clive (Cambridge, Mass.: Belknap Press of Harvard University Press, 1960), is practically silent about Pennsylvania's political system. The only relevant remark contains a serious error: "Every six years a new governor is chosen by the King and Parliament in England and is sent to Pennsylvania to rule in the name of the King" (ibid., 48). Since Mittelberger's journal was published too late to have an impact on the image of Germans it is not considered here in any detail. Another important printed German source widely available in Germany was the extracts from Muhlenberg's and other Lutheran pastors' letters sent to A. G. Francke and published in the *Halle'sche Nachrichten*; yet these, too, discussed only religious and moral problems.

11. See for Württemberg, Hartmut Lehmann, *Pietismus und weltliche Ordnung in Württemberg vom 17. bis zum 20. Jahrhundert* (Stuttgart: Kohlhammer, 1969); Walter Grube, *Vogteien, Ämter, Landkreise in der Geschichte Süddeutschlands*, ed. Landkreistag Baden-Württemberg (Stuttgart: Kohlhammer, 1960), 18–41; Hans Eugen Specker, "Die Verfassung der Württembergischen Amtsstädte im 17. und 18. Jahrhundert dargestellt am Beispiel Sindelfingen," in Erich Maschke and Jürgen Sydow, eds., *Verwaltung und Gesellschaft in der südwestdeutschen Stadt des 17. und 18. Jahrhunderts. Protokoll über die VII. Arbeitstagung des Arbeitskreises für südwestdeutsche Stadtgeschichtsforschung, Sindelfingen 15.–17. November 1969*, Veröffentlichungen der Kommission für Geschichtliche Landeskunde in Baden-Württemberg, Reihe B: Forschungen, vol. 58 (Stuttgart: Kohlhammer, 1969), 1–21. The best discussion of the modes of property transfer in southern Germany and its practical aspects is Albrecht Strobel, *Agrarverfassung im Übergang. Studien zur Agrargeschichte des Badischen Breisgaus vom Beginn des 16. bis zum Ausgang des 18. Jahrhunderts*, Forschungen zur Oberrheinischen Landesgeschichte, C. Bauer et al., eds., vol. 23 (Freiburg: K. Alber, 1972), 95–128. The villages are the subject of Karl S. Bader, *Studien zur Rechtsgeschichte des mittelalterlichen Dorfes*, 3 vols. (Weimar: Böhlau, 1957–73), vols. 2 and 3; Bader, "Dorf und Dorfgemeinde im Zeitalter von Naturrecht und Aufklärung," in Wilhelm Wegener, ed., *Festschrift K. G. Hugelmann zum 80. Geburtstag* (Aalen: Scientia Verlag, 1959), 1:1–39; Peter Blickle, "Bauer und Staat in Oberschwaben," *Zeitschrift für Württembergische Landesgeschichte* 31 (1972):104–20. For an excellent summary of research on central and local government in the seventeenth and eighteenth centuries, see Kurt G. A. Jeserich et al., eds., *Deutsche Verwaltungsgeschichte*, vol. 1: *Vom Spätmittelalter bis zum Ende des Reiches* (Stuttgart: Kohlhammer, 1983), 215–467, 552–74, 615–33. Complaints against officials are mentioned in Renate Vowinckel,

Ursachen der Auswanderung gezeigt an badischen Beispielen aus dem 18. und 19. Jahrhundert, Vierteljahresschrift für Sozial- und Wirtschaftsgeschichte, supplement 37 (Stuttgart: Kohlhammer, 1939). There is a sorry lack of solid regional church history. Yet for Württemberg see Lehmann, *Pietismus und weltliche Ordnung*, and Martin Brecht, *Kirchenordnung und Kirchenzucht in Württemberg vom 16. bis zum 18. Jahrhundert*, Quellen und Forschungen zur Württembergischen Kirchengeschichte, vol. 1 (Stuttgart: Calwer Verlag, 1967); for the Palatinate in 1690–1716, see B. G. Struve, *Ausführlicher Bericht von der pfälzischen Kirchenhistorie* (Frankfurt a.M.: J. B. Hartung, 1721), 721–1364.

12. John Hughes, *An Ephemeris for the Year 1726* (Philadelphia, 1725). On German immigration see Marianne Wokeck, "The Flow and Composition of German Immigration to Philadelphia, 1727–1775," *Pennsylvania Magazine of History and Biography* 105 (1981):249–78; for the settlement process see Williams, *Lower Jordan Valley*, 64–66; Wood, *Conestoga Crossroads*, chap. 1; *The Remainder of the Observations Promised in the Mercury*, 2.

13. See Tully, "Englishmen and Germans," 242–43; Stephen L. Longenecker, *The Christopher Sauers: Courageous Printers Who Defended Religious Freedom in Early America* (Elgin, Ill: Brethren Press, 1981), 35–94; Willi Paul Adams, "The Colonial German-Language Press and the American Revolution," in Bernard Bailyn and John B. Hench, eds., *The Press and the American Revolution* (Worcester, Mass.: American Antiquarian Society, 1980), 151–228, esp. 154–60. Christopher Sauer was politically influential largely because a considerable majority of naturalized Germans shared his and the Quakers' pacifism. Thus of the 367 persons naturalized under a law passed in 1743, 278 (75.7 percent) "affirmed" allegiance instead of taking the oath; of 850 persons naturalized between 1740 and 1749, 54 percent "affirmed" (MacMaster, Horst, and Ulle, *Conscience in Crisis*, 53, 67; see also n. 38, below). The increasing number of German Lutherans did not share Sauer's or the Quakers' positions; see H. M. Muhlenberg to G. A. Francke and F. M. Ziegenhagen, June 6, 1743, Muhlenberg Korrespondenz, MS vol. 1, no. 19, 151–58, and Muhlenberg to Francke and Ziegenhagen, May 24, 1747, ibid., no. 65, 475–93, esp. 482–90. I am much indebted to Professor K. Aland, Münster, for letting me peruse volume 1 of the manuscript of the Muhlenberg Correspondence to be published in 1985. Conrad Weiser, *Ein Wohlgemeindter und Ernstlicher Rath an unsere Lands-Leute, die Teutschen* (Philadelphia: B. Franklin, 1741), 1; an English translation is printed in Paul A. W. Wallace, *Conrad Weiser, 1696–1760: Friend of Colonist and Mohawk* (Philadelphia: University of Pennsylvania Press, 1945), 113–14.

14. For the Mennonites' anguished reactions to this threatening situation, see letters of 1742 and 1745 to their brethren in Amsterdam in MacMaster, Horst, and Ulle, *Conscience in Crisis*, 84–86. On the dispute between the proprietary's supporters and Quaker politicians see Hermann Wellenreuther, "The Quest for Harmony in a Turbulent World: The Principle of 'Love and Unity' in Colonial Pennsylvania Politics," *Pennsylvania Magazine of History and Biography*, 107 (1983): 537–76.

15. *Gewissenhaffte Vorstellung Vom Mangel Rechter Kinder-Zucht, Und zugleich Wie solche zuverbessern wäre* (Germantown: C. Saur, 1740), 24–26.

16. Georg Neisser, *Aufrichtige Nachricht ans Publicum, Über eine Von dem Holländischen Pfarrer Joh. Phil. Böhmen bei Mr. Andr. Bradford edirte Lästerschrift Gegen die sogenannten Herrnhuter, Das ist, Die Evangelischen Brüder aus Böhmen, Mähren u.s.f.* (Philadelphia: B. Franklin, 1742), 3. English authors shared the view that public morals in Pennsylvania were declining but did not assign all the blame to a malfunctioning of government; see the dialogue between two girls in *Poor Robin's Almanack for 1745* (Philadelphia: William Bradford, 1744); the principal reasons for this decline in

morals were thought to be the decay of education. The Disciples' Conference resolve: "Wer eine Kirche Christi ist, da muss subordination und Gehorsam seyn oder wir müssen uns nicht rufen eine Kirche Christi zu seyn," Disciples' Conference Protocolls [Jünger-Tags Conference], under August 7, 1754, Bethlehem Moravian Archives; the best studies of Bethlehem are Joseph Mortimer Levering, *A History of Bethlehem, Pennsylvania, 1741–1892, with some Account of its Founders and their early Activity in America* (Bethlehem, Pa.: Times Publishing Co., 1903); and Helmut Erbe, *Bethlehem, Pennsylvania: Eine kommunistische Herrnhuter Kolonie des 18. Jahrhunderts* (Stuttgart: Ausland und Heimat Verlag, 1929).

17. For frequent requests of church bodies that governments intercede to settle controversies within churches, see Waldemar Humburg and Albert Rosenkranz, eds., *Generalsynodalbuch. Die Akten der Generalsynoden von Jülich, Kleve, Berg und Mark 1610–1793*. Part 1: *Die Akten der Generalsynoden von 1610–1755*, section 2: *1701– 1755* (Düsseldorf: Presseverband der Evangelischen Kirche im Rheinland, 1970), 17, 54, 66, 75–77, and passim; Hans Ammerich, *Landesherr und Landesverwaltung. Beiträge zur Regierung von Pfalz-Zweibrücken am Ende des Alten Reiches*, Veröffentlichung der Kommission für Saarländische Landesgeschichte und Volksforschung, 11 (Saarbrücken: Minerva Verlag, 1981), 95–101; Lehmann, *Pietismus und weltliche Ordnung*, 82–94. For comments of Muhlenberg see *The Journals of Henry Melchoir Muhlenberg*, 3 vols., trans. Theodore G. Tappert and John W. Doberstein (Philadelphia: Evangelical Lutheran Ministerium of Pennsylvania and Adjacent States, 1942–58), 1:104–8, 111–16, 153–55, and passim; Muhlenberg to G. A. Francke and F. M. Ziegenhagen, December 3, 1742, Muhlenberg Korrespondenz, MS vol. 1, no. 14, 63– 71, esp. 68, and Muhlenberg to A. G. Francke, March 17, 1743, ibid., no. 17, 94–143, esp. 117:"In religious matters the authorities provide no help at all. Rather, each individual has the utmost freedom in such matters."

18. *Eine Nützliche Anweisung Oder Beyhülfe vor die Teutschen um Englisch zu lernen: Wie es vor Neu-Ankommende und anders im Land gebohrne Land- und Handwercks-Leute welche der Englischen Sprache erfahrne und geübte Schulmeister und Preceptores ermangeln, vor das Bequemste erachtet worden; mit ihrer gewöhnlichen Arbeit und Werckzeug erläutert. Nebst einer Grammatic, vor diejenigen, Welche in andern Sprachen und deren Fundamenten erfahren sind* (Germantown: C. Saur, 1751), 171; three years earlier G. Armbrüster had reprinted Theodore Arnold, *Grammatica Anglicana Concentrata, Oder, Kurtz-gefasste Englische Grammatica. Worinnen die zur Erlernung dieser Sprache hinlänglich-nöthige Grundsätze Auf eine sehr deutliche und leichte Art abgehandelt sind* (Philadelphia: Gotthard Armbrüster, 1748), originally published at Leipzig.

19. "Die Teutschen seyen vormahls geliebt worden wegen ihrer Redlichkeit; nun aber übertrafen viele die Eyrischen selbst," *Der Hoch-Deutsch Americanische Calender auf das Jahr 1752* (Germantown: C. Saur, 1751); for other complaints about misuse of freedom and excessive unruliness see Georg Michael Weiss, *Der in der americanischen Wildnusz unter Menschen von verschiedenen Nationen und Religionen hin und wieder herum wandelte und verschiedentlich angefochtene Prediger* (Philadelphia: A. Bradford, 1729), 2; *Gewissenhafte Vorstellung vom Mangel rechter Kinder-Zucht, Und zugleich Wie solche zu Verbessern wäre*, 24, 26, see note 15; *Jacob Lischys Reformirten Predigers Declaration seines Sinnes. An seine Reformirte Religions-Genossen in Pennsylvania* (Germantown: C. Saur, 1743), 4; Muhlenberg to G. A. Francke and F. M. Ziegenhagen, December 3, 1742; Muhlenberg to J. Ph. Fresenius, November 15, 1751, Muhlenberg Korrespondenz, MS vol. 1, no. 14, 63–71 and no. 106, 744–64, esp. 752–53.

20. *Journals of Muhlenberg*, 1:72, 116, 136, 137; see also C. Lee Hopple, "Spatial

Development of the Southeastern Pennsylvania Plain Dutch Community to 1970, Part I," *Pennsylvania Folklife* 21 (Winter 1971–72):18–40, esp. 22–25; Williams, *Lower Jordan Valley*, plate III: "Warrants and Patents." Muhlenberg to G. A. Francke and F. M. Ziegenhagen, December 3, 1742; Muhlenberg to J. B. Gabler, December 22, 1749, Muhlenberg Korrespondenz, MS vol. 1, no. 14, 63–71 and no. 77, 577–89, esp. 586; *Journals of Muhlenberg*, 1: 235.

21. *Der Hoch-Deutsch Americanische Calender auf das Jahr 1751* (Germantown: C. Saur, 1750); *Journals of Muhlenberg*, 1: 136; Solon J. Buck and Elizabeth Hawthorn Buck, *The Planting of Civilization in Western Pennsylvania* (Pittsburgh: University of Pittsburgh Press, 1939), 356–58.

22. Labaree et al., eds., *Papers of Benjamin Franklin*, 4:117–21, 477–85.

23. Weiss, *Der in der americanischen Wildnusz*, 2; *Gewissenhaffte Vorstellung Vom Mangel rechter Kinder-Zucht*, 1, 24, 26; *Der Hoch-Deutsch Americanische Calender. Auf das Jahr 1742* (Germantown: C. Saur 1741); *Der Hoch-Deutsch Americanische Calender. Auf das Jahr 1743* (Germantown: C. Saur, 1742). In both almanacs Sauer printed lengthy essays entitled "Vom Krieg und Frieden" on which my analysis is based.

24. Labaree, et al., eds., *Papers of Benjamin Franklin*, 3:200–204; Christopher Sauer, *Klare und Gewisse Wahrheit, Betreffend den eigentlichen Zustand, sowohl der Wahren Friedliebenden Christen und Gottesfürchtigen, als auch der Verfallenen, Streit- oder Kriegs-Süchtigen, zusammen ihrer beyder Hoffnung und Ausgang. Schrifftmässig dargelegt von einem Teutschen Geringen Handwercks-Mann* (Germantown: C. Saur, 1747), 12–13.

25. [Christopher Sauer], *Verschiedene Christliche Wahrheiten, und Kurtze Betrachtung über das kürzlich herausgegebene Büchlein genannt: Lautere Wahrheiten, Aufgesetzt zur Überlegung von einem Handwercksmann in Germantown* (Germantown: C. Saur, 1748), 19–20.

26. *Kurtze Verteidigung der Lautern Wahrheit gegen die so genannte Unterschiedliche Christliche Wahrheiten, Welche der Buchdrucker C. S. in Germantown ohnlängst ausgestreut. Vorgestellet in einem Brief von einem 3ten Handwercksmann in Philadelphia an seinen Freund im Lande geschrieben, und Welche beyde Wahrheiten der Author dieses Briefes denen Verständigen Teutschen zur Beurtheilung in Druck vorgeleget* (Philadelphia, 1748), 9–10; the terminology of the pamphlet points to an English author. Historians have thus far ignored the larger issues in this debate and have treated the controversy as a debate between Sauer and Franklin over the issue of pacifism; see Glenn Weaver, "Benjamin Franklin and the Pennsylvania Germans," *William and Mary Quarterly*, 3d ser. 14 (1957):536–59, esp. 538–39; Tully, "Englishmen and Germans," 243–44; Parsons, *Pennsylvania Dutch*, 83. The debate is not mentioned by Rothermund, *Layman's Progress*; the latest discussion of the exchange as a conflict over pacifism is in MacMaster, Horst, and Ulle, *Conscience in Crisis*, 69–70.

27. Rothermund, *Layman's Progress*, 90, believes that Sauer "incessantly admonished them [German settlers] to take out naturalization papers and to make use of their political rights in order to preserve their newly gained freedom," a position I find at odds with the evidence.

28. For naturalization statistics see sources cited in note 13. Tully, *William Penn's Legacy*, 49, 93–94, believes that a significant number of Germans in the 1740s and 1750s went to the polls, that not only proprietary supporters but Quaker politicians shared the fear that Pennsylvania would be "germanized" but that while the proprietary group indulged in hysterics the Quakers solved the issue by gerrymandering.

29. *Kurtze Verteidigung der Lautern Wahrheit,* 9–10, 11, 15; Wokeck, "Flow and Composition," 260.

30. Richard Peters, *A Sermon on Education* (Philadelphia: B. Franklin and D. Hall, 1751), 25.

31. William Smith, *Some Thoughts on Education* (New York: J. Parker, 1752); for a closer analysis of this pamphlet see William D. Andrews, "William Smith and the Rising Glory of America," *Early American Literature* 8 (1973): 33–43. On the concept of empire see Richard Koebner, *Empire* (Cambridge: Cambridge University Press, 1961); Norbert Kilian, "New Wine in Old Skins? American Definitions of Empire and the Emergence of a New Concept," in Erich Angermann, Marie-Luise Frings, and Hermann Wellenreuther, eds., *New Wine in Old Skins: A Comparative View of Socio-Political Structures and Values Affecting the American Revolution* (Stuttgart: Klett, 1976), 135–52. Smith was intimately involved in efforts to anglicize German settlers; see Michael Schlatter, *The Case of the German Protestant Churches Settled in the Province of Pennsylvania, and in North America* (London, 1753); Whitfield J. Bell, Jr., "Benjamin Franklin and the German Charity Schools," *Proceedings of the American Philosophical Society* 99 (1955): 381–87; and for a letter by Smith in which he stressed the necessity of a homogeneous society based on intraethnic "acquaintances and connections," "a conformity of manners," a common "enjoyment of liberty," "intermarriages," and the "acquisition of a common language," see Lawrence A. Cremin, *American Education: The Colonial Experience, 1607–1783* (New York: Harper & Row, 1970), 261–62.

32. William Smith, *A Brief History of the Rise and Progress of the Charitable Scheme, Carrying on by a Society of Noblemen and Gentlemen in London, for the Relief and Instruction of poor Germans, and their Descendants, settled in Pennsylvania, and the Adjacent British Colonies in North-America* (Philadelphia: B. Franklin and D. Hall, 1755), 4–5, 14.

33. See sources cited in note 19.

34. *Journals of Muhlenberg,* 1:68, 282–83, 277, 304. For other complaints see *Der Hoch-Deutsch Americanische Calender auf das Jahr 1756* (Germantown: C. Saur, 1755); Gov. James Hamilton to Thomas Penn, September 24, 1750, Thomas Penn Papers, microfilm, roll 7, unpaginated, Historical Society of Pennsylvania.

35. *Der Hoch-Deutsch Americanische Calender auf das Jahr 1753* (Germantown: C. Saur, 1752); *Der Hoch-Deutsch Americanische Calender auf das Jahr 1756* (Germantown: C. Saur, 1755); *Der Hoch-Deutsch Americanische Calender auf das Jahr 1758* (Germantown: C. Saur, 1757).

36. *Der Hoch-Deutsch Americanische Calender auf das Jahr 1754* (Germantown: C. Saur, 1753); Disciples' Conference Protocolls, June 19, 1754, Bethlehem Moravian Archives (Bethlehem, Pa.).

37. *Journals of Muhlenberg,* 1:287; printer's introduction to Arnold, *Grammatica Anglicana-Concentrata.*

38. Thomas Barton, *Unanimity and Public Spirit: A Sermon Preached at Carlisle, and Some Other Episcopal Churches, in the County of York and Cumberland, Soon after General Braddock's Defeat. To Which is Prefixed a Letter from the Reverend Mr. Smith, Provost of the College of Philadelphia, Concerning the Office and Duties of a Protestant Ministry, especially in Times of Public Calamity and Danger* (Philadelphia: B. Franklin and D. Hall, 1755), xi–xii, 2–3; see also the more bizarre pamphlet *Kawanio Che Keetere: A True Relation of a Bloody Battle Fought between George and Lewis in the Year 1755* (Philadelphia: William Bradford, 1756).

39. Samuel Finley, *The Curse of Meroz; Or, The Danger of Neutrality, in the Cause*

of God, and Our Country: A Sermon, Preached the 2nd of October 1757 (Philadelphia: James Chattin, 1757), 8, 14, 16, 24–25.

40. [Christopher Sauer], *Eine zu dieser Zeit höchst nöthige Warnung und Erinnerung an die freye Einwohner der Provinz Pensylvanien von Einem, dem die Wohlfahrt des Landes angelegen und darauf bedacht ist* (Germantown: C. Saur, 1755); in 1754 Sauer had published a pamphlet that advocated complete retreat from the world, *Christian Education Exemplified under the Character of Paternus Instructing his Only Son* (Germantown: C. Saur, 1754), 4–7; *Der Hoch-Deutsch Americanische Calender auf das Jahr 1755* (Germantown: C. Saur, 1754); *Der Hoch-Deutsch Americanische Calender auf das Jahr 1756* (Germantown: C. Saur, 1755).

41. Disciples' Conference Protocolls, October 28, 1755, Bethlehem Moravian Archives; ibid., 1756–60, for Moravian defense efforts; MacMaster, Horst, and Ulle, *Conscience in Crisis*, 90–150.

42. Labaree et al., eds., *Papers of Benjamin Franklin*, 6:357–60; Wood, *Conestoga Crossroads*, 75–76; MacMaster, Horst, and Ulle, *Conscience in Crisis*, 111–12, 120–27; *Die Erzählungen von Maria le Roy und Barbara Leininger, welche vierthalb Jahr unter den Indianern gefangen gewesen und am 6. May in dieser Stadt glüklich angekommen. Aus ihrem eigenen Munde niedergeschrieben und zum Druck befördert* (Philadelphia: Teutsche Buchdruckerey, 1759), 13–14 and passim.

43. *Der Hoch-Deutsch Americanische Calender auf das Jahr 1759* (Germantown: C. Saur, 1758), for a balanced view of the Indians. Tales of Indian cruelty are in *Der Hoch-Deutsch Americanische Calender auf das Jahr 1758* (Germantown: C. Saur, 1757); William Fleming, *Eine Erzählung von den Trübsalen und der Wunderbahren Befreyung* (Germantown: C. Saur, 1756); Disciples' Conference Protocolls, May 12, 1757, Bethlehem Moravian Archives.

44. Philo-Pennsylvania, *A Serious Address to the Freeholders and Other Inhabitants of Pennsylvania* (New York, 1758), 8; and *A True and Impartial State of the Province of Pennsylvania* (Philadelphia: W. Dunlap, 1759), 168–70, were the two most important pamphlets defending Quakers and Germans; a production of the proprietary party was *Tit for Tat, or the Score Wip'd off. By Humphrey Scourge, Esq., No. 1* (Philadelphia: James Chattin, 1758), 6.

45. *Der Hoch-Deutsch Americanische Calender auf das Jahr 1760* (Germantown: C. Saur, 1759); *Der Hoch-Deutsch Americanische Calender auf das Jahr 1761* (Germantown: C. Saur, 1760).

46. David H. Fränckel, *Eine Danck-Predigt wegen des wichtigen und wundervollen [Prussian] Sieges* (Philadelphia: Anton Armbrüster, 1758); this sermon was reprinted in English in Boston (1758), where within the year ten editions appeared, in New York in 1758, and in Philadelphia in 1763. *Höchstmerckwürdige Prophezeiung von wichtigen Kriegs- und Welthändel: In welcher vornehmlich von dem glorreichen Könige von Preussen geweissagt wird* (Philadelphia: Henrich Miller, 1760).

47. *Der Hoch-Deutsch Americanische Calender auf das Jahr 1763* (Germantown: C. Saur, 1762).

48. Johann Conrad Steiner, *Liebes- und Ehren-Denkmahl, Unserm weyland Allergnädigsten und Glorwürdigsten Könige von Grossbritannien Georg dem Zweyten, nach Seiner Majestät tödlichem Hinschiede, so erfolgt den 25. Oktober 1760, aufgerichtet in der Hochdeutsch-Reformirten Gemeine zu Philadelphia* (Philadelphia: Henrich Miller, 1761), 21, 28–29, 31.

49. David Henderson, *Des Landmanns Advokat. Das ist: Kurzer Auszug aus solchen Gesetzen von Pennsylvania und England welche daselbst in völliger Kraft, und*

einem freyen Einwohner auf dem Lande höchst nöthig und nützlich zu wissen sind . . .
zusammengetragen von einem Rechtsgelehrten. Und zum Besten der hiesigen Deutschen
in ihre Muttersprache übersetzt (Philadelphia: Henrich Miller, 1761), i–viii; *Der Neu-*
este, Verbessert- und Zuverlässige Americanische Calender auf das Jahr 1764 (Philadelphia: Henrich Miller, 1763).

50. *Der Neueste, Verbessert- und Zuverlässige Americanische Calender auf das*
Jahr 1764.

51. *Eine Anrede an die Deutschen Freyhalter der Stadt und County Philadelphia*
(Philadelphia: Anton Armbrüster, 1764); *Eine andere Anrede an die Deutschen Frey-*
halter der Stadt und County Philadelphia (Phila-
delphia: Anton Armbrüster, 1764); *Anmerckungen über ein noch nie erhört und gesehen*
Wunder Thier in Pennsylvanien, genannt Streit- und Strauss-Vogel, Heraus gegeben
von einer Teutschen Gesellschaft freyer Bürger und getreuer Unterthanen Seiner Gross-
Britannischen Majestät (Germantown, C. Saur, 1764); *An Answer to the Plot* (Philadelphia, 1764), probably the most scurrilous attack on Franklin accusing him of seducing
little German girls.

7.

The Plain People: Historical and Modern Perspectives

JOHN A. HOSTETLER

BECAUSE THERE ARE MANY DIVERSITIES among the German sectarians, I have chosen to focus my observations on the "plain people."[1] On the surface "plain" brings to mind an image of conservative groups often designated as "Old Order." By some they are considered "strange people," who come from another world or who have remained frozen while the world marched on. "Plain" most obviously refers to distinctive dress and grooming patterns. The term "plain people," however, refers to more than simple clothing or broad-brimmed black hats. Beneath the surface these people share a value system radically different from that of worldly society. Since their first settlement in Germantown three centuries ago, the Mennonites have spread to many parts of the United States and into other regions of the Americas. The world membership of the Mennonites today is approximately 650,000 with roughly half that number in North America. About 150,000 maintain some form of "plain" living. They include groups designated by the prefix "Old" or "Old Order," thus Old Order Mennonite, Old Order Amish, and various branches of these traditional groups. Most are distinguished by their horse-and-buggy culture, their Pennsylvania German dialect, and their plain attire.

Main-line European theologians labeled the Mennonites as heretical and seditious; sociologists classified them as a sectarian society. Social scientists have contrasted the social structure of the "sect" with that of the "church."[2] The established church was viewed as hierarchical and inclusive. The state church served the ruling classes, administered grace to all people in a territorial domain, and was the main institution of social control. By contrast, the sect was essentially a voluntary religious movement, its members separating themselves from others on the basis of beliefs, practices, and institutions. The Anabaptists, for example, attempted to model their lives after the spirit of the Sermon on the Mount (Matt. 5, 6, 7) while also exercising the power to exclude and discipline members. Absolute separation from all other religious loyalties was required. All members were considered equal, and none were to take oaths, participate in war, or take part in worldly government. The sects rejected the authority of the established religious organizations and their leaders. Sociologists viewed the tensions between sect and church as a dialectical principle at work within Christianity. The church-sect typology, however, is a structural designation fraught with limitations for understanding the essence of Mennonite communities in the New World.

The use of an "ideal type" helped to clarify particular characteristics of the sectarian groups. Members of the sect remain segregated in various degrees, chiefly by finding a group whose philosophy of history contradicts the existing values so drastically that the group sustains itself for a generation or more. To the onlooker, sectarianism, like monasticism, may appear to serve as a shelter from the complications of an overly complex society. For its participants, it provides authentic ways of realizing new forms of service and humility as well as protection from mainstream culture.

Ethnologists in America have conceptualized the Mennonite community as a folk society in contrast to civilization.[3] As an ideal type, folk societies are traditional, small, isolated, and simple, made up of people who are marginal to the mainstream of modernization. They exist because of "accidents" of habitat, that is, they are insulated from the developing centers of civilization. Conventionalized ways are important factors in integrating the whole of life. Shared practical knowledge is more important than science, custom is valued more than critical knowledge, and associations are personal and emotional rather than abstract and categoric. The folk model lends itself well to understanding the tradition-directed character of the "plain" Mennonite community society. The Amish, for example, have retained many of the customs and small-scale technologies that were common in rural society in the nineteenth century. Through a process of syncretism,[4] religious values have been fused with an earlier period of simple country living when everyone farmed with horses and on a scale that permitted family members to work together. But this view does not explain the dynamics of the community.

University teachers have traditionally taught their students to think of the plain people as one of many cultural islands left over in the

The Old Order Amish at a barn-raising, the contruction of a barn by the entire community. Four hundred men will attend a "barn frolic," and women come to prepare a meal. The carriages are equipped with rear-view mirrors and turn signals. The Amish consider themselves highly successful in moderating the influences of industrialization. (Richard Reinhold, Lancaster)

modern world. The Amish, for example, have been considered a "sacred society," a "familistic society" maintaining "organic solidarity," an "integrative social system" with "primary" (face-to-face) rather than "secondary" relationships. The Amish may be viewed from any one of these perspectives, but such abstractions ignore elements that are important for understanding the whole. All such perspectives are synthetic views from the exterior, having the quality of half-truths. To understand their viability, we must turn to the view of reality from within.

From Krefeld to the present time, the plain people have rejected worldly structures and are attempting to create their own cosmos in the *Gemeinde* as a redemptive community.[5] Community-building is central to the redemptive process. Like all human beings, they use signs and symbols to cope with everyday life in order to make their world more meaningful and desirable. They are engaged in a social discourse with reality, the meaning of which is revealed in the analysis of the "unconscious" structure of their religious ideology. Such an analysis takes into account the mythological, the ritual process, and the charter of the community, thus enabling one to comprehend how the Mennonites view themselves as a people and how they regard their mission in the world.

The plain people view themselves as a Christian body suspended in a tension field between obedience to an all-knowing and all-powerful Creator on the one hand and the temptations of the carnal world on the other. The mythology is the story of Creation in the Genesis account. As a result of the fall, mankind acquired a sinful nature. The Creator, however, provided a way of escape for the spiritual life of man. He took pity on man in his sinful plight and provided a way of redemption from death.

The love of God requires an appropriate response. That response is a "brotherly community" living in obedience. This "love community" emphasizes sacrificial suffering, obedience, submission, humility, brotherly love, and nonresistance. Not only is this community made up of surrendered members, but Christ himself is incarnated into the community. As a corporate offering to God, the brotherly community must be "without spot or blemish" (Eph. 5:27; 1 Pet. 1:19; 2 Pet. 3:14) and must be "a light to the world" (Matt. 5:14). Living in a state of unity and constant struggle to be worthy as "a bride for the groom" (Rev. 21:2), the community must be vigilant, on the edge of readiness. Within the community the "gift" of God is shared and reciprocated among the members, for because God loves all, "we ought also love each other" (John 3:23). This reciprocation commits the members to an indivisible unity according to which each lives in harmony with all other members.

Separation must naturally exist between those who are obedient to God and those who are proud and disobedient. The Mennonites are mandated to live separate from the "blind, perverted world" (Phil. 2:15) and to have no relationship with the "unfruitful works of darkness." There is, therefore, a continuous tension between the obedient and the unbelieving. The plain people are "in the world but not of it" and hence claim the status of "strangers" and "pilgrims" (1 Pet. 2:11). As a believing community, they strive to be a "chosen generation" (1 Pet. 2:9), a "congregation of the righteous," and a "peculiar people" (Titus 2:14) prepared to suffer humiliation or persecution.

Unworthy members and those who are disobedient or cause disunity must be expelled, for they cannot be part of the "bride" offered to God. The "old leaven" must be purged from the group (1 Cor. 5:7). Periodically the church community enacts the necessary ritual to cleanse and purify the corporate body through the observance of communion. Two of the important tensions felt by the individual in daily life are pride versus humility and love versus alienation.

Pride leads to knowledge that is counterproductive to the knowledge of God. The knowledge that comes from disobedience to God comes from the "evil one" and will lead to the broad path of destruction. By contrast, the knowledge of God comes from obedience, and obedience leads to the narrow path of redemption. The educational goals for their children and their antipathy toward philosophical and worldly knowledge are grounded in this dialectic.

The practice of community was prevented in the Old World by the established system of landholding, by the limitation on association, and by compulsory territorial religion. Nonconformists were denied the right of ownership. Individual families who fled from authorities rented land or sold their services to noblemen in exchange for protection. The extended family, not the community, was the dominant form of organization. After coming to America the Mennonites formed compact neighborhoods and geographic communities. Before the American War of Independence the Mennonites had purchased large blocks of land in Lancaster County. The Amish had already formed eight separate settlements in Pennsylvania.[6]

In the New World the Mennonites maintained a strong affinity for agriculture and manual skills. Tilling the soil was not one of the founding principles that gave rise to the Anabaptist movement but became a basic value, acquired during the process of persecution and survival. In the hinterlands they developed their unique skills for work incentives and crop production.[7] The basic techniques devised in the Palatinate, Alsace, and elsewhere in Europe, such as rotation of crops, stable feeding of cattle, meadow irrigation, using natural fertilizers, and raising clover and alfalfa as a means of restoring soil fertility were transplanted to Pennsylvania. They had combined animal husbandry with intensive cultivation on the lands they rented. The family occupied a farm, and the entire household worked there. Married children sometimes lived with the family in anticipation of renting the farm. The parents would help their children financially, spending their later years helping the young couple take over. In this manner all the generations of a farming family were integrated by agricultural labor. Improvement of the soil and the dwellings was made feasible by long-term leases. The principles of family occupancy, family entrepreneurship, continuity, and motivation for labor were combined in the management of the farms.

Those who came to Pennsylvania showed a strong preference for family-sized holdings on soils that were suited to intensive cultivation. Furthermore, they wanted to combine agriculture with a preferred way of life, not to farm primarily for commercial gain. They sought limestone soils, which they believed to be superior. Although the Amish located on large acreages, ranging from one hundred to four hundred acres at the outset, they gradually reduced their holdings to a size that could be managed with family labor. Plantations or large-scale farms did not interest them.

The agricultural practices of the two major immigrant groups of the colonial period—the English-speaking Scotch-Irish and the Swiss-Germans—were very different.[8] The Scotch-Irish were mobile, "forever changing," and inclined to move to cheaper land.[9] The Swiss-Germans, who settled in communities, soon made the land valuable. In 1785 Pennsylvania's famous physician and citizen Benjamin Rush observed that the German farms were "easily distinguishable from those of others, by good fences, the extent of orchards, the fertility of soil, productiveness of the fields, and luxuriance of the meadows."[10] This observation is still apt today, for the plain people have maintained these characteristics, as can be seen when driving through their settlements. The Germans tended to secure the farms of the Scotch-Irish after they had moved and to improve and restore the depleted land.[11]

The Mennonites set high standards of work for themselves.[12] Work patterns took on the characteristics of ritual. "To fear God, and to love work," wrote Benjamin Rush, "are the first lessons the Pennsylvania Germans teach their children, preferring industrious habits to money itself."[13] Communities today differ, however, in the tempo of work and in motivation. Few hire an outsider to do farm work. Outsiders, they say, do not know enough and do not work hard enough.

As farmers in America the plain people might be classed as small-scale capitalists, but they differ from Max Weber's description of the Protestant ethic as expressed in Calvinism, Pietism, and Methodism.[14] Manual labor, frugality, industry, and honesty are valued, but such moral virtues do not give assurance of salvation. Wealth does not accrue to the individual for his enjoyment or for the advancement of his social standing, but rather enhances the well-being of the community. The Amishman, for example, is embarrassed by outward signs of social recognition. Similarly, the calling is not that of seeking worldly success, for neither the individual nor the family depends on material success for assurance of salvation. The ascetic limitations on consumption, combined with the compulsion to save, provide the economic basis for a people "in the world, but not of it."

To the casual observer, the plain people appear remarkably uniform. In reality there are many differences within the structure of most geographic settlements. Diversity, divisions, and schisms are characteristic of the American Mennonite community structure. Their faith, in an environment of religious toleration, gave rise to many varieties of Mennonites. Yet these diverse groups are related and supportive of one another. Sociologists have often drawn the premature conclusion that any change within a group means assimilation into the larger society. In reality, the ministructure persists despite a flow of personnel across the boundaries. Separate group identities are maintained by social processes of exclusion, not by the absence of mobility. Here I need only mention the function of sign and symbol: the many shapes and colors of horse-drawn carriages among the Amish (white, black, gray, or no tops), the varieties of suspenders and hats that distinguish one group from others, and the variation in hymn singing.

The Mennonites, who work so hard to maintain unity and uniformity, nevertheless suffer the consequences of a fragmented social order. The symbols over which they divide appear to be diverse. Some have polarized over the shape or color of a garment, the style of a house, carriage, or harness, or the use of labor-saving farm machinery. The list is mind-boggling. Beneath the surface are opposing family lines, frequently fraught with envy or jealousy. At the root of many divisions are members who suffer from stagnation and others who suffer from too much change.[15] Members tend to suppress their feelings because no one wishes to become the cause of disunity. Eventually the unfulfilled members migrate to more liberal or more orthodox affiliations.

Symbols are not the cause of disunity. Rather, they are the indicators of a change in collective feeling, frequently signaling a gradual shift from traditional to modern ways of living. During their early period in colonial America, the Mennonites were influenced by the Pietist movement, for both Anabaptism and Pietism were concerned with renewal. Mennonites emigrated with and often settled alongside German Quakers, German Lutherans, Reformed, and Tunkers or German Baptist groups. The Pietist movement tended to diminish denominational loyalties, for all of the "awakened" shared a common "experience," and for pietists, experience was paramount.[16]

Immigrant families did well if they reared one son to remain with the faith and some families lost all their children to other denominations. As Joseph Beiler notes: "After the War of Independence there was a steady flow of Amish converts to the Tunkers or Brethren group, German Baptists, and even to the Lutherans as well as to the Moravians."[17] Anabaptism from the sixteenth century stressed obedience, hardship, and willingness to suffer. To some in the newly formed Mennonite communities, feeling comfortable and free from persecution in America, the language of Pietism seemed natural.[18]

The plain Mennonite groups are community people. Individual experiences, whether through dreams or inspiration, are for them not the most important indicators of faith. Members are nurtured to live by example, not to develop a specific, patterned vocabulary with respect to conversion. Under the sway of articulate revivalists, some have fallen prey to other denominations, especially those who have entertained doubts about their way of life. One sign of taking on an alien belief today is seeking "assurance of salvation." When a person in the plain community embraces this teaching, it is disruptive to the community and considered a manifestation of pride rather than humility.

The Amish teach the "newbirth" and "regeneration," but the understanding of the language of religious commitment is different from that of revivalistic groups. The biblical texts are the same, but the interpretations are different. The Amish understanding of regeneration, in the words of Dirk Philips, is "submissiveness, obedience, and righteousness," without "flowery and embellished rhetoric" or "lofty and arrogant language."[19] The Amish emphasize "partaking of the divine nature" (2 Pet. 1 : 4), being "made heirs of the hope of salvation" (Titus 3 : 5–7), and taking on the attributes and sufferings of Christ.

Revivalistic movements stress individual liberation from sin more than submission to the corporate community of believers. They stress enjoyment rather than suffering, assurance of salvation rather than hope, a subjective rather than a submissive experience, a vocal rather than a nonverbal (silent) experience. As can be demonstrated from historical sources, the plain groups stress the Anabaptist theme of *Gelassenheit* with its many meanings: resignation, calmness of mind, composure, staidness, conquest of selfishness, long-suffering, collectedness, silence of the soul, tranquillity, inner surrender, yieldedness, equanimity, and detachment.[20] *Wir müssen in Christus still halten* (We must reside quietly in Christ) has supported the basic fabric of the plain Mennonite groups during the centuries.

Mennonite communities have functioned as mediating structures within the tensions that make a pluralistic society possible. During the centuries, the Mennonites and Amish have often seemed to
thwart the objectives of the nation-state. Though they have paid their
taxes, they have consistently refused military service and public office.
They have often turned their backs on the notion of progress. By some
they were regarded as a stubborn sect living by oppressive customs.
They have resisted the influence of the modernizing processes and industrialization along with modern secular schools.[21] They do not train
their members for upward mobility in the world of science or the intellectual professions. What meaning must be attached to these tendencies? On matters of family, church, neighborhood, working place, and
commitment they have maintained a clear line of thinking within
worlds of tension and worlds of meaning.[22]

The Mennonite communities have stood midway between the individual in his private life and the large-scale, alienating bureaucracies
of public life.[23] The growing antibureaucratic mood in industrializing
societies is not without foundation. Too many megastructures result in
widespread alienation. Meaning and identity for the individual are
thwarted. The loss of community and the trusting relationships nurtured in family, neighborhoods, church, voluntary associations, and
cultural pluralisms threaten the health of the wider democratic society.
As mediating structures Mennonite communities have functioned as
the value-generating and value-maintaining agencies essential in the
wider society.

Mediating structures not only check the excesses of government
but expand familial love to wider, more distantly related human groups.
Healthy ethnic and religious communities make members feel specifically bound and responsible to others. Instead of being a hindrance to
the wider society, they can be ennobling, strengthening, healing, and
satisfying. Mediating human associations are roadblocks to totalitarian
governments, whether socialist or capitalist, for they view ethnic (and
religious) subcultures as disruptive, evil, irrational, and corruptive. On
the contrary, it is linguistic and ethnic diversity that makes human beings distinctly human.

Over the past three centuries the plain people, like other ethnic
groups, have been suspended between two opposing forces: the elements in the nation-state that would eliminate ethnicity from the face
of the earth and those who regard ethnicity as a natural and necessary
extension of the affective familial bonds that integrate human activi-

ties. Caught between these forces, the plain people have sometimes prospered and sometimes suffered for their faith.

Those who would eliminate ethnicity argue that it is restrictive, narrow, corruptible, and fraught with nepotism and family jealousies. To totalitarian state systems, ethnic movements are disruptive and evil. Today some of our bureaucratic elements who view the ethnic communities from the windows of our skyscrapers see diversity in language, dress, and morality as an unmanageable problem. They ask: "Would it not be more civilized if all those queer people out there spoke one language, obeyed all our regulations, and got 'cleaned up' like the rest of us?"[24]

Ethnicity, on the other hand, as peoplehood and as an extension of familial love, informs us who we are, where we came from, and what is special about us. The plain people found in America conditions that were essential to the practice of the free exercise of religion. They have enjoyed, for the most part, the fundamental right to be left alone, a right which Justice Louis Brandeis called "the most comprehensive of rights and the right most valued by civilized man."[25]

Like other ethnic groups, the plain people run the risk of ethnocentrism, that is, developing an inflated view of their own culture. Excessive ethnocentrism can lead to nationalistic arrogance and to racism. The checks against such excesses are not the destruction of the mother group but self-correction from within. One such check is the pervasive practice of humility and moderation in human associations. Among plain people the old saying "self-praise stinks" has worked effectively in checking both individual and group arrogance.

Notes

1. See Don Yoder, "Plain and Gay Dutch," *Pennsylvania Dutchman* 8 (1956): 35–55; also his "Sectarian Costume Research in the United States," in Austin Fife, Alta Fife, and Henry H. Glassie, eds., *Forms on the Frontier*, Monograph Series 16, no. 2 (Logan: Utah State University Press, 1969), 41–75. The term "plain" was applied to the early Pennsylvania Quakers and to other distinctive religious subcultures. The smaller subdivisions among American Mennonites who qualify for this definition include the Old Order Amish, several divisions among the Old Order Mennonites, the River Brethren, German Baptists, and to some extent the Old Colony Mennonites and the Hutterian Brethren. For identifying social characteristics of the plain people see Calvin Redekop and John A. Hostetler, "The Plain People: An Interpretation," *Mennonite Quarterly Review* 51 (1977): 167. See also Melvin Gingerich, *Mennonite Attire through Four*

Centuries (Breinigsville, Pa.: Pennsylvania German Society, 1970); and Fritz Berthold, *Das Glück vom einfachen Leben: Siedlerkulturen in USA* (Munich: Herbig, 1979).

2. Ernst Troeltsch, *The Social Teaching of the Christian Churches* (New York: Macmillan, 1931); Helmut Richard Niebuhr, *The Social Sources of Denominationalism* (New York: Holt, 1929).

3. For the folk society concept as applied to the Amish see John A. Hostetler, *Amish Society*, 3d ed. (Baltimore: Johns Hopkins University Press, 1980), 8–17.

4. For a recent study of syncretism in dress and grooming tradition among the Amish see Werner Enninger, "Nonverbal Performatives: The Function of a Grooming and Garment Grammar in the Organization of Nonverbal Role-Taking and Role-Making in One Specific Trilingual Social Isolate," in W. Hullen, ed., *Understanding Bilingualism: Life Learning and Language in Bilingual Situations* (Frankfurt: Lang, 1980), 25–64.

5. For the significance of the redemptive community see Sandra Cronk, "Gelassenheit: The Rites of the Redemptive Process in Old Order Amish and Old Order Mennonite Communities" (Ph.D. dissertation, University of Chicago, 1977); published in part in *Mennonite Quarterly Review* 55 (January 1981): 5–44.

6. See John A. Hostetler, "Old World Extinction and New World Survival of the Amish," *Rural Sociology* 20 (1955): 212–19; also *Amish Society*, 54–58.

7. Jean Séguy, *Les assemblées anabaptistes-mennonites de France* (Paris: Mouton, 1977), 503–7; Ernst Correll, *Das schweizerische Täufermennonitentum* (Tübingen: Mohr, 1925).

8. Richard H. Shryock, "British versus German Traditions in Colonial Agriculture," *Mississippi Valley Historical Review* 26 (1939): 39–54.

9. Walter M. Kollmorgen, "The Pennsylvania German Farmer," in Ralph Wood, ed., *The Pennsylvania Germans* (Princeton: Princeton University Press, 1942), 33.

10. Benjamin Rush, *An Account of the Manners of the German Inhabitants of Pennsylvania, Written in 1789*, ed. I. Daniel Rupp (Philadelphia: S. P. Town, 1875), 11–12.

11. S. W. Fletcher, *Pennsylvania Agriculture and Country Life, 1640–1840* (Harrisburg: Pennsylvania Historical and Museum Commission, 1955), 124.

12. For seasonal work schedules see Kollmorgen, "Pennsylvania German Farmer," 42–46.

13. Rush, *Account of the Manners*.

14. Max Weber, *The Protestant Ethic and the Spirit of Capitalism* (New York: Charles Scribner's Sons, 1958), 144–54.

15. For a discussion of fragmentation, see Hostetler, *Amish Society*, 270–91.

16. See Beulah Stauffer Hostetler, "Franconia Mennonite Conference and American Protestant Movements, 1840–1940" (Ph.D. dissertation, University of Pennsylvania, 1977), 21.

17. Joseph F. Beiler, "Revolutionary War Records," *The Diary* 3 (March 1971): 71.

18. Richard McMaster, *Land, Piety, and Peoplehood: The Establishment of Mennonite Communities in America, 1683–1790* (Scottdale: Herald Press, 1985), chap. 6.

19. Dirk Philips, *Enchiridion or Hand Book* (LaGrange, Ind.: Pathway, 1966), 295.

20. For these pertinent observations I am indebted to Robert Friedmann, "Anabaptism and Protestantism," *Mennonite Quarterly Review* 24 (1950): 22. See also his book, *Mennonite Piety through the Centuries* (Goshen, Ind.: Mennonite Historical Society, 1949).

21. For a description of schooling see John A. Hostetler and Gertrude E. Huntington, *Children in Amish Society* (New York: Holt, Rinehart, and Winston, 1971).

22. Changes are not always considered worldly but are evaluated for their effect on the welfare of the redemptive community. See Thomas E. Gallagher, Jr., "Clinging to the Past or Preparing for the Future? The Structure of Selective Modernization among Old Order Amish of Lancaster County, Pennsylvania" (Ph.D. dissertation, Temple University, 1981).

23. For the concept of mediating structures see Peter L. Berger and Richard J. Neuhaus, *To Empower People* (Washington, D.C.: American Enterprise Institute for Public Policy Research, 1977).

24. Observations gleaned from Joshua Fishman, "Language, Ethnicity, and Racism," *Georgetown University Round Table on Languages and Linguistics* (1977): 297–309.

25. *Olmstead* v. *United States*, 277 U.S. 438, 478 (1928).

8.

Pietism Rejected: A Reinterpretation of Amish Origins

LEO SCHELBERT

THE AMISH OCCUPY A SPECIAL PLACE among the "extraordinary groups" of the United States.[1] Popular articles periodically feature their separate ways in dress, lifestyle, and ways of farming,[2] and many scholarly books explore the fabric of Amish life.[3] Amish origins, in contrast, have received far less attention,[4] and they deserve to be probed further. In this chapter, first, the events of 1693–94 and the interpretations they received shall be touched upon, then a reassessment of their meaning shall be attempted.

In 1693 the Swiss Brethren[5] Elder Jakob Ammann[6] from Erlenbach near Thun in Switzerland's Bernese Oberland went on a visiting tour of Swiss and Alsatian congregations. Driven by a deep conviction that the Brethren were in danger of losing the very core of their faith, he had issued a "Warning Message" that was as curt as it was authoritative. It read in part:

I, Jakob Ammann, together with Deacons [Diener] and Elders [Aeltesten][7] send this writing and shall make known to everyone, be it woman's—or man's-person [Weibs—or Mannsperson], deacon or common disciple [Jünger] that you shall come forth by February 20 [1693] and announce to us, that is those [only] who are not yet banished by decision and counsel from the commune [gemein], and shall give account whether you can confess with us the controversial articles, namely to avoid those that are under the ban, and that one shall exclude liars from the commune, and [that one] shall proclaim no one saved outside of God's word or, [if] you can by the word of God inform us otherwise, [then] we will let us be convinced.[8]

In the company of like-minded Brethren such as Ulrich Ammann, Christian Blank, and Niklaus Augspurger, Jakob Ammann visited congregation after congregation. He put three issues before those who had bothered to assemble: the demand of total avoidance of those that were excommunicated, the necessity of the ban for those caught lying, and the impossibility of salvation for those outside the Brethren fold. In strict conformity with the scriptures as he understood them, Ammann made sure that each was "warned" at least three times and in the presence of witnesses before he put the ban on those dissenting.[9]

The reaction to Ammann's call was mixed. Hans Reist, an elder from Obertal near Zäziwil, led the opposition to the younger man's reforming zeal. He responded to Ammann's insistence on total avoidance of those who had been put under the ban by pointing out: "Christ also ate with publicans and sinners."[10] On March 10, 1694, an assembly of Swiss and Palatine elders issued a reply to Ammann and his followers. They insisted that Paul's admonition in 1 Corinthians 5:11—"you shall not associate" with sinners and "not even eat a meal with such people"—did not refer to "everyday [äusserlich] eating . . . but [to] eating the Easter Lamb [Oster-Lamm]." Despite some later efforts at reconciliation, the Swiss Brethren divided permanently into two groups; their interpretation of what constituted true Christianity revealed significant differences, despite the common bonds of a shared early history and of adult baptism as a central event in the true believer's life. The Brethren and Sisters of the Emmental Valley and of the Palatinate generally sided with Hans Reist; those of the Bernese Oberland in the region of Thun and the Alsatian congregations followed Jakob Ammann's lead.[11]

Renewed pressures from established ecclesiastical and secular authorities as well as the continued search for affordable arable land led to the dispersal of both Brethren groups. They settled as separate communities in Holland, Bavaria, Galicia, and Volhynia. Their descendants emigrated from these regions or directly from Swiss, Alsatian, and Palatine areas also to North America. There Ammann's followers came to be known as Amish; they split into various subgroups because of differing views on how to respond to secular challenges around them. Hans Reist's followers came to be known as Swiss Mennonites although they had only loose ties to the followers of Menno Simons.[12]

In European regions the Brethren of the Amish persuasion were too scattered and too mobile to survive as separate denominational communities. By 1900 the Swiss Brethren groups had reunited, and they are known today simply as *taufgesinnte Gemeinden*. Between 1727 and 1790 some five hundred and between 1815 and 1865 some three thousand Amish are estimated to have settled in North America.

Today their descendants number about eighty thousand and reside in twenty states and the Canadian province of Ontario; 75 percent of them are in Pennsylvania, Ohio, and Indiana.[13] The Amish continue to be mobile to escape the intrusive world of unbelievers and to search for land for their offspring who are to follow exclusively the God-ordained farming way of life.

The schism of the 1690s among the Swiss Brethren has received various scholarly interpretations. C. Henry Smith attributed the split to "the same strong individualism" that led these men and women not only to suffer martyrdom for their beliefs but also "to hairsplitting arguments over unimportant questions of policy and practice." Milton Gascho wondered "just how a controversy could continue in the midst of . . . persecution and distress"; to him the division exemplified "what may take place . . . when a few people begin to dispute religious questions." Discussing the various schisms suffered by the Amish during the nineteenth century in the United States, John C. Wenger praised Europe's Swiss Brethren for their "earnestness," brotherly love, and "ample tolerance" that had prevented all "but one division." Delbert L. Gratz found it surprising that, although in a precarious state as a persecuted minority, the Brethren "nevertheless had found occasion to disagree among themselves." John A. Hostetler feared that "the exact details of the division may not increase the reader's respect for the sect groups."[14]

Such concern, however, seems unnecessary. James M. Stayer's observations on Martin Luther and Huldreich Zwingli also apply to Jakob Ammann and Hans Reist; they were all "confident that they *did* have differences worth struggling over"; and one cannot understand their situation if one "refuse[s] to take them seriously."[15] If the division in the 1690s of the Swiss Brethren is placed in its proper theological and historical perspective, the contrasting views emerge as anything but "hairsplitting arguments over unimportant questions";[16] to the contrary, they appear as fundamental issues in attempts at defining "true" Christianity.

In the 1670s the established churches faced a new challenge. For some 120 years the various denominations that had arisen from the ashes of the medieval church between 1520 and 1550 had been able to maintain their respective synthesis of faith and reason, heart and mind, true doctrine and proper practice. Johannes Arndt's *True Christianity*, published between 1605 and 1610,[17] foreshadowed what was to come to full fruition in the spirituality of Angelus Silesius (1624–77), Johann Georg Gichtel (1638–1705), and above all, Philipp Jacob Spener

(1635–1705) and his most ardent follower August Hermann Francke (1663–1727).[18] The movement came to be known as Pietism.[19] In Germany it found "its very point of departure" in Spener's *Pia Desideria* but took separate forms in various parts of Christendom and emerged as Hasidism in the Jewish faith. Among Christian Pietism's noted representatives, according to the modern editor of *Pia Desideria*, were "the English Puritan John Bunyan, the Dutch Reformed Willem Teelinck, the German Lutheran Philip Jacob Spener, the Moravian Nicholas Zinzendorf, the Methodist progenitor John Wesley, the American Presbyterian Gilbert Tennent and the Roman Catholic Blaise Pascal."[20]

In German-speaking regions the so-called *collegia pietatis* gained special importance. Spener, a native of the Alsatian village of Rappoltstein near Strasbourg, had exhorted people to form special groups devoted to the practice of piety. "How much good it would do," he declared, "if good friends would come together on a Sunday and instead of getting out glasses, cards, or dice would take up a book and read from it for the edification of all." They could explore "the divine mysteries," especially those "who by God's grace have a superior knowledge of Christianity," and could "by virtue of their universal priesthood" edify each other.[21]

Despite its multiple expressions, Pietism pursued some common "essential concerns."[22] Faith was a matter of experience. God, the active mystery of salvation, poured out his wondrous grace into the hearts of those who not only strove for the "knowledge of the Christian faith" but also knew that *"Christianity consists rather of practice."*[23] Everyone was immediate to God, and the conversion of each was part of the coming Kingdom of God. Thus the importance of trained and ordained ministers was lessened, the division between clergy and laity became blurred, and the universal priesthood of all believers was fervently proclaimed anew. Pietism dissolved "the orthodox synthesis from within," stressed the virtuous life, and defined the minister's role less as a teacher of valid doctrine than as a *Vorbild der Gottseligkeit*, that is, a "model of Godblissfulness."[24]

Between 1690 and 1720 the Pietist movement also transformed the South German and Swiss churches. Lay people as well as students of theology and young clergymen, commoners as well as patricians, experienced powerful awakenings that brought them into direct conflicts with those who remained faithful to the ideals of post-Reformation orthodoxy and advocated a *via media* or balance between charisma and authority, true faith and spiritual experience, obedience to given rules and free-flowing devotion. They looked askance at "the running [of parishioners] to pietist ministers . . . the whole conventicle thing in the evening with laypeople as teachers, the secret network [of pietists] . . . the new way of preaching" that even made use "of dialect phrases" and of such "strange" works as those of Jakob Boehme. Some Pietist clergymen lost their positions, but others bowed sufficiently to the demands of the established authorities to remain at least in marginal posts. By the 1750s, however, the movement had spent its main force and inner-churchly Pietism had gained full acceptance.[25]

The rise of Pietism had a double impact on the Swiss Brethren. The authorities viewed the new dissenters as simply another version of the old Anabaptist evil; to them "Quaker," "Pietist," and "Wiedertäufer" were synonymous. As guardians of what they understood as the only valid Christianity, they renewed their efforts to stamp out all heresy, be it old or new, and to safeguard the purity of the church as well as proper civic behavior.[26]

But Pietism also affected the Swiss Brethren from within. It challenged the foundations of their faith as it had evolved between 1525 and 1527 and had been crystallized in the Schleitheim Confession of the latter year. Jakob Ammann had perceived that challenge. Had Brethren not reported that some held that "a good life was all that was necessary for salvation"?[27] Had not a sister who had been found lying gone unpunished? Had not the view gained acceptance that the *Treuherzigen* could also be saved, that is, those outside the *Gemein* who assisted its members in time of need? Ammann viewed these matters not as trifling opinions but as threatening the very essence of the Brethren creed.

The most fundamental assumption of the Swiss Brethren faith was cosmological. It interpreted the world as thoroughly and irreconcilably dualistic. The Schleitheim Confession had expressed this view with stark and concise beauty:

Nun ist ye nütt anders in der welt
und aller creatur dan
gütz und bös,
glöubig and unglöubig,
finsternüs und liecht
welt und die uss der welt sind,
tempel gottes and die götzen,
Christus und Belial,
und keins mag dem andern kein
    teil han.[28]

(Now there is nothing other in the world
and all creatures than
good and bad,
believing and unbelieving,
darkness and light,
world and those [who] are outside the world,
temples of God and the idols,
Christ and Belial,
and none may have no part in the other.)

This ontological view led the Brethren to a radical separation not only from the secular domain but also from "the horrors" (*grüwel*) of "all papal and antipapal work and divine service, meetings, and church attendance." "Winehouses," "citizenships and duties of unbelief," "the sword," and "armor" were secular realities that were no more the domain of "Belial" than were all the known ecclesiastical institutions, regardless of whether they were part of the Catholic, Lutheran, or Reformed persuasion. In brief, the Brethren declared the whole of Christendom outside the *Gemein*, secular and ecclesiastical, as the domain of Satan. This view denied the very foundation of society and branded the belief in the *corpus christianum*, that is, the basic unity of the religious and the secular under God, as idolatrous. The resulting bitter persecution is, at least from this vantage point, understandable, just as the steadfast sincerity of the Brethren and their nonresistant suffering are admirable.[29]

The basic cosmological dualism led the Brethren to a rejection of all ecumenism that soon emerged as a hallmark of the Pietist persuasion, which "did not recognize Reformed and Lutherans, but only awakened Christians." The Christian Enlightenment, Pietism's contemporary countermovement, similarly made light of denominational boundaries.[30] The Swiss Brethren congregations did not remain untouched by the new ecumenical spirit. Occasional attendance at Reformed services was not uncommon and was tolerated; many Brethren viewed the *Treuherzigen* as also saved, and members of the *Gemein* who had outwardly sinned were not shunned. Yet the Schleitheim Confession had clearly defined the people of the *Gemein* as the only "true implanted members of Christ" and as the only truly "obedient children of God and sons and daughters who have become separate"; in contrast, all others, but especially false Brethren and Sisters, served not God but "their father, the devil."[31] Whereas the emerging Pietist movement tended toward a monistic and thus ecumenical stance, the original Brethren faith had espoused a radically dualistic and separatist attitude.

Yet there was a further irreconcilable difference between the two interpretations of what constituted true Christianity. The Pietist movement was individualist and experiential whereas the Brethren faith demanded unquestioned communal obedience; a true believer had "to reject, hate, and curse all plans, word use, and good thinking of all people, also of one's own," and to embrace only that which the *Gemein* had "found in clear bright scripture" (*das in heiterer, clarer schrift erfunden werden mag*).[32] The true *Gemein* was led not by "awakened souls," but by its "guardians" (*Hirten*) whose duty it was "to read and admonish and teach . . . and to observe in all things the lips of Christ" (*Sölich ampt sol sin lesen und ermanen und leren . . . und in allen dingen des lips Christi acht haben*).[33] The Brethren *Gemein* as envisioned by those at Schleitheim had thus left no room for the experiential individualism that was to become a pronounced trait of Pietist traditions. When Jakob Ammann and his followers adopted uniform dress, regulated the width of men's hats, and demanded that beards remain untrimmed and hooks and eyes replace buttons, they were not obsessed by trifling externals; they hoped that by such daily tests of obedience the *Gemein* would remain dedicated to paying attention in all ways only "to the lips of Christ" as spoken in Holy Writ. This, then, was not religion that had turned outward and replaced true godliness with adherence to external trivialities; rather, the Amish posture was an attempt to safeguard the radical separation of Christ's people from those of Belial, in literal observance of what the Brethren viewed as God's command.[34]

From this vantage point, Jakob Ammann's zeal appears not as a young hothead's divisive obsession with trifles but as an attempt to protect the Brethren *Gemein* from Pietism's undermining force. He had sensed that the two forms of Christianity had antithetical traits, as the following list of contrasts highlights:

Swiss Brethren Faith	*Pietist Movement*
Dualist	Monist
Exclusivist	Ecumenical
Communal	Individualist
Obedient	Experiential
Scripturally literal	Inspirational
Conservative	Innovative

If there is merit in such an interpretation, Jakob Ammann's three questions about avoidance, the liar, and the *Treuherzigen* were merely crystallizations of fundamentals of Swiss Brethren beliefs as they had been formulated at Schleitheim in 1527 and challenged in the 1690s by the Pietist movement. Thus the Amish persuasion within the fold of the *Taufgesinnten* fulfilled then, and continues to fulfill to this day, a major mission: it reminds the Brethren groups who absorbed impulses from Pietism or, in the nineteenth century, from American evangelicalism or laissez-faire liberalism, of the fundamentals of their original creed. Thus the Amish are neither quaint nor queer; rather, they embody in their unique Christian vision a formidable challenge not only for the Swiss Brethren traditions but for all forms of religious life.

Notes

1. William M. Kephart, *Extraordinary Groups: The Sociology of Unconventional Life-Styles* (New York: St. Martin's Press, 1976), 6–51.
2. A recent example is Jerry Irwin (photo essay) and Douglas Lee (text), "The Plain People of Pennsylvania," *National Geographic* 165 (April 1984):492–519. A graphic popular portrait is offered by William I. Schreiber, *Our Amish Neighbors* (Chicago: University of Chicago Press, 1962).
3. An authoritative study is John A. Hostetler, *Amish Society* (Baltimore: The Johns Hopkins University Press, 1963; rev. ed. 1968; 3d ed., 1980); all three editions contain an extensive bibliography; the 1968 edition has been used throughout.
4. Basic is Milton Gascho, "The Amish Division of 1693–1697 in Switzerland and Alsace," *Mennonite Quarterly Review* (hereafter cited as *MQR*) 11 (October 1937): 235–66; an extensive discussion of the available primary sources appears on pp. 237–43. Among them the following are especially important: Joseph Stuckey, *Eine Begebenheit die sich in Deutschland und in der Schweiz von 1693–1700 zugetragen hat*, 4th ed. (Arthur, Ill.: A. M. Publishing Association, 1936); an English translation is John B. Mast, ed. and trans., *The Letters of the Amish Division, 1693–1711* (Oregon City: C. J. Schlabach, 1950).
5. An incisive essay is James M. Stayer, "The Swiss Brethren: An Exercise in Historical Definition," *Church History* 47 (June 1978):174–95. The so-called Radical Reformation may be divided into the "loud" and the "still" Anabaptists; the former were led by Thomas Müntzer, a sixteenth-century revolutionary, "driven by a sincere zeal for the salvation of souls" (James M. Stayer, "Thomas Müntzer's Theology and Revolution in Recent Non-Marxist Interpretations," *MQR* 43 [April 1969]:152). The "still" Anabaptists formed three separate denominational communities: the Swiss Brethren of Swiss, Alsatian, and South German regions; the Hutterian Brethren of Moravia, and the Mennonites or Doopsgezinde of the Lower Rhine regions, the Netherlands, and northern Germany. These subgroups had multiple origins but were united in their belief in the centrality of adult baptism; see Ernst H. Correll, *Das schweizerische Täufertum* (Tübingen: J. C. P. Mohr [Paul Siebeck], 1925), 14; incisive is James M. Stayer, Werner O. Packull, and Klaus Deppermann, "From Monogenesis to Polygenesis: The Historical Discussion of Anabaptist Origins," *MQR* 49 (April 1975):83–121.
6. Ammann's dates are uncertain; he had certainly died before 1730; see Delbert L. Gratz, "The House of Jacob Ammann in Switzerland," *MQR* 25 (April 1951):137–39.
7. Hostetler, *Amish Society*, 33, translates *Diener und Aelteste* as "ministers and bishops." An Amish *Gemein*, congregation, is composed of some ten to twenty-five families who are led by a *Volle Diener* or bishop, two *Diener zum Buch* or preachers, and an *Armen Diener* or deacon; they do not receive formal training and engage in farming like other members; see Kephart, *Extraordinary Groups*, 23–24.
8. Translated from the German text as given in Hostetler, *Amish Society*, 32; see also Gascho, "Amish Division," 239.
9. Stuckey, *Begebenheit*, 65; Ammann invoked Matthew 18:15–17 and Titus 3:10:"Avoid any heretic after one or two warnings."

10. Ibid., 59.

11. Gascho, "Amish Division," 262, has the complete text; the declaration is signed by nine Swiss and seven Palatine ministers.

12. The migrations of the Brethren are featured by John C. Wenger, *Glimpses of Mennonite History and Doctrine* (Scottdale, Pa.: Herald Press, 1947); most authoritative is Delbert L. Gratz, *Bernese Anabaptists and Their American Descendants* (Scottdale, Pa.: Herald Press, 1953); the eighteenth- and nineteenth-century migrations of the Reist group to the United States are described in Leo Schelbert, *Swiss Migration to America: The Swiss Mennonites* (New York: Arno Press, 1980), 143–261.

13. John A. Hostetler, "Amish," in Stephan Thernstrom et al., eds., *Harvard Encyclopedia of American Ethnic Groups* (Cambridge, Mass.: Belknap Press of Harvard University Press, 1980), 123.

14. C. Henry Smith, *The Story of the Mennonites* (Berne, Ind.: Mennonite Book Concern, 1941), 139; Gascho, "Amish Division," 252, 235; Wenger, *Glimpses*, 109; Gratz, *Bernese Anabaptists*, 44; Hostetler, *Amish Society*, 28. In his third edition, pp. 33 and 42, Hostetler views the schism as "a Family squabble" between the Bernese mother church and the Alsatian diaspora; he also suggests that Ammann may have been a convert to the Brethren faith.

15. James M. Stayer, "Swiss Brethren," *Church History* 47 (1978):176, n. 9.

16. Smith, *Story of the Mennonites*, 139.

17. A recent edition is Johann Arndt, *True Christianity*, trans. and intro. Peter Erb (New York: Paulist Press, 1979); Erb's valuable introduction profiles the origin and impact of the book.

18. See F. Ernest Stoeffler, *German Pietism during the Eighteenth Century* (Leiden: E. J. Brill, 1973), 1–87, for a discussion of Francke and the "Spener Halle Movement in Germany"; Stoeffler comments: "As a religious genius he [Francke] fashioned Spenerian Pietism into the most self-assured theologically compact, as well as dynamic religious movement of his day" (p. 36).

19. For the origin of the term see Kurt Müller, "Feller," *Neue Deutsche Biographie*, 13 vols. (Berlin: Dunker und Humblot, 1953–82): 5:73; also Johann Heinrich Zedler, *Universal-Lexicon*, 64 vols. (Halle: J. H. Zedler, 1732–50), 28:122, 130.

20. Emmanuel Hirsch, "Die Grundlegung der pietistischen Theologie durch Philipp Jakob Spener," in Martin Greschat, ed., *Zur neueren Pietismusforschung* (Darmstadt: Wissenschaftliche Buchgesellschaft, 1977), 34. For an English edition see *Pia Desideria*, trans., ed., and intro. Theodore G. Tappert (Philadelphia: Fortress Press, 1964); the Introduction gives a valuable overview of Spener's life and ideas. The quote is on p. 1.

21. Ibid., 13; the origins of the *collegia pietatis* are explored in Johannes Wallmann, "Das Collegium Pietatis," in Greschat, ed., *Zur neueren Pietismusforschung*, 167–223, taken from his *Philipp Jakob Spener und die Anfänge des Pietismus* (Tübingen: J. C. B. Mohr [Paul Siebeck], 1970).

22. This discussion follows Martin Schmidt, "Pietismus," in Kurt Galling, ed., *Die Religion in Geschichte und Gegenwart*, 7 vols. (Tübingen: J. C. B. Mohr [Paul Siebeck], 1957–65); 5: cols. 370–81.

23. Tappert, ed., *Pia Desideria*, 95.

24. Schmidt, "Pietismus," col. 376:"Das konfessionelle Selbstbewusstsein der Orthodoxie löste er von innen her auf," col. 377.

25. Paul Wernle, *Der schweizerische Protestantismus im XVIII. Jahrhundert*, 5 vols. (Tübingen: J. C. B. Mohr [Paul Siebeck], 1923), 1 : 121, 124. This thorough study explores the various types of Pietism in Swiss regions in the context of general German developments.

26. Gratz, *Bernese Anabaptists*, 37–38, 56–59.

27. Stuckey, *Begebenheit*, 13; Gascho, "Amish Division," 252.

28. Beatrice Jenny, *Das Schleitheimer Täuferbekenntnis 1527* (Thayngen: Karl Augustin, 1951), 12, lines 114–18; my translation is as literal as possible. For an English version see John C. Wenger, "The Schleitheim Confession of Faith," *MQR* 19 (October 1945): 247–53; also in Wenger, *Glimpses*, 206–13.

29. Ibid., 12, lines 126–30.

30. Wernle, *Der schweizerische Protestantismus*, 1 : 477.

31. Jenny, *Das Schleitheimer Täuferbekenntnis*, 9, lines 14, 24–28; 10, lines 47–48.

32. Letter of Conrad Grebel and friends to Thomas Müntzer, September 5, 1524, in Leonard von Muralt and Walter Schmid, eds., *Quellen zur Geschichte der Täufer in der Schweiz* (Zurich: S. Hirzel, 1952), 1 : 14. See also Hostetler, *Amish Society*, 55 : "The Amish Vow"; Jean Runzo, "Communal Discipline in the Early Anabaptist Communities of Switzerland, South and Central Germany, Austria and Moravia, 1525–1550" (Ph.D. diss., University of Michigan, 1978), abstract in *MQR* 53 (January 1979): 78–79.

33. Jenny, *Das Schleitheimer Täuferbekenntnis*, 13, lines 147–51.

34. Smith, *Story of the Mennonites*, 139.

PART III:
Ethnicity and Politics

9.

German-Americans and the Invention of Ethnicity

KATHLEEN NEILS CONZEN

IN OCTOBER 1883 the New York German humor magazine, *Puck*, ran an elaborate full-page color cartoon entitled "A Family Fest— the 200th Birthday of the Healthiest Lad among Uncle Sam's Adoptive Children." In a mild parody of Last Supper iconography, the artist depicted Uncle Sam, Miss Liberty, and figures representing twelve immigrant groups gathered around a banquet table under portraits of Baron von Steuben, George Washington, and the Marquis de La- fayette. Each immigrant figure is stereotypically garbed: the Swede in rough laborer's clothes, the Frenchman as a chef, the Italian with mu- sic box and monkey. Sitting in the Judas seat is the disgruntled cari- cature of an Irishman. In the deferential role of the beloved apostle to the right of the Christ figure is the Englishman in loud checks. And the Christ figure in the center of the picture? It is the German: tall, blond, smilingly confident, a wine glass on the table before him, a cigar in his hand, his beard and slouch hat reminders of the glory days of 1848 and of his ethnic heritage, his evening dress a symbol of his full integration into American society. He accepts as his due the toasts of Miss Liberty and Uncle Sam and the homage of his neighbors; he leaves no doubt as to either the rightfulness of his central place or his pride in his dual loyalties.[1]

The cartoon succinctly captures German self-perceptions of the place they had attained within American society after two hundred years of settlement in the New World. It is often argued that German- Americans never constituted a "real" ethnic group within America, di- vided as they were by dialect, region of origin, religion, class, time of emigration, and place of American settlement. Rather, they re- mained, as Heinz Kloss put it, an *"unvollendete Volksgruppe,"* an un-

Ein Familienfest. — Der 200. Geburtstag des gesündesten Jungen unter Onkel Sam's Adoptiv-Kindern.

fulfilled ethnicity.[2] But such a perspective assumes a monolithic and all-encompassing definition of ethnicity that few groups in America ever achieved. To so limit the concept is to lose the ability to analyze and compare the various forms that ethnic identity has taken in the United States. If ethnicity is regarded as a form of social identity resulting from a continuing process of core definition and boundary maintenance, which persons of a given national descent accept in varying numbers and with varying degrees of commitment, then we may speak in a very real sense of a German-American ethnicity.[3] Indeed, as the *Puck* cartoon suggests, by the time of their Bicentennial celebration German-Americans had consciously invented an ethnicity for themselves and, in attempting to win acceptance for the legitimate role of such a group identity, had helped also to invent ethnicity itself as a category within American society.

This dual "invention" emerged in the course of extensive debates within the German community regarding the appropriate role and future of Germans in America. Historiography has accustomed us to analyze the process of immigrant integration in terms of the changing assimilation norms imposed by the host society. For much of the nineteenth century, Americans fairly unthinkingly assumed a benign melting process leading to the fusion of immigrants and native-born alike into a new American culture. By the late nineteenth century, explicit insistence on complete conformity to prevailing American norms became more prevalent, to be ultimately succeeded in the later twentieth century by widespread acceptance of a pluralist norm positing the enduring survival of distinctive ethnic cultures.[4]

Germans shaped their own ethnicity in part by reacting to the assimilation norms held out to them by American society. But theirs was more than a passive, reactive role. As an Anglo-American commentator noted in 1883, even if English-speaking Americans seldom indulged in serious inquiry into the process of immigrant assimilation, "the destiny of the German element in America has long been a theme for argument and speculation among the more cultivated and thoughtful representatives of that element. . . . In the German newspapers and the German clubs which are found in all our principal cities the questions, Will the Teutonic race lose its identity in the New World? and, Will its language become extinct here? are often discussed with feel-

Facing page. Cartoon in the magazine *Puck* (October 3, 1883) on the occasion of the German-American Bicentennial. The caption reads: "A Family Fest—the 200th Birthday of the Healthiest Lad among Uncle Sam's Adoptive Children."

ing and interest." Indeed, as early as 1857 a German-American commentator sighed that German life in America was "a theme that has already been discussed hundreds of times and can lay claim to almost anything but the charm of novelty and originality."[5] Through the medium of these interminable discussions, German-Americans sought to define their own assimilation norms and shape the content of a group identity capable of serving the needs of the largest possible proportion of the German immigration yet still consonant with American ideals and circumstances.

Discussion occurred on two levels. First, they tried to understand what assimilative processes were actually under way. With such understanding, they could then proceed to the second level, defining norms for the processes that were both realizable and philosophically defensible in accordance with the needs of both immigrants and host society and designing policies to achieve them. Their discussions canvassed the possibilities of all three of the basic models of assimilation that American society has exhibited. Three separate phases of debate can be identified in the period stretching from the 1840s to the 1880s, logically though not chronologically distinct from one another. In each phase, a certain degree of consensus was achieved, which was further refined in the next phase in a cumulative process of self-definition. In the initial phase, those arguing for the necessity of preserving German culture in America drowned out voices favoring Anglo conformity. In the second phase, ethnic separatism was rejected on both logical and pragmatic grounds in favor of an ethnic presence within American society defined and defended in melting pot terms. In the third phase, as German-Americans refined their definitions of the content of their ethnicity, they attempted to replace the melting pot model with a cultural pluralist ideal whose realization they found elusive.

These debates can be traced in the pages of German-American books and journals of opinion. Those who participated were hardly representative of the mass of German-Americans. It is clear, however, that the limitations posed by the attitudes of the ethnic rank and file strongly influenced their discussions. Moreover, the arguments they formulated were retailed to a wider audience by countless local journalists, politicians, and public speakers, and they framed the terms within which German-Americans contemplated their ethnic situation. If not all agreed with the tenor of their conclusions, those who rejected their position rejected the only formal ethnic identity Germans in America ever achieved.

The discussion opened in the mid-1840s as German immigrants

multiplied, German neighborhoods expanded, German associations proliferated, and the German press found its voice. Emil Klauprecht defined the basic issue for his Cincinnati readers in 1847: "Which of the characteristics of our nation have been retained to the present, and have its members . . . left behind any lasting traces . . . of their former culture and of their influence as a race, which could give their successors the comforting assurance that he who exchanges his homeland for America's free soil does not also have to leave behind his nationality, to live and die as a stranger among strangers?"[6] Many who attempted to answer this question were not very sanguine. They saw in the descendants of the colonial German immigration a confusing mixture of peasant German and crude American without any real cultural influence. In the majority of more recent immigrants they discerned a no more felicitous "mania to Americanize": "Their highest aspiration is to reach the point where you cannot tell them from an American." But such immigrants seemed only to lose all the German virtues while acquiring only American vices, attracting the contempt of native Americans who came to regard Germans as little more than cultural manure, fit only to fertilize the creativity of others.[7]

But representatives of this immigration of the 1830s and 1840s could advance a strong case for the necessity of as rapid and complete an Americanization as possible. On the one hand, the same logic of romantic nationalism that urged a united Germany implied that to maintain German cultural distinctiveness was unfair to the need of their new homeland for national unity. On the other, the tyranny, submissiveness, and national disunity engendered by German culture in Europe argued that Germans had little cultural baggage worth importing to a free nation.[8] Julius Fröbel rehearsed a sophisticated version of such arguments for Anglo conformity in 1857. Most Germans, he pointed out, would gain culturally through Americanization. They would replace dialect German with decent English and exchange provincial small-mindedness for the pride of American national vision. What in any case did they know of the glories of German culture, of Kant or Schiller? Moreover, the "interests of the Republic" could demand rapid assimilation to educate immigrants to participate in American politics, to preserve the illusion of cultural equality upon which belief in the political system rested, and to avoid introducing class-specific customs into a classless society.[9]

But then Fröbel finessed his case. Such arguments, he noted, rested on the Whiggish belief that American society was closed, its development essentially complete, its territory given, its character set.

But he found this Whiggish stance premature. The final form of the republic was not yet determined, and thus possible cultural dangers did not have to be taken into account and the path for distinctive immigrant cultural contributions was not yet barred. "We too, even though we are not Anglo-Saxons, believe in 'manifest destiny' and—we add for the benefit of the nativists—'manifest destiny' also believes in us."[10]

Like most new immigrants of his ilk after 1848, Fröbel could not bring himself to accept an America that had no place for what he regarded as a superior German culture. Earlier immigrants, largely lower class, had assimilated rapidly in part because they lacked sufficient numbers to support familiar customs and institutions but also because they found America superior to what they had known in Germany. Most of the exiles of 1848 judged American society far more harshly. They saw much that was praiseworthy in German culture, much that was crass, materialistic, and hypocritical in America. This view made the general American scorn for Germans all the more intolerable. Hence their rejection of the Anglo-conformist model was generally immediate and instinctive, based more on their sense of cultural superiority than on any reasoned theory of ethnic interaction.[11]

Nevertheless, the arguments they marshaled to support the correctness and the necessity of maintaining a German cultural presence in America remained basic to all subsequent German ethnic theorizing. First, they achieved agreement on the essentially political character of American nationhood. "What is it," Christian Esselen queried, "that permits us to pursue our own most German ways and habits in a land in which we or our fathers were not born, whose language is not ours. . . ? It is the grand concept of eternal and inalienable human rights, which was set down in the Declaration of Independence, the legal basis of this great Republic." Founded not on a national or dynastic basis, the American state required for naturalization only a renunciation of former allegiance and an oath to uphold the Constitution. Indeed, among the rights of man protected by the Constitution was, effectively, the right of cultural freedom. Consequently, "one need not chew tobacco, nor go bankrupt, nor speculate in lots, nor become a temperance fanatic, nor run into church or chase after Negroes. The decision, the firm will, and the capability to become a free man, Americanizes us completely." Nor, they agreed, was the national character of the United States yet determined, inasmuch as the nation was founded on a purely political basis and settled by people from every quarter of the globe; hence the romantic nationalist argument for cultural conformity was fallacious. Nationalism could even be viewed as incompatible with America's foundation solely upon a unity of belief: "To vindicate individualism against nationality, is the office of America."[12]

They also agreed on a second basic tenet: since a person cannot change his nationality along with his national loyalties, he could have cultural needs which his new homeland's culture might be unable to fulfill. This, of course, was the heart of the matter for most commentators. Germans in the South, according to one disillusioned observer, frequently found themselves so starved for accustomed sociability that they jeopardized their status within white society by resorting to the company of slaves. Even if it were possible to strip oneself of one's nationality, as Gustav Struve noted, it would not be advantageous for the new homeland: he who readily throws away one set of values will as readily throw away another, becoming a slave to the highest bidder. Some, like the pre-Forty-eighter Klauprecht, even propounded an early version of an almost purely pluralist position: cultural diversity, he argued, was valuable in itself: "Everything already bears too great a mask of factory-like uniformity. Every pronounced, picturesque peculiarity of the various groups within the population here should be sacredly preserved."[13] But above all, commentators agreed that Americans would never learn to respect Germans and accord them equality until Germans learned to respect themselves and their culture, and that meant cultivating differences rather than rooting them out.[14]

Thus provoked by Americanizing immigrants on the one hand and Yankee scorn on the other, various German-Americans in the 1840s and 1850s groped their way toward a defense of ethnic difference in American society and an argument for the conservation of their own culture. By the late 1850s, their reasoning had acquired the status of self-evident postulates. But in the meantime, the practical problem remained: theoretical agreement was well and good, but how were German values and customs to be preserved in the face of assimilative pressures? For those most repelled by American reality, the favorite solution was ethnic separatism: establishing isolated German settlements, dominating an entire state or states, or even creating a separate German colony beyond the western boundaries of the nation.[15] The debate over the feasibility of such separatism constitutes the second phase in the rhetorical evolution of German ethnicity and engendered a specifically German version of the melting pot model.

Separatists maintained that when the immovable object of German nationality confronted the irresistible force of American society, the outcome could only be "degeneration and devastation." Only in isolation from Americans could the German be truly American, preserving his virtue as well as his cultural values while enjoying the blessings of free American institutions; only in isolation was there any hope that the second generation would remain German. Switzerland demonstrated that two or more nationalities could live separately within the same nation-state. But proponents of separatism were forced to concede that real isolation was a practical impossibility, given the inevitable use of English in American public institutions and the intrusive penetration of Yankee entrepreneurs wherever they sniffed opportunity. Moreover, most Germans seemed to prefer the economic options within American society to cultural continuity outside it. But ironically, most ascribed the practical failure of separatist plans mainly to the stubborn retention by Germans of one of their least admirable traits: their inability to unite for the common good.[16]

A New York popular weekly summarized the lesson most Germans drew from the failure of such plans: "German colony, German state—yes . . . if only a German sense of community had first been created. . . . Wherever the German element attempts to separate itself and stand on its own two feet, the result is a fiasco. . . . Instead of enthusing about a state within a state—insisting on a policy of isolation— wouldn't it be wiser to seek the cultural-historical task of the German emigration in a melting of Germanic idealism with the realism of the Anglo-Saxons?"[17] The metaphor of the melting pot—Christian Essellen used the term *Schmelztiegel* in 1857, a good half-century before it became current in English[18]—accorded well with midcentury American rhetoric on immigrant assimilation and proved ideal for German-Americans seeking a middle way between an Anglo conformity that stripped them both of self-respect and much that they considered superior and indispensable in German culture, and an impracticable, impotent separatism. The melting pot explained observed processes of cultural change among immigrants and the Americanization of their children and flowed naturally from assumptions concerning the nature of the American state. Yet it left a role in America for German culture. As Carl Schurz put it in his 1859 Faneuil Hall speech, "It is true, the Anglo-Saxon establishes and maintains his ascendancy, but without absolutely absorbing the other national elements. They modify each other, and their peculiar characteristics are to be blended together by the all-assimilating power of freedom."[19]

Midcentury American acceptance of the melting pot imagery rested on two critical assumptions. Individualistic Americans took for granted the individualistic nature of the melting and were unable to visualize assimilation as a collective, group process. And they relied upon the transforming effects of the American environment and America's free institutions to ensure that undesirable traits would be eliminated before the melting began.[20] Both of these assumptions were unacceptable to most Germans. With their increased numbers and with the solidarity and self-confidence engendered by resistance to nativist and temperance attacks had come also, by the mid-1850s, a richly articulated German-American community life that was beginning to fulfill many of their perceived social and cultural needs. It seemed clear that German culture could be preserved in America only with the support of such group institutions and collective identity. It was becoming equally clear that what Germans most wished to preserve of German culture, particularly their distinctive modes of socializing, was, in many instances, precisely what Americans found most objectionable.

German theorizers, therefore, converted the vague, cosmopolitan melting pot model of the Crèvecoeur tradition into an aggressive doctrine designed not only to reassure German-Americans that it was possible to survive as Germans in the midst of American society but also to assert the German right to enter the melting pot collectively and on their own terms. The result was a Germanocentric argument, not so much for the right of all groups to coexist but for the special right of Germans to support an ethnic existence in America because of the special gifts that they would ultimately bring into the melting pot.

The argument rested on perceived differences between German and American national traits. Americans were seen as active, practical achievers with a genius for business and politics but with no sense for the higher things in life. Germans, by contrast, were dreamers, artists, thinkers, impractical perhaps, but able to enjoy life and cultivate warm personal relationships. The cultural-historic mission of the Germans in America, therefore, was to bring to Americans "in return for the freedom guaranteed us as citizens of the new homeland and the easier material advancement that we find among them . . . certain gifts that they are lacking and that can contribute materially to their ennoblement."[21]

But if Germans were to contribute to America the gifts of sociability, public morality, and an appreciation for the good, the true, and the beautiful, they would have to preserve and cultivate these traits among themselves, apart from the dross of German or American culture. They would have to unite to preserve their community, as Friedrich Münch argued, "with sufficient self-sufficiency to ensure that it will not be absorbed, but rather gradually flow, healthy and unweakened, into the American way of life [*hiesiges Volksleben*]." Translated into a program of action, that meant above all supporting the German language and its teaching in the schools and defending German sociability from attacks by temperance and Sunday observance fanatics.[22]

The melting pot rhetoric initially formulated in the debates over separatism and nativism in the 1850s thus contained a self-definition of ethnicity in exclusively cultural terms, a justification for tolerance of German ethnic difference based on the benefits it would bring America, and a consolation for the cultural loss of the second generation in the higher mission of Germans in America. Only by remaining solidly within American society, reminded Philip Schaff in 1855, could Germans fulfill that holy mission:

Beyond all question the German has a great work to do in the New World, though he is as yet hardly aware of it. He will not fully meet the demand, however, if he coldly and stiffly shuts himself out from the Anglo-Americans, and thinks to form a state within a state. . . . He must rather, by his native cosmopolitan, universal spirit, boldly and energetically master the Anglo-American nature, appropriate its virtues, and then breathe into it, as far as it may be desirable, the breath of his own spirit and life. In this way he will work in a larger and richer field; whereas by selfish seclusion, he robs himself of all influence on the central stream of American life. . . . Amerika is the grave of all European nationalities; but a Phenix [sic] grave, from which they shall rise to new life and new activity in a new and essentially Anglo-Germanic form.[23]

But after the Civil War, with their right to a place in American society now purchased in blood, German-Americans found it increasingly difficult to accept the ethnic suicide, however Phoenixlike, that the melting pot ideal held out to them. In German-American culture, they had convinced themselves, lay the salvation of the nation. "Without a deep, ardent inner life the American nation will be tested time and again as it was in the late conflict; without a sound, lively popular way of life rooted, German fashion, in the ethical sentiments of the heart . . . the temple of true freedom may never be ornamented with the cupola of completion and will appear to coming generations little more than a desolate ruin." America was already beginning to "Germanize," they noted, and pride was buoyed by German victories in Europe; why should an ethnic culture so patently superior not survive indefinitely?[24]

With the post–Civil War search for an enduring pluralist alternative to the melting pot, therefore, the German-American "invention" of ethnicity moved into its third phase. The contours of debate can be traced in the controversy generated by the 1867 publication of Friedrich Kapp's history of the Germans in colonial New York. Kapp, an old Forty-eighter, had concluded by emphasizing that "there cannot be a German nation within America, but Germans can contribute the rich contents of their inner life, the treasures of their thought; the greater the field on which they choose to fight, the greater their contribution. . . . If this happens, there will be nothing painful, nothing tragic about the disintegration of Germanness in America." It might even, he argued, be a kind of resurrection: "For on this point we can harbor no illusions: he who emigrates gives up his fatherland and is lost to it. One can no more have two fatherlands than two fathers. Therefore either German or American: the German-American is only a transitional figure, who disappears in the second generation. He who wishes to remain German must either stay in the homeland or return to it, for emigration is for the individual who resorts to it a national death."[25]

German-American critics throughout the country rushed to the defense of a durable ethnicity, charging Kapp with hatred of his own people and ignorance of the true situation within German-American communities.[26] To distance themselves from the implications of the melting pot, they groped their way toward justifications for the perpetuation of ethnic difference. Some took the complete step to a principled defense of permanent ethnic diversity. A Milwaukeean, for example, argued in 1883 that history had shown that ethnicity in no way interfered with patriotism: "We fought in the War of the Rebellion at your side . . . on the other hand, we were 'partners' in the whiskey rings . . . we have all gained from one another and we have all lost. . . . But still, must we all go the same way?"[27] Most, however, remained content to stress pragmatically the advantages to the nation of citizens able to appreciate the treasures of two cultures and the insight thereby gained in international dealings. Their vision, influenced by the racial beliefs and German chauvinism of the period, was not really of a pluralist America but of an America codominated by German and Anglo culture.[28]

But as more sober analysts noted, it was one thing to argue that German ethnicity had a right to survive in American society and another to demonstrate that it had a reasonable chance of so doing. To assert that large-scale immigration could continue indefinitely, or that German language in the schools could guarantee a lasting ethnic influence, was wishful thinking. Kapp and others cited numerous indications that the second generation was rapidly Americanizing, culturally as well as politically. The speech and customs of the homeland were a "bridge," they argued, that eased the process of initial amalgamation,

Hermann's Monument in New Ulm, Minnesota
(above). Construction was begun in 1888 and completed in 1897. The monument was modeled after the
"Hermannsdenkmal" (facing page) at Detmold in the
Teutoburger Forest of Germany which was begun in
1838 and dedicated with considerable pomp and cir-
cumstance in 1875. Inspired by the story of Hermann
the Cherusker (Arminius), who unified the Germanic
tribes and led them to a victory over the Roman le-
gions in the Teutoburger Forest in A.D. 9, German-
Americans founded the Order of the Sons of Hermann
and contributed to the erection of the New Ulm monument with a nationwide fund drive. Julius Bernd, an
architect from New Ulm, designed the American version at approximately half the size of the German
original. At the time of the dedication of the monument, New Ulm was a town of 3,000 people, almost all
of German background. It has since quadrupled in
size and celebrates "Heritage Days" every year in July,
during which the history of the original Hermann is
interwoven with New Ulm's local story in an open-air
theater presentation. (Minnesota Historical Society;
Bildarchiv Foto Marburg)

but resistance to ultimate assimilation would mean degeneration into a sterile and fossilized cultural fragment.[29]

In attempting to clarify the actual operation of the melting pot, therefore, some German-American theorists began to formulate a realistic understanding of the actual process of cultural change in terms that resembled what John Higham has called "pluralistic integration."[30] But most, unwilling to abandon the ethnic community so laboriously created, preferred rather to abandon altogether any effort to integrate theory and reality in favor of simply asserting—as they did in the call to the 1883 Bicentennial celebrations—both their contributions to America and the cultural equality and group perpetuation to which they consequently felt entitled.[31]

In many ways, 1883 was a high-water mark of German culture in America. German immigration peaked during that decade, and with it the influence of the immigrant generation and the ethnic institutions they had created.[32] I have attempted to argue that in the half-century preceding that symbolic date, German-American theorists had consciously attempted to "invent" both a place for ethnicity within American society and a content for German ethnicity sufficiently broad to include all of German background while distinguishing them from non-Germans. The ethnic boundaries that they erected were limited cultural ones, which emerged naturally from perceptions of what separated Germans from Americans but also from the realization, generally acknowledged by the late 1850s, that any all-inclusive unity or corporate identity was not only impossible but un-American.[33] The rhetoric helped define what it was to be a German-American, for those who cared. Large numbers did not, of course, or rejected the ethnicity so defined in favor of more limited subgroup loyalties.

What, then, is the significance to be derived from the shifting rhetoric of German-American ethnic invention? First, it provides important contemporary evidence for the nature of immigrant integration. The pluralist model enjoys widespread acceptance today.[34] Try as they might, however, German-American theorists could find little basis for such a model in nineteenth-century America, not because Americans imposed forced integration but because, except in limited cultural spheres, the mass of German immigrants perceived few benefits to be gained by remaining separate.

Second, for all its hot air, the rhetoric provided German-Americans with an indispensable philosophic unity and righteous conviction necessary to defend forcefully through politics those areas of cultural distinctiveness that they chose to retain. Third, as a result, through the medium of politics German assumptions regarding the limits of required cultural integration and the legitimacy of ethnic group activity were widely canvassed, if not always accepted, within American society. When Americans later came to debate and study the problem of immigrant integration more systematically, such concepts as developed within the ethnic groups had become part of the nation's vocabulary and thus deserve a place in our analysis of those debates today.

But, finally, the ways in which the ethnic core was defined were critical also for German-Americans themselves. By expanding the cultural umbrella of ethnicity to shelter beer gardens alongside Kant and Schiller, theorists could attract the allegiance of a large core of faithful, but at the price of alienating others, and tying group energies to efforts that did not necessarily improve the group image. Moreover, in choosing to fight their battle on grounds of expediency—defending German ethnicity on the grounds of what it could do for the nation—they were left with no fall-back position when the nation later rejected the gifts they had to bring. The ultimate irony, however, may be that the melting pot theorists were only too accurate: a major reason why Germans in the long run were unable to retain succeeding generations within the definitions of the ethnicity they "invented" was because America proved ready to accept so much of what that ethnicity was designed to keep alive. For at the 1983 Tricentennial celebration, "Uncle Sam's healthiest stepson" can no longer take central place at the immigrant banquet table; he is one of the hosts.

Notes

I gratefully acknowledge the support of the Woodrow Wilson International Center for Scholars and the Stiftung Volkswagenwerk for the research on which this essay is based.

1. *Puck* 8 (October 3, 1883): 40–41. All translations are my own.

2. Heinz Kloss, *Um die Einigung des Deutschamerikanertums: Die Geschichte einer unvollendeten Volksgruppe* (Berlin: Volk und Reich Verlag, 1937).

3. Fredrik Barth, "Introduction," in Fredrik Barth, ed., *Ethnic Groups and Boundaries: The Social Organization of Cultural Difference* (Boston: Little, Brown, 1969), 9–38; John Higham, *Send These to Me: Jews and Other Immigrants in Urban America* (New York: Atheneum, 1975), 8–13; Arthur Mann, "The City as a Melting Pot," in Arthur Mann, Neil Harris, and Sam Bass Warner, Jr., *History and the Role of the City in American Life* (Indianapolis: Indiana Historical Society, 1972), 18–19.

4. Milton M. Gordon, *Assimilation in American Life* (New York: Oxford University Press, 1964); Philip Gleason, "American Identity and Americanization," in Stephan Thernstrom et al., eds., *Harvard Encyclopedia of American Ethnic Groups* (Cambridge, Mass.: Belknap Press of Harvard University Press, 1980), 31–58; John Higham, "Integrating America," *Journal of American Ethnic History* 1 (1981):7–22; Higham, *Strangers in the Land* (New York: Atheneum, 1973); Higham, *Send These to Me*, 196–230; Arthur Mann, *The One and the Many* (Chicago: University of Chicago Press, 1979).

5. E. V. Smalley, "The German Element in the United States," *Lippincott's Magazine*, n.s., 5 (1883):356, 362; Christian Essellen, "Das Deutsche Leben in America," *Atlantis* 6 (1857): 1. See also Johann Eggers, "Hat das deutsche Element in den Vereinigten Staaten von Nordamerika eine Zukunft?" *Atlantis* 5 (1856):33. For the initial emergence of these debates, see Franz Löher, *Geschichte und Zustände der Deutschen in America* (Cincinnati: Verlag von Eggers und Wulkop, 1847), 286–89.

6. "Ueber deutsche Nationalität in den Vereinigten Staaten," *Fliegende Blaetter* 1 (February 20, 1847):25.

7. Theodor Griesinger, *Land und Leute in Amerika: Skizzen aus dem amerikanischen Leben*, 2 vols. (Stuttgart: Kröner, 1863), 1:293, 285; Dr. A. Kirsten, *Skizzen aus den Vereinigten Staaten von Nord-amerika* (Leipzig: F. A. Brockhaus, 1851), 284, 282, 286; Ernst Ludwig Brauns, *Amerika and die moderne Völkerwanderung* (Potsdam: Vogler, 1833), 323–34; Löher, *Geschichte und Zustände*, i.

8. These arguments, as advanced by organs such as the *Anzeiger des Westens* and the *New Yorker Staatszeitung*, are summarized in Löher, *Geschichte und Zuständ*, 287, 243.

9. Julius Fröbel, *Aus Amerika* (Leipzig: J. J. Weber, 1857), 510–16.

10. Ibid., 524–30, quotation, 530.

11. See, for example, "B," "Die Auswanderer in Amerika," *Atlantische Studien* 3 (1853): 16–31.

12. *Atlantis* 7 (1857): 55–58; 7 (1857): 6; 2 (1855): 108–11; 7 (1857): 398–400; 4 (1856): 496–73; H. L., "Yankeethum und Deutschthum," *Meyers Monats-Hefte* 3 (1854): 456–59; Klauprecht in "Ueber deutsche Nationalität in den Vereinigten Staaten," *Fliegende Blaetter* 1 (February 20, 1847): 26; Theodore Poesche and Charles Goepp, *The New Rome; or, The United States of the World* (New York: G. P. Putnam and Co., 1853), 71.

13. Otto K., "Der Nativismus," *Atlantische Studien* 3 (1853): 81–90; Gustave Struve, *Diesseits und Jenseits des Oceans* (Coburg: F. Streit, 1864), 2: 20; *Fliegende Blaetter* 1 (February 20, 1847): 26.

14. Kirsten, *Skizzen aus den Vereinigten Staaten*, 282, 296–300; Samuel Maclea, in *Deutsch-Amerikanische Didaskalia* 1 (1848): 3–6.

15. For a contemporary summary of these various shades of ethnic separatism, see William Weber, "Die Zeitungen in den Vereinigten Staaten," *Das Westland* 1 (1837): 200–205. For extended discussion of such schemes, see John A. Hawgood, *The Tragedy of German-America* (New York: G. P. Putnam's Sons, 1940), 93–224; Kloss, *Um die Einigung*, 103–218 passim.

16. *Meyers Monats-Hefte* 5 (1855): 217; *Atlantische Studien* 3 (1853): 16–34; Johann Eggers in *Atlantis* 5 (1856): 33–44; Griesinger, *Land und Leute in Amerika*, 309.

17. *Illustrierte Welt* 2 (December 31, 1859): 196.

18. *Atlantis* 8 (1857): 6; Gleason, "American Identity," 38.

19. "True Americanism," *The Speeches of Carl Schurz*, collected and revised by the author (Philadelphia: J. B. Lippincott and Co., 1865), 57.

20. Richard Conant Harper, *The Course of the Melting Pot Idea to 1910* (New York: Arno Press, 1980); Gleason, "American Identity," 32–39.

21. "H. L.," "Yankeethum und Deutschthum," *Meyers Monats-Hefte* 3 (1854): 456; Essellen, in *Atlantis* 8 (1858): 409.

22. Hermann Lindeman, "Die europäisch-amerikanischen Ideen in der deutschen Einwanderung," *Meyer's Monats-Hefte* 5 (1855): 383–89; Friedrich Münch, "Ist die Erhaltung des deutschen Elementes innerhalb der Vereinigten Staaten für die Fortentwickelung derselben erförderlich oder nicht?" *Gesammelte Schriften* (St. Louis: C. Witter, 1902), 384–91, quotation 390.

23. Dr. Philip Schaff, *America: A Sketch of the Political, Social, and Religious Character of the United States of North America* (New York: Scribner, 1855), 58.

24. Dr. J. G. Eberhard, "Festrede," *Deutsch-Amerikanische Monatshefte* 2 (1865): 462; see also Friedrich Lexow, "Die Deutschen in Amerika," ibid. 3 (1866): 149–54, 255–61; Friedrich Kapp, "Rede," ibid. 2 (1865): 182–88; Adolf Douai, *Land und Leute in der Union* (Berlin: O. Janke, 1864), 53–57, 255; "Rede des Herrn Johann Bernhard Stello" (1867), *Deutsch-Amerikanisches Magazin* 1 (1886): 113–18. "H" in *Steiger's Literarisches Magazin* 1 (1869): 30–32, took the German-American press to task for exaggerating German achievements and denigrating those of Americans. For expressions of German-American belief in their position and the respect that they had gained from

Americans, see Benno Haberland, *Das deutsche Element in den Vereinigten Staaten von Nord-Amerika* (Leipzig: H. Matthes, 1866), 53–55, 84–87; Daniel Hertle, *Die Deutschen in Nordamerika und der Freiheitskampf in Missouri* (Chicago: Druck der 'Illinois Staatszeitung', 1865), 24–35, 112; *Steiger's Literarisches Magazin* 1 (1869): 33.

25. Friedrich Kapp, *Geschichte der Deutschen im Staate New York*, 3d ed. (New York: E. Steiger, 1869), 369–70.

26. Cf. ibid., i–xiii; "Reisebriefe," *Steiger's Literarischer Monatsbericht* 1 (1869): 26–27.

27. "Die Assimilation der Deutschen," *Der Deutsche Pionier* 15 (1883): 329–31.

28. Friedrich Münch, "Die künftige deutsche Auswanderung nach Nordamerika," *Der Deutsche Pionier* 3 (1871): 203–8; "Frau Clara Neymann über den Beruf der Deutschen in Amerika," *Deutscher Volksfreund* 3 (February 15, 1873): 55–56; "Zunehmende Macht der Deutschen," *Der Deutsche Pionier* 6 (1874): 265–67; "Amerikanisirung," *Der Deutsche Pionier* 13 (1881): 202–3.

29. Kapp, *Geschichte*, i–xiii; see also Dr. Edmund Spiess, "Ueber die Zukunft und Aufgabe der Deutschen in Amerika," *Deutscher Volksfreund* 4 (May 14, 1874): 158–59; (May 21, 1874): 166–67; (May 28, 1874): 174–75; (June 4, 1874): 182–83; (June 11, 1874): 190–91; (June 18, 1874): 198–99; (June 25, 1874): 207; (July 2, 1874): 214–15; quotation (May 28, 1874): 174; *Steiger's Literarisches Magazin* 1 (1869): 30–32; Dr. Adolf Douai, "Die Zukunft der deutschen Sprache im Auslande," *Der Deutsche Pionier* 12 (1880): 256–62; "Eine deutschamerikanische Schriftstellerin über Deutsch-Amerika," *Der Deutsche Pionier* 14 (1882): 208–11.

30. Higham, *Send These to Me*, 240–43.

31. "Aufruf an die Deutschen in America," Executive Committee of the German-American Pionier-Jubiläum zu Philadelphia, *Der Deutsche Pionier* 15 (1883): 212–13.

32. Kathleen Neils Conzen, "Germans," in Thernstrom et al., eds., *Harvard Encyclopedia of American Ethnic Groups*, 402–25.

33. *Atlantis* 9 (1858): 403.

34. Cf. Stephen Steinberg, *The Ethnic Myth: Race, Ethnicity, and Class in America* (Boston: Beacon Press, 1981); John Higham, "Current Trends in the Study of Ethnicity in the United States," *Journal of American Ethnic History* 2 (1982): 5–15.

10.
Ethnic Leadership and the German-Americans

WILLI PAUL ADAMS

THE ROLE OF ETHNIC LEADERS is, of course, only one element in the much larger social process we call the rise, maintenance, and disintegration of ethnic communities. But it is a crucial element. Recent emphasis on history "from the bottom up" and on mass political behavior as reconstructed with the help of the computer notwithstanding, leadership functions played a decisive role in the formation and disintegration of ethnic groups. In German-American ethnic communities, the individuals with the capacity and time for dealing with more than their own daily tasks took the lead by speaking out and influencing their fellow immigrants' opinions about their situation. Through the local singing society's and Turnverein's organizing committees, the priest saying more than mass, the editor reflecting on nativism or other hardships of immigrant life, the lawyer and merchant running for election to the school board, the city council, the state legislature, or a judgeship many men (and few women) gave public expression and direction to the abstraction called a community's development. Discontent alone, as Robin Williams put it in the context of analyzing relative deprivation, does not produce collective action. "Unorganized and dispersed masses of discontented people are not in a position to generate effective political pressure. Only through communication and the subsequent emergence of leadership, authority, and division of functions—that is, organization—can discontent be mobilized and focused into collective dissent, protest, and structured opposition."[1] The same holds true for collective action in support of the goals of ethnic groups. And yet, immigration historians have only lately discovered the topic.

Pre-1920 filiopietistic historiography was by no means unaware of the role of individuals. On the contrary, out of a need to people the group's past with heroes and role models, to create a usable past, German-American chroniclers—like those of any other immigrant group—loved to publish thumbnail sketches of exemplary business-men, lawyers, and engineers under such headings as "Deutsche im öffentlichen Leben, im Handel und Wandel" and "Deutsche Männer, die sich verdient gemacht haben." They wanted to measure the suc-cess and demonstrate the contribution of their own ethnic group to American culture so as to bolster their group's sense of achievement and pride.[2] Albert Faust and his predecessors wasted no time in-vestigating the interaction between the exemplary individual and the ethnic group, the group's meaning for the successful, how opinion leadership within the group worked, and so on.[3] Nor did the chroni-clers of the American nation as a whole—even when they began to worry about the nation's capacity to absorb the swelling tide of people from alien cultures—stop to think about possible internal structures of what they perceived as one threatening mass; they neglected the role of spokesmen and potential mediators between (and among) immi-grant groups and Anglo-American society.

It was not historians but sociologists, social workers, and social psychologists who first discussed the role of leaders in and of ethnic groups. Their concern for solving social problems of minority groups led them to see the special contribution which particularly active members of these groups could make to social reform. In the early phase of this discussion attention often focused on leadership among urban blacks. The more or less explicit message was that black leaders should do for their group what other minority group leaders had done for theirs. An early statement of the issue was made at the annual meeting of the American Sociological Society at Minneapolis in 1913. Robert A. Woods, director of South End House in Boston, declared in a discussion of how the lot of the black population could be bettered:

The lesson of the progress of the different racial groups in the American popu-lation is that they gain strength first by a very strong offensive and defensive inner loyalty. The most capable members of each group develop the power of leadership in intimate relation with this clannish coherence. In due time a suf-ficient power of leadership, political, economic, and even intellectual, is gained, so that the group leaders begin to qualify as leaders of the general community. By that time the group so represented begins to have general social power and general social respect.[4]

The underlying assumptions were clear: American society is a conglomeration of competing interest groups, and the more cohesive, organized, and well led a group is, the more gains it will make. The upward mobility of the group and the growth in experience of its leaders will then be rewarded by the rest of society, "the general community," and former ethnic leaders will become leaders without the restrictive adjective. Because Woods was concerned with the future of American blacks and did not anticipate their disappearance by assimilation, he felt no need to think about what might happen to ethnic leaders when their group not only enjoyed "general social power" and "general social respect" but began to disintegrate because of its very success.

This question became the focus of concern a generation later, when in 1941 social psychologist Kurt Lewin in his essay on self-hatred among Jews discussed the fear of American Jews that their group might disintegrate, or at least be severely weakened, because more and more of its members were pulled away from the confined life of orthodox practitioners of Judaism. It was in this context that Lewin pointed out a dilemma that exists not only for Jewish-American leaders. Among minority groups, as in society at large, persons who have distinguished themselves through professional or economic achievement are often called upon to fill leadership positions. Frequently, however, these individuals are culturally marginal to the group because they are not eager to cultivate the values and behavior that define the group's identity. They become leaders "from the periphery." This trend is strongly reinforced because the majority group tends to prefer to deal with them instead of others who are closer to the cultural core of their ethnic group and because they seek these leadership roles as part of their striving for acceptance by the majority. In this context Lewin also employed the helpful metaphor of concentric circles, with the group's defining cultural traits forming the core and increasingly peripheral zones of "belonging" surrounding it.[5]

The authoritative summary of the state of leadership studies in the *International Encyclopedia of the Social Sciences* of 1968 focused on the dimensions of power, authority, personality, organization, and participation; it ignored the special questions of leadership in and of ethnic groups. But discussion of the active role of the followers and the multiplicity of interactions and interdependencies of leaders and followers contains a number of observations that the historian of migration and ethnicity will find fruitful to apply and test. Especially to the point is the statement: "Leadership defines, initiates, and main-

Frederick Augustus Conrad Muhlenberg (1750–1801) as Speaker of the House of Representatives of the United States Congress in 1790. Portrait by Joseph Wright (1756–1793). As the first elected Speaker of the House, Muhlenberg was one of the earliest Pennsylvania Germans to gain national prominence in politics. The Muhlenberg family provided leaders in many areas, both before and after the founding of the United States. (National Portrait Gallery, Smithsonian Institution, Washington, D.C.)

tains social structure. The social system is, so to speak, 'programmed' through leadership."

It was left to immigration historians to focus attention on ethnic leadership. They did so in the second half of the 1970s under the leadership of John Higham, whose Johns Hopkins Symposium in Comparative History in 1976 became the starting point of the current discussion. The volume of essays on a dozen ethnic groups commissioned by Higham, which included Frederick C. Luebke's essay on German-Americans in the twentieth century, amply documented the active role of leaders, not only in articulating and organizing existing interests but also in projecting a sense of shared values and interests and thereby defining and strengthening the group's identity. Higham summed up his understanding of the process in a metaphor (more suitable than that of the melting pot to our stage of technological development): An ethnic group is like a magnetic field that fades at the periphery; and leaders provide its core.[6] Higham's efforts apparently convinced the editors of the *Harvard Encyclopedia of American Ethnic Groups* (1980) to include an extensive entry on leadership, written by Higham, parallel to articles on such established topics as Americanization, language maintenance, and German-Americans.[7] The context in which ethnic leadership thus became a topic was no longer the engagement of the social worker or that of the sociologist of minority groups. The new context was a resurgence—at least in print—of ethnic awareness among Americans of eastern and southern European background, the wave of a "new ethnicity" of the 1960s and 1970s.

To prevent a misunderstanding I encountered in Germany, where the terms *Führer* and *Führertum* do not seem to lend themselves to cool, analytical usage, the intention here is not to contribute to the study of the "power elites," or of "men who make history," or of more or less "dominant classes." I consider leadership a functional need in the preparation of action by any group, by no means limited to an elite, great men, or classes, however defined. I see—following Robert C. Tucker—three tasks to be taken on by political leadership in particular. First, "leaders are expected to define the situation authoritatively for the group." For an ethnic group, this is a particularly challenging task. Second, "they must prescribe a course of a group action, or action on the group's behalf, that will meet the situation as defined." Third, leaders are expected to mobilize support for the implementation of the suggested policy.[8]

As for the special circumstances of ethnic leadership, I plead for a strict construction of the term "ethnic." Since we can usefully distinguish four elements or sets of variables that make up the process of leadership—the leader(s), the followers, the situation in which they interact, and the tasks the leader(s) and followers confront[9]—we could say that ethnic leadership occurs when the leader(s) and the followers, and especially when the task they confront, are all characterized by a genuinely ethnic dimension. What is a genuinely ethnic dimension? Instead of construing a contorted or circular abstract definition, let me simply say that in the American context it is useful to label as "ethnic," and in my particular case as "German-American," those qualities of a person, a group, or a public issue that clearly derive from and would not exist without the shared experience or memory of migration. Electing a competent lawyer to the state legislature is not an assertion of ethnicity per se, even if he was born in Germany. But the deal struck between Irish and German politicians which led to that lawyer's candidacy for the Democratic party in a Chicago district in the 1870s was ethnic politics and a result of and means of German-American ethnic leadership.

Our understanding of ethnic leadership can be further developed by bringing together theory and a wide variety of case studies from many ethnic groups, applying hypotheses to history, and then perhaps going back to improve the theory. I will comment on nine elements of ethnic leadership, building upon ideas proposed by Higham and others by applying them to the German-American case.[10]

1. A clear distinction between ethnic leaders and "culture-heroes" is as appropriate in the German-American case as for most other groups. Culture-heroes are of importance to their group because they have gained recognition outside of it. They may never have aspired to ethnic leadership and may never have wanted to be perceived as members of their ethnic group. But with or without their approval, they are claimed by the group and held up to society at large as proof of its collective ability, its contribution to the building of America, and so forth. To members of the group they are held up as role models to inspire group pride and individual exertion. Baron von Steuben, John Jacob Astor, John Roebling, and Carl Schurz are prime examples of German-American culture-heroes; Schurz represents the rare case of a divisive political leader who in his later years acquired the functions of a consensus-supporting culture-hero. The German-language press throughout the nineteenth century heavily contributed to fixing culture-heroes in the group's collective memory. Monument-building served the same purpose. No chapter in Congressman Richard Bartholdt's memoirs conveys a deeper sense of satisfaction than his account of how in 1910 he got the Steuben statue erected next to that of Lafayette and Rochambeau in Lafayette Park across from the White House.[11] The category of the ethnic culture-hero has limits. Once an individual has achieved universal recognition in a field essentially indifferent to ethnic dimensions, attempts by an ethnic group to hitch its wagon to the star no longer seem convincing. I would therefore not number Albert Einstein among any ethnic group's culture-heroes.

2. How important were effective central leadership and professionalized and institutionalized ethnic leadership? In the German-American case, there seems to be an inverse relationship between the existence of live, grass-roots ethnicity and nationwide organization with a professionalized and institutionalized leadership at the top. It is very difficult to establish what the activities of the Nationalbund meant for most of the German-born Americans and their children and grandchildren or how much activity on the national level was an artificial media event, especially in the decade leading up to World War I. H. L. Mencken was referring to this situation in his devastating assessment of 1928: "The German Americans as a group are in the process of rapid disintegration. The disintegration began long before the

War. The War even interrupted it for a while. . . . German culture in America became a toy for third-rate 'leaders,' most of whom had something to sell; except for them it was dead. . . . The Melting Pot has devoured [the German-Americans] as it has no other group, not even the Irish."[12] In the postwar decade the Steuben Society theoretically could have become the center for cool but effective German-American interest-group politics. It did not. Leadership from other areas was probably more important in the German-American case.

3. The central place of churches and religious convictions in the lives of many immigrants is well known, but we know too little about the long-range integrating or Americanizing effect the various attitudes and policies of German-American Protestant, Catholic, Jewish, and Freethinking religious leaders had on the ethnic group as a whole. The role of the rabbi as mediator or "ethnic broker" between Jews and mainstream Anglo-America and other ethnic groups has been demonstrated.[13] Group cohesion and resistance to Americanization strongly motivated Mennonite leadership.[14] The German Catholics, who made up about one-third of the German immigrants, were led by the episcopate—or were all propelled together—along the road from the German-speaking "national" parish to the English-speaking and often ethnically mixed congregation without a lasting schism such as that of the Polish National church; yet how did Pope Leo XIII's condemnation in 1899 of "Americanism" in church government affect the relationship between the hierarchy and lay leaders in America?[15] Even the conservative Lutheran Missouri Synod, to mention only the most ethnically persistent of the great Protestant churches, was forced by 1920 to "Americanize in order to survive."[16] The way spiritual leaders became followers in this secular process needs further clarification. Only the central question all of them faced is clear: "As a German abroad, do I not have to give up and overcome the separation of our people into denominations; but on the other hand, as a Protestant Christian, do I not have to be cosmopolitan?"[17]

4. The same is true for the much discussed German-American *Vereinswesen*. Here we need to reexamine the issue of the extent of the "cultural baggage" of the immigrants. As Kathleen Conzen showed in the case of early Milwaukee, it is hard to believe that the rich associational life of German-Americans sprang up only in response to the immigrant situation.[18] A far greater part of the club life of German-Americans than is often assumed probably crossed the Atlantic fully developed. This fact, however, need not make the immigrant associations any less important instruments and forms of expression of

ethnic leadership in the various spheres of cultural, social, and political life.

5. An ethnic press or foreign-language press as an instrument of ethnic leadership was as highly developed by the German-Americans as by any other group. Publishers, editors, and other journalists did more than provide a forum for all comers; they pursued editorial policies with the intention of influencing public opinion and action in certain directions. A recent study of several German-language Chicago newspapers by Annelie Edelmann of the Free University of Berlin confirmed the very active role of editors of various political persuasions. They took advantage, for instance, of the opportunities provided by the crises in the homeland—from the Franco-Prussian War to the Samoa crisis—to mobilize German-Americans for their own purposes, to awaken and increase the sense of identification with the ethnic group, to stimulate support for certain *bürgerliche*, socialist, or labor union demands, and for other purposes.

6. Another highly developed form of ethnic leadership among German-Americans was exercised by members of the group who had become influential in nonethnic institutions, especially holders of public offices on the local and regional levels but also on the national level. The filiopietistic chroniclers loved to enumerate officeholders to prove the rising importance of German-Americans in public life. As with culture-heroes, however, individuals were often claimed by the group although they did not want to be identified with it and did not use their public office to further the particular goals of their ethnic group. When, for instance, we look more closely at the forty-three German-born members of the U.S. House of Representatives who served before 1930 and apply a strict definition of ethnic leadership, only seven can be said to have been German-American ethnic political leaders. I examined the following four factors to measure the degree of ethnicity of their leadership: constituency (number of German-born in electoral district and other information about the strength of the German-American community); political career and involvement in German-American issues; intellectual life (concern with German and German-American historical or current questions); and family life (use of German, socializing with German-Americans, and the like). I found that it was possible, as Gustav Finkelnburg of St. Louis did in the 1870s, to be elected by a constituency with a high percentage of Germans without becoming a German-American ethnic leader. The extreme case of a German-born and Jewish United States senator who disavowed any connection with German-Americans was Joseph Simon

of Oregon (1897–1903). He wanted his official biography to begin with the sentence: "Born in 1851, has resided in the city of Portland, Oregon, since 1857."[19] The other extreme, perhaps the most successful mediator between his ethnic group and American politics on the national level, was Carl Schurz. His most recent biographer characterized his role as that of a "guide" across the bridge from Germany to America, who showed his fellow German-Americans "how to become good Americans without abandoning their German heritage, how to master the English tongue without giving up their *Muttersprache*." Schurz's philosophy in this respect was "a combination of the idea of the melting pot with that of the retention of ethnicity."[20]

7. The German-Americans shared two of the special services that are expected to be provided by ethnic leaders of all groups: material advancement and status advancement of the group. But because of the size, diversity, and geographic scattering of the Germans, this attribute could never apply to the group as a whole but only to the locally relevant part of it. Doing something for the group in the German-American case often came to be inseparable from doing something for the community, as can be seen in the numerous schemes for public and private local development in nineteenth-century state politics. Editors, state legislators, congressmen, and senators were deeply involved in allocating state and federal resources for dredging rivers and harbors, building bridges, post offices, courthouses, and army installations, and routing railroads. The ethnic politician who joined the process and wanted to be an effective servant of his constituency could not limit himself to acting as ambassador of his ethnic group. He had to participate fully in the all-American political game. By achieving the ultimate, bringing a world's fair to his hometown, as St. Louis Congressman Richard Bartholdt did in 1904, a leader scored many points for his group by doing something for the entire community. The pursuit of status clearly was a preoccupation of leading German-Americans. The exaltation of German culture, so irritating to Yankees and others who were trying to establish an American national cultural identity, should be seen in the context of competitive status-seeking.

8. Defense of lifestyle is another of the major tasks of ethnic leaders. The German-American case demonstrates that questions of lifestyle, such as freedom to do the same activities on a Sunday that one may do on a weekday and to drink what one likes best where one likes to drink it, assumed great importance for this ethnic group's self-definition and, consequently, for its politics.

9. Defense of the homeland as a task for ethnic leaders took on

a tragic dimension in the German-American case. With the exception of Spanish-Americans, only the Japanese, German-Americans, and Austrian-Americans had to cope with the temptations and divided loyalties, the hysteria, hatred, and suppression that were aroused by war between the new and the old homelands.[21] The increasing tensions between the rising world power and the European Continental empire, afflicted with leaders who had a dangerously exaggerated sense of their country's role in the world, demanded responsible leadership of the highest quality on the part of the German-Americans. Absence of that leadership cannot be fully explained by personal shortcomings. The decreasing quality of leadership on the national level in the decades preceding American entry into World War I was one of the consequences of a disintegration of the German-Americans as an ethnic group. Representation of German-American interests on the national level had been allowed to become, as Mencken put it, "a toy for third-rate 'leaders.'" These men failed to foresee the consequences for German-Americans of the unleashed forces of American nationalism and contributed to the destruction of what they had hoped to preserve.

On the national level institutionalized German-American leaders failed to face the homeland issue and the assimilation dilemma realistically. On the local, community level, leadership among German-Americans seems to have succeeded much better in providing useful services to make immigrant life easier. Most American interest-group politics took place on the community and regional levels, and so did the conflicts over conditions of work, education, language maintenance, religious concerns, and political-cultural issues such as Sunday closing laws. It is in more detailed community studies, therefore, that we will find further insight into the significant role that ethnic leaders played in the rise, maintenance, and disintegration of German-America.

Notes

1. Robin M. Williams, Jr., "Relative Deprivation," in Lewis A. Coser, ed., *The Idea of Social Structure: Papers in Honor of Robert K. Merton* (New York: Harcourt Brace Jovanovich, 1975), 355–78, quotation, 372.

2. Representative examples are Herman Julius Ruetenik, *Berühmte deutsche Vorkämpfer für Fortschritt, Freiheit und Friede in Nord-Amerika* (Cleveland, Ohio: Forest City Bookbinding Co., 1888), and Max Heinrici, ed., *Das Buch der Deutschen in Amerika* (Philadelphia: German-American National Alliance, 1909).

3. Albert Bernhardt Faust, *The German Element in the United States, with Spe-

cial Reference to Its Political, Social, and Educational Influence, 2 vols. (1909; rev. ed. New York: Steuben Society of America, 1927).

4. American Sociological Society, *Papers and Proceedings* 8 (1914):100.

5. Kurt Lewin, *Resolving Social Conflicts: Selected Papers on Group Dynamics* (New York: Harper, 1948), 195–97.

6. John Higham, ed., *Ethnic Leadership in America* (Baltimore: Johns Hopkins University Press, 1978), 2.

7. Higham, "Leadership," in Stephan Thernstrom et al., eds., *Harvard Encyclopedia of American Ethnic Groups* (Cambridge, Mass.: Belknap Press of Harvard University Press, 1980), 642–47.

8. Robert C. Tucker, *Politics as Leadership* (Columbia: University of Missouri Press, 1981), 18–19 and chap. 2.

9. Cecil A. Gibb, "Leadership," *International Encyclopedia of the Social Sciences* (1968), 9:91.

10. E.g. Victor Greene, "'Becoming American': The Role of Ethnic Leaders—Swedes, Poles, Italians, and Jews," in Melvin G. Holli and Peter d'A. Jones, eds., *The Ethnic Frontier: Essays in the History of Group Survival in Chicago and the Midwest* (Grand Rapids, Mich.: Erdmans, 1977), 143–75.

11. Richard Bartholdt, *From Steerage to Congress: Reminiscences and Reflections* (Philadelphia: Dorrance, 1930), chap. 14.

12. H. L. Mencken, "Die Deutschamerikaner," *Die neue Rundschau* 39 (1928): 493; my translation.

13. Mark K. Bauman and Arnold Shankman, "The Rabbi as Ethnic Broker: The Case of David Marx," *Journal of American Ethnic History* 2 (1983):51–68; and Mark K. Bauman, "Role and History: The Illustration of Ethnic Brokerage in the Atlanta Jewish Community in an Era of Transition and Conflict," *American Jewish History* 73 (1983):71–95.

14. Beulah Hostetler, "Franconia Mennonite Conference and American Protestant Movements, 1840–1940" (Ph.D. dissertation, University of Pennsylvania, 1977).

15. Kathleen Neils Conzen, "Germans," in Thernstrom et al., eds., *Harvard Encyclopedia of American Ethnic Groups,* 418.

16. Ibid., 419. See Reinhard R. Doerries, "Church and Faith on the Great Plains Frontier: Acculturation Problems of German-Americans," *Amerikastudien/American Studies* 24 (1979): 275–87.

17. E. W. Bussmann, "Schranken der nationalen und religiösen Aufgaben. Das Grundproblem der Diasporaarbeit," *Der Deutsche Aussiedler: Monatliche Mitteilungen über die Lage des evangelischen Deutschtums im Auslande* 46 (February 1980):10; my translation.

18. Kathleen Neils Conzen, *Immigrant Milwaukee, 1836–1860: Accommodation and Community in a Frontier City* (Cambridge, Mass.: Harvard University Press, 1976), 204–5. See Hartmut Bickelmann, "Zwischen Einwanderungshilfe und Einwanderungsförderung: 'Deutsche Gesellschaften' und ihre Funktion im deutsch-amerikanischen Wanderungsprozess," in a forthcoming and as yet untitled anthology on German-American migration edited by Günter Moltmann (Wiesbaden: Steiner Verlag). For *Vereine* in rural southwestern Germany see Dieter Jauch, "Die Wandlung des Vereinslebens in ländlichen Gemeinden Südwestdeutschlands," *Zeitschrift für Agrargeschichte und Agrarsoziologie* 28 (1980):48–77.

19. U.S. Congress, Office of the Joint Committee on Printing, file "Deceased Members."

20. Hans L. Trefousse, *Carl Schurz: A Biography* (Knoxville: University of Tennessee Press, 1982), vii–viii.

21. Frederick C. Luebke, *Bonds of Loyalty: German-Americans and World War I* (De Kalb, Ill.: Northern Illinois University Press, 1974), and Phyllis Keller, *States of Belonging: German-American Intellectuals and the First World War* (Cambridge, Mass.: Harvard University Press, 1979).

11.

The German-American
Immigrants and the Newly
Founded Reich

HANS L. TREFOUSSE

IT HAS OFTEN BEEN POINTED OUT that the restoration of German unity in 1871 had an electrifying effect on the German-American population. Almost without exception, the immigrants rejoiced at Germany's victories, the overthrow of Louis Napoleon, and the establishment of a united German Empire. This was as true of the liberal Forty-eighters as of their more conservative predecessors. Priests, ministers, and rabbis offered thanks to God, and a general feeling of euphoria and pride enveloped the German-speaking population of the United States.[1] In fact, as Heinrich Börnstein pointed out, Germans abroad were much more inspired with national feeling than those within the Reich, a tendency they richly proved during the war.[2] Yet whether they, or at least a prominent group of liberals among them, were willing to forget their republican principles and overlook the shortcomings of Bismarck's Germany is a different question.

It is not surprising that almost all German-Americans hailed with joy the victories of their compatriots in Europe. German unity had been an age-old dream. The Romantic movement had given a nationalistic interpretation to the disappearance in 1806 of the Holy Roman Empire, and students, intellectuals, and countless patriots in the old country had long been fighting for the reestablishment of a strong and united fatherland. National unity had been one of the goals of the democratic, liberal revolutionaries of 1848. Their failure had forced many of them to flee to the United States, where they often remained loyal to the ideals of their youth. Although German-Americans had severely condemned the actions of both Prussia and Austria during the

1864 war against Denmark, they had made no secret of their endorsement of an all-German cause.[3] Two years later, though deploring the outbreak of the "fratricidal" war between Prussia and Austria, after Prussia's quick victory they applauded the renewed movement toward unity implicit in the creation of the North German Confederation under Prussian leadership.[4] After the convocation of a customs parliament had increased hopes for unification, even Otto von Bismarck, whose autocratic ways German-Americans had often criticized, appeared less liable to censure. Describing the Prussian prime minister in an article in the *North American Review* in 1869, Henry Villard wrote: "With all his failings, he has been of great service to his countrymen, who will ever remember him as the trenchant instrument of Providence which hewed a way to national unity, and made their fatherland more respected abroad than it had been since the reign of Charles V."[5] When the first news of the outbreak of war with France reached America, German-American enthusiasm for the German cause and sympathy with the German armies knew no bounds.

For Americans of German heritage, Napoleon III was a natural antagonist. They remembered the unprincipled adventurer who had overthrown the French Republic. They recalled the great men of letters who had been forced to flee because of him. And had he not taken advantage of America's troubles during the Civil War to violate the Monroe Doctrine by attempting to set up a puppet monarchy in Mexico? These events were not forgotten, to say nothing of more recent reports of the emperor's greed for the acquisition of the left bank of the Rhine. "The time has come. The German has awakened and is restoring his ancient empire, eternally hated by France," exulted the German Soldiers' Aid Society in its appeal in the *Milwaukee Seebote*.[6]

The conservative Catholic newspaper was expressing the feelings of most German-Americans. "When you thank God that you have lived to see this rising or resuscitation of Germany, you can imagine what must be my feelings," Francis Lieber wrote to the political scientist Johann Kaspar Bluntschli in August 1870. "We will sing a still louder Te Deum when the German nation places the imperial crown on William's head. It is the first step which should be taken after all the bloodshed is at an end. William I, Emperor of the Germans. It does not sound bad."[7] The war was an example of the struggle between the German and the Latin races, German-Americans read in their newspapers. All Latin races had long been in decline, and now France would see the logic of history. The German-American press assured the public that all the blessings of the Germans in America accompanied the

German armies.[8] The enthusiasm of America's Germans for the cause of their old fatherland "against the usurper not only of France but of Europe" was said to be as general as it was fundamental,[9] and even though the immigrant press, quoting from the *Nation*, conceded that Prussia had "a strong feudal artery" in its institutions, the *Milwaukee Seebote* believed that these were rapidly being superseded.[10] German-Americans held mammoth meetings in the principal cities of the country; they raised money for the succor of the German wounded, and they greatly rejoiced when the French emperor surrendered at Sedan. They printed extras, distributed patriotic calendars showing Germania keeping watch on top of the Vosges, and vigorously defended the fatherland against a rising tide of sympathy for the newly proclaimed French Republic.[11]

Even the projected annexation of Alsace and Lorraine was hailed by the German-American press. Asserting that both areas were ancient German provinces, German-language newspapers reminded their readers that the majority of the population spoke German, and if the inhabitants were no longer German in sentiment, they would soon be brought back to their ancestral allegiance.[12] As for a proposed plebiscite, Francis Lieber considered it completely out of the question. No plebiscites had been held when the United States annexed territory—Louisiana, Florida, Texas, California, and New Mexico had all become American without popular referendums. In fact, he insisted, not only Alsace and Lorraine but Luxembourg as well was German and ought to be annexed to the Reich, an opinion others shared.[13]

This general feeling of triumph and joy lasted throughout the winter while the South German states joined with the North to form the new empire. In the midst of celebrations, German-Americans were looking forward to the end of the war, and when in 1871 it finally came, they again observed the event in proper style. By and large, most of the refugees of 1848 joined in the general rejoicing.[14]

There were a few exceptions. The irrepressible Carl Heinzen, radical of radicals, refused to be reconciled to the Prussian monarchy. Those who toasted the kaiser were not real Americans, he maintained, consistently keeping up his opposition in his newspaper, the *Pionier*. Calling William I "the hoary assassin of heroes," he refused to attend dinners in honor of the empire.[15] The *Neue Zeit*, a left-wing, feminist periodical, took a similar position. War was wrong, it insisted, although it conceded that if war were unavoidable, the magazine would have to be sympathetic to the Germans. In any case, it was the rulers who were to blame for war, such men as "this William of Prussia . . . this pious, senile actor . . . the same Prince of Prussia who in the year 1849 ordered the execution . . . of dozens of the best sons of Germany in Saxony and in Baden." Not even the victory at Sedan was able to convert the publication. Warning that the establishment of a republic in France would cause the sympathy of the world to turn toward Germany's enemy, it predicted that the annexation of Alsace and Lorraine would be a curse for the German people. Moreover, emphasizing that the victory march into Paris was bound to constitute a great obstacle to later efforts at reconciliation, it prophesied that these measures would cause another war, one in which Germany, and not France, would be isolated.[16] A few socialist organizations were also critical, but all these manifestations of dissent were purely marginal. The overwhelming majority of German-Americans remained totally unaffected by them.[17]

In spite of the enthusiasm of most German-Americans, however, the far left was not the only group to express misgivings. Many German newspapers in the United States were in the hands of Forty-eighters or other liberals, who had never trusted the Prussian monarchy. And Bismarck's subversion of the Prussian constitution in 1862 in his struggle for a larger army budget had not endeared him to them. Unity was a desirable goal for Germany, they thought, but so was freedom. "Prussia, that of Herr von Bismarck, is neither capable nor worthy of leading Germany," asserted the New York *Belletristisches Journal* in 1866; other publications also deplored the militaristic state's authoritarian government, and suggested that its king and prime minister, instead of being committed to a united Germany, seemed interested merely in the aggrandizement of Prussia.[18] As the philosopher Arnold Ruge explained in October 1866 to Franz Sigel, it was true that Germany had gained a great advantage because of the collapse of Austrian military might and the establishment of Prussian military hegemony. Nevertheless, "the old police tyranny . . . keeps going. Although an amnesty has been granted, in general the system continues, with all its odiousness and uselessness for the state and the estrangement of other Germans."[19] Mathilde Anneke, the radical feminist, wrote to her husband that much as he thought Prussia was to be Germany's salvation, she could not rid herself of distrust of the militarist state.[20]

Nor was the new constitution of the North German Confederation encouraging. True, Bismarck had introduced universal male suffrage, but there was a general feeling of unease about his refusal to pay a salary to the deputies. Only the wealthy would be able to serve. Maybe there was some hope for the future, but for the time being Prussian militarism seemed to reign supreme, as was indicated by the treatment of such smaller states as Hanover and the Free City of Frankfurt. The Prussians were riding roughshod over the freedom of these states, limited though these liberties might have been. Even if Francis Lieber, despite earlier republican convictions, insisted that Germany needed a monarch, others expressed their hope for a future republic.[21]

When in the summer of 1870 war broke out with France, these feelings were temporarily muted. Gustave Koerner spoke for many of his associates when he sent a telegram from a mass meeting in Belleville, Illinois, to the Prussian envoy in Washington. Emphasizing that most of those present were South Germans and old Forty-eighters, Koerner expressed his satisfaction that they nevertheless fully supported the war.[22] Democratic newspapers even found good words for the institution of monarchy in Germany. They rationalized that different peoples required different forms of government and that monarchy could be combined with freedom.[23] After the new German Empire had been proclaimed, however, the old suspicions returned. Despite its enthusiasm for Germany's regained unity, the *New-Yorker Staats-Zeitung* admitted that "the German structure of unity" was no model fabric. "It is an emergency structure which will have to undergo a number of changes as time goes on," the paper wrote, expressing its hope that with its firm foundation, the new Germany would experience slow reforms instead of revolution.[24]

The New York *Belletristisches Journal* was less sanguine. It, too, hailed Germany's unification but pointed out that it was illegal for the king of Prussia to take upon himself the German crown without the previous sanction of the legislature. "The Emperor's religiosity causes him to see in everything only the hand of God when he must know that in addition the people also contributed materially," it cautioned. "The imperial dignity which he now claims was made possible for him by the blood, the tears, the thousand-fold sacrifice of the people." Criticizing the deputies' traveling to Versailles to congratulate the emperor, it called their action most unfitting because "the usurpation, the circumvention of the people" could not be denied and popular representatives had no reason to be happy about such actions. Whatever the hurry in accepting the North German constitution by the southern states, the resulting structure was a ramshackle fabric, and it could not last forever.[25] Many old liberals agreed. Friedrich Hecker, the fiery Forty-eighter, asked to deliver the principal oration at a German victory celebration in Chicago, accepted but could not refrain from giving vent to his reservations. As he put it, "Should not the man who loves his people, his homeland, the law of nations and freedom worry when he looks at a constitution . . . which contains no bill of rights to protect the people from enslavement? A constitution which is hardly worth more than Bassermann's popular representation at the Federal Council plus an emperor and minus Austria? A parliament without power, in which poor intellectuals have no place because they are not rich enough to pay their own salaries; a right to vote taxes with an iron unchangeable military budget and a constitution with a double life of modern feudalism, imperial vassalage, and state sovereignty!" Continuing, he expressed the hope that Germany, as it secured its independence abroad, might also be able to achieve its internal freedom.[26] Even Francis Lieber, though enthusiastic, was worried about the Prussian spirit of authoritarianism.[27] Fritz Anneke, who in 1870 had differed with his radical wife's strictures on German affairs, as he had earlier during a trip to Germany in 1872, also expressed doubts. "People don't realize here . . . ," he wrote from Dortmund, "that they don't as yet have free speech, a free press, that they are still watched by the police from cradle to grave, led around by leading strings like a child."[28] For those who cherished ideas of freedom it was difficult to be wholly enthusiastic about the new Germany.

Most of the German-Americans who had doubts about the new constitution, of course, cherished hopes of seeing a further development toward free institutions as time went on. Bismarck's introduction of universal manhood suffrage seemed to presage other democratic changes. But as E. J. Passant in his *Short History of Germany* has correctly pointed out, they were grossly deceiving themselves. The chancellor had always been determined to preserve the power of the monarchy and the ruling classes, and his concessions to democracy were merely means to an end. He saw the need to enlist the support of the liberals in the southern states.[29]

These truths continued to perturb disappointed German-Americans. Catholics were jolted by the *Kulturkampf*, and the cautious *Milwaukee Seebote* in 1873 pointed out that conscription contributed greatly to the continuing emigration from the old country, which was draining it of its strength.[30] Liberals were even more critical. Especially in 1878, their sympathies were put to a test when the Reichstag attempted to repress Germany's socialists by passing severe anti-socialist laws. "Victory of Reaction," the *New-Yorker Staats-Zeitung*, which no one could accuse of Marxist sympathies, headlined its report of the measures. "How must the German nation feel," it lamented, "when it sees that now, after unity has been successfully fought for, its elected representatives in the Reichstag have agreed to become the blind instruments of government without taking into account the voice of the people in order to inaugurate once again a full-fledged police state . . . and to open the gates to brutal police despotism?"[31] Freedom was being shackled again, it appeared, and Bismarck's high-handed action in ordering the arrest of two Social-Democratic deputies was roundly condemned by German-Americans. "Bend or Break," appeared to be his motto. And the uproar in the Reichstag about socialist leader Wilhelm Liebknecht's remark, "When Germany will be a republic," seemed especially silly. Socialists were not the only ones harboring such thoughts.[32]

New disappointments followed. Bismarck's reshuffling of the political situation in the Reichstag, his abandonment of his erstwhile National Liberal supporters, and his alliance with protectionists struck German-Americans, liberals as well as those interested in the export of American agricultural products, as another setback for Germany's hoped-for democratic development. A "fateful Christmas present," the *Milwaukee Herold* called Bismarck's turn toward protection,[33] and when in the 1880s a "pig war" started between the two countries concerning the importation of American pork, midwestern German newspapers, warning that not a nation in the world with the least trace of feelings of honor could allow itself to be subjected to such malevolent harm to its trade, called upon the United States to resist Bismarck's outrageous behavior.[34] The chancellor had almost succeeded in making his will law, the *Cincinnati Union* pointed out. He could always find lackeys to do his bidding.[35]

The renewal of anti-Semitism in Germany in the late 1870s and 1880s also made a bad impression in liberal German-American circles. In a letter to the German-American writer Udo Brachvogel, the author Friedrich Martin von Bodenstedt compared the agitation against Germans in Bohemia with the Jew-baiting in Prussia, a scandal which others also condemned in unmistakable terms. News from Germany was depressing, as German-Americans continually found out from their European correspondents.[36]

The disappointment in developments in Germany was dramatized in 1884 by the heart attack and death in New York of the progressive party leader Eduard Lasker, the chancellor's bitter opponent, after a lengthy visit to the United States, during which Lasker carefully sought to refrain from active criticism of the state of affairs in the fatherland. His body was returned to Germany amid general mourning, and Congress passed a resolution of sympathy. Bismarck, however, considering this mark of esteem for his critic an insult and an interference in Germany's internal affairs, refused to accept it.[37] German-Americans dep-recated this exhibition of pettiness. "The great Bismarck showed himself very small concerning the memory of Lasker," commented Gustave Koerner, whose compatriots in Chicago pointed out that "no Richelieu, no Napoleon, no Metternich ever exercised power with more wanton lack of consideration than the great, absolute ego which is now called the Iron Chancellor."[38] The resulting diplomatic contre-temps caused further consternation in the German-American commu-nity, and the prospect of strained relations between the two countries they cared so much about made German-Americans uneasy. Even those who had criticized others for attacking Bismarck because of the "pig war" now warned the chancellor to beware. Germany needed friends.[39] That Aaron Sargent, the American minister in Berlin, whom Bismarck disliked, was denounced by the German press did not help. All that liberal German-Americans could hope for was that the situa-tion would improve in the future.[40]

Hopes for the future, however, suffered a setback when, after a brief reign of only ninety-nine days, Emperor Frederick III died in June 1888. Frederick was widely regarded as a liberal, and after his ascent to the throne following the death of his father he had seemed to hold out expectations of a brighter future.[41] His untimely passing was regarded as a blow to the development of liberal institutions in Ger-many. "Had he lived," one German-American commented, "we could have counted with certainty upon the Germanization of Prussia; his much too early death, on the other hand, raises the curtain upon the Prussianization of Germany."[42] Other editorials in the German-language press pointed out that if Frederick had not died he "would have led Germany toward a peaceful, joyful, happy, and internally free future." What his son, William II, might do was uncertain, but he was known to be much less liberal.[43]

Carl Schurz provides perhaps the best example of the reaction of literate and liberal German-Americans to the events in the fatherland. Without doubt the best-known German-born citizen of the United States, Schurz was often, rightly or wrongly, considered the spokes-man for his compatriots. Indeed, he served as a role model for them, and they had every reason to be proud of him. Reaching the highest political offices open to foreign-born citizens, he hobnobbed with states-men, presidents, and leading intellectuals. Famous when he arrived in America at twenty-three because of his successful rescue of his pro-fessor, Gottfried Kinkel, from Spandau prison, Schurz was a model Forty-eighter. He himself had taken part in the 1849 campaign against the forces of reaction in southwestern Germany. Escaping from the vengeful Prussians by fleeing from the besieged fortress of Rastatt through a sewer toward the Rhine and freedom in France, he had returned to Germany to effect Kinkel's liberation. The deed seemed especially praiseworthy because the professor had been condemned to life imprisonment as a result of his revolutionary activities. Schurz, who eventually settled in Watertown, Wisconsin, dabbled in journalism, real estate, and the law. Deeply committed to the struggle against slavery, he became a spokesman for the Republican party, and with his excellent oratorical gifts, weaned away a number of his compatriots from their habitual Democratic allegiance. Believing that Schurz's support had been so important that he merited a diplomatic plum, Abraham Lincoln appointed him U.S. minister to Spain, a post from which Schurz returned after half a year to join the army. He became a brigadier and later major general and participated in the second battle of Bull Run, as well as the battles of Chancellorsville, Gettysburg, and Chattanooga. Moving to Missouri after the war, he assumed the editorship of the *St. Louis Westliche Post* and in 1869 was elected U.S. senator. He soon broke with President Ulysses S. Grant because of his disapproval of the attempted purchase of the Dominican Republic, his devotion to civil service reform, and his rift with the regular Republicans in his home state. This break led to the founding of the Liberal Republican movement in which Schurz played an important role, though he was severely disappointed by the nomination of Horace Greeley for the presidency. By 1877, however, he was back within the Republican fold and became Rutherford B. Hayes's secretary of the interior.[44]

Like other German-Americans, at first Schurz was delighted with the progress of German unification. He was horrified at the outbreak of the Austro-Prussian War in 1866, which he believed showed the irresponsibility of Germany's reactionary governments. There seemed to be no leadership except Bismarck's, but the Prussian leader was on the wrong side. Nevertheless, Schurz entertained hopes that eventually some statesman might appear in Germany to give it a parliament that the princes would have to accept.[45]

Of course, events did not take that course, and when the Franco-Prussian War started, Schurz fully shared the general enthusiasm. Having overcome his prejudices against Bismarck, who two years earlier had cordially received him in Berlin, he made it clear at a great mass meeting in Baltimore on July 21, 1870, that he had no compunctions about taking sides in a war between kings. The question was one

Carl Schurz als Kabinettszimmermann!

"Carl Schurz Tinkering with the U.S. Cabinet." Cartoon by Thomas Nast. Schurz (1829–1906), a "Forty-Eighter" who emigrated to the U.S. in 1852, served as Secretary of the Interior from 1877 to 1881, the highest-ranking position ever held by a German-American immigrant in the United States. Thomas Nast (1840–1902), who also emigrated from Germany, became the leading American political cartoonist in the second half of the nineteenth century. His cartoons appeared in *Harper's Weekly* and other leading periodicals and changed American political iconography by creating new symbols such as the Democratic Party's donkey and the Republican's elephant. (*Harper's Weekly*) of nationality, he said, and though loyal to the United States, he was German-born with a German heart beating for a German victory. As he put it, "If we despise the old fatherland, our love for the new one can only be a lie and deception."[46]

After this beginning, Schurz became increasingly caught up in patriotic feeling for his old country. The initial German successes delighted him. "Today Germany is the world's leading military power," he wrote to his wife. "Long live the old fatherland!"[47] After more victories, he raised his newspaper's big new black, white, and red German flag from the window of the editorial room and had the entire building decorated with bunting. As he acknowledged to Mrs. Schurz on August 27, "I have to confess that since the beginning of the war I have been living on the other side much more than here. Every free moment finds me with maps in front of me. . . . The German armies seem to be much stronger and the French much weaker than had been thought. . . . It is a great, glorious work." A few days later, he boasted that German banners would soon be seen in front of Paris, and when the French emperor surrendered to the Prussians at Sedan, Schurz's enthusiasm knew no bounds. "The Germans are now the greatest and mightest nation of the Old World, and nobody can dispute this position anymore," he exulted. "This fact forms such a huge contrast with the past that the Germans themselves can hardly grasp it. And yet, no matter how coolly we face the truth today, it is so. And may it remain so! Hallelujah!" He had even been thinking of going back to Europe to take part in the war.[48]

Nevertheless, Schurz retained some political good sense. Regretting that the king of Prussia continued to treat with Napoleon III as a fellow sovereign, the senator admitted that no matter how great the Germans' heroic deeds, political conditions seemed to look better from the outside than from within, and he stressed his pride in his American citizenship. He even welcomed the creation of a republic in hostile France—the word "republic" might do some good in Germany with its current monarchical enthusiasm. Acknowledging that ever since Napoleon III's capture, the war had lost much of its attraction for him, he was hoping for its speedy end.[49]

By the beginning of 1871, Schurz, though still optimistic, had become very cautious. "You ask me what I think," he wrote to his brother-in-law in Hamburg. "You are now the great nation, and now that you have shown that you can beat the world, you will still have to prove that at home too you can't be led around by the nose. The federal constitution is really a sad specimen of patchwork." Believing that national unification would create problems that could not be solved by a military state, he concluded, "Indeed, not everything by far is the way it ought to be, but I have to say that I entertain great hopes for Germany, even for its internal development."[50]

These hopes were often disappointed. To be sure, he still remained optimistic, as he made clear in a lecture in Brooklyn on the results of the Franco-Prussian War in December 1871. Germany would eventually move toward free institutions, he predicted, and acknowledged that his visit to Europe had made him an admirer of Bismarck.[51] By the beginning of the 1880s, however, he was much less sanguine. "Your conditions over there," he admonished his brother-in-law, "make me feel quite uncomfortable, so uncomfortable in fact that I don't like to think about them. What the papers have been printing here about [your] Jew-baiting we Germans could not read without being ashamed. And then your muddled economic conditions, the reactionary movement and the very insecure international relations which won't allow the maintenance of an unarmed peace." Contrasting these shortcomings with American prosperity, he boasted of his country's peaceful elections and its rapid economic development.[52]

Between 1881 and 1883, Schurz was one of the editors of the *New York Evening Post*, then a mouthpiece of the "best men," the genteel reformers of the Gilded Age. Still upset about developments in Germany, he used his newspaper for all-out attacks against anti-Semitism. The *Evening Post* pointed out that although Jew-baiting was worse in Russia, it occurred in Germany as well. Rejoicing at every setback suffered by anti-Semitic parties in the Reich, the newspaper asserted that it was ridiculous to maintain that 44 million gentiles could be swallowed up by fewer than 1 million Jews.[53]

The Lasker affair gave Schurz a renewed opportunity to voice his outrage against German anti-Semitic excesses. Long sympathetic to the German democrat, Schurz consented to deliver an oration at a commemorative service in a New York synagogue. "At a German's bier a German word is appropriate," he began. Then he launched into a paean of praise for the departed German statesman with a scathing attack upon the anti-Semitic insults to which Lasker had been subjected. German liberals thanked Schurz for his stand, and when Bismarck refused to accept the congressional resolution, Schurz's German-American correspondents labeled the chancellor's behavior an outrage. Let the German-American community show its disagreement, they suggested. Especially incensed at the shabby treatment accorded to the American minister in Berlin, Schurz proposed to Senator

George Edmunds that Sargent be recalled and the post left vacant as a sign of American dissatisfaction.[54]

In spite of Schurz's disappointments, reinforced by the bad news he received from German progressives furious at Bismarck's insistence upon long-term military budgets, the German-American leader never wholly lost faith in the future of the old fatherland. When Emperor William I died, Schurz agreed to deliver a eulogy. Frankly admitting his reservations, he said that he had lost many friends under the iron hand of the prince now being mourned and that he himself had escaped from that iron hand with difficulty and peril. William's system had not been popular in America, but he had presided over the rebirth of a great nation. Thus he had become Germany's national hero and was now honored by all Germans.[55] Clearly pleased with this attitude, German officials received Schurz with full honors when in 1888 he came to Europe. Bismarck welcomed him again and flattered him; the crown prince, about to ascend the throne as William II, granted him an interview, and the visitor was delighted with the attention. It was obvious that the new emperor, Frederick III, was already mortally ill and could not live long. Commenting on the reactionaries' hatred for the sovereign, Schurz called Frederick's expected death a tragedy. After the brief reign came to an end in June, Schurz attended a festival in Hamburg, where he met William II, who was friendly but at times struck the German-American as almost sinister.[56]

Events after 1890 are beyond the chronological span of this inquiry. It might be noted, however, that Schurz was distressed at Bismarck's dismissal. Consenting to deliver an oration on the occasion of the Iron Chancellor's death a few years later, he expressed his opinion that it might have been better had Bismarck left domestic affairs to others, although otherwise highly praising the departed statesman. After 1891, Schurz never returned to the land of his birth. Continuing to do everything in his power to further German-American understanding, he nevertheless wrote to his sister-in-law that she was the only attraction Germany still held for him. The old country's illiberal tendencies, its power-hungry Junkers, and their strong influence on the government were distasteful to him.[57]

Schurz's attitude was not unique. Franz Sigel shared it; Gustave Koerner expressed similar frustration; and the lifelong German-American patriot Philipp Wagner, when seeing Europe during the Bismarckian era, regretted that the fruits of the patriotic struggle against France were not what he had hoped for.[58] As early as 1872, when Hecker visited Germany again, he was unpleasantly affected by the ubiquitous presence of military uniforms.[59] If there were some German-Americans who blindly praised everything that was happening in the old fatherland, their outstanding representatives tended to maintain their perspective.

Clearly, then, during the exciting years leading to the unification of Germany the German-American community shared and at times exceeded the enthusiasm of its kinsmen overseas. But at the same time this fervor was often tempered by a healthy skepticism about conditions in the new Reich. The leading German-Americans proved to be good democrats whose convictions could not be changed by nationalistic fanaticism.

Notes

1. John Gerow Gazley, *American Opinion of German Unification* (New York: Columbia University Press, 1926), 425–508; John A. Hawgood, *The Tragedy of German-America: The Germans in the United States of America during the 19th Century—and After* (New York: Putnam's, 1940), 2–9, 280–81; Georg von Skal, *Die Achtundvierziger in Amerika* (Frankfurt am Main: Frankfurter Societätsdruckerei, 1923), 8–9; Carl Wittke, *Refugees of Revolution: The German Forty-Eighters in America* (Philadelphia: University of Pennsylvania Press, 1952), 352ff.

2. Heinrich Börnstein, *Fünfundsiebzig Jahre in der alten und neuen Welt*, 2 vols. (Leipzig: O. Wigand, 1884), 2:423.

3. *New-Yorker Staats-Zeitung*, January 23, February 1, 2, 4, August 11, 18, 26, 1864; Gazley, *American Opinion of German Unification*, 462ff, 453ff.

4. *Belletristisches Journal*, May 4, June 29, July 6, September 7, December 19, 1866, March 8, 1867; *New-Yorker Staats-Zeitung*, March 2, 9, 1867; Thomas J. McCormack, ed., *Memoirs of Gustave Koerner, 1809–1896: Life Sketches Written at the Suggestion of His Children*, 2 vols. (Cedar Rapids, Ia.: Torch Press, 1909), 2:454–56.

5. *Belletristisches Journal*, May 1, 1868; Henry Villard, "Karl Otto von Bismarck-Schoenhausen," *North American Review* 112 (1869): 220–21.

6. *Die Welt* 6 (July 26, 1870): 686; *Milwaukee Seebote*, August 10, 1870. For an example of the dislike of Napoleon III, see Carl Schurz, *The Reminiscences of Carl Schurz*, 3 vols. (New York: McClure, 1907–8), 1:361–62, 2:201–2.

7. Thomas Sergeant Perry, ed., *The Life and Letters of Francis Lieber* (Boston: James Osgood, 1882), 398.

8. *New-Yorker Staats-Zeitung* (weekly), July 23, 1870.

9. *Die Welt* 6 (July 26, 1870): 686.

10. *Milwaukee Seebote*, August 10, 1870.

11. Alexander I. Schem, ed., *Deutsch-amerikanisches Conversations-Lexikon*, 11 vols. (New York: Steiger, 1869–74), 11:285–86; McCormack, ed., *Memoirs of Koerner*, 2:507–18; *Milwaukee Seebote*, September 19, 1870; *Die Welt*, October 19, 1870; *Philadelphia Fair-Zeitung*, December 7, 1870–January 2, 1871; *New-Yorker Staats Zeitung* (weekly), August 2, 30, September 4, 1870; J. B. Stallo, *Reden, Abhandlungen und Briefe* (New York: Steiger, 1893), 270–73.

12. *New-Yorker Staats-Zeitung* (weekly), August 13, 1870; *Philadelphia Fair-*

Zeitung, December 30, 1870; *Friedrich Gerhard's Deutsch-Amerikanische Gartenlaube* 7 (1870): 528.

13. Perry, ed., *Life and Letters of Lieber*, 400–401; Francis Lieber, *Contributions to Political Science* (Philadelphia: Lippincott, 1881), 301–5; *Philadelphia Fair-Zeitung*, December 30, 1870; *Belletristisches Journal*, May 12, 1871.

14. *Belletristisches Journal*, April 2, 1871; *New-Yorker Staats-Zeitung* (weekly), April 15, 1871; McCormack, ed., *Memoirs of Koerner*, 2:530.

15. *Der Pionier*, February 1, 1871; Carl Wittke, *Against the Current: The Life of Karl Heinzen (1809–80)* (Chicago: University of Chicago Press, 1945), 299–300, 272ff.

16. *Neue Zeit*, July 30, September 10, 17, October 1, 22, 29, 1870, January 28, March 4, 1871.

17. Gazley, *American Opinion of German Unification*, 507–8; Carl Wittke, *The German Language Press in America* (Lexington: University of Kentucky Press, 1957), 164ff.

18. *Belletristisches Journal*, May 4, 1866; *New-Yorker Staats-Zeitung*, July 4, August 16, 1866.

19. Arnold Ruge to Franz Sigel, October 2, 1866, Sigel Papers, New York Historical Society, New York.

20. Maria Wagner, *Mathilde Franziska Anneke in Selbstzeugnissen und Dokumenten* (Frankfurt am Main: Fischer, 1980), 256.

21. *New-Yorker Staats-Zeitung* (weekly), February 16, 1867; *Belletristisches Journal*, May 4, August 17, 1866, January 4, 1867; Schem, ed., *Deutsch-Amerikanisches Conversations-Lexikon*, 5:164; Perry, ed., *Life and Letters of Lieber*, 377.

22. McCormack, ed., *Memoirs of Koerner*, 2:507–13.

23. For example, *New-Yorker Staats-Zeitung* (weekly), September 3, 1870.

24. Ibid., December 31, 1870.

25. *Belletristisches Journal*, December 23, 30, 1870, January 27, April 7, 1871.

26. Friedrich Hecker, *Reden und Vorlesungen von Friedrich Hecker* (St. Louis: Witter, 1872).

27. Perry, ed., *Life and Letters of Lieber*, 415–16.

28. Wagner, *Anneke*, 286–87, 296–97.

29. E. J. Passant, *A Short History of Germany, 1815–1945* (Cambridge: Cambridge University Press, 1969), 87.

30. *Milwaukee Seebote*, February 24, 1873.

31. *New-Yorker Staats-Zeitung* (weekly), October 26, 1878, February 28, 1879.

32. *Belletristisches Journal*, February 28, March 21, 28, 1879.

33. *Milwaukee Herold*, May 1, 1879.

34. *Illinois Staats-Zeitung*, January 3, 1884.

35. *Cincinnati Union*, July 10, 1879.

36. Friedrich Martin v. Bodenstedt to Udo Brachvogel, March 1, 1881, Brachvogel Papers, New York Public Library, New York; Theodor Barth to Schurz, January 11, 1887, Schurz Papers, Library of Congress, Washington, D.C.

37. Louis L. Snyder, *Roots of German Nationalism* (Bloomington: Indiana University Press, 1978), 134–56.

38. McCormack, ed., *Memoirs of Koerner*, 2:709–10; *Illinois Staats-Zeitung*, February 19, 1884.

39. *Um die Welt*, January 26, March 22, 1884.

40. Ibid.; *New-Yorker Staats-Zeitung* (weekly), February 27, 1884; *Belletristisches Journal*, April 2, March 19, 1884.

41. Golo Mann, *The History of Germany Since 1789* (New York: Praeger, 1968), 245–46.

42. *Illinois Staats-Zeitung,* June 16, 1888.

43. *Belletristisches Journal,* June 21, 1888.

44. Hans L. Trefousse, *Carl Schurz: A Biography* (Knoxville: University of Tennessee Press, 1982).

45. Schurz to Heinrich Meyer, June 10, 1866, Schurz Collection in possession of Arthur R. Hogue, Bloomington, Indiana. Hereafter cited as Hogue Collection.

46. Trefousse, *Schurz,* 165–66; *Missouri Democrat,* July 24, 1870; Baltimore *Der Deutsche Correspondent,* July 21, 1870.

47. Schurz to Mrs. Schurz, August 9, 1870, Hogue Collection.

48. Schurz to Mrs. Schurz, August 15, 27, 29, September 3, 6, 1870, ibid.

49. Schurz to Mrs. Schurz, September 10, 1870, ibid.

50. Schurz to Adolph Meyer, February 3, 1871, ibid.

51. *New York Times,* December 28, 1871.

52. Schurz to Adolph Meyer, January 2, 1881, Hogue Collection.

53. John G. Sproat, *"The Best Men": Liberal Reformers in the Gilded Age* (New York: Oxford University Press, 1968), 236; *New York Evening Post,* August 22, November 2, 1881, January 23, 1882.

54. *Westliche Post,* May 9, 1884; Schurz to Fanny Chapman, February 27, 1884, Schurz-Chapman Correspondence, University of Münster (microfilm); John Ruhm to Schurz, February 22, 1884; Schurz to George Edmunds, March 9, 12, 1884, Schurz Papers, Library of Congress; Andrew Dickson White, *Autobiography of Andrew Dickson White,* 2 vols. (New York: Century, 1905), 1: 200–201.

55. Theodor Barth to Schurz, January 11, 1887, Schurz Papers, Library of Congress; Frederick Bancroft, ed., *Speeches, Correspondence and Political Papers of Carl Schurz,* 6 vols. (New York: Putnam's, 1913), 4: 495–506.

56. Schurz, Diary, May–October 1888, Schurz Papers, Library of Congress.

57. Hermann Freiherr von Eckardstein, *Lebenserinnerungen und politische Denkwürdigkeiten,* 3 vols. (Leipzig: Paul List, 1919), 1: 11–12; *New-Yorker Staats-Zeitung,* October 19, 1893; Schurz to William McKinley, September 22, 1898, McKinley Papers, Library of Congress; Schurz to Emilie Meyer, February 25, 1905, Schurz Papers in possession of Cissa Morlang, Hamburg, Germany.

58. Philipp Wagner, *Ein Achtundvierziger: Erlebtes und Gedachtes* (Brooklyn: Johannes Wagner, 1882), 390; Skal, *Die Achtundvierziger in Amerika,* 9; McCormack, *Memoirs of Koerner,* 2:709–10; M. C. Becker, *Germans of 1849 in America: An Address before the Monday Club of Columbus, Ohio, March 14, 1887* (Mt. Vernon, Ohio: Republican Printing House, 1887), 23.

59. Wittke, *Refugees,* 361–62.

12.
Whose Celebration? The Centennial of 1876 and German-American Socialist Culture

CAROL POORE

ON THANKSGIVING DAY IN 1875, the *New York Arbeiter-Stimme*, official newspaper of the Sozialdemokratische Arbeiterpartei von Nordamerika, rhetorically asked its German working-class readers what they had to be grateful for. Should they give thanks for the depression that had lasted for three years? Should they be satisfied that their political options were still restricted to a choice between Republicans and Democrats? Should they welcome the corruption of the press, or be grateful that the number of millionaires was steadily increasing? Or should they look forward proudly to the upcoming Centennial, with its predictable displays of hypocrisy and tastelessness?[1] Earlier in the year, this same newspaper had characterized the Fourth of July as an occasion for the bourgeoisie to celebrate its independence from the British monarchy and had attempted to discourage German workers from celebrating the occasion with their employers.[2] Such editorials were typical before 1876; the German-American socialist press either took no notice of Independence Day or urged its readers not to participate in official festivities. The interest which all sectors of the population took in the Centennial, however, with its mood of national self-congratulation, extravagant festivities, and the impressive international exposition in Philadelphia, caused immigrant German socialists to reinterpret the meaning of this holiday for workers and to offer alternatives to the official celebrations—a sort of "People's Centennial."

Labor historians have recognized the crucial political role German immigrants played in introducing the theory of scientific socialism to the United States, helping to organize the American labor movement after the Civil War, and founding this country's first enduring socialist party, the Sozialistische Arbeiterpartei (Socialist Labor party) in 1877. Only recently, however, have social historians begun to study the complex cultural framework created by German socialists as the largest and most significant group of ethnic radicals in nineteenth-century America.[3] In addition to electoral and union activities, these socialists— along with other members of their communities—created workers' theaters, workers' singing societies, socialist literature and journalism, and periodic festivals, as well as workers' gymnastic societies (Turners), producers' and consumers' cooperatives, workers' insurance societies, special organizations for women, workers' educational societies, and socialist schools for children and adults. This cooperative social network provided a cushion against culture shock and economic difficulty and served the same hegemonic function—inspiring, informing, and entertaining—as its middle- and upper-class counterparts.[4] Particularly in the situation of exile and immigration, these cultural and social activities assumed crucial importance in unifying the working class within the German ethnic group and helping establish a sense of solidarity with workers of other nationalities.

The "Workers' Fourth of July" celebrations in 1876 were part of these expanding opportunities for alternatives to mainstream American cultural expression and were a significant indication of how German immigrant radicals viewed the United States. Although German-American socialists arranged such activities in several large cities with sizable German working-class populations, the largest and most commented-upon, the *Arbeiter-Juli-Feier*, took place in Chicago on July 3, 1876. A preliminary editorial in the *Chicago Vorbote* on July 1 described the pompous preparations being undertaken around the country for celebrating the independence of the "American exploiters" from the "English exploiters."[5] It painted a grim picture of the sufferings of American workers under the capitalist economic system and stated that they had no reason to commemorate the centennial of a republic that was the political instrument of the "monied aristocracy." As the editorial proclaimed: "For *us* it was not a republic, not a fatherland." Rather than joining with the well-to-do, the newspaper urged that workers attend the festival planned by Chicago's socialists and trade unionists, a gathering that would promote the spirit of genuine liberty, equality, and fraternity.

According to reports in the socialist press, the parade and celebration on July 3 were an impressive workers' demonstration. Fifteen hundred strong, the marchers were led through Chicago by the Lehr-

"On the Fourth of July, 1877." An allegorical representation of the United States which appeared in the Chicago *Vorbote* on July 7, 1877, and which typified the sentiments of German-American socialists toward the Fourth of July celebration. Columbia (to Mr. Moneybags): "You have my blessing and good-will,/My dear, prominent son;/Here the poor man whom you fleeced/Gets all the *work*; While you get the *returns*!" (Chicago *Vorbote*)

und Wehrverein, an armed self-defense organization of German socialists formed to protect workers against the police and military,[6] and it included socialists from the Arbeiterpartei von Illinois, various trade unions, and Turner societies. When the parade arrived at a popular Chicago park, the ten thousand people who attended enjoyed music, a tableau or *lebendes Bild*, speeches, and socializing far into the night. The tableau provided an especially striking illustration of the socialists' view of the present and hopes for the future. It was entitled "The Old and the New World," but it did not contrast—as some in the audience might have expected—exploitation and misery in Europe with freedom and plenty in the United States. Rather, one side depicted the present exploitation of man by man under capitalism, showing, on the lowest level, a group of workers in chains; on the second level, two women representing poverty and misery; and above these figures, two men standing for the reign of money and religion. In contrast, the reverse side presented the New World, the hoped-for future of labor under socialism. The first level showed productive agriculture and the happy, secure family life of liberated humanity. On the second level, three women represented industry, science, and art in the service of all and accessible to all. On the third level, reigning over the New World, justice and freedom were portrayed by a woman holding scales and a sword and another woman wearing the Jacobin cap and waving the red flag.

The main German-language speaker of the evening, the socialist journalist Joseph Brucker of Milwaukee, chose to amplify on this theme of the Old and New Worlds.[7] He characterized the Old World as a class society ruled by discord, hypocrisy, and inequality, which the socialists sought to replace by a New World promising liberty, justice, education, and security for all. Brucker then asked what course of action would be appropriate for socialists to pursue in the United States, their adopted homeland. In a moving personal statement, he described his first impressions of America after immigrating from Austria several years earlier. Like most in his audience, he stated, the love of freedom and the longing for a better life had driven him to leave his homeland. He did not want to seem ungrateful to the United States, for this republic had offered the new arrivals freedom of speech and the press and a better existence. He was amazed to see what human efforts had created in such a short time: the populous cities, the transcontinental railway, scientific and artistic achievements. But, he stated, the longer he resided in America, the more it seemed to him that there was not such a stark contrast here with his native land after all. Disillusioned with the reality underlying the promised freedoms of the United States, he pointed with dismay to a rapid decline in the standard of living and to increasingly stringent restrictions on liberty and equality. Nevertheless, Brucker urged that socialists not despair or resign themselves but attempt to contribute their part toward improving the conditions they found in the United States. As "men of the revolution," they stood in the proud tradition of the signers of the Declaration of Independence and had a unique opportunity to work for the true realization of its principles. Thus the Centennial could be the occasion for "workers, Turners, and party comrades" to commit themselves to the tradition of Washington, Jefferson, Franklin, and Thomas Paine, so that the principles of socialism would first be realized under the Stars and Stripes.

After Brucker's speech, socialists read a second Declaration of Independence which proclaimed the independence of labor from capital, enumerating the ways in which the capitalist economic system prevented workers from enjoying their inalienable rights to "life, liberty, and the full benefit of their labor."[8] Under present conditions, it claimed, property and monied interests enjoyed a disproportionate share of representation and control over legislation, and consequently, the two major parties did not work for the welfare of all the people. Justice was not impartial, wealth was unequally distributed, and employers used the grand inventions in labor-saving machinery to subjugate workers further rather than to reduce the hours of labor. As a final measure of injustice, workers assembled to discuss their grievances and course of action had been dispersed and shot down. The framers of this declaration stated in closing that, having tried in vain to work cooperatively within the existing political parties, workers would now endeavor to acquire the power to make their own laws, manage their own production, and govern themselves. They doubtless referred to the Socialist Unity Congress that was held in Philadelphia in this same month, July 1876, bringing together several predominantly German regional parties into the Arbeiterpartei der Vereinigten Staaten.

In view of these extremely negative statements about the United States and the disillusionment with its political and economic system, we might wonder how representative this festival was. After all, it has almost become a cliché to say that German-American socialists failed to establish a large, enduring socialist movement because of their refusal to incorporate specifically American experiences (such as upward mobility and a higher living standard) into their theory and strategies.[9] Was the Chicago Workers' Centennial merely a gathering of an insignificant group of foreign radicals who clung tenaciously to ways of thinking appropriate to Europe but inapplicable to the reality immigrant workers experienced in the United States? We may approach this question from several angles: What was the state of the economy in 1876, and were the socialists' assertions of increasing impoverishment justified?[10] How did such "Workers' Fourth of July" festivals evolve as a response to American tradition in German and other ethnic groups? What was the place of this event within the context of German-American socialist festivals and culture?

In the centennial year, the United States was in the midst of the most severe depression it had yet experienced. The failure of the banking house of Jay Cooke and Company in September 1873 ushered in an economic crisis that would last for the rest of the decade. By 1877 3 million workers were unemployed, and many of those permanently out of work had taken to the road as tramps. The centennial year witnessed large demonstrations of the unemployed, including one of fifty thousand people in August in New York City. In San Francisco, the press reported that hundreds of people were living off the city garbage dump, while in Manhattan about ninety thousand homeless workers were called "revolvers" because of their practice of staying at different police stations for one or two days in the coldest months.[11] During the depression, many working-class organizations, which might have made economic security more possible to attain, disbanded and employers drastically reduced wages and lengthened hours for those who were still employed.[12] The sudden fall in the standard of living led to widespread unrest and disillusionment among workers who could remember a better past or even an irretrievable artisan way of life that had offered some of them more self-sufficiency. Accordingly, papers sympathetic to labor such as the *Pittsburgh National Labor Tribune* questioned the appropriateness of the centennial celebration of freedom when workers were in fact experiencing more limited opportunities. It editorialized: "The dreams have not been realized. . . . The working people of this country . . . suddenly find capital as rigid as an absolute monarch. . . . Capital has now the same control over us that the aristocracy of England had at the time of the revolution."[13] The growing unemployment and impoverishment culminated in the national railroad strike of 1877, which escalated in St. Louis into the first American general strike for the eight-hour day and an end to child labor. The size and violence of these strikes led to a hysterical reaction in the press and public opinion, which compared events in the United States to the recent Paris Commune and divined the sinister guiding hand of the foreign-dominated International behind it all.[14] In con-

trast, labor and socialist organizers long remembered the brutal treatment of strikers as yet another example of class justice in the United
States. For example, it was the experience of helplessness in the 1877
strike which caused *Lehr- und Wehrvereine* like the one that marched
in the Chicago socialists' parade to spring up in cities around the country. Thus, within the context of economic depression, unemployment,
and escalating conflicts between capital and labor in the 1870s, the
criticisms of the United States voiced at the Chicago meeting appear
representative of the experience of many recent immigrants as well as
native-born workers.

As an attempt to provoke reflection on American history and to
change accepted ways of commemorating the American heritage, this
Workers' Fourth of July was part of a tradition of countercelebrations
among both native-born American and immigrant groups. Beginning
as early as the 1790s, the Fourth of July was claimed by American labor as its day, and by the 1830s, it was fixed as a day for workers to
voice their demands and proclaim themselves the legitimate heirs of
the spirit of '76.[15] In particular, the Declaration of Independence served
workers and other disadvantaged groups as a model for stating their
grievances and their programs for continuing the goals of the American Revolution. Numerous workers' organizations published alternative declarations during the nineteenth century, and these were
supplemented by declarations from other groups, especially blacks
and women, who felt that America was not living up to the principles
proclaimed in the original document. In tones foreshadowing those of
the Chicago socialists' celebration, the great black abolitionist Frederick Douglass had spoken on the meaning of the Fourth of July for the
American Negro on July 5, 1852, saying: "I am not included within the
pale of this glorious anniversary! . . . This Fourth of July is *yours*, not
mine. You may rejoice, but I must mourn."[16] And at the official centennial ceremony in Philadelphia on July 4, the suffragist Susan B. Anthony, who had been denied a place on the program, disrupted the
proceedings to read a "Declaration of Rights for Women" and articles
of impeachment against the all-male government.[17]

In contrast to many of these alternative declarations, the Chicago
festival of 1876 was not geared primarily toward voicing specific workers' demands but rather toward urging reflection on America's past
within the context of a countercelebration. After the Centennial, however, immigrant and native-born socialists and workers took the Fourth
of July as the major occasion to voice their demand for the eight-hour
day. Organized by trade unions and the Sozialistische Arbeiterpartei,

these demonstrations were similar to the one held in Chicago in 1876, but they were larger and revealed a more hopeful mood, a feeling that the workers' movement was growing as the depression of the 1870s ebbed. The socialist press reported most extensively on the eight-hour demonstrations held on July 4, 1879, in cities such as Philadelphia (eight thousand participants), Chicago (nine thousand men and five hundred women in the march), and New York (fifteen thousand participants).[18] These events were noteworthy for the heterogeneity of participating organizations and the realization of class interests transcending ethnic boundaries which they signified. The parade through New York and Brooklyn, for example, included German, English-speaking, French, and Czech sections of the Socialist Labor party, unions representing many trades, and workers' singing societies, gymnastic societies, and other social clubs. In Chicago, 130 workers' organizations participated, including groups of Germans, native-born Americans, Swedes, French, Czechs, Irish, and Poles. Reminiscent of the Chicago tableau, a decorated wagon in the Brooklyn parade showed the "Fraternity of all Nations" as the solidarity of workers from all ethnic groups under the red flag. Banners in German, English, and Czech proclaimed slogans such as "Tenement-house work is slavery, but united we will be free," and "Down with Republican thieves and Democratic robbers." But this affirmation of international working-class solidarity did not entail a blanket rejection of American tradition. On the contrary, speakers at all of these demonstrations praised the revolutionary past of the United States and claimed this heritage as their own. Accordingly, the German speaker at the Brooklyn meeting, Georg Winter, recalled to his audience a time of more self-sufficient artisan life in the United States before the spread of the factory system and called for establishment of the eight-hour day as a first step toward realizing for all the principles upon which the nation had been founded.

The Fourth of July remained an occasion for foreign- and native-born workers to demonstrate for the eight-hour day through the 1880s. The *New York Volkszeitung* reported on July 4, 1883, that a growing number of English-speaking workers were participating in the event, but by 1889 the *Chicago Vorbote* stated that the eight-hour demonstration in that city on July 4 was much smaller than in previous years.[19] This decline in the Workers' Fourth of July celebrations does not necessarily imply a waning militancy among the groups that had participated in them. Rather, these groups created new occasions for asserting solidarity and voicing labor's demands, and German socialists, social revolutionaries, and unionists were foremost in these efforts. May Day originated in the national strike and demonstrations for the eight-hour day held on May 1, 1886. The widespread support for this strike, its climax in the Haymarket Affair in Chicago, and the subsequent hanging of four leading Chicago labor organizers (three German-born) made this into a tragically unforgettable day for the workers' movement. Accordingly, the *Chicago Vorbote* wrote in 1887 that May 1, 1886—rather than the Fourth of July—marked the beginning of a new era, the birth of the new workers' movement for freedom.[20] During these years, the practice of celebrating Labor Day early in September was also becoming accepted, from its beginning in 1882 as a New York holiday initiated by the heavily German Central Labor Union to its proclamation as a national holiday in 1894.

The Chicago workers' Centennial gathering was not only one of the more impressive events in the dynamic tradition of alternative Fourth of July celebrations. It was also part of the ongoing festival activity which working-class organizations of all ethnic groups created in the nineteenth century as alternative opportunities for cultural expression. These festivals provided a source of entertainment, enjoyment, and escape from the rigors of the working day and a place for the renewal of strength and courage in the company of friends, family, and comrades.[21] Another function of these festivals was to increase awareness of progressive historical traditions and strengthen solidarity among the participants and with workers from other ethnic groups. German-American socialists customarily held countercelebrations not only on the Fourth of July but also on religious holidays such as Christmas (when they would invoke socialism as the new Messiah[22] or omit the religious aspect altogether) and Thanksgiving. In 1884, for example, five thousand American and German workers and tramps marched through Chicago under red and black flags to protest the hypocrisy of celebrating Thanksgiving while so many were poor and unemployed.[23] All of this activity may sound negative, as if these immigrant socialists were reacting only with hostility toward established customs. As alternatives to these occasions, however, festivals commemorating outstanding events in the international workers' movement were also a central part of German-American socialist culture. These included some dates from their European heritage, such as the fervent commemorations of the Paris Commune each March and of Ferdinand Lassalle's birth and death. Furthermore, along with other progressive groups, German-American socialists proposed and created celebrations originating in their experiences in the United States and aimed toward influencing workers' perspectives on American history.

Some of these occasions were critical responses to traditional, affirmative ways of celebrating the Fourth of July. On this date in 1885, for example, the New York newspaper *Der Sozialist* suggested that January 1, the date of Lincoln's Emancipation Proclamation, would be a more appropriate national holiday because until then the Declaration of Independence had secured freedom only for whites. After the four labor organizers convicted of murder in the Haymarket Affair were hanged on November 11, 1887, this date became an occasion for large demonstrations to honor their memory, especially in Chicago, where the execution was carried out. This date was a rallying point for Chicago workers for many years, although by the time of the twentieth anniversary in 1907—after May Day and Labor Day had become fixed working-class holidays—the annual ceremony seemed more like a gathering of the veterans from the labor struggles of the 1880s.

The year 1983 marks not only the Tricentennial of German immigration to the United States but also the anniversary of another important event: the centennial of Karl Marx's death. On March 19, 1883, Cooper Union in New York City was the scene of the largest memorial event held anywhere in the world immediately following the death of Marx. Coming at a time of sharpening class conflict in the United States, the meeting was significant both for its size (six thousand men and women attended and several thousand were turned away) and because groups that were often at odds with each other were willing to put aside their differences on this occasion. Organized by the Central Labor Union of New York and the Sozialistische Arbeiterpartei, the meeting featured songs by a German workers' chorus and speeches in English, German, Russian, Czech, and French. Stressing the spirit of proletarian internationalism, the speakers praised Marx as a "man who belonged to no nation," and the exiled former Reichstag deputy Johann Most surmised that after national heroes were long forgotten, Marx would still be remembered. Along these lines, an article in the *New York Volkszeitung* suggested that the first weeks in March would be appropriate holidays for the "supporters of the International" in memory of 1848, 1871, and Marx's death. The speakers also took care to point out the applicability of Marx's theories to the social question in the United States, which—in Johann Most's words—was just as pressing as in Europe. In language reminiscent of the "Workers' Fourth of July" celebrations, speakers asserted the need for a radical reconstruction of society to create a truly just republic, in which armies would be disbanded, poverty would be unknown, and government would become cooperative.[24]

The central problem which German-American socialists raised in all of these efforts to establish critical, alternative festivals was the relevance of historical tradition—specifically, the American revolutionary heritage—to their present situation and hopes for the future. In their statements on the function of such festivals and in the make-up of the celebrations themselves, they reflected on which historical events they should commemorate and how these events could be meaningful to immigrant workers. German-American socialists always praised the principles contained in the Declaration of Independence but also always declared that the Fourth of July should be a time to reflect on what else needed to be accomplished so that these principles would be realized for all Americans. Thus they criticized orators and politicians who used this day as an opportunity for uncritical self-congratulation and who avoided reminding citizens of their right to revolutionary change. As one socialist newspaper stated: "The revolution of our ancestors is celebrated at the same time as the people's right to revolution is extinguished. It is for precisely this reason that the orators speak of *temporal* events as if they were *eternal*."[25] That is, rather than viewing the Fourth of July and celebrations of other dates as occasions to reminisce nostalgically or to advance a static view of history, these immigrant socialists saw historical commemorations as occasions to reflect on the relevance of the past for the present and future, on history as struggle, and on possibilities for social change. Along these lines, an editorial in the *New York Volkszeitung* in July 1883 took issue with the assertion that workers had no homeland, saying: "The fatherland still means something to us, not only because of what it *is*, but also because of what we hope to make out of it."[26] Declaring socialists and workers to be the true heirs of 1776, the article went on to say that the Fourth of July had even more meaning for them than for followers of other parties. Just as the United States had been the cradle of freedom, they hoped that it would become the place where this freedom would be fully realized. With its great natural resources and diverse immigrant population, this country could offer a chance to overcome the barriers of nationality and race. The editorial concluded: "In spite of everything, we love the New World and people because of what they will become through our efforts." For a number of years, German immigrant socialists and workers took the Fourth of July as an occasion to establish solidarity, determine their needs, and voice their demands. In so doing, they took their place in progressive American tradition. As Joseph Brucker said in Chicago: "Let us be socialists in the true sense of the word, then we will also be the best citizens of this republic . . . and we will not have celebrated the Centennial in vain."[27]

Notes

1. *New York Arbeiter-Stimme*, November 28, 1875, p. 1.
2. Ibid., July 11, 1875, p. 2.
3. See Hartmut Keil and John B. Jentz, eds., *German Workers in Industrial Chicago, 1850–1910: A Comparative Perspective* (DeKalb, Ill.: Northern Illinois University Press, 1983); and Carol Poore, *German American Socialist Literature, 1865–1900* (Bern: Lang, 1982).
4. See Lee Baxandall, preface to *The Origins of Left Culture in the U.S., 1880–1940, Cultural Correspondence/Green Mountain Irregulars*, special issue, Spring 1978, p. 2.
5. *Chicago Vorbote*, July 1, 1876, p. 1.
6. See Philip Foner, *We, the Other People: Alternative Declarations of Independence by Labor Groups, Farmers, Woman's Rights Advocates, Socialists, and Blacks, 1829–1975* (Urbana: University of Illinois Press, 1976), 99; Christine Heiss, "German Radicals in Industrial America: The Lehr- und Wehr-Verein in Gilded Age Chicago," in Keil and Jentz, *German Workers*, 206–24.
7. Brucker's speech was reprinted in the *Chicago Vorbote*, July 22, 1876, p. 3.
8. An English version of this alternative Declaration of Independence is printed in Foner, *We, the Other People*, 100–103.
9. This assessment has been offered by observers of the American scene from Engels to some contemporary historians; see Friedrich Engels to Friedrich Sorge, February 8, 1890, in Karl Marx and Friedrich Engels, *Letters to Americans, 1848–1895* (New York: International Publishers, 1953), 224–25; Daniel Bell, *Marxian Socialism in the United States* (Princeton: Princeton University Press, 1967).
10. For a careful sociological study of poverty among German immigrants, see John B. Jentz and Hartmut Keil, "From Immigrants to Urban Workers: Chicago's German Poor in the Gilded Age and Progressive Era, 1883–1908," *Vierteljahrschrift für Sozial- und Wirtschaftsgeschichte* 68 (1981):52–97.
11. See John Bergamini, *The Hundredth Year: The United States in 1876* (New York: Putnam, 1976), 224.
12. See Philip Foner, *History of the Labor Movement in the United States*, 4 vols. (New York: International Publishers, 1947–65), 1:439.
13. Quoted in Philip Foner, *The Great Labor Uprising of 1877* (New York: Monad, 1977), 7.
14. Allan Pinkerton, *Strikers, Communists, Tramps and Detectives* (New York: Dillingham, 1878).
15. Foner, *We, the Other People*, 2–40.
16. Quoted in ibid., 15.
17. See ibid., 21, 105–15; Bergamini, *Hundredth Year*, 190.
18. For accounts of these demonstrations, see the *New York Volkszeitung*, July 5, 1879, and the *Chicago Vorbote*, July 12, 1879.
19. *Chicago Vorbote*, July 10, 1889.
20. Ibid., May 4, 1887, 4.

21. For a discussion of the importance of such opportunities for communal leisure, see Gottfried Korff, "Volkskultur und Arbeiterkultur. Überlegungen am Beispiel der sozialistischen Maifesttradition," *Geschichte und Gesellschaft* 5 (1979): 83–103.

22. See Ludwig Geissler, "Allegorisches Weihnachtsfestspiel," *Volksstimme des Westens*, January 18, 1880, p. 3.

23. *Chicago Vorbote*, December 3, 1884, p. 8.

24. See Philip Foner, ed., *When Karl Marx Died: Comments in 1883* (New York: International Publishers, 1973), 83, 70 (quotation), 105, 198–99, 100–101.

25. *New York Sozialist*, July 11, 1885, p. 1.

26. *New York Volkszeitung*, July 5, 1883, p. 2.

27. *Chicago Vorbote*, July 22, 1876, p. 4.

13.

German Immigrant Workers in Nineteenth-Century America: Working-Class Culture and Everyday Life in an Urban Industrial Setting

HARTMUT KEIL

THREE TRADITIONAL ASSUMPTIONS have dominated historians' perceptions of the impact of German immigrant workers on America's industrializing society: (1) They were industrious artisans and skilled workers who contributed scarce and valuable work experiences to the new country. (2) They were an important element in the early period of industrialization but, partly because they assimilated and moved out of the working class so quickly, they did not play a significant role in this group after the 1880s. (3) German working-class radicalism, which was rampant in America's urban industrial centers in the 1870s and 1880s, was an imported ideology inappropriate to American conditions.[1] These views were reinforced by a predominantly ethnic approach to the study of immigrant groups, which tended to emphasize common national characteristics and experiences and to downplay social class divisions within an immigrant group.[2] Only recently have social historical approaches contributed new focuses of analysis, and the new urban history and the new labor history have provided insights that place the study of German immigrant workers in a different analytical context. Thus the new urban history sees the spatial dimension and the functional differentiation of specific urban centers as determining factors in allocating economic and social resources to populations, and this structure of opportunity decisively affected the job careers and patterns of everyday life of German immigrant workers.[3] For the first time the new labor history paid attention to the mass of workers, organized as well as unorganized, applying the method of community study as the necessary interdisciplinary tool for relating industry, work, everyday life and leisure, institutions, politics, and culture of the working class.[4]

Two serious limitations remain, however. Concentrating on long-range economic, demographic, and social developments, new urban history studies have tended to neglect the perspective of the people experiencing these changes. The widespread use of quantitative data at the expense of sources that reveal the norms and values of persons reacting to structural developments reduces these people to mere statistical figures.[5] Community studies, on the other hand, have so far focused on the early phase of industrialization in the New England and Atlantic regions and on relatively small industrializing towns. This temporal and regional limitation largely excludes German workers, who were most important in the towns and cities of the Midwest during the decisive phase of industrialization before and after 1880.

The Chicago Project, a research effort with the goal of writing a social history of German workers in Chicago from 1850 to World War I and funded by the Volkswagen Foundation, has tried to overcome these limitations by selecting the most important industrial boom city of the Midwest and by combining the indispensable quantitative analysis with the study of records of German workers' institutions, particularly the German-language press.[6] This essay will emphasize aspects of German workers' everyday life and culture in an effort to relate results of this research to the experience of other German immigrant groups. Class must be a central variable when analyzing the experience of an immigrant group because class contributes a necessary dimension for understanding the processes of acculturation and integration. These processes were affected not only by a common cultural heritage but also by the social position immigrants held before and after emigrating. Thus German workers shared many problems and characteristics with other German immigrants vis-à-vis the receiving society. But at the same time, their entrance into a multiethnic American working class in the process of formation and development set them apart from the German immigrant middle class and forced them to interact with workers of many national backgrounds. I therefore proceed from the assumption of a class-specific process of integration which did not necessarily end with German workers entering the broad American middle class, but often led to their firm positioning in the American working class.

Chicago, not incorporated as a town until the 1830s, profited from its superb geographic location at the end of the waterway across the Great Lakes and the southern tip of Lake Michigan to become the Midwest's leading transportation, trade, and industrial city in the course of the nineteenth century.[7] German immigrants and their children contributed significantly to this development. In 1850, before the great wave of German emigration to the United States, almost five thousand Germans lived in Chicago; their numbers more than quadrupled in the next decade and continued to increase in proportion to the overall population growth, except in the decade from 1890 to 1900 after the end of mass emigration from Germany. If the children of German immigrants are included, one detects an astonishing degree of continuity in the proportion of Chicago's German population over a period of fifty years despite a tremendously fluctuating urban population also significantly shifting in its ethnic makeup. Except for 1850, German immigrants and their children always made up between 25 and 30 percent of Chicago's population between the middle of the nineteenth century and World War I. This high level was achieved by constant mass immigration. In particular, the last immigration wave of the 1880s ensured the continued impact of the immigrant generation beyond the turn of the century. Even in 1900 more than three-fourths of the heads of households of German families in Chicago had been born in Germany, a clear reason why there were more German institutions in Chicago around the turn of the century than ever before. It would thus be wrong when studying the process of acculturation to accept the periodization offered by historians of migration, who see the 1880s as the dividing line between the "old" and the "new" immigration. For this process took much longer and extended over more than one generation.

Continuity is also apparent in the social composition of Chicago's German population.[8] As early as 1850, all classes were represented, the professions to the same degree as in 1900 (2.9 percent). Small businessmen (8.8 percent) were an indispensable element of the German population. Artisans and skilled workers were by far the largest group (48.1 percent), followed by unskilled laborers and service workers (36 percent). Over the next fifty years, the proportion of workers decreased by the same degree (from 84.1 to 67.7 percent) by which that of small businessmen and white-collar employees increased (25.9 percent in 1900). Structural changes in the city's economy help account for these less than spectacular occupational developments within Chicago's German work force. Even in 1900 more than two-thirds of all German households still were working class.

At the same time, important changes occurred within Chicago's German population which help explain why this national group was only rarely able to translate its relative predominance in the city into a powerful political force. The evidence in 1850 of complete internal social stratification suggests the early maturity of the German community and different economic, political, and cultural interests within it. Germans at the time of their immigration were not nearly so homogeneous as, for example, the Irish and Poles. The long period of immigration from Germany created additional regional and cultural as well as social and economic differences. It is therefore not necessary to attribute the lack of political unity among Chicago's German population to the German mentality. Instead, sharp conflicts of interest and class prevented a lasting ethnic solidarity.

Generational changes were an equally important factor of internal differentiation, especially the transition from the immigrant generation to the second generation of children of German immigrants born in America. The ratio of first and second generation for three census years impressively reflects this development. It changed from 4:1 in 1850 to 1:1 in 1880 and 2:3 at the turn of the century. Although three-fourths of the second generation in 1900 were still unmarried sons and daughters living in German immigrant households, their impact after 1900 must have increased rapidly because mass immigration from Germany, which had been replenishing the ranks of the first generation until the early 1890s, had ended.[9] These demographic changes point to the increasing abandonment of German institutions by the young generation and its orientation toward American lifestyles. Although World War I may have served as a catalyst for the expeditious and often forced integration of German immigrants, demographic developments had already paved the way.[10]

German immigrant workers brought with them diverse occupational experiences. They joined the American labor force at different stages of industrialization.[11] The major changes in the regions of origin from southwestern to northeastern Germany reflect occupational as well as social and cultural shifts over fifty years. The initial immigration from the Southwest was soon superseded by that from the Prussian, especially the East Elbian, provinces, which meant that artisans, traders, and skilled workers were increasingly joined by un-skilled workers and agricultural laborers. Thus in Chicago's German working class in 1880, one could find day laborers from a quasi-feudal society who were placed for the first time in an urban context and who worked in one of Chicago's mass production industries, as well as highly skilled workers with industrial experience in Germany and ar-tisans who had been deprived of their traditional occupations because of the impact of early industrialization and who hoped to conserve their threatened status by emigrating. In addition, the significant numbers of workers who had reached maturity in Chicago after hav-ing come to the city as young children of German immigrant families or who had been born in America contributed to a working class of heterogeneous occupational backgrounds.

Despite this diversity, and especially through the 1880s, one com-mon ground for working-class solidarity existed: a lively artisan tra-dition that had surpassed regional boundaries in Germany and had become international in orientation. During their obligatory years of travel journeymen moved across practically all regional and national boundaries in Europe, meeting fellow workers on the basis of a com-mon craft and becoming imbued with this tradition despite different ethnic and regional backgrounds. In Chicago, where German skilled workers made up almost 50 percent of the German labor force in 1850, the same tradition could serve to integrate new arrivals into the rapidly growing German artisan community.[12] So long as skilled workers were in the center of the production process, in small craft shops as well as in the few large manufacturing plants such as McCormick's Reaper Works, they provided the natural leadership in Chicago's early labor movement. So central was this artisan tradition that it not only domi-nated Chicago's local production but extended beyond the work sphere to influence many facets of the everyday life of German workers. One can justifiably speak of a viable artisan culture sustained by a net-work of educational, supportive, fraternal, recreational, and political institutions.

At first glance, the situation had seemingly not changed much by 1900. Never before had so many German workers been concentrated in the skilled crafts.[13] The enormous number of almost 175,000 Ger-mans in the Chicago labor force affected practically all skilled jobs, which were often dominated by German workers: in four-fifths of seventy-five occupations listed in the published census for Chicago, German workers were the largest national group.[14] But decisive struc-tural changes had taken place under the impact of industrialization that severely affected the skilled crafts, even if in some instances indirectly and with a time lag. Thus small neighborhood bakeries continued to serve their customers well into the twentieth century, but from the 1880s on they came under heavy pressure from Chicago's West Side baking factories and often existed precariously as sweatshops.[15] This competition did not necessarily mean the loss of a job—the percentage of Germans among bakers remained high—but it resulted in financial and social degradation. In larger plants, it usually led to the redefinition of work, even if the occupational designation remained the same, thereby masking the actual changes of work content taking place. In this process of "homogenization of work"[16] the next step often was the replacement of skilled workers by recently arrived immigrant workers with lower skill levels and lower wage demands. Industrial changes thus led to the displacement of traditional skilled workers from the center of production.

A typical example is meat packing. From the early years in Chicago, it was concentrated in large industrial plants rather than small neighborhood butcher shops, especially after the establishment of the Union Stockyards on the South Side in the mid-1860s. Skilled butchers remained indispensable even in large-scale meat packing, however, until the system of subdividing the process into small repetitive tasks on a "disassembly" line was perfected in the 1870s. As a consequence, the percentage of German butchers working in the meatpacking houses drastically declined after 1880, and new immigrant workers of other nationalities took over their jobs. In 1900 only a few German skilled workers were left in highly specialized occupations, for example as splitters or sausage makers.

Industrial changes had different consequences for German unskilled workers. Their considerable importance in Chicago as well as in other midwestern towns tends to be overlooked.[17] Although the percentage of unskilled workers in Chicago's German labor force dropped from more than one-third in 1850 to one-fourth in 1900, Germans still contributed the largest number of "laborers," surpassing the Irish and Poles.[18] Whereas the majority of these common laborers in 1850 worked in building and construction, brickyards, breweries, and tanning, as well as in teaming, private services, and as day laborers on farms, they increasingly found employment in the expanding industrial plants in later years. Cases in point are again the baking and meat industries. The slow rise in the importance of occupations in these two industries from 1880 to 1900 for German workers was solely attributable to the growing number of unskilled workers finding employment in them, whereas the percentage of skilled workers declined during the same time.[19] Similarly, the high percentage of German workers in the labor force of the McCormick Reaper Works in the early 1880s—almost half of its workers were Germans in those years—can be explained only because many of them were unskilled or semiskilled, for example machine workers.[20] In contrast to skilled workers, these unskilled German laborers profited from the homogenization of work, which opened up new jobs.

Occupational changes occurring in the transition from the immigrant generation to the second generation point to a further consequence of the industrialization process. In 1880 the generational succession was still the order of the day in many trades.[21] Sons followed their fathers into such traditionally German trades as furniture making, brewing, baking, and butchering. In addition, tobacco and clothing—neighborhood-based sweatshop industries requiring low levels of skill or none at all—offered entry opportunities into the labor market for children and adolescents who had to help supplement the family income. By 1900, this occupational succession as well as the rush into those unskilled jobs were disrupted. The second generation tended to look for highly qualified positions in new growth areas, such as the metal, electrical, and chemical industries. The second typical development, already under way in 1880 but accelerating toward the turn of the century, was the move into low white-collar jobs. In 1900, second-generation heads of household were to be found in the lower middle class almost as frequently (36.2 percent) as in the skilled category of the working class (36.7 percent). If one includes unmarried sons and daughters working as clerks, salesmen, saleswomen, and typists, low white-collar employees outnumbered small businessmen and storekeepers—who are also counted in the lower middle class—by three to one. This preponderance as well as the changes in skilled work illustrate the improved occupational opportunities for the second generation. English-language skills particularly qualified one for low white-collar jobs.[22]

These occupational developments within Chicago's German working class do away with the myth of its quick disappearance. They indicate, however, that the artisan tradition had weakened by the turn of the century, so that it was now removed from the center of production. German immigrant workers clinging to their old trades and this tradition could in the future play only a marginal role in the Chicago labor movement. On the other hand, many first-generation immigrants, and especially the second generation, had adapted to the new system of industrial production and become a part of the modern American working class.

Community studies of small industrial towns during the early phase of industrialization have demonstrated the usefulness of integrating the analysis of family, household, workplace, culture, and politics. Enormous problems of numbers and scale arise, however, when applying this method to a city like Chicago. Using findings on the spatial differentiation of American cities during the nineteenth century, the Philadelphia Social History Project has worked out a sophisticated method of relating workplace and home and has contributed detailed and rich knowledge of their relationship.[23] Such a systematic procedure is so costly, however, that other solutions had to be found for the Chicago Project.

Fortunately, the development of Chicago's industrial locations is sufficiently known.[24] Since the middle of the nineteenth century, an industrial belt formed along both branches of the Chicago River and gradually extended into the adjacent neighborhoods. In addition, in cases where industrial plants were located beyond settled areas, neighborhoods soon developed with an occupational structure that clearly indicates that the overwhelming majority of their populations worked in the nearby industries.

This obvious connection between the location of home and work suggests that it should be possible through selected neighborhood analyses to find similar evidence for other occupations. Such a procedure also allows for closely relating the work sphere and the everyday life of workers. Neighborhood analysis has therefore been a central tool in the work of the Chicago Project;[25] for it was in the neighborhoods that the population experienced, and reacted to, structural industrial and social changes. Such an analysis cannot be confined to reconstructing the demographic and industrial structures but has to include institutions, group activities, manifestations of the political will, leisure, and social events. The study of the network of communication in a neighborhood will thus reveal how people tried to cope with larger structural changes.

Although German households were predominantly working class even at the turn of the century, the three German neighborhoods on the North, Northwest, and Southwest Sides showed substantial differences in their social composition. To a certain degree, they all needed the same basic supplies and services and offered job opportunities in similar occupations: in decentralized trades such as building and construction, in craft shops (shoemakers, plumbers), in stores (bakeries, meat markets, retail, hardware, and grocery), and in trades that employed children and youths (tobacco, cigarmaking, clothing). But characteristic neighborhood differences of industrial location created occupational and class differences. The North Side, the oldest of Chicago's German neighborhoods, had a distinctly middle-class structure even in 1880.[26] Small businessmen, stores, and craft shops were strongly represented, and skilled workers employed in machine shops, shoemaking, baking, furniture-making, printing, and publishing predominated in the working class. It was here that the emerging German-American middle class lived, setting itself apart from other classes even within the neighborhood by its ability to afford the more expensive homes closer to Lake Michigan, whereas unskilled laborers working in the lumber and coal yards along the North Branch of the Chicago River lived in the cheaper quarters bordering the industrial belt. In contrast, leather and tanning, iron and steel, furniture and machines were the large industries employing German workers on the Northwest Side, where home and neighborhood industries were relatively less important. It was a typical working-class neighborhood, with craftsmen, skilled workers, and laborers equally represented. The Southwest Side, although also a working-class neighborhood, differed from the Northwest Side in that its occupational structure was almost exclusively dominated by the metal industries and the lumber yards on the South Branch of the Chicago River. Its percentage of unskilled workers was the highest of the three German neighborhoods.

The associational life of Chicago's German community was also clearly embedded in the neighborhoods. Except for a few efforts, most of them futile, by the German middle class to establish citywide elite organizations, all institutions and associations were founded on a neighborhood basis. (The German Aid Society, founded in 1854, was the only exception, probably because it reached across classes, supporting needy individuals and families especially from the lower classes.[27]) Parishes are the most obvious example, but gymnastics clubs, lodges, and even building associations followed the same pattern. Geographic and population expansion did not result in membership congestion in the well-established institutions. Instead, similar associations were founded—again on a neighborhood basis—which helps to explain the hundreds of German parishes, aid societies, lodges, singing societies, and ethnic, literary, and educational clubs listed in the Chicago directories around 1900. This diversity of neighborhood institutions made for a dense network of institutional and personal interrelations.

Institutions of the working class were no exception. To the contrary, their dependence on the workplace as well as on neighborhood life was especially close. Trade unions were founded in the working-class neighborhoods where the shops were located and the workers lived. Thus the strongholds of the largely German Furniture Workers' local were the North and Northwest sides, whereas the Metal Workers Union had its largest membership on the Southwest Side. The Socialist Labor party also depended upon a strong neighborhood basis for its election successes from 1877 to 1880, and the working-class neighborhoods of the Southwest and Northwest sides sent socialist aldermen to the city council. Demonstrations, boycotts, and strikes were successful to the extent that determined workers were supported by a neighborhood population and its institutions. Even if such institutions (such as gymnastics clubs) served other purposes, they openly sympathized with the concerns of the working class. Thus the Aurora Turnverein on Chicago's Northwest Side as well as other gymnastics clubs in Chicago raised funds for the defense of the anarchists in 1886. August Spies was a member of the Aurora Turnverein, which let the Lehr- und Wehr-Verein, an armed workers club, use its facilities for meetings.[28] There were also lodges with an overwhelmingly working-class constituency, such as the Harugari and the Sons of Hermann, in contrast to the Freemasons and Odd Fellows, which catered to the middle class. These and other associations were the institutional expression of an alternative cultural system functioning in working-class neighborhoods.[29] But the neighborhood basis also reinforced the ethnic character of labor organizations. It has been argued repeatedly that German immigrant workers deliberately held fast to their national culture and language.[30] There can be no doubt, however, that the labor movement in the Gilded Age was successful only on the basis of such neighborhood solidarity. It was much more difficult, for example, to effect permanent organization in large industrial plants—in the bread bakeries, meat-packing houses, or metal works—that usually lacked the determined support of a homogeneous neighborhood.

Changes occurring as a consequence of the further geographic and population expansion of the city point toward the gradual weakening of this close relationship between workplace and neighborhood everyday life. By 1900 the move of Germans to outlying areas had taken on major dimensions. Only 45.5 percent of the German population still lived within the Chicago city limits of 1880, whereas more than half lived in areas incorporated since then. This trend does not mean that the population in the old neighborhoods declined. In fact, more Germans lived within the old city limits in 1900 than in 1880. The population increase accounts for much of this outward move. But the relative importance of the old neighborhoods (including working-class neighborhoods) had begun to change because the working class, especially on the North and Northwest Sides, contributed most to the move to outlying areas. In 1900, more than two-thirds of German working-class households in these parts of town were located there, thus over-representing German workers. The well-established families with middle-aged fathers as well as the second generation tended to live farther from the center of the city. The relocation of industries, the expansion of the industrial belt, the increase of other ethnic groups, such as the Poles on the Northwest Side, the availability of land and homes, and the desire to escape congested districts all contributed to this development. As a result, German workers became dispersed over larger areas and had to cover longer distances between their homes and places of work. Thus the world of work on the one hand and family and home on the other were becoming more distinctly separated; and as time went on, common working-class activities such as social gatherings, picnics, and celebrations would no longer be bound into the everyday life of German working-class neighborhoods. This development raises the issue of the changing function of German working-class culture.

Working-class culture can be defined as the material and lived manifestations of common norms and values of the working class. This general definition, however, does not help clarify, but rather tends to obscure, the problems that arise when one tries to analyze a specific working-class culture in a concrete social setting. German workers in Chicago were only one element within a heterogeneous working-class population in the city, whose important ethnic differences indicate the lack of a common cultural tradition. The emergence of an American tradition was therefore accompanied by the more or less intense clash of various national backgrounds. Such instances of potential and often open conflict represent an additional determinant for the position of German working-class culture in Chicago (in contrast to the situation in Germany). It supplements the central problems of this class's relationship to the dominant society as well as to the German-American middle class, which viewed German cultural traditions in a different light. Several problems arise from this position of German working-class culture in a complex social order.[31]

In its explicit restriction to one class, the term "working-class culture" implies alternative and even oppositional meanings. Its institutional strongholds are, of course, the economic, social, and political organizations of the labor movement. A new tradition had yet to be created, and it was articulated in deliberate contrast to the values of the dominant culture. In this process, however, working-class culture of necessity had to take into account the existing social structure and cultural forms, even if it rejected them. Thus it took advantage of the social spaces not of central importance to, and therefore not tightly controlled by, the hegemonic society.[32] In addition, it incorporated lower-class traditions of feudal and early bourgeois origin by reinterpreting them for its own purposes. Thus working-class culture was embedded in lower-class lifestyles and in a folk culture, from which it drew in significant ways and with which it had much in common.

Therefore it is imperative to know the everyday life experience of German workers to which German working-class culture in Chicago referred. The process of becoming settled initially meant finding a means of existence: permanent work, if possible, as well as a decent place to live. But it also meant adapting to the hectic pace of an urban industrial world and to the ways of life in an ethnic working-class neighborhood. To cope with the new circumstances, immigrant workers tried to keep to familiar habits. It was not so much the material and the work sphere, however, that provided emotional security, because one was forced to adapt to conditions, for example, working in a new occupation. Emotional security was sought instead in the sphere of kin, family, and friends. A young coppersmith, Nikolaus Schwenck, immigrating to Chicago in 1855, was typical in relying on a large circle of relatives and friends from his hometown in Württemberg for his first social contacts.[33] Likewise, all German associations independent of their special goals sought common forms of leisure-time activities and entertainment so long as their membership belonged largely to the lower middle and working classes. Picnics were family events for young and old folks; dancing, drinking, games, and lotteries prevailed. Picnics held by labor associations characteristically offered additional elements such as a demonstration preceding the event, pictorial or performed agitation or a political speech, using the celebration to present and enact a specific political culture. In using folk cultural forms on such occasions, these picnics continued common German lower-class traditions and thus were able to relate to a public that transcended the more limited labor movement.

This relation between working-class culture and the everyday life of the lower classes has important repercussions for the question of the transfer of such traditions. After all, the young generation growing up in working-class households in urban Chicago had never known the original cultural forms but only their modifications. Different ways of life prevailed in Chicago, and the dominant society offered a different cultural tradition. A dispute in the Schwabenverein in 1905 concerning the selection of a new park for the annual Cannstatter Volksfest exemplifies how much the second generation of German immigrants was already attracted by American culture.[34] To the younger generation, profit-oriented institutions of popular mass entertainment seemed fully compatible with the festival, whose traditional folk character the older generation wanted to preserve. Changes in the everyday life of the German-American lower and middle classes in this case as in other instances show that German working-class culture had to relate to a changed population as well as to a changed tradition.

Since German workers in Chicago used familiar German traditions, including the German language, they were part of a cultural tradition transcending class lines in which the German-American middle class and the emerging small upper class participated as well. The large percentage of German workers in Chicago at the same time resulted in German cultural traditions having a significant impact on the city's working class. Thus the ambiguous relation between working-class culture and ethnicity contains two aspects that should be kept separate. On the one hand, a common cultural tradition tended to blur class antagonisms within Chicago's German community. On the other hand, the narrow self-interests of one national group within the working class threatened to prevent the solidarity of all workers.

A consensus among the Germans of Chicago did indeed exist, but it was confined to efforts at preserving German instruction in the public schools, fighting Sunday and temperance laws, and protecting basic forms of the German way of life and of German conviviality. Whenever coalitions, which had been formed for these purposes, were to be put to political uses, they broke apart. Parochial schools, important mediators of German language and instruction, were not tolerated by the German labor movement for this function, but instead were heavily attacked for ideological reasons. Likewise, the labor movement clearly judged German associations by their specific functions and goals, in contrast to efforts by leaders of the German-American middle class after 1900 to exploit ethnicity for political purposes and to stem the impending fossilization and disintegration of cultural traditions through an ethnic interest group. The labor movement, by contrast,

202 Ethnicity and Politics

regarded itself as the guardian of classical German culture, to which it claimed to add significant new impulses, whereas it detected only Babbit-like qualities in the profit-oriented German-American middle class.[35]

That German workers in the Chicago labor movement drew upon their cultural tradition does not mean they were ethnically isolated. What else should they have fallen back on? In the second half of the nineteenth century, there was no generally established working-class culture in America, into which German and other immigrants could have been readily integrated. After 1880, immigrants and their children made up more than 80 percent of the working class in Chicago. They contributed diverse cultural traditions to a working class continually supplemented and changed by new national groups, which actively participated in the emergence of an "American" working-class culture. Therefore it is not the question of ethnic fragmentation that should be the center of attention, but the question of how particular traditions were overcome by incorporating them into an emerging common tradition. The decisive test for the success or failure of such incorporation occurred during the transition from the immigrant culture to a German-American culture already changed by various influences in the adopted country.

This question brings up the issue of the relation between German working-class culture and the dominant American culture. This relation was ambivalent. On the one hand German working-class culture fully accrued American political rights and liberties as guaranteed by the Constitution as an inalienable part of the country's political culture. The Declaration of Independence, above all, was referred to as the symbol of the continuity between radical European and American republican traditions. Like other groups in American society, German workers engaged themselves to their utmost for the preservation of these rights during the Civil War, when they, along with artisans and liberal intellectuals, joined the Union army in disproportionate numbers, or during the Gilded Age, when they actively opposed the all-powerful plutocracy. Likewise, German workers defended the public school system as guarantor of the liberal education of all citizens. "Free" Sunday schools were founded by German workers' clubs in Chicago in the late 1880s, when this goal seemed to be threatened by church institutions pursuing their own particular interests.[36]

On the other hand, German working-class culture was faced with the twofold pressure to modify German traditions in the direction of a puritanical Protestant way of life and to give up its class character as incommensurate with American reality. In the historical process this pressure varied. The culmination of an oppositional German working-class culture in Chicago certainly occurred in the 1870s and 1880s, when German workers were still at the center of Chicago's working class and when they were severely threatened by the structural changes in industry and society taking place at that time. After other immigrant groups had begun to displace German workers from the center of production, German working-class culture began to lose its oppositional stance. These changes are usually taken as indicators of social mobility and successful integration. There can be no doubt, of course, that German working-class culture, as German immigrant culture in general, with the ascent of the second generation began to lose its most important medium, the German language. It would be wrong, however, to see this development as the indiscriminate immersion into the American melting pot. Rather, it has to be seen in the context of larger economic and social changes, in the course of which the integration into the dominant society took different directions depending on the social and class positions people held. Thus German working-class culture did not disappear without a trace into a homogeneous middle-class culture but contributed to an American working-class culture differing in significant ways from the norms and values of the hegemonic society.

Notes

1. The literature dealing with these issues is widely dispersed and often only touches upon them. See Daniel Bell, *Marxian Socialism in the United States* (Princeton: Princeton University Press, 1967); Morris Hillquit, *History of Socialism in the United States* (New York: Dover, 1971); John R. Commons et al., *History of Labour in the United States*, vol. 2 (New York: Macmillan, 1918); Philip S. Foner, *History of the Labor Movement in the United States*, vols. 1 and 2 (New York: International Publishers, 1947, 1955); John H. M. Laslett and Seymour Martin Lipset, eds., *Failure of a Dream? Essays in the History of American Socialism* (New York: Anchor Press, 1974); Philip S. Foner and Brewster Chamberlin, eds., *Friedrich A. Sorge's Labor Movement in the United States: A History of the American Working Class from Colonial Times to 1890* (Westport, Conn.: Greenwood Press, 1977); Hermann Schlüter, *Die Anfänge der deutschen Arbeiterbewegung in Amerika* (Stuttgart: J. H. W. Dietz, Nachf., 1907); Hermann Schlüter, *Die Internationale in Amerika: Ein Beitrag zur Geschichte der Arbeiterbewegung in den Vereinigten Staaten* (Chicago: Deutsche Sprachgruppe der Sozialistischen Partei der Vereinigten Staaten, 1918); John H. M. Laslett, *Labor and the Left: A Study of Socialist and Radical Influences in the American Labor Movement, 1881–1924* (New York: Basic Books, 1970).
2. For a review of the literature on German immigration, see Willi Paul Adams, ed., *Die deutschsprachige Auswanderung in die Vereinigten Staaten. Berichte über Forschungsstand und Quellenbestände* (Berlin: John F. Kennedy-Institut für Nordamerika-

studien, Freie Universität Berlin, 1980). For an overview of German immigration and problems of integration, see Kathleen Neils Conzen, "Germans," in Stephan Thern-strom et al., eds., *Harvard Encyclopedia of American Ethnic Groups* (Cambridge, Mass.: Belknap Press of Harvard University Press, 1980), 405–25.

3. For the most relevant recent example, see Theodore Hershberg, ed., *Phila-delphia: Work, Space, Family, and Group Experience in the 19th Century* (New York: Oxford University Press, 1981).

4. Examples are Bruce Laurie, *Working People of Philadelphia, 1800–1850* (Philadelphia: Temple University Press, 1980); Alan Dawley, *Class and Community: The Industrial Revolution in Lynn* (Cambridge, Mass.: Harvard University Press, 1976); Paul Faler, "Workingmen, Mechanics, and Social Change: Lynn, Massachusetts, 1800–1860" (Ph.D. diss., University of Wisconsin, 1971); Daniel J. Walkowitz, *Worker City, Company Town: Iron and Cotton-Worker Protest in Troy and Cohoes, New York, 1855–84* (Urbana: University of Illinois Press, 1978); John Cumbler, *Working-Class Community in Industrial America: Work, Leisure, and Struggle in Two Industrial Cit-ies, 1880–1930* (Westport, Conn.: Greenwood Press, 1979); Susan E. Hirsch, *Roots of the American Working Class: The Industrialization of Crafts in Newark, 1800–1860* (Philadelphia: University of Pennsylvania Press, 1978); John Bodnar, *Immigration and Industrialization: Ethnicity in an American Mill Town, 1870–1940* (Pittsburgh: Uni-versity of Pittsburgh Press, 1977).

5. An exception is Kathleen Neils Conzen, *Immigrant Milwaukee, 1836–1860: Accommodation and Community in a Frontier City* (Cambridge, Mass.: Harvard Uni-versity Press, 1976). Her study does not go beyond 1860, however, and therefore does not cover the important period of industrialization during the Gilded Age.

6. Analyses of the manuscript schedules of the U.S. census of population were made for the years 1850, 1880, and 1900. For 1850, the entire German population was included; for the other years representative samples were drawn of 2,222 German households with more than 11,000 persons in 1880 and of 6,116 households, including 1,532 German households with more than 8,000 persons, in 1900. Numerous other sources were used including German- and English-language labor and middle-class newspapers as well as trade union publications, records of associations, government publications, and private papers and letters.

7. For the history of Chicago in the nineteenth century, see the "traditional" work by Bessie Louise Pierce, *A History of Chicago*, 3 vols. (New York: Knopf, 1937–57). The following figures were taken from there as well as from the published census and the Chicago Project samples.

8. For a more detailed analysis of the demographic structure of the German popu-lation and working class, see Hartmut Keil, "Chicago's German Working Class in 1900," in Hartmut Keil and John B. Jentz, eds., *German Workers in Industrial Chicago, 1850–1910: A Comparative Perspective* (DeKalb, Ill.: Northern Illinois University Press, 1983), 19–36.

9. According to the published census of 1910, the relationship between the first and second generations was close to 1:2 already; the exact percentages are 36.3 and 63.7 (Bureau of the Census, *U.S. Thirteenth Census 1910, Population I*, 946).

10. For studies of the impact of World War I, see Frederick C. Luebke, *Bonds of Loyalty: German-Americans and World War I* (DeKalb, Ill.: Northern Illinois University Press, 1974), and Melvin G. Holli, "The Great War Sinks Chicago's German *Kultur*," in Peter d'A. Jones and Melvin G. Holli, eds., *Ethnic Chicago* (Grand Rapids: Erdmans, 1981), 260–311.

11. For German migration to the United States, see Mack Walker, *Germany and the Emigration, 1816–1885* (Cambridge, Mass.: Harvard University Press, 1964); Peter Marschalck, *Deutsche Überseewanderung im 19. Jahrhundert* (Stuttgart: Klett, 1973); Wolfgang Köllmann and Peter Marschalck, "German Emigration to the United States," *Perspectives in American History* 7 (1973): 449–554.

12. Bruce C. Levine gives the following percentages of German-born in Chicago's work force in selected trades for 1860: painters 30 percent, masons, bricklayers, stone-cutters, and marble polishers 32 percent, carpenters 33 percent, blacksmiths 39 percent, saddlers and harness makers 53 percent, tailors 54 percent, tanners and curriers 55 percent, wagonmakers and carriage makers, butchers, and shoemakers 56 percent each, miscellaneous woodworkers 66 percent, bakers 68 percent, cabinetmakers 74 percent, cigarmakers 78 percent ("Free Soil, Free Labor, and *Freimänner*: German Chicago in the Civil War Era," in Keil and Jentz, eds., *German Workers*, 164).

13. Of all German heads of household, 41.2 percent were skilled workers in 1900; the respective figure for 1880 is 37.5 percent (Chicago Project samples).

14. Bureau of the Census, U.S. Twelfth Census 1900, Special Report, *Occupations at the Twelfth Census* (Washington, D.C., 1904), 516–19.

15. John B. Jentz, "Bread and Labor: Chicago's German Bakers Organize," *Chicago History* 12 (1983): 25–35.

16. The term is taken from David M. Gordon, Richard Edwards, and Michael Reich, *Segmented Work, Divided Workers: The Historical Transformation of Labor in the United States* (Cambridge: Cambridge University Press, 1982).

17. For a comparison of the social status of Germans in different American cities, see Nora Faires, "Occupational Patterns of German-Americans in Nineteenth-Century Cities," in Keil and Jentz, eds., *German Workers*, 37–51.

18. The absolute numbers were 17,442 Germans, 14,500 Irish, and 11,768 Poles (U.S. Bureau of the Census, Twelfth Census 1900, *Occupations at the Twelfth Census*, 517).

19. The percentage of all German workers employed in baking rose from 1.8 in 1880 to 2.0 in 1900. The number of skilled workers declined from 3.1 to 2.7 percent, whereas that of the unskilled increased from 0.6 to 1.2 percent. In meat, the percentage rose from 2.9 to 3.3, that of skilled workers declined from 5.1 to 3.9, and that of unskilled workers increased from 0.9 to 2.5 (Chicago Project samples for 1880 to 1900).

20. Hanns-Theodor Fuss, "Massenproduktion und Arbeiterbewusstsein. Deutsche Arbeiter in den McCormick Reaper Works, 1873–1886," *Amerikastudien/American Studies* 29 (1984): 149–68.

21. For the pattern of generational succession in two trades in Chicago, see J. B. Jentz, "Skilled Workers and Industrialization: Chicago's German Cabinet Makers and Machinists, 1880–1900," in Keil and Jentz, eds., *German Workers*, 73. For a thorough analysis of generational succession among the Irish and Germans in Philadelphia, see Bruce Laurie, Theodore Hershberg, and George Alter, "Immigrants and Industry: The Philadelphia Experience, 1850–1880," in Hershberg, ed., *Philadelphia*, 93–119.

22. Hartmut Keil, "Die deutsche Amerikaeinwanderung im städtisch-industriellen Kontext: das Beispiel Chicago 1880–1910," in Klaus J. Bade, ed., *Auswanderer—Wanderarbeiter—Gastarbeiter: Bevölkerung, Arbeitsmarkt und Wanderung in Deutschland seit der Mitte des 19. Jahrhunderts* (Ostfildern: Scripta Mercaturae Verlag, 1983), 378–405; Keil and Jentz, "German Workers in Industrial Chicago: The Transformation of Industries and Neighborhoods in the Late 19th Century," Paper presented at the Organization of American Historians meeting, Detroit, April 1–4, 1981.

23. See, for example, Theodore Hershberg, Harold E. Cox, Dale B. Light, Jr., and Richard R. Greenfield, "The 'Journey-to-Work': An Empirical Investigation of Work, Residence and Transportation, Philadelphia, 1850 and 1880"; and Stephanie W. Greenberg, "Industrial Location and Ethnic Residential Patterns in an Industrializing City: Philadelphia, 1880," both in Hershberg, ed., *Philadelphia*.

24. Again, the respective chapters in Pierce's three-volume *History of Chicago* provide the best general introduction.

25. For a more detailed discussion of this method, see Keil and Jentz, "German Working-Class Culture in Chicago: A Problem of Definition, Method, and Analysis," *Gulliver: German-English Yearbook* 9 (1981): 128–47.

26. Keil, "Chicago's German Working Class in 1900"; Christiane Harzig, "Chicago's German North Side, 1880–1900: The Structure of a Gilded Age German Neighborhood," in Keil and Jentz, eds., *German Workers*, 127–44.

27. For an analysis of these support activities see Jentz and Keil, "From Immigrants to Urban Workers: Chicago's German Poor in the Gilded Age and Progressive Era, 1883–1908," *Vierteljahrschrift für Sozial- und Wirtschaftsgeschichte* 68 (1981): 52–97.

28. Christine Heiss, "German Radicals in Industrial America: The Lehr- und Wehr-Verein in Gilded Age Chicago," in Keil and Jentz, eds., *German Workers*, 206–23.

29. Richard Oestreicher in this context uses the term "competing cultural systems" ("Industrialization, Class, and Competing Cultural Systems: Detroit Workers, 1875–1890," in Keil and Jentz, eds., *German Workers*, 52–69).

30. Severe criticism was voiced by Friedrich Engels and some of his correspondents; see Karl Marx and Friedrich Engels, *Letters to Americans, 1848–1895: A Selection* (New York: International Publishers, 1953).

31. Hartmut Keil und Heinz Ickstadt, "Elemente einer deutschen Arbeiterkultur in Chicago zwischen 1880 und 1890," *Geschichte und Gesellschaft* 5 (1979): 103–24; Keil and Jentz, "German Working-Class Culture in Chicago," and Klaus Ensslen and H. Ickstadt, "German Working-Class Culture in Chicago: Continuity and Change in the Decade from 1900 to 1910," in Keil and Jentz, eds., *German Workers*, 236–52.

32. The term "hegemonic society" is taken from Raymond Williams, see his "Base and Superstructure in Marxist Cultural History," *New Left Review* 82 (1973): 3–16.

33. Letters of Nikolaus Schwenck, Schwenck private archives, Langenau, Württemberg.

34. "Cannstatter Volksfest," *Chicagoer Arbeiter-Zeitung*, January 19, 1905.

35. See Keil and Ickstadt, "Elemente einer deutschen Arbeiterkultur," and Ensslen and Ickstadt, "German Working-Class Culture in Chicago."

36. For a description of the free schools in Chicago, see "Die socialistischen Sonntagsschulen in Chicago," *Sonntagsblatt der New Yorker Volks-Zeitung*, July 28, 1889, pp. 4–5.

14.

Images of German Immigrants in the United States and Brazil, 1890–1918: Some Comparisons

FREDERICK C. LUEBKE

IN THE 1890s, following a decade of unprecedented immigration from Europe, the United States experienced a period in which national identity was greatly stressed. The term "Americanization" came into frequent usage as many citizens, privately and through various organizations, stressed conformity to the dominant culture in language, manners, and religious belief.

During these same years a similar development, in some respects stronger than in the United States, could be detected in Brazil. In 1889 the empire of Brazil ended when Pedro II went into exile and Brazilian leaders introduced a republican form of government. During the preceding decade Brazil, like the United States, had experienced heavy immigration from Europe.[1] The abolition of slavery in 1888 had created a labor shortage, chiefly in the central and southern states, that the government had sought to relieve through the recruitment of Italian, Spanish, Portuguese, and German immigrants. During the 1890s the Brazilian Republic, unsure of itself in its first years, experienced a wave of nativism much like that in the United States. The new Brazilian leaders, motivated strongly by doctrines of Comtean Positivism, insisted on a new national unity. They felt strongly that immigrants should resist the natural tendency to remain separate. To speak a different language, to wear different clothing, to eat different foods, to attend different schools, and to worship a different god all seemed undesirable because such behavior threatened to alter national identity and to undermine the confidence of the republicans to govern their huge, diverse, and undeveloped country.[2]

German immigrants and their children were conspicuous in both countries. Approximately 5 million Germans had arrived in the United States during the nineteenth century. In each of the peak years of 1854 and 1882 more than two hundred thousand persons arrived. Although 85 percent of the Germans settled in the northeastern quarter of the country, they could be found in all states of the Union. Two-thirds lived in urban places (a proportion much higher than that for the American population generally at that time), but they were also strongly attracted to agriculture, especially dairy farming in the Midwest. By the end of the century there were about 8 million first- and second-generation Germans in the United States, roughly 10 percent of the total population. Unusually diverse in origin, occupation, residence patterns, and religious belief, they were easily the largest non-English speaking group in America.[3]

The Brazilian pattern was similar but on a much smaller scale. The German immigration to Brazil had begun in the 1820s, largely as a consequence of vigorous recruitment efforts sponsored by the Brazilian government. The annual totals seldom exceeded two thousand, yet after seventy-five years the Germans had multiplied and prospered until they numbered nearly four hundred thousand persons, mostly Brazilian-born and German-speaking. Although important colonies developed in the large cities and seaports of Brazil, the majority of Teuto-Brazilians (as they were called) settled in rural regions, where they founded exclusive settlements chiefly in the two southernmost states of Rio Grande do Sul and Santa Catarina, in which they accounted for one-fifth of the population by 1910. There, even more than in the United States, they created a society within a society—a large, isolated, diverse, structured community with its own values, attitudes, language, and folkways. They adapted their agricultural practices to subtropical realities, raised large families, and built churches, schools, and towns. Like the German-Americans, the Teuto-Brazilians were of diverse provincial origins and were divided between the Catholic and Protestant faiths. Like their American counterparts, the Teuto-Brazilians developed a substantial German-language press and an amazing array of voluntary associations.[4]

Stereotypes naturally developed in both countries. Each receiving society tended to regard the Germans in their midst as a unified group with common characteristics. Provincial differences, linguistic variations, religious divisions, and social and political distinctions were usually lost on the native-born, who tended to lump all German immigrants together on the basis of their presumably common language. Since

Germany did not exist as a unified state until 1871, a German was simply someone who spoke the German language.

There was no uniform or consistent content to the images of the German immigrant. Wealthy and educated Americans, for example, generally registered more favorable impressions than did the lower classes. Rarely rubbing shoulders with ordinary newcomers, these Americans more often encountered persons who had adapted quickly to American ways and who, like themselves, were educated and successful. Moreover, their impressions were conditioned by notions about Germany itself, such as the preeminence of German learning. In the nineteenth century, approximately ten thousand Americans had studied in various German universities. They discovered a quality of scholarship, a depth of thought, and an appreciation for learning and academic freedom that led them to place Germany on a cultural pedestal. Although such impressions of Germany and its institutions must be separated from ideas about German immigrants, they contributed to a generally high regard for them among the upper strata of society.[5]

The ordinary American of the nineteenth century, however, had little contact with the products of German universities and still less with their books and essays. He gained his impressions of things German from the immigrants who lived next door or on a nearby farm, worked in the same factory, shopped in his store, clipped his beard, repaired his shoes, or deposited savings in his bank.

Perhaps the most prominent elements in the American stereotype of German immigrants were industriousness, thrift, and honesty—admirable virtues in the American value system. The German seemed strongly attached to his family; he was orderly, disciplined, and stable. A bit too authoritarian by American standards, he was nonetheless admired for his ability to achieve material success through hard work. Similarly attractive was his reputation for mechanical ingenuity. The Germans were usually perceived as an intelligent people, though somewhat plodding in their mental processes. And if they tended to be unimaginatively thorough, they sometimes also seemed stubborn and graceless in manner. But the German wife and mother was commonly regarded as a model of cleanliness and efficiency; her daughter was valued as a reliable house servant or maid. Although some native Americans thought that the Germans treated their women badly, on the whole they considered these newcomers desirable additions to the American population.

But there were negative elements in the image as well. Some felt that Germans were unwarrantably proud of their origins and culture.

Others had ambivalent feelings about German festivities. It seemed as though the Germans had a celebration for every occasion, complete with parades and contests both athletic and cultural. Even their church affairs often took a festive air. Especially offensive was what puritanical Americans perceived as abandoned dancing and boorish swilling of beer, especially on the Sabbath, the day that God had set aside for worship, rest, and spiritual contemplation. Still others were put off by the apparent radicalism of German immigrants. The American labor movement seemed to have among its leaders an unusually large number of Germans who preached alien doctrines of communism, anarchism, and varying degrees of socialism. Impressions drawn from such unfortunate and widely publicized affairs as the Chicago Haymarket Riot of 1886 strengthened the image of at least some Germans as dangerous revolutionaries.[6]

Clashes between native and immigrant cultures produced some of the most potent political issues of the late nineteenth century. Although many German immigrants were interested in political reform, economic development, and the tariff and currency questions, they responded more strongly to issues related to ethnocultural conflict. In addition to political and economic liberties, they wanted social and cultural freedom. By the 1890s prohibition had become the dominant political manifestation of cultural conflict. Woman suffrage, Sabbatarianism, and efforts to regulate (if not close down) parochial school education were closely related issues that were capable of producing remarkable, though temporary, levels of uniformity in the voting behavior of German immigrants.[7]

Ethnocultural politics had an impact on nativist attitudes. Awareness of ethnic group identities was greatly intensified among immigrants and nativists alike. Thinking in stereotypes and symbols was encouraged; tolerance and understanding diminished. The live-and-let-live attitudes common in earlier decades were weakened by organized political action. Changes in attitudes toward immigrants were also fostered by some of the most respected social scientists of the day, whose study of the immigration question led them to conclude that socially undesirable characteristics were hereditary and were more typical of some ethnic groups than others. Both negative and positive qualities were thus thought to be fixed or rigid.[8]

Still, as such ideas gained currency at the end of the nineteenth century, the German-Americans fared well. Although there were dissents from the general view, most Americans considered the Germans to be a desirable people. Moreover, as racial thinking became increas-

Germantown as "Germanopolis." The title page of the souvenir program for the 225th anniversary of the first German settlement in America reveals the proud—and sometimes haughty—mood of German-Americans at that time. The parades in celebration of "German Day" in 1908 were particularly elaborate and fancy and in Germantown the foundation-stone of the Pastorius monument was laid. However, at the same time the ethnic press began to take note of the fact that the reduced numbers of immigrants coming to the United States from Germany threatened to alter the character and substance of the German-American community. (Roughwood Collection)

ingly common early in the twentieth century, some German-American intellectuals were stimulated, in countless speeches and articles, to laud and magnify the achievements of their group, ranging from such early contributions as those of Baron von Steuben in the Revolutionary War to the more recent accomplishments of such engineers as John Roebling and his American-born son, who designed and built the Brooklyn Bridge. This indulgence in cultural chauvinism was partly an effort to lay claim to a share in American greatness, but it was also intended to balance Anglo-Saxonist notions of racial superiority and preeminence in world affairs.[9]

By the beginning of World War I, the leaders of the rapidly assimilating German element in the United States, understandably proud of their cultural heritage, were encouraged in their ethnocentrism by the stereotypes native-born Americans generally held of them. Some were even prompted to promote their heritage as a culture counter to the dominant Anglo-American. But this was a dangerous course in a period of resurgent nativism. Deviations from American norms were but lightly tolerated by persons unwilling or unable to distinguish cultural chauvinism from the political or nationalistic variety.

In Brazil, German immigrants were generally perceived favorably in the nineteenth century, especially by the ruling classes, who regarded them as desirable additions to Brazilian society. The Germans, they thought, would not only bring valued skills to Brazil but would also "whiten" the population, which in 1890 was only 44 percent white. The Brazilian elite, like the American, was strongly influenced by racist theories based on presumably scientific criteria that gave the highest rating to so-called Nordic peoples, which, of course, included the Germans.[10] As in the United States, they were admired for their industry, orderliness, and stability.

Even though the Germans were welcomed and valued for the contributions they were making to Brazilian development, the Brazilian image, even more than the American, rested on inadequate and distorted information, rhetorical exaggeration, and myth[11] because the multiracial Brazilian society was considerably more divided than the American between rich and poor, the literate and the illiterate. German immigrant society in Brazil was both more concentrated spatially and more isolated socially than in the United States, especially in the rural settlements. Moreover, the German enclaves in the Brazilian cities were often dominated by wealthy, educated *Reichsdeutsche* (subjects of the German kaiser). Such persons—bankers, industrialists, merchants, journalists, technicians, and various representatives of large German firms—frequently considered life in Brazil to be temporary. Moreover, they were often contemptuous of Luso-Brazilian culture,[12] an attitude that did not go unnoticed by the Brazilians with whom they were in frequent contact.

Some Teuto-Brazilian leaders also shared this attitude of condescension for Brazilian culture. Feeding on ethnocentric German nationalist propaganda of the turn of the century, they considered Brazilian culture to be decidedly inferior to their own. In one example of such literature, a German writer on Brazil recommended stout resistance to assimilation on the ground that Brazilian culture was worthless. "What the Lusitanians have created in America," he wrote, "is a country that has produced nothing memorable in any field, including economics and culture; in the economic sphere . . . this state . . . is crippled, . . . a poorly organized community of seventeen million people. And these seventeen million, who rule over a rich and productive area the size of Europe, are unable to colonize anything, nor are they able to establish a properly functioning means of transportation and communication, regulate their financial affairs, guarantee justice, build a fleet, nor maintain an army other than one that is really nothing more than a privileged band of robbers."[13] This statement is so extreme, of course, that it cannot be considered typical. Still, many Teuto-Brazilians regarded Brazilian culture as weak and ineffectual; the Luso-Brazilians themselves seemed to combine indolence and ignorance with ridiculous conceit. The Portuguese language was useful to know for practical reasons, they thought, but it seemed to offer few literary treasures compared to the German.[14] Like the most extravagant of German-American cultural chauvinists, some Teuto-Brazilians insisted that the Germans would perform their best service as loyal citizens by infusing the culture of their adopted country with their presumably superior German qualities. If German language and culture were allowed to fade from use, they argued, Brazil would be deprived of the invaluable German sense of duty and commitment to the work ethic. Many felt that the chances for successful maintenance of German language and culture were greater in Brazil than in the United States, where, they believed, Anglo-American Protestant culture was so strong that German immigrants were virtually unable to withstand its assimilative power.[15]

The status of the Germans in Brazilian society was not a topic of national debate. At most it was a regional issue discussed in the states where the Germans were concentrated and where upper-class perceptions were drawn primarily from the behavior of unrepresentative persons who perpetuated immigrant culture because it served their economic interests and psychological needs. Hence most educated Brazilians had little comprehension of the diversity of the German immigrant group, such as the differences that divided Catholics from Protestants or the disparate values and behaviors that distinguished the rural farmers from the urban workers and the economic and social elite. Moreover, they failed to understand how the physical environment, in conjunction with unique events in Brazilian history, promoted German isolationism. They were often mystified by the German spirit of separatism. They could not understand why the Germans would want to perpetuate their own language and culture indefinitely, especially since Brazilian culture was so attractive. In their view, Brazilian culture was open, tolerant, hospitable, adaptable, nonideological, humane, and free of rigid stratification. Brazilians, they believed, were motivated by a spirit of conciliation that sought compromise and rejected extremist measures. Above all, they considered themselves to be a nonviolent people.[16]

It is not possible to determine the extent to which the illiterate and unskilled classes in Brazilian society shared the concerns of the elite. Because of the isolated character of most German rural settlements, the social interaction of the Germans with other Brazilians was infrequent and often superficial. Furthermore, the Germans, like any other social group, differed widely in education, skills, health, and working habits, and large numbers experienced a deterioration in social and economic circumstances as they struggled to survive in the Brazilian environment. But the prevailing image was that the Germans were better housed and fed; that their system of private and parochial schools was often superior to what passed for public education in Brazil at that time; and that their homes and persons were cleaner and healthier. The Germans also seemed willing to work very hard, at least in contrast to the impoverished *caboclos* (persons of mixed Indian and Portuguese descent), among whom labor was intermittent and subject to frequent and long interruptions. One may assume that some Brazilians of the less privileged classes regarded the Germans with resentment and jealousy, but even so, there is no record of persistent cultural conflict based on ethnic differences.[17]

Of course, most Brazilians, rich or poor, white, black, mulatto, or *caboclo*, rarely thought about the Germans at all, much less in any systematic way. Similarly, the ordinary Teuto-Brazilian people went about their daily business, adapting to their surroundings and rarely giving the problems of assimilation any consideration. Like any other immigrant group, the Germans included many persons who were favorably disposed toward the language and culture of the host society and wanted to become part of it as quickly and painlessly as possible. Through daily contacts at work, at the store, at church, in school, or even in the home, they learned Portuguese readily. Whether they learned quickly or slowly depended upon individual circumstances and whether they had good or poor opportunities for interaction with speakers of Portuguese. Obviously, the isolated, exclusive rural colonies offered few such chances.

The existence of colonies where there were no Portuguese-language schools and where hundreds of second- and third-generation children had only rudimentary knowledge of Portuguese began to concern members of the Brazilian elite as the nineteenth century drew to a close. When they tried to identify typical German attitudes they naturally paid attention to the most conspicuous persons—the articulate German-Brazilian idealists who made speeches and wrote editorials, essays, and letters demanding their right to maintain their cultural separatism. Some persons in government were eager to break up the rural German enclaves, especially in Rio Grande do Sul, and to guarantee that new settlements would consist of a mixture of ethnic groups. Several efforts were made on both the state and national levels to restrict the growth of the colonies, but none were effective. In Santa Catarina the attack on immigrant institutions centered on private schools. For example, a law enacted in 1913, mild by present-day standards, ordered inspection by state officials and required that statistics of attendance be reported. It further specified that any schools that accepted subventions from either state or local governments were required to use Portuguese as the language of instruction.[18]

Luso-Brazilian fears that the Germans in the southern states were becoming so numerous that they could never be assimilated were heightened by much discussion of the so-called "German peril"—a commonly held belief that Germany had set itself upon a course of worldwide imperialism, based in part on the presence of German immigrants in various underdeveloped countries, including Brazil. At the same time, German aggressiveness was observed in the South Pacific, China, the Philippines, and the Caribbean. When in 1904 the Germans threatened the integrity of Venezuela in a debt-collection controversy, alarmists saw the first steps in a plan designed to create a German protectorate over southern Brazil and possibly a state that would be German in language and culture.[19]

Meanwhile in Germany the noisy, supernationalistic Pan-German League fueled new fears of German imperialism. In its widely distributed publications, this organization emphasized the cultural kinship of Germans all over the world and agitated vociferously for a colonial empire, for an enlarged navy, for war as an instrument of national policy, and for the preservation of German language and culture in German settlements overseas. A symptom rather than a cause of the rampant nationalism of the time, the Pan-German League was identified by English and French propagandists as the coordinating agency of German imperialism. Although the league's importance was grossly exaggerated, a flood of articles exposing the alleged Pan-Germanist conspiracy soon appeared in newspapers and periodicals in Europe and America. In Brazil, the noted Brazilian literary critic Sylvio Romero produced a lengthy tract entitled *O Allemanismo no sul do Brasil* (1906). Although he welcomed the influx of German immigrants,

Romero warned his countrymen of the German peril, outlined steps that could be taken to combat the threat, and urged that measures be taken to assimilate the German colonists into Brazilian society.[20] Other Brazilian writers expressed similar fears.

When world war engulfed Europe in 1914, the governments of both the United States and Brazil declared their neutrality. For most ordinary people in both countries, but especially in Brazil, the war in Europe was a distant affair of no particular consequence. It seemed to affect their daily lives in no direct or discernible fashion. Still, the war tended to evoke sympathies for one side or the other. Immigrants and their descendants naturally felt an emotional bond with their ancestral homeland and were convinced of the justice of its cause. Leaders of the German ethnic groups in both countries tended to be extravagant in their partisanship for Germany. Opinion among the educated or "established" groups in both the United States and Brazil, however, tended to favor the Allied powers. In Brazil, even more than in the United States, the press was disposed against Germany.

In 1917 the neutrality period came to an end when both the United States and Brazil declared war on Germany, ostensibly because vessels in their respective merchant marines had been torpedoed by German submarines. Although there were strong similarities in the behavior of Brazilians and Americans toward the Germans in their midst, the differences are striking.

In the United States, the war introduced a period of persecution for German-Americans. Many citizens of German origin were suspected of disloyalty. Individuals were harassed in various ways as the American people were swept up in a wave of anti-German feeling. In effect, there was a war against German language and culture. The climate of suspicion produced such measures as bans on German-composed music and the renaming of persons, foods, streets, parks, and towns. German-language instruction in the schools was restricted or eliminated, and German-language newspapers were closely regulated. There were scores of patriotic demonstrations in which German-Americans were forced to kiss the American flag, buy war bonds, or sing the national anthem. Ceremonies were held at which German-language books were burned. There were frequent instances of vandalism, beatings, arrests for allegedly unpatriotic utterances, and even a lynching of a German alien in Illinois.[21]

But the American behavior pales in contrast to the Brazilian. Following the Brazilian break in diplomatic relations with Germany in April 1917, German-Brazilians were victims of numerous destructive riots. Property damage was enormous as hundreds of residences, German-language newspaper offices, churches, schools, clubhouses, businesses, factories, and warehouses were damaged or destroyed by mobs. Six months later, following Brazil's declaration of war in October, a second series of riots resulted in more destruction. Martial law was declared in Rio de Janeiro and all southern states, where the great majority of the Teuto-Brazilians lived. All publications in the German language were forbidden. All instruction in the German language was banned in all schools at all levels. All German-language church services were outlawed. The president was empowered to seize the property of enemy aliens and to sell all goods consigned to them. Enforcement of these repressive measures was inconsistent and sometimes haphazard, but Brazilian behavior was remarkably violent and repressive compared with the American.[22]

It is easy to explain the Brazilian response to the German problem in terms of the classic stereotype of the Latin temperament as irresponsible, unrestrained, volatile, emotional, and spontaneous. But such a simple interpretation would explain very little. It is more useful to compare Teuto-Brazilian circumstances with the American. Although Germans represented a much smaller proportion of Brazilian society than of the American, their settlement patterns were more highly concentrated, exclusive, and isolated in Brazil. Usually better educated and often wealthier than the average Brazilian, the Germans were more slowly assimilated than in America. As northern Europeans, the Teuto-Brazilians, in contrast to the more numerous Italian, Spanish, and Portuguese immigrants in Brazil, had a language and a culture that were significantly different from those of the host society. Differentness in turn promoted a heightened sense of minority group identity in addition to a full complement of ethnic institutions—churches, schools, social organizations, a German-language press—that tended to be more closely tied to Germany than were their equivalents in the United States. All these elements combined to promote a general sense of cultural superiority that had no equal in the United States. Moreover, leadership was more often vested in *Reichsdeutsche*, whose bonds with Germany were close. Finally, compared to their American cousins, the Germans in Brazil wielded greater economic power, but their political influence was weaker.

The comparison should be carried a step further. Brazilian society, compared to the American, was more highly stratified: its rich were richer and its poor poorer. Its economy was less developed and its political institutions less democratic; it had no long-standing constitutional tradition. Illiteracy was pervasive. In such a social setting, the relatively prosperous Germans naturally tended to evoke antagonism, the Brazilian reputation for tolerance and goodwill notwithstanding.

As the spirit of nationalism swelled early in the twentieth century, the Brazilians, like the Americans, naturally acted on the basis of stereotypes that obscured individual differences and beclouded interpersonal relationships. Lacking both knowledge and understanding of the separatistic German subsociety, its manners and institutions, they demanded an unprecedented measure of conformity to established Brazilian ways. When war came in 1917, they treated their Germans with a severity surpassing anything generally experienced by Germans in the United States. Had the German-Americans been as divergent from the American norms as the Teuto-Brazilians were from Brazilian, it is likely that they too would have suffered from destructive riots, as did nineteenth-century Chinese in mining camps of the American West, or American blacks in Chicago, East St. Louis, Tulsa, and elsewhere in the immediate postwar period. Had their number been small enough, they might have been herded into concentration camps, as were Japanese-Americans in World War II.

Notes

1. For the Brazilian portion of this essay, I have relied heavily on my article "A Prelude to Conflict: The German Ethnic Group in Brazilian Society, 1890–1917," *Ethnic and Racial Studies* 6 (January 1983): 1–17. For accessible statistics of German immigration to Brazil, see Imre Ferenczi, comp., and Walter F. Willcox, ed., *International Migrations*, vol. 1: *Statistics* (New York: National Bureau of Economic Research, 1929), 695, 700–701.

2. Gilberto Freyre, *Order and Progress: Brazil from Monarchy to Republic*, ed. and trans. Rod W. Horton (New York: Knopf, 1970); E. Bradford Burns, *A History of Brazil* (New York: Columbia University Press, 1970), 250–54; Fernando de Azevedo, *Brazilian Culture* (New York: Knopf, 1966), 159–60, 414–18; Gilberto Freyre, *New World in the Tropics: The Culture of Modern Brazil* (New York: Knopf, 1966), 154; José Honório Rodrigues, *The Brazilians: Their Character and Aspirations* (Austin: University of Texas Press, 1967), 96. European immigration is placed within the context of racist thought and Brazilian nationalism in Thomas E. Skidmore, *Black into White: Race and Nationality in Brazilian Thought* (New York: Oxford University Press, 1974), 38–68, 124–44.

3. For the American portion of this essay, I have drawn extensively on my book *Bonds of Loyalty: German Americans and World War I* (DeKalb, Ill.: Northern Illinois University Press, 1974), esp. chap. 2. See also U.S., Bureau of the Census, *Historical Statistics of the United States, Colonial Times to 1957* (Washington, D.C.: U.S. Government Printing Office, 1960), 57; Edward P. Hutchinson, *Immigrants and Their Children, 1850–1950* (New York: Wiley, 1956), 123–24.

4. The most comprehensive study of Germans in Brazil is by Jean Roche, *La colonisation allemande et la Rio Grande do Sul* (Paris: Institut des Hautes Études de l'Amerique Latine, 1959). Among useful surveys is Karl Fouquet, *Der deutsche Einwanderer und sein Nachkommen in Brasilien: 1808–1824–1974* (São Paulo: Instituto Hans Staden, 1974). See also Karl H. Oberacker, Jr., *Der Deutsche Beitrag zum Aufbau der brasilianischen Nation* (São Paulo: Herder, 1955); Oberacker, "Die Deutschen in Brasilien," in Hartmut Fröschle, ed., *Die Deutschen in Lateinamerika*, (Tübingen: Erdmann, 1979), 169–300.

5. Walter P. Metzger, *Academic Freedom in the Age of the University* (New York: Columbia University Press, 1955), 93–107, 119–24; Clara E. Schieber, *The Transformation of American Sentiment toward Germany, 1870–1914* (Boston: Cornhill, 1923), 256.

6. Luebke, *Bonds of Loyalty*, 59–63.

7. A considerable literature has been produced on ethnocultural conflict in the last decades of the nineteenth century. See, as examples, Paul Kleppner, *The Cross of Culture: A Social Analysis of Midwestern Politics, 1850–1900* (New York: Free Press, 1970); Richard Jensen, *The Winning of the Midwest: Social and Political Conflict, 1888–1900* (Chicago: University of Chicago Press, 1971); and Frederick C. Luebke, *Immigrants and Politics: The Germans of Nebraska, 1880–1900* (Lincoln: University of Nebraska Press, 1969).

8. See the writings of Josiah Strong, Edward A. Ross, John R. Commons, Edward Channing, John W. Burgess, and many others. The voluminous reports of the Immigration Commission, published in 1911, also reflect these attitudes.

9. Luebke, *Bonds of Loyalty*, 47–51.

10. Skidmore, *Black into White*, 38–77. See especially the tendency of Brazilian writers to compare Brazilian experience with that of the United States, 69–77.

11. Egon Schaden, "Die Deutschbrasilianer—Ein Problem," *Staden-Jahrbuch: Beiträge zur Brasilkunde* 2 (1954):184.

12. Portuguese-Brazilian. The term derives from Lusitania, the name of the ancient province virtually coterminous with modern Portugal. Its usage is comparable to Anglo-American in the United States.

13. Walter Kundt, *Brasilien und seine Bedeutung für Deutschlands Handel und Industrie* (Berlin: Siemenroth, 1903), 18.

14. *Deutsche Zeitung* (Porto Alegre), October 20, 1917; Oskar Canstatt, *Brasilien: Land und Leute* (Berlin: Ernst Siegfried Mittler, 1877), 251, 416; Ernest Tonnelat, *L'expansion allemande hors d'Europe* (Paris: Armand Colin, 1908), 125, 141; Clarence H. Haring, *The Germans of South America* (New York: Oxford University Press, 1920), 43.

15. Schaden, "Die Deutschbrasilianer," 183–84; Emílio Willems, "Immigrants and Their Assimilation in Brazil," in T. Lynn Smith and Alexander Marchant, eds., *Brazil: Portrait of Half a Continent* (1951; rpt. Westport, Conn.: Greenwood Press, 1972), 209.

16. Rodrigues, *The Brazilians*, 60–61; A. H. Neiva and M. Diegues, Jr., "The Cultural Assimilation of Immigrants in Brazil," in W. D. Borrie, ed., *The Cultural Integration of Immigrants* (Paris: UNESCO, 1959), 185.

17. Although Emílio Willems is in no way responsible for my interpretation here, I have relied in part on his numerous works and have modified my views in consequence of private correspondence with him. See Emílio Willems, *A aculturaçaõ dos alemães no Brasil*, 2d ed. (São Paulo: Companhia Editora Nacional, 1980). Among his English-language articles, see his "Assimilation of German Immigrants in Brazil," *Sociology and*

Social Research 25 (1940):125–32, and "Some Aspects of Cultural Conflict and Acculturation in Southern Rural Brazil," *Rural Sociology* 7 (1942):375–84.

18. G. Entres, ed., *Der Staat Santa Catharina in Vergangenheit und Gegenwart unter besonderer Berücksichtigung des Deutschtums* (Florianopolis: Livraria Central, 1929), 223; Ferdinand Schröder, *Brasilien und Wittenberg: Ursprung und Gestaltung deutschen evangelischen Kirchentums in Brasilien* (Berlin: Walter de Gruyter, 1936), 356; Martin Braunschweig, "Die rechtliche Stellung des deutschen Schulwesens in Südbrasilien," in Bruno Geissler, ed., *Die Kulturbedeutung der evangelischen Kirche in Brasilien* (Leipzig: Hinrichs'sche Buchhandlung, 1922), 51.

19. Schieber, *Transformation of American Sentiment*, 88, 136, 171, 177, 178.

20. Mildred S. Wertheimer, *The Pan-German League, 1890–1914* (New York: Columbia University, 1924), 65, 74, 117, 126; Sylvio Romero, *O allemanismo no sul do Brasil, seus perigo e os meios de os conjurar* (Rio de Janeiro: Ribeiro, 1906). See also Skidmore, *Black into White*, 32–37, 56.

21. Luebke, *Bonds of Loyalty*; Carl Wittke, *German-Americans and the World War* (Columbus: Ohio State Historical Society, 1936); Donald R. Hickey, "The Prager Affair: A Study in Wartime Hysteria," *Journal of the Illinois State Historical Society* 62 (Summer 1969):117–34. A variety of other studies on the local level have been published during the past decade. See also Phyllis Keller, *States of Belonging: German-American Intellectuals and the First World War* (Cambridge, Mass.: Harvard University Press, 1979).

22. Detailed accounts of the Brazilian riots may be found in various metropolitan newspapers, April 16–18, 1917, for example, *A Federação* and *Correio do Povo* of Porto Alegre and *Jornal do Commercio* of Rio de Janeiro. For summary accounts of the April riots in the German-language press, see *Deutsche Post* of São Leopoldo, April 24, 1917, and *Germania* of São Paulo, April 25, 1917. Because publication in the German language was forbidden in November 1917, comparable accounts for the November riots do not exist. The *New York Times* published numerous translations of dispatches from Brazilian newspapers. The full text of *Lei da guerra* (War Law) is given in English translation in Andrew Boyle, ed., *The Brazilian Green Book: Consisting of Documents Relating to Brazil's Attitude with Regard to the European War, 1914–1917* (London: George Allen & Unwin, 1918), 99–102. For a useful survey of Brazil's role in the war, see Percy Alvin Martin, *Latin America and the War* (Baltimore: Johns Hopkins University Press, 1925), 30–106.

PART IV:

The German Language

15.
The German Language in America

JÜRGEN EICHHOFF

THE HISTORY OF THE GERMAN LANGUAGE in America dates back to the founding of the first stable and distinctly German settlement some six miles north of what were then the city limits of Philadelphia. It is significant that the settlement was named *Germantown*, not *Neu/New Krefeld* after the home of most of the first settlers, or with *Neu/New* affixed to the name of the mother country's capital as was done in the case of the earlier Dutch settlement, *Nieuw Amsterdam*. No German mother country capital existed after the Thirty Years' War, which left the German-speaking areas of central Europe divided into a multitude of kingdoms, principalities, and other worldly or church territories. More important, the immigrants from Krefeld came into an environment in which the English language was already firmly established as the means of communication in administration, law, and business transactions. The name *Germantown* had no German predecessor. It was an English name from the very beginning.[1]

The Germantown settlers were followed by tens of thousands of other German immigrants during the eighteenth century. A study sponsored by the American Council of Learned Societies established that in 1790 roughly 277,000 Americans were of German ancestry.[2] About 141,000 of these lived in Pennsylvania, where they constituted almost one-third of the total population. According to government statistics, between 1820 and 1980 more than 7 million German men, women, and children arrived on American shores.[3] That is more than the total United States population in 1808.[4] Their geographical distribution in 1890 is shown in Map 1.

In addition, hundreds of thousands of German-speaking immigrants came from Austria, Switzerland, Russia, Poland, Romania, and other European countries. The number of persons for whom German was the native language in 1910 is estimated to have been about 9 mil-

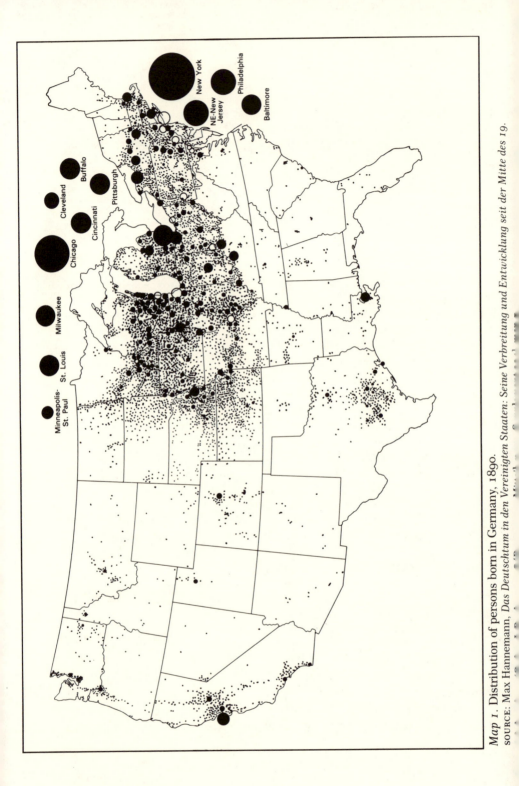

Map 1. Distribution of persons born in Germany, 1890.
SOURCE: Max Hannemann, *Das Deutschtum in den Vereinigten Staaten: Seine Verbreitung und Entwicklung seit der Mitte des 19.*

lion.[5] When asked about their ancestry in the 1980 census, 188 million Americans reported one or more ethnic ties. "Germany" was the answer of more than 49.2 million persons, only slightly fewer than the 49.6 million who claimed English ancestry. Seventeen states along the northern tier of the United States, plus Alaska, had more persons listing Germany as their ancestral origin than any other country (see Map 2).[6]

With such large numbers, was there ever a chance for the German language to hold its own in the United States or possibly to become the country's national language? There is a popular notion that the latter was indeed the case. It surfaced, for example, in the "Letters" section of *Playboy*'s March 1969 issue (p. 38):

Have you heard this one? During revolutionary days (or immediately thereafter), a convention was held in the Colonies for the purpose of deciding what our national language would be. English and German were the most popular choices and, when the matter came to a vote, English won—but only by a single vote. Ironically, the deciding vote was cast by a German, who is regarded in some German circles as a Benedict Arnold.

The story is widespread in Germany and seems to be ineradicable in spite of media efforts to set the record straight.[7] That it is nothing but a legend was proved by Otto Lohr more than fifty years ago.[8] But like all legends, this one is based on actual events. In 1794, upon a petition submitted by German-speaking citizens of Virginia, two congressional committees discussed the possibility of printing an official German version of Union laws in addition to the English version. A year later, the petition was denied by the full Congress. There is some evidence that the Speaker of the House, a German-American by the name of Frederick A. Muhlenberg, cast the decisive vote. This seems to have been the origin of what among scholars is now known as the Muhlenberg legend.

During the following decades several attempts were made to allow German official status in public documents, in schools, and in the courts in places where there was a strong German-speaking element in the population.[9] The legend seems to have been fostered by a discussion that took place in Pennsylvania. In 1837, when a new constitution was debated, a delegate named Ingersoll submitted an amendment calling for the legislature to "provide by law for the immediate establishment of common schools wherein all persons may receive instruction at the public expense, at least three months in every year, in the

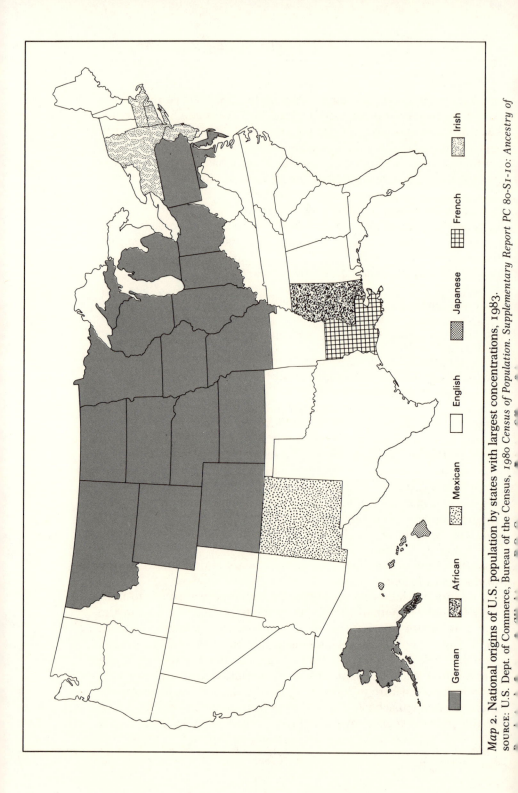

Map 2. National origins of U.S. population by states with largest concentrations, 1983.
SOURCE: U.S. Dept. of Commerce, Bureau of the Census, *1980 Census of Population. Supplementary Report PC 80-S1-10: Ancestry of*

| German | African | Mexican | English | Japanese | French | Irish |

English and German language, as may be by law directed." The discussion makes it clear that either German or English was meant, depending on the preference of the parents. Supporters and opponents of the amendment were by no means divided along the lines of their own ancestries. Men with such names as Porter and Merrill pointed out the richness and elegance of the German language, as well as its importance in the sciences. But others stressed that many Germans preferred their children to learn and use English as the most important means to get ahead. Finally, William Hiester, a delegate of German background, became the most outspoken advocate of English-only instruction: "All the public records of every kind are kept in the English language, and it seems right to me that the Germans should be made to accommodate themselves to it."[10]

If discussions such as those in Virginia and Pennsylvania gave rise to the legend, it should be emphasized that there never was a proposal to substitute the German language for English in the United States. All proposals were aimed at allowing German in addition to English, and then only locally or in narrowly limited areas.

From early on, unbiased observers were aware that there was hardly a chance for the German language to survive in this country. As early as 1789, Jedidiah Morse, in his book *The American Geography*, observed that

the English language is the one which is universally spoken in the United States, in which business is transacted, and the records kept. . . . Intermingled with the Anglo-Americans, are the Dutch, Scotch, Irish, French, Germans, Swedes and Jews; all these, except the Scotch and Irish, retain, in a greater or less degree, their native language, in which they perform their public worship, converse and transact their business with each other. The time, however, is anticipated when . . . the language, manners, customs, political and religious sentiments of the mixed mass of people who inhabit the United States, shall have become so assimilated, as that all nominal distinctions shall be lost in the general and honourable name of AMERICANS.[11]

But what about Benjamin Franklin's apparently fearful question of 1751, "Why should Pennsylvania, founded by the English, become a colony of aliens, who will shortly be so numerous as to Germanize us instead of our Anglifying them?"[12] We can only assume that this sentiment was motivated by Franklin's having lost the support of the German-speaking population for his ambitious political plans. If the Germans were so dangerous, why then would Franklin, in 1732, have published this country's first German-language newspaper, the *Phila-delphische Zeitung*? In the eighteenth and early nineteenth centuries large numbers of German immigrants and their descendants were already giving up their mother tongue. During the Pennsylvania debate on whether to allow German schools, one delegate noted that "in the city of Lancaster, twenty years ago, you heard nothing but German spoken; now, however, you hardly hear a word of it. So, in the town of York, twenty years ago, you would hear nothing but the *bauren sprache* of the country; but now it has all passed away and you hear nothing but English spoken. The young Germans don't wish to continue to speak it." Another delegate predicted that "the day will soon come, in my opinion, and it is also the opinion of many intelligent Germans, when the German language will be unknown in this state."[13] The speaker was unaware of the resistance that would be raised by religious groups such as the Amish, but the general observation is certainly correct. Nor was the trend restricted to Pennsylvania. In the Milwaukee Turnverein, when the question of whether the German element in America had a future was discussed in 1858, hardly a single person could be found who would argue in the affirmative.[14] The most prominent nineteenth-century German-American, Carl Schurz, insisted that German be spoken in his family and expressed the wish that all Americans learn German as a second language but nevertheless stressed that one could not get ahead in America without a good command of the English language. The decisions of men such as Muhlenberg and Hiester must be seen with this truth in mind. Schurz dared submit that he who prevented German from becoming the official language in Pennsylvania had "rendered the Germans [that is, the Americans of German descent] a service."[15]

Under the circumstances, the transition from German to English was a natural process, which often took place between the bilingual older and a more or less monolingual younger generation, whose parents supported the change. Certain situations accelerated the transition. The contact with English-speaking fellow servicemen in the army is one. A report from the 1890s, referring to the Civil War of 1861–65, reads, "*Before the war* and *after the war* was her constant keyword. She was of the opinion that before the war unpretentious simplicity, good behavior, and in German homes the dear German language were the rule; but that now showy dresses, insubordinate behavior among the young, and the disagreeable English prattle were more and more prevalent."[16]

The Americanization hysteria generated by World War I "has-

A German-language version of "Yankee Doodle," the popular patriotic song of the American Revolution. The tune originated in the mid-eighteenth century and by 1767 there were many versions of the song. It was sung by American soldiers during the Revolution as a symbol of defiance toward the British, who had first used the song to deride the American colonials. Its first kown publication in America occurred in 1795 as part of Benjamin Carr's *Federal Overture*. The single-page print pictured above originated in the early nineteenth century. (Roughwood Collection)

tened the natural urge of the American-born to abandon their special traditions." This observation, made by Einar Haugen with regard to Norwegian-Americans, is even more true for Americans of German ancestry. When it became apparent that the use of the German language could mean harm to their property and themselves, many parents decided to bring up their children with English as their first language. After all, they were Americans. If they spoke German, it was often a matter of the immediate linguistic environment rather than choice. Some may even have revered the German language because it was the language of their ancestors, their childhood, their Bibles and their prayers. But it was not worth getting beaten up or even killed for. And so it came about that "the continual flight of the bilinguals . . . from bilingualism" came to a climax which left few active bilinguals behind. It had been "a special kind of bilingualism, in that the advantages were all on the side of the [English] language." [17] The almost total extinction of the German language in America reflects "the largest assimilation process that ever occurred in a single speech community, in a single nation, in one century." [18]

While it survived, the German language in America was not uniform. Rather, it moved in different directions in different parts of the country. In Pennsylvania, the history of German settlement dates back to colonial times. Mass immigration, beginning in 1710, as well as the proverbial fertility of the Pennsylvania Germans led to a rapid increase of the German-speaking population. When the use of Pennsylvania German reached its climax sometime between 1870 and 1880, it was the everyday language of about 750,000 people, [19] about 600,000 of whom lived in Pennsylvania. The remainder were spread in secondary settlements in western Maryland, the Shenandoah Valley of Virginia, and many speech islands in various parts of the North American continent.

Although the founders of Germantown hailed from Krefeld in the lower Rhineland, most of the eighteenth-century immigrants came from the Palatinate, about 150 miles south in the central Rhineland. Additional immigrants originated from Württemberg, Baden, the Alsace, and Switzerland. The political division of the German-speaking areas of central Europe resulted in the formation and consolidation of local and regional dialects. A standard language was only slowly emerging through cultural, economic, and religious impulses. For immigrants arriving in groups, it was natural to continue using their native dialects. But there were times when a Württemberger needed to converse with a Swiss or a Swiss with someone speaking a Palatinate dialect. It would have been possible for them to use High (Standard) German. They had learned it to some extent in school, they heard it in church, read it in their Bibles and perhaps in their newspapers. But most immigrants were not well versed in it. High German also lacked pliability for the needs of a predominantly agricultural society. "In all likelihood," Lester W. J. Seifert concludes, "it was simpler for each partner to use his dialect; with a little practice, accompanied by patience and good will, communication was quite possible."[20]

Toward the end of the eighteenth century, immigration came to an end because of revolutionary upheavals on both sides of the Atlantic. It was during this time that the dialects grew closer together through a process known as leveling. Features that were distinctive for one dialect but incomprehensible to speakers of the other dialects were gradually eliminated in favor of the more common ones. This process led to the development of a new dialect, which was uniform enough to be understood beyond local and regional boundaries. Because it significantly differs from the Old World dialects, it deserves its own designation: *Pennsylvania German* or *Pennsilfaanisch*, or in the popular tongue, because of a mixup of *Deutsch* and *Dutch*, *Pennsylvania Dutch*.

Pennsylvania German is based primarily on the dialect of settlers from the Palatinate. But there are Alemannic (= Swiss) and, of course, English admixtures. The preeminence of the Palatinate dialect results from the large number of immigrants from that area. But there is also good reason to believe that the relative closeness of this dialect to Standard German was a supportive factor. As Werner Veith was able to show, among the various subdialects of *Pfälzisch*, the ones closest to the written language (= High German) were able to gain the upper hand.[21] Veith found that in the Pennsylvania German of Lancaster County the sounds and lexical items were similar to those found in the southeastern Palatinate in the area now dominated by the city of Mannheim.

Even though Pennsylvania German is understood in all German-speaking areas of Pennsylvania, it is not totally uniform. Carroll E. Reed and Lester W. J. Seifert have pinpointed many regional phonological varieties in their *Linguistic Atlas of Pennsylvania German*.[22] Seifert is working on an atlas of lexical variants in the central areas of Pennsylvania German.[23] An extensive study of Pennsylvania German speech items encompassing Pennsylvania as well as the outlying Pennsylvania German settlements is in progress under the directorship of Wolfgang W. Moelleken.[24]

German immigration to Texas is the only one that was planned and supported by German authorities.[25] In April 1842, fourteen German noblemen meeting at Biebrich on the Rhine founded a society to purchase land for a German settlement in Texas. Two years later, in March 1844, the Adelsverein was formally established in Mainz. Among the twenty-one founding members were rich and respected men such as Count Adolf of Nassau, August Ernst of Saxony-Coburg, Prince Friedrich Wilhelm Ludwig of Prussia, and Prince Ferdinand of Solms-Braunfels. The society was charged with financing and organizing the emigration of thousands of Germans within a short time.

Between October 1845 and April 1846, 5,247 immigrants landed at Galveston in thirty-three ships. In March 1845 a settlement had been laid out, which, in honor of Prince Karl of Solms-Braunfels, was given the name New Braunfels. A year later, Fredericksburg was founded, named after Prince Friedrich Wilhelm of Prussia. After initial difficulties were overcome, the settlements began to prosper. Around 1850, more than 30,000 German immigrants lived in Texas. Between 1865 and World War I, Texas experienced several waves of German immigration. By 1907, the number of German-speaking Texans may have been between 75,000 and 100,000. In 1965, Glenn Gilbert estimated their number to be around 70,000.[26] German is still heard spoken in public in places such as Fredericksburg and New Braunfels.

The large majority of German immigrants in Texas originated from central and northern Germany: northern Hessia, Nassau, the Waldeck, the Rhineland including the Palatinate, and Alsace. We may assume that, like the earlier immigrants, they spoke their accustomed dialects in everyday life. For them, too, it soon became necessary to communicate with speakers from other parts of the German speech area. It is significant that contrary to the development in Pennsylvania, leveling did not occur with one of the dialects involved as common denominator but rather on the basis of Standard German. Glenn Gilbert found few traces of German dialects. He reports:

With the exception of Alsatian and East Friesland Low German in Medina County and isolated survivals of Mecklenburg and Pomeranian Low German in counties such as Fayette and Washington, it is indeed a rare event to find someone who can consciously speak a type of language markedly different from that which prevails among his neighbors, or in the entire county and in adjoining counties. The trend is clearly toward a dissolution of the old fragmented, mutually unintelligible (or at best partially intelligible) dialects either by outright replacement or by gradual modification to form a new type of speech which, although far from uniform, enjoys sufficient common characteristics to merit the generic name, *Texas German.*[27]

Among the grammatical developments that set Texas German off from Standard German is the tendency to have only one form for both the dative and the accusative with articles, adjectives, and pronouns. Remaining regional differences in Texas German are presented in Gilbert's *Linguistic Atlas of Texas German.*

For the development of the German language in the Midwest, Wisconsin is a good example. There was no German effort to organize immigration to the state, but according to the census enumerations of the years 1880, 1890, 1900, and 1910, Wisconsin had a higher percentage of German-born inhabitants than any other state in the nation—15 percent in 1880 and 10 percent in 1910. No less than 37 percent of the population was of first- or second-generation German ancestry in 1890, 34 percent in 1910. The absolute numbers were very high, too, if compared with those of Texas.[28] In 1890, 259,819 of the state's residents were born in Germany; in 1910, 233,384.

One might expect that with such a high number of speakers, the German language would have been preserved particularly well in Wisconsin, but it has not been. There is today not a single area where German is heard as the everyday language in the public domain. To be sure, many older persons in areas heavily settled by Germans are still able to speak the language. But they rarely do. Many of those born before about 1920 reported that they were unable to speak a sentence of English until they learned it in school. The language of their parental homes and their neighborhoods was German. In Wisconsin, the settlements of German immigrants were scattered over the entire state. When they arrived, Yankees and Irish already occupied large areas. Many other nationalities arrived and settled side by side with the Germans. Learning English was not only a necessity but also a very natural development.

Wisconsin's German-speaking immigrants came from nearly all areas of Germany. Although those from the province of Pomerania were in the majority, there were sizable numbers from Bavaria, the Rhineland, Lippe-Detmold, Switzerland, Hannover, and Schleswig-Holstein. Many spoke the North German dialects known as Low German or *Plattdeutsch.* For speakers from central and southern Germany, this was almost a foreign, unintelligible language. Cultural consciousness was probably already too advanced, and development too rapid, for dialect leveling to take place. But the Texas solution of converging on Standard German did not work in Wisconsin. Most speakers of Low German could understand the standard language, but they were unaccustomed to speaking it. It was too far removed from their own dialect. There are countless reports that among speakers of different German dialects, the English language soon became the easiest and most available means of communicating. Only in urban areas of eastern Wisconsin, along the shores of Lake Michigan, was Standard German in wider use among German immigrants and their descendants. But modern times and the wave of Americanization closed in on these developments before the language had time to adjust to the new environment.

The dialects still extant in rural areas preserve practically all the distinctive marks of the mother dialects in the German areas from which they originated. With the exception of the borrowing of lexical items from the English language, little if any development occurred. It is obvious that there is not and never was a language variety that had enough characteristics to deserve the generic name "Wisconsin German." Instead, there are German dialects spoken in Wisconsin.

The German language lived for three centuries in Pennsylvania before succumbing. In Texas, it was alive and relatively well until the recent past. But Pennsylvania and Texas are exceptions. More typical was the languid extinction of the language as sketched out for Wisconsin. The center of the much quoted melting pot was located in the Midwest, in Ohio, Illinois, Kansas, Michigan, Minnesota, and Iowa. Pennsylvania German developed in seclusion and at a time when life was still centered around family, neighborhood, and church. Once it was consolidated, it survived for more than a century. The relatively strong position of Texas German is the result of the coincidence of favorable circumstances first seen and described by Heinz Kloss:

The Texas-German identity came into being when Texas was not yet a part of the Union and joined it with a strong feeling of equal rights; Texas-Germans as a group lived on the border between Latin and Anglo-America where bilingualism was nothing extraordinary; and where linguistic rights were almost taken for granted; they lived far removed from the German-American areas of Pennsylvania and the Midwest and were for this reason, and through their distinctive history, disposed to consider themselves as a group of its own and not just part of German-America; less than most of the Midwestern areas did they have to suffer from tensions between groups of a different world view, especially Lutherans and Freethinkers (although they were by no means spared these); geographically they were concentrated in a relatively small area. City and country were not totally separated as was the case in the Midwest. Rather, there were cities with a predominantly German population within the pre-dominantly German rural areas. They had a relatively strong educated upper class which spoke for the rural Germans. Last, but not least, there had been, during the founding of the early Texas-German settlements, a strong desire to foster the continued existence of the German language, which lingered on for some time.[29]

It is only in groups that practice language maintenance as part of a religious survival strategy that German continues to be used in everyday communication and is passed on to the children. There are three such groups: the Old Order Amish, the Old Order Mennonites, and the Hutterites. The Old Order Amish are the most conservative offshoot of the Mennonites. Under the leadership of Jakob Ammann, a Swiss Mennonite bishop, they broke away from the parent church around 1695 and are recorded in Pennsylvania as early as 1727. Their largest concentrations today are in Lancaster County, but there are also groups of significant size in Ohio and Indiana and smaller ones in other parts of the United States and Canada. Their total number is about ninety thousand. None are left in Europe. The women of the Old Order Amish wear simple dresses, bonnets, and shawls, and the men traditionally wear hats and do not shave. They avoid using electricity and automobiles, depending on their black horse-drawn buggies for transportation. The smaller group of the Old Order Mennonites is somewhat less strict about not using electricity, but they still shun the automobile. The Hutterites, an Anabaptist sect like the Amish, did not come to this country until the 1870s, after a long odyssey through southern and eastern Europe. Estimates put their number at more than twenty-two thousand living in 229 *Brüderhöfe* (colonies) concentrated in South Dakota, Montana, and the Canadian provinces of Alberta, Manitoba, and Saskatchewan.[30]

For the Old Order Amish, the Old Order Mennonites, and the Hutterites, language loyalty is part of their belief in the specific significance of the language in which their religious convictions were founded. In addition, it is a shield against the influences of the outside world. Still, all members also learn to speak English reasonably well. My own observation is that although most speakers of the Old Order Amish and Old Order Mennonites insist that among themselves they feel most comfortable speaking Pennsylvania German, their proficiency in English covers more domains more adequately, especially with regard to the vocabulary. An English word is always available (if necessary, by asking a neighbor); this is not the case for the Pennsylvania German. Consequently, English vocabulary is making rapid, not to say disastrous inroads into these speakers' native "Dutch." The language of the Hutterites, too, has been subject to impoverishment because of cultural isolation. The complicated function of language varieties in group identification within the Hutterite community was analyzed in Kurt Rein's voluminous study.[31]

Whether these religious groups will continue to find the German language an indispensable means to preserve religious or group identity remains to be seen. When the Beachy Amish broke away from the Old Order Amish in 1927, permitting the use of automobiles, they also gradually but irrevocably began abandoning their loyalty to the German language. They follow the example of another religious group, the so-called Russian Mennonites. These German-speaking Mennonites from Russia had retained their German identity and the Low German language for more than a hundred years while settling in the Ukraine, and for several decades after they emigrated to central Canada and the northern plains states in 1873 and in the early 1920s. In an attempt not to lose the younger generation, which gradually turned to speaking English, and especially during World War II, they introduced English in their church services. English has been used more and more in their community life ever since.

There are many reasons why the German language never had a real chance to retain importance in American life and culture. English was already established as the country's language long before German-speaking immigrants arrived in sizable numbers. The number of English speakers was increased by the speakers of minor languages who switched to English. With the exception of the ill-fated Texas undertaking, there was no effort on the part of German governments to direct the stream of emigrants to certain areas. Many of them fled religious or political persecution; most of them wanted to escape miserable economic conditions. There were differences, often deemed insurmountable, in religion (Protestants, Catholics, and Freethinkers) and dialects. A Catholic German could have more in common with a Catholic Irishman than with a German freethinker. Under these circumstances, it was difficult to establish and convincingly defend a "German" identity in America.

The widespread use of dialects and the changes the German language underwent in contact with English were detrimental to whatever chances at survival may have existed. The nineteenth-century

Der Deutschen

allgegenwärtiger

Englischer Sprachlehrer

des

Wortes Gottes,

welcher diese Sprache in Fragen und Antworten, auf eine ganz
neue, kurze, leichte, deutliche und gründliche Art lehret.

Eingerichtet

wie der allgegenwärtige Deutsche Sprachlehrer des Wortes Gottes,
nach der Ordnung der Englichen Buchstabirbücher, und den Regeln
der Sprachlehre, zum Gebrauch der Schulen und zu Hause,

für

Lehrer und Schüler.

Lehrend
das Buchstabiren, Lesen und Sprechen.

Enthaltend in

Englisch und Deutsch:

1) Ein vollständiges Buchstabir=
buch welches über 4600 englische
Wörter enthält, welche nach dem
Plan der englischen Buchstabir=
bücher, von drey Buchstaben bis zu
sieben Sylben, säulenförmig oder
in Kolumnen gestellet, und durch
Tabellen nach den Regeln der
Sprachlehre in ihre unterschied=
lichen Arten abgetheilet sind; de=
ren Aussprache, stumme Buchsta=
ben, Sylbentheilung, Sylbenton,
vielfache Zahl, Geschlecht, Abän=
derung, Abwandelung, Veral=
tungs Grade und Abkürzungen
gezeiget und gelehret wird.

2) Ein vollständiges Lesebuch,
enthaltend 70 Leseselectionen, über
welchen die Namen der unter=
schiedlichen Arten der englichen
Wörter zu sehen sind: die Ab=
wandelung der 12 Hülfszeit=
wörter; 83 auserlesene Sprüch=
wörter; 9 gewöhnliche Unterredun=
gen; der Gebrauch der Lesezeichen;
31 lehrreiche Fabeln; 14 ausgesuchte
Briefe; eine Erklärung des Buch=
stabirtheils; und eine Anweisung
wie man die Englische Sprache
hinterm Ofen, oder im Schatten
seines Baumes erlernen kann.

Man sucht hier stets vollkommener am Verstand † zu werden;*
Denn das ist unsere erste Christenpflicht* auf Erden.
*Matth. 5, 48.   † 1 Cor. 14, 20.

Von Christ. Becker, Lehrer in Pennsylvanien.

Easton, (Penns.)
Gedruckt bey C. J. Hütter.

Christian Becker's *Englischer Sprachlehrer* (Primer of the English Language),
printed in 1808 by C. J. Hütter in Easton, Pennsylvania. This text documents
the rise of English among the Pennsylvania Germans in the early nineteenth
century. (Roughwood Collection)

immigrants found virtually no way of linking up linguistically with the large block of Pennsylvania Germans. Educated speakers who arrived after 1848 following the aborted attempt at establishing a democratic form of government in Germany soon contributed to a rich cultural life in America. But they failed to reach the majority of the earlier, conservative, church-affiliated, and rural German-Americans, whom they often criticized because of their "debased German." This criticism has maintained its negative effects on the speakers' self-consciousness to this very day. "I don't speak the right German, I am a *Deutschverderber*," is a frequent statement made by speakers of German in this country.

This is not the place to present the controversies that surrounded the founding and mission of German-language schools in America. Suffice it to say that many speakers never received any formal training in handling Standard German. As early as 1837, representatives from German-speaking communities in Pennsylvania requested that official documents, of which one-third had traditionally been printed in German, be published in English only. They argued that the translations were too bad, or they could not read German.[32] The language of higher education was English; Pennsylvania German had become degraded to a "bauren sprache." When Pennsylvania German reached its climax around 1880, its speakers were largely illiterate in written German.[33] Unless they had attended a parochial German school, the same held true of most other German-speaking Americans.

What, then, remains of the German language in America? Eventually, probably not much more than a few loan words and names. The majority of the German loan words adopted into American English refer to eating and drinking (for example, *sauerkraut* and *schnapps*), but there are also some that testify to the German contributions to American life and culture (*fest* in compounds such as *songfest*, and *kindergarten*).[34] There is even a dialect word that never found its way into written German, the word *nix*, meaning "nothing," which has become popular as a verb in contexts such as "The President's staff nixed the idea because, they said, it created logistic problems."[35]

Because they settled mostly in areas with an established administration, German immigrants were rarely in a position to choose their own name for a settlement. If they were, they often preferred bibilical names such as Salem or Bethlehem. The small number of German place names was further diminished by official name changes during World War I. Few remain, such as New Holstein and New Berlin in Wisconsin, New Braunfels and Fredericksburg in Texas. Much more ubiquitous are German family names. Although their number has been constantly eroded by name changes and assimilation to English orthography, family names, for many Americans, provide the first and sometimes only reason to learn about, and become interested in, their ethnic origin.

Notes

1. We do not know who named the settlement. There is no record of a ground-breaking or name-giving ceremony. But whether the name originated with William Penn and his administrative agents or was selected by the intellectual and organizational mastermind of the settlement, Francis Daniel Pastorius, is ultimately irrelevant.

2. American Council of Learned Societies, *Report of the Committee on Linguistic and National Stocks in the Population of the United States* (Washington, D.C.: Government Printing Office, 1932), p. 305; reprinted as *Surnames in the United States Census of 1790* (Baltimore: Genealogical Publishing Co., 1969).

3. U.S., Bureau of the Census, *Historical Statistics of the United States, Colonial Times to 1970*. Bicentennial Edition, Pt. 2 (Washington, D.C.: Government Printing Office, 1976), 105–6; *Annual Report 1977*, 54. Information for 1976–80 was received from the U.S. Department of Justice, Immigration and Naturalization Service, August 1983.

4. The population of the United States in 1808 is estimated to have been 6,838,000; the estimate for 1809 is 7,031,000 (United States Bureau of the Census, 1976, pt. 2:8).

5. Heinz Kloss, "German-American Language Maintenance Efforts," in Joshua A. Fishman et al., eds., *Language Loyalty in the United States: The Maintenance and Perpetuation of Non-English Mother Tongues by American Ethnic and Religious Groups* (The Hague: Mouton, 1966), 213.

6. U.S. Department of Commerce, Bureau of the Census, *1980 Census of Population. Supplementary Report PC 80-S1-10: Ancestry of Population by State: 1980* (Washington, D.C.: Government Printing Office, 1983).

7. For example, *Die Zeit*, March 19, 1971, p. 6, and April 16, 1971, p. 68.

8. Otto Lohr, "Deutsch als 'Landessprache' der Vereinigten Staaten?" *Mitteilungen der Akademie zur wissenschaftlichen Erforschung und zur Pflege des Deutschtums* 4:(1931), 283–90.

9. See Heinz Kloss, *Das Volksgruppenrecht in den Vereinigten Staaten von Amerika*, 2 vols. (Essen: Essener Verlagsanstalt, 1940–42), 1:93–129, 247–53, 440–41.

10. *Proceedings and Debates of the Convention of the Commonwealth of Pennsylvania to Propose Amendments to the Constitution . . .* , 13 vols. (Harrisburg, 1837–39), 5:186, 281.

11. Jedidiah Morse, *The American Geography: Or, A View of the Present Situation of the United States of America* (Elizabethtown: Shepard Kollock, 1789), 67–68.

12. Allen Walker Read, "Bilingualism in the Middle Colonies," *American Speech* 12 (1937):93.

13. *Proceedings of the Convention of 1838*, 5:228, 224.

14. Wilhelm Hense-Jensen, *Wisconsin's Deutsch-Amerikaner bis zum Schluss des neunzehnten Jahrhunderts*, 2 vols. (Milwaukee: Die Deutsche Gesellschaft, 1900–1902), 1:32.

15. Carl Schurz, Untitled contribution in "Zum Schutze deutscher Kultur," *New Yorker Staatszeitung*, June 28, 1886; also *Der deutsche Pionier* 18 (1886):21.

16. Margarete Lenk, *Fünfzehn Jahre in Amerika* (Zwickau: J. Herrmann, 1911), 34.

17. Einar Haugen, *The Norwegian Language in America: A Study in Bilingual Behavior*, 2 vols. in one (Bloomington: Indiana University Press, 1969), 28, 2, 52.

18. Heinz Kloss, "Deutsche Sprache ausserhalb des geschlossenen deutschen Sprachgebiets," in Hans Peter Althaus, Helmut Henne, and Herbert Ernst Wiegand, eds., *Lexikon der Germanistischen Linguistik*, 2d ed. (Tübingen: Niemeyer, 1980), 543.

19. Lester W. J. Seifert, "The Word Geography of Pennsylvania German: Extent and Causes," in Glenn G. Gilbert, ed., *The German Language in America: A Symposium* (Austin: University of Texas Press, 1971), 17.

20. Ibid., 18.

21. Werner Veith, "Pennsylvaniadeutsch. Ein Beitrag zur Entstehung von Siedlungsmundarten," *Zeitschrift für Mundartforschung* 35 (1968):254–83.

22. Carroll E. Reed and Lester W. J. Seifert, *A Linguistic Atlas of Pennsylvania German* (Marburg: N.p., 1954).

23. See Seifert, "Word Geography of Pennsylvania German."

24. Wolfgang Moelleken, "Language Maintenance and Language Shift in Pennsylvania German: A Comparative Investigation," *Monatshefte* 75 (1983):172–86.

25. The following account is based on Glenn G. Gilbert, "The German Dialect of Kendall and Gillespie Counties, Texas," *Zeitschrift für Mundartforschung* 31 (1964):138–72, and Gilbert, "German Regional Dialects in the United States," 8 pp., typescript.

26. Glenn G. Gilbert, "English Loan Words in the German of Fredericksburg, Texas," *American Speech* 40 (1965):102.

27. Glenn G. Gilbert, *Linguistic Atlas of Texas German* (Austin: University of Texas Press, 1972), 1.

28. There were two states with higher numbers of German immigrants than Wisconsin. Wisconsin's numbers are not exceptionally high compared with those in other states. In 1890, the number of persons born in Germany was 498,602 in New York, 338,382 in Illinois, 235,668 in Ohio, and 230,516 in Pennsylvania. But their share of the total population was only 8.3 percent in New York, 8.8 percent in Illinois, 6.4 percent in Ohio, and 4.4 percent in Pennsylvania. See Jürgen Eichhoff, "German in Wisconsin," in Gilbert, ed., *German Language in America*, 45.

29. Heinz Kloss, *Das Nationalitätenrecht der Vereinigten Staaten von Amerika* (Vienna: Braumüller, 1963), 196.

30. John A. Hostetler, *Hutterite Society* (Baltimore: Johns Hopkins Press, 1974).

31. Kurt Rein, *Religiöse Minderheiten als Sprachgemeinschaftsmodelle. Deutsche Sprachinseln täuferischen Ursprungs in den Vereinigten Staaten von Amerika* (Wiesbaden: Steiner, 1977), 13.

32. *Proceedings of the Convention of 1838*, 5:224, 228.

33. Ralph C. Wood, "Pennsylfaanisch (Pennsylvaniadeutsch). Eine neudeutsche Sprache Nordamerikas," in Wolfgang Stammler, ed., *Deutsche Philologie im Aufriss*, 2d ed., 3 vols. (Berlin: E. Schmidt, 1956–62), 1:1934.

34. Karl-Heinz Schönfelder, *Deutsches Lehngut im amerikanischen Englisch* (Halle/Saale: Max Niemeyer, 1957).

35. *Time*, December 6, 1976, p. 27.

16.
Language-Maintenance Efforts Among German Immigrants and Their Descendants in the United States

MARION L. HUFFINES

LANGUAGE MAINTENANCE among German immigrants and their descendants in the United States depended on three main supports: the school, the church, and the press; for postcolonial immigrants secular clubs and organizations also played a role. Each of these institutions succeeded for a time in providing support for the use of the German language, but each was subject to counterpressures from within and without the German-American community. The following remarks will deal with language-maintenance efforts of various subgroups that constitute the German-Americans in the United States. These remarks are based on the general observations of Heinz Kloss,[1] whose basic outline I have followed in this essay, those of Jürgen Eichhoff on Wisconsin Germans,[2] my own on the Pennsylvania Germans,[3] and those found in other case studies cited below.

The German community in America is composed of a variety of subgroups, each having a different relationship to the dominant Anglo culture. Lifestyles differ widely from the very visible conservatism of the separatist religious groups to German-Americans whose lifestyle and language cannot be distinguished from those of Anglo-Americans in the same area. Language-maintenance efforts have been more or less successful in these subgroups at various times in their history. It is clear, however, that very large numbers of Germans have assimilated into American society, that for them Americanization was also Anglification, and that the German language in America has declined to the point of virtual extinction in spite of the numerical strength of the Germans in America and a relatively tolerant and even favorable legal and political environment.

The German-Americans most successful at maintaining German are, of course, the separatist religious sects. The Old Order Amish and a majority of the Old Order Mennonites in farm communities in Pennsylvania, Ohio, Indiana, Kansas, and other states speak Pennsylvania German at home and in the community but use a variety of High German in their church services and English in their parochial schools and in discourse with outsiders. The Hutterites, who live in colonies (or *Bruderhöfe*) in North and South Dakota and Montana, have vigorously maintained their German although Kurt Rein states that his investigations "reveal a very delicate equilibrium in which German in its variant forms remains unassailed as the spoken language even among young people, while English is advancing to replace the retreating standard German in its partial function as the language of education and writing."[4] Hutterite children attend both an English school and a German school. The Amanites of Iowa maintain their language with the support of public schools in which German is taught from grades 4 to 6 and in senior high school. Kloss cites this case as the only remaining public school in the United States in which German is taught because it is the mother tongue of the pupils.[5] Amanite church services are conducted in German, but English services have been introduced. These four religious groups, the Old Order Amish, the Old Order Mennonites, the Hutterites, and the Amanites (and perhaps a few smaller sects) maintain their German language as part of the lifestyle that sets them apart from the dominant society. Within that lifestyle, German fulfills communicative functions not served by English. The prospects for continued maintenance of German in America are best among these groups.

During the colonial period and postrevolutionary decades Germans settled in language islands along the Atlantic coast and particularly in Pennsylvania. The Pennsylvania German language island was large enough and self-contained enough that for a long time no special efforts were necessary for language maintenance. German was spoken because it was appropriate and convenient. German church schools founded by the Moravians, Lutheran and Reformed churches, Mennonites, Dunkards, and other sects multiplied rapidly. Generally these schools provided only an elementary education. Secondary schools and institutions of higher learning were conducted in English. This arrangement distanced the educated from their German mother language and diminished intellectual support for German language usage.

The 1834 free public school law is seen by many to have severely crippled German language-maintenance efforts for descendants of colonial immigrants. A motion to provide for common schools in English and German did not pass the 1837 Pennsylvania State Convention, nor did petitions to grant official status to the German language in the form of bilingual court officials. Scholars today find no support for the widely circulated story that a proposal to declare German an official language of Pennsylvania (some say of the nation) failed to pass by one vote.

Although German lost ground in the schools, it was maintained in the churches and by an active German press, especially in the eastern part of Pennsylvania. Lobbying on the part of the Verein der deutschen Presse von Pennsylvanien, founded by S. K. Brobst in 1862, resulted in the enactment of a law mandating that all official notices be published in German newspapers in eight, later nine, designated counties. This press association also promoted bilingual public schools in some cities and German as a branch of study in other cities, and it founded Sunday and weekday schools to supplement the free public schools. Brobst's death in 1876 brought most of these efforts to an end. The German press diminished in importance, and by the outbreak of World War I it had almost disappeared in Pennsylvania. High German in the churches met a similar fate, and by World War II it had also disappeared.

The Pennsylvania German dialect persisted much longer than did the use of High German in Pennsylvania, and it can be heard today in isolated areas of Pennsylvania, even among the nonsectarians. Certainly the dialect suffered the same attrition as did High German because of the free public school law and the anti-German hysteria associated with World War I. In the 1930s, however, the dialect enjoyed a resurgence of interest. Numerous new dialect plays were performed, dialect newspaper columns appeared, and the number of Pennsylvania German radio broadcasts increased significantly. Organizations sponsored *Fersomlinge* and meetings of the Grundsow Lodges for fun and merrymaking in the dialect. Scholars founded the Pennsylvania German Society and the Pennsylvania German Folklore Society; in 1950 a teaching grammar of Pennsylvania German was published along with a Pennsylvania German translation of the Gospel according

Auf Oeffentlicher Vendu

Zu Versteigern

Montags den 29ten März,
An dem Hause von Samuel Haller, in Elisabeth
Taunschip, etwa eine halbe Meile von Neuephrata, nemlich:

Ein breiträderiger

Plantasche-Wagen, Rindsvieh

und Schweine, Pferdsgeschirr, ein Drawr, Better und
Bettladen, Tisch und Stühl, nebst einer grossen Verschieden-
heit von Haus-und Baurengeräthschaften, zu weitläuftig
alles zu melden.
Die Vendu geht an um 10 Uhr Vormittags, da alsdan
gute Aufwartung und billiger Credit gegeben wird, von

Michael Klein, ju'r.
Richard A. Heitler.

Asseinnies von Samuel Haller.

März 18, 1824.

Joseph Bauman, Drucker, Ephrata.

Announcement of a public auction in Lancaster County, Pennsylvania, in 1824. Written in so-called Pennsylvania-High German, the text contains a number of loan words, showing the encroachment of other languages on this dialect: *Vendu* for "auction" (*Versteigerung*); *Plantasche* for "farm" (*Bauernhof, Plantage*); *Asseinies* for "assignees" (*Bevollmächtigte*). (Roughwood Collection)

to St. Matthew. In spite of these successes, the efforts proved ultimately futile. No provisions were ever made to provide elementary education in the dialect; native speakers were doomed to remain functionally illiterate in their mother tongue. Pennsylvania German suffers in no small measure from the lack of a standard orthography and a dignified literary tradition; its speakers are indifferent to the linguistic and historical relationships between Pennsylvania German and varieties of High German. Pennsylvania German speakers also suffer from a widespread attitude characterized by the stereotype of the "dumb Dutchman," an attitude the Pennsylvania German community has internalized, which has led to the belief that Pennsylvania German is not only useless but inferior.[6] The continued existence of Pennsylvania German among nonsectarians can be attributed to the rural isolation and self-sufficiency of its speakers. The prospects of continued Pennsylvania German maintenance among nonsectarians are dim indeed.

In my research covering communities in seven Pennsylvania counties, I have found no nonsectarian native speaker under the age of forty-one years.[7]

The postcolonial immigrants of the nineteenth and twentieth centuries included Roman Catholics, Orthodox Lutherans, and other Protestants; these groups formed self-contained religious congregations to which individuals tied their primary loyalties. This population, the church Germans, was rural and settled chiefly in the Midwest and Texas. The postcolonial immigrants also included a small but ideologically active group of liberals or freethinkers. They tended to settle in the cities and were particularly active in forming secular clubs for the promotion of German culture. The Roman Catholics and the Lutherans concerned themselves with language maintenance by founding parochial schools. The Roman Catholics stressed bilingual education, but in time English predominated as the language of instruction. The

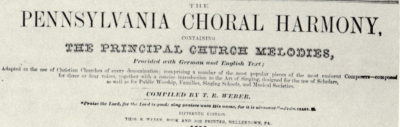

For many generations Pennsylvania Germans were bilingual, using both High German and English. Thomas R. Weber's popular *Pennsylvanische Choral Harmonie*—here in its 15th printing (Hellertown, 1888)—was used in hundreds of "Union Churches," which served both Lutherans and members of the Reformed Church. (Roughwood Collection)

Lutherans tried to preserve the use of German over English. German was the language used in the church and within these semiautonomous German communities.

The nineteenth-century German immigrants were numerically strong and settled in some areas that were still in pioneering stages. Unlike the Pennsylvania Germans, whose original dialect differences had leveled out to form a common vernacular, these Germans were linguistically heterogeneous. When they could no longer control High German, they had no common vernacular except English. Planned language-maintenance efforts became necessary if German was to survive.

The 1830s brought political refugees from Germany who were well educated and determined to keep their language alive. They founded newspapers, established secular organizations such as glee clubs and lodges, and were responsible for a considerable body of German writing in science and the humanities. The years 1848 to 1880 brought still larger numbers of highly cultured, intellectual Germans to the United States. With these immigrants (the so-called Forty-eighters) came unparalleled expansion of parochial and independent German schools as well as greater emphasis on the teaching of German in public schools. Other strides were made in the public school arena. In Ohio, for instance, an 1839 law provided for German to be taught in elementary schools. German areas in other states followed suit. These efforts were aimed not only at having German taught locally but also at preventing state authorities from intervening in local educational policies. With the Forty-eighters came an increase of publications: German newspapers, German literature, German books on religion and philosophy. The Forty-eighters founded theater and choral groups, discussion groups, and a new type of club, the Turnverein, which were centers of cultural as well as physical activity. For these Germans, Americanization did not mean Anglification. During this period until 1914, newspapers and clubs flourished as never before. Eichhoff reports that publications in Wisconsin reached a peak in 1900, when approximately one hundred newspapers of general interest and thirty-four of special interest were printed in German.[8] Language-maintenance efforts appeared eminently successful.

The appearance was deceptive. During this time of unprecedented growth, the Germans were not united. The liberals, the Catholics, and the Protestants formed separate camps. The church people distanced themselves from the National Alliance of secular clubs (the

Nationalbund, founded in 1901), whose resources were spent mainly in the struggle against prohibition; the clubs did little to promote German language education. A trend toward English became visible in the church: English services began to be held regularly. Rural language islands settled by Germans whose lives centered around the church managed to preserve the use of German in the church beyond World War I, but by 1910 these areas were losing population as people sought work in the cities.

The Anglo-Americans were not indifferent to the heightened visibility of the Germans. Vociferous protests were raised against the use of German as the language of instruction in public schools. In Wisconsin an 1846 law mandated that English be taught in all Milwaukee schools, even in German areas. An 1854 law prohibited teaching in any language other than English. In 1889 both Indiana and Illinois passed laws prescribing instruction in English for most subjects even in nonpublic schools. The Forty-eighters with their stress on German ways became active just as intense feelings against foreigners were spreading nationally. Anglo-Americans feared the growing political strength of the Germans and opposed the German habits of celebrating a festive Sunday and of drinking beer. The antiforeign nativist movement had the effect of creating a renewed ethnic awareness among Germans in America, and oppositions that would have balanced out peacefully became serious barriers between the Germans and their Anglo neighbors.

Pressures within the German-American community also undermined the success of German language-maintenance efforts. New waves of German immigrants hindered the settled Germans from stabilizing their lifestyle and developing pride in their uniquely German-American way of life by reminding them of how un-German they had become and how defective and corrupted their language had become. Kloss observes that the greatest German language persistence has been in areas where since 1890 there have been the fewest immigrants, specifically in Texas and parts of rural Wisconsin and Minnesota.[9] German-language newspapers, as Eichhoff points out, softened the initial shock for the new immigrants but essentially facilitated their ultimate assimilation by slowly introducing new immigrants to the American way of life.[10] The more successful the press was at facilitating assimilation, the less it was needed, and as successive waves of new immigrants dwindled, so did German-language newspapers. In 1910, 54 percent of the non-English dailies and 56 percent of the non-

English weeklies were published in German; by 1960, German dailies accounted for only 7 percent of the total number of dailies and 15 percent of the weeklies.[11]

The unparalleled political and cultural growth of German-America and the seeming successes of its language-maintenance efforts before 1917 were followed by an equally unparalleled downfall with the outbreak of World War I. Major secular German associations dissolved. The teaching of German was forbidden in many private as well as public schools. Germans heard speaking their native language were suspect. Language-maintenance efforts after World War I never regained the vigor they had had before. New German-American organizations either failed or resorted to using English. New immigrants arriving before 1933 sought improved economic conditions and were indifferent to language maintenance. After 1933 the political refugees from Nazi Germany willingly embraced Americanization and Anglification. The German press also continued to decline. After World War II even the supplementary *Sprachschulen* of the churches ceased to exist although a few opened in the 1950s. Kloss reports twenty-three in existence in 1961. The transition of the Lutheran church to the use of English, which had begun before World War II, was rapid. After World War II German services were occasional: monthly, annually, or not at all.

The prospects for the survival of the German language in America are poor. Eichhoff describes areas in Wisconsin where German is still spoken.[12] Sixty-eight of his informants had spoken German before they went to school, but only eight claimed to be fluent in German. The youngest informant brought up speaking German was born in 1937. Joseph Wilson observes about a German community in Texas: "Only in the last decades, after surviving for over a hundred years, has the German language in Texas begun to decline, but the decline has been rapid, and with the current older generation, Texas German as a living language will die."[13] William Pulte, on German in Valley View, Texas, observes, "One class of the weekly *Sabbatschule* is still conducted in German. It is attended, however, by only a few elderly people who have difficulty reading English, or who have a sentimental attachment to the use of German in religious services." He also describes informant selection in Corn, Oklahoma: "It did not seem feasible to select informants according to age, since the generally moribund condition of the German language in the communities in question caused most of the informants to be, of necessity, members of the older generations. It seemed also that the various German dialects spoken in the communities studied had been better retained by women than by men; the typical informant was female and over sixty years of age."[14] Klaus Wust comments on the Virginia Germans: "The failure of German-Americanism is nowhere more evident than in its inability to retain German schools. The multifarious organizations now became wholly dependent on new immigrants for their existence. Once this source of continued strength dried up, it was only a matter of time before the German element disappeared into the American amalgam. More and more families gave in to the inevitable and found it good."[15]

The reasons for the failure of German language maintenance efforts are by no means straightforward. Few scholars today point to World War I as the determining factor in the loss of the German language in America. The trends toward English were well in place before 1917; the war served only to accelerate them. The survival of any ethnic language resides in its ability to fulfill unique communicative functions within the ethnic community not served by the dominant language. To use Joshua Fishman's word, the language must have its own domain. Language-maintenance efforts are successful only insofar as they create or preserve domains for the language. As social, educational, and occupational concerns draw German-Americans into mainstream American society independent of the ethnic group, ethnic affiliation diminishes and the language functions previously allocated to German disappear. The shift from German to English appears deceptively slow because of the dispersion of German-American communities throughout large areas of the United States, but the shift in any individual community is rapid once it begins. The community seems to approach a threshold of contact with the dominant society beyond which it becomes impossible to retain the ethnic language. The school systems do not support the mother tongue of children who are raised speaking German; churches must meet the religious needs of younger generations who can no longer follow the teachings in German; the German press cannot cater to a readership unable to read German; secular clubs are irrelevant to German-Americans who comfortably interact with the dominant society and have come to accept its values. The isolation imposed by religious separatism can effectively retard the assimilation process and preserve the domains in which the German language uniquely functions. Rural self-sufficiency and residential clustering in the form of language islands also retard language shift by preserving the domains of German language usage. Without the institutional support of German schools, German-language churches, and a strong German press, increased interaction with the dominant society is accompanied by a language shift to English.

Notes

1. Heinz Kloss, "German-American Language Maintenance Efforts," in Joshua A. Fishman et al., eds., *Language Loyalty in the United States: The Maintenance and Perpetuation of Non-English Mother Tongues by American Ethnic and Religious Groups* (The Hague: Mouton, 1966), 206–52.

2. Jürgen Eichhoff, "Wisconsin's German-Americans: From Ethnic Identity to Assimilation," *German-American Studies* 2 (1970):44–54; see also Eichhoff's "German in Wisconsin," in Glenn G. Gilbert, ed., *The German Language in America: A Symposium* (Austin: University of Texas Press, 1971), 43–57.

3. Marion Lois Huffines, "Pennsylvania German: Maintenance and Shift," *International Journal of the Sociology of Language* 25 (1980):43–57. See also my article "Language Contact across Generations: The English of the Pennsylvania Germans," in Wolfgang Moelleken, ed., *Dialectology, Linguistics, Literature: Festschrift for Carroll E. Reed* (Göppingen: Kümmerle, 1984), 93–103.

4. Kurt Rein, "German Dialects in Anabaptist Colonies on the Great Plains," in Paul Schach, ed., *Languages in Conflict: Linguistic Acculturation on the Great Plains* (Lincoln: University of Nebraska Press, 1980), 108–9. See also Robert H. Buchheit, "Language Maintenance and Shift among Mennonites in South-Central Kansas," *Yearbook of German-American Studies* 17 (1982):111–21.

5. Kloss, "German-American Language Maintenance Efforts," 244.

6. Huffines, "Pennsylvania German: Maintenance and Shift," 52–53.

7. Huffines, "Language Contact across Generations," 95.

8. Eichhoff, "German in Wisconsin," 49.

9. Kloss, "German-American Language Maintenance Efforts," 233.

10. Eichhoff, "Wisconsin's German-Americans: From Ethnic Identity to Assimilation," 48–49.

11. Joshua A. Fishman, Robert G. Hayden, and Mary E. Warshauer, "The Non-English and the Ethnic Press, 1910–1960," in Fishman et al., eds., *Language Loyalty in the United States*, 52, 54–55.

12. Eichhoff, "German in Wisconsin," 50.

13. Joseph Wilson, "The Earliest Anglicisms in Texas German," *Yearbook of German-American Studies* 16 (1981):103.

14. William Pulte, "An Analysis of Selected German Dialects of North Texas and Oklahoma," in Glenn G. Gilbert, ed., *Texas Studies in Bilingualism* (Berlin: de Gruyter, 1970), 107, 110.

15. Klaus Wust, *The Virginia Germans* (Charlottesville: University Press of Virginia, 1969), 238.

17.
Demographic and Institutional Indicators of German Language Maintenance in the United States, 1960–1980

JOSHUA A. FISHMAN

THERE IS MORE GERMAN LANGUAGE MAINTENANCE in the United States today than meets the eye and far more than meets the mood of many German-American scholars, who are still intellectually focused on better days in former years. That awareness, based upon a factual familiarity with the magnitude of German-American language maintenance in the second half of the nineteenth century and a realization of the declines that have been experienced since World War I, however, must not lead to erroneous, self-punishing convictions that the German language has died or is about to die in the United States. Such "cocktail party wisdom" is unbecoming the tradition of German-American scholarship, a tradition that should be more aware than most that language maintenance and language shift are subtle and changeable social processes that have been part and parcel of the American scene ever since the arrival of the Pilgrims. Indeed, careful examination of recent American ethnolinguistic phenomena reveals far more life on the German language scene in the United States than many had expected.[1]

From 1940 to 1960, a decrease of 36 percent marked German mother tongue claiming in the United States. The 3,145,770 claimants of German as a mother tongue in the latter year (Table I) were resisting a trend to deny any and all associations with the history and culture of Nazi Germany. Never before in this century had the ranks of German mother tongue claimants been so depleted.[2] In the context of

Table I. *Persons Claiming Mother Tongue for Twenty-three Languages, 1940–1970*

Language	1940	1960 (est.)	1970	Change, 1940–1960		Change, 1940–1970		Change, 1960–1970	
				Number	Percent	Number	Percent	Number	Percent
Arabic	107,420	103,910	193,520	−3,510	−3.27	+86,100	+80.15	+89,610	+86.24
Czech	520,440	217,770	452,810	−302,670	−58.16	−67,630	−12.99	+235,040	+107.93
Danish	226,740	147,620	194,460	−79,120	−34.89	−32,280	−14.24	+46,840	+31.73
Dutch	289,580	321,610	412,630	+32,030	+11.06	+123,050	+42.49	+91,020	+28.30
Finnish	230,420	110,170	214,170	−120,250	−52.19	−16,250	−7.05	+104,000	+94.40
French	1,412,060	1,043,220	2,598,410	−368,840	−26.12	+1,186,350	+84.02	+1,555,190	+149.08
German	4,949,780	3,145,770	6,093,050	−1,804,010	−36.45	+1,143,270	+23.10	+2,947,280	+93.69
Greek	273,520	292,030	458,700	+18,510	+6.77	+185,180	+66.97	+166,670	+39.95
Hungarian	453,000	404,110	447,500	−48,890	−10.79	−5,500	−1.21	+43,390	+10.74
Italian	3,766,820	3,673,140	4,144,320	−93,680	−2.49	+377,500	+10.02	+471,180	+12.83
Lithuanian	272,680	206,040	292,820	−66,640	−24.45	+20,140	+7.39	+86,780	+42.12
Norwegian	658,220	321,770	612,860	−336,450	−51.12	−45,360	−6.89	+291,090	+90.47
Polish	2,416,320	2,184,940	2,437,940	−231,380	−9.58	+21,620	+8.95	+253,000	+11.58
Portuguese	215,660	181,110	365,300	−34,550	−16.02	+149,640	+69.39	+184,190	+5.52
Romanian	65,520	58,020	56,590	−7,500	−11.45	−8,930	−13.63	−1,430	−2.46
Russian	585,080	460,830	334,620	−124,250	−21.24	−250,460	−42.81	−126,210	−26.39
Serbo-Croatian	153,080	184,090	239,460	+31,010	+20.26	+86,380	+56.43	+55,370	+30.08
Slovak	484,360	260,000	510,370	−224,360	−46.32	+26,010	+5.37	+250,370	+96.28

Slovenian	176,640	67,110	82,320	−111,530	−62.43	−96,320	−53.92	+15,210	+22.66
Spanish	1,861,400	3,335,960	7,823,580	+1,474,560	+79.22	+5,962,180	+320.31	+4,487,620	+134.52
Swedish	830,900	415,600	626,100	−415,300	−49.98	−204,800	−24.65	+210,500	+50.65
Ukrainian	83,600	252,970	249,350	+169,370	+202.60	+165,750	+190.27	−3,620	−1.43
Yiddish	1,751,100	964,610	1,593,990	−786,490	−44.91	−157,110	−8.97	+629,380	+65.25
Total	21,786,340	18,356,400	30,434,870	−3,429,940	−15.74	+8,648,530	+39.70	+12,078,470	+65.80
Total minus Spanish	19,924,940	15,020,440	22,611,290	−4,904,500	−24.61	+2,686,350	+13.58	+7,590,850	+50.54
Total U.S. Population	132,165,129	179,325,671	203,210,158	+47,160,542	+35.68	+71,045,029	+53.75	+23,884,487	+13.32
Total English mother tongue	93,039,640	149,219,776	160,717,113	+56,180,136	+60.38	+67,677,473	+72.74	+11,497,337	+7.70
Total Non-English mother tongue	22,036,240	19,381,786	33,175,172	−2,654,454	−12.05	+11,138,932	+50.55	+13,793,386	+71.17

SOURCES: U.S. Census of Population, 1970. Report PC(2)-1A: National Origin and Language, 1973. Referred to in the following tables as PC(2)-1A. Data for 1940 and 1960 are from Joshua A. Fishman et al., eds., Language Loyalty in the United States: The Maintenance and Perpetuation of Non-English Mother Tongues by American Ethnic and Religious Groups (The Hague: Mouton, 1966), in which original sources are cited and estimation procedures described. The twenty-three languages included in this table are the only ones for which data for 1940, 1960, and 1970 are available.

the general ethnic revival that characterized American life from the mid-1960s to the mid-1970s, however, the number of claimants of German mother tongue rose to a phenomenal 6,093,050, an increase of 93.7 percent in 1970. This increase cannot be explained on either natural demographic or immigrational grounds.[3] It is almost entirely attributable to a redefinition of self-concept on the part of many who had previously denied German mother tongue. Although many of these people were of advanced age, and therefore their number declined to 5,486,186 by 1979 (a drop of 10 percent relative to 1970), this figure is still huge and higher than that of 1960 (Tables II and III). Certainly, a language claimed by 5.5 million individuals of whatever age deserves to be studied carefully and characterized more sensitively than by the term "demise" alone.

One swallow does not make a summer, and one index does not make a revival. Mother tongue claiming is exactly that: an attitudinally colored indicator of self-concept. It is not the same as an indicator of overt language use, although many overt indicators along institutional lines also reveal that there is considerable life left in the German language on American shores. After registering a sizable decrease from 1940 to 1960, the German-language press in the United States remained stable at fifty-some periodical publications (Table IV), not even counting the Pennsylvania German ones, and their overall circulation remained almost unchanged with a third of a million subscribers in 1980. German-language radio also increased from 104 stations in 1960 to 169 in 1980 (Table V), an increase of some 60 percent. Although we do not have comparable 1960–80 data for ethnic community schools and churches in which German is taught and used, their numbers are still appreciable, 183 and 261 respectively (Tables VI and VII). In these latter two areas, the sidestream German contribution is huge indeed (585 schools for Pennsylvania Germans plus 61 for Hutterites and 1,705 local religious units for Pennsylvania Germans alone), demonstrating the different dynamics that characterize the mainstream and the sidestreams among German-Americans as a whole. These indicators of German language use also imply that the language has recently pulled out of its former nosedive and is not ready to give up the ghost.

I must admit, however, that on all measures of intensity of use, the German language appears weak. Less than 5 percent of all grandchildren of German-speaking grandparents in the United States can speak German.[4] Although the total circulation of the German press has

Table 11. Persons Claiming Ancestry (1980) and Mother Tongue (1979) for Certain Ancestries or Languages

Ancestry or language	Claiming mother tongue (age 14+) 1979	Claiming ancestry[a] (age 14+) 1980	Percent of those claiming ancestry also claiming mother tongue	Claiming single ancestry[a] (age 14+) 1980	Percent of those claiming single ancestry also claiming mother tongue
Chinese[b]	514	609	84.40	444	116.03
Czechoslovak	511	1,644	31.08	743	68.78
French[c]	2,417	14,692	16.45	3,231	74.81
Filipino	442	632	69.94	393	112.47
German	5,138	49,432	10.39	14,943	34.38
Greek	475	896	53.01	473	100.42
Italian[d]	4,100	11,160	36.74	5,514	74.29
Japanese	449	596	64.51	445	100.90
Norwegian	590	4,013	14.70	1,125	52.44
Polish	2,452	8,148	30.09	3,225	76.03
Portuguese	409	880	46.47	427	95.78
Spanish[e]	7,652	9,469	80.81	6,738	113.56
Swedish	550	4,819	11.41	1,149	47.87
Total	38,534	132,863	29.00	36,367	105.94

[a] "Claiming ancestry" means claiming a particular ancestry among others. "Single ancestry claiming" means claiming only the particular ancestry indicated.

[b] Chinese includes Taiwanese.

[c] French includes Franco-Canadian.

[d] Italian includes Sicilian.

[e] Spanish includes Cuban, Mexican, Puerto-Rican, other Latin American, and other Spanish.

Table III. Estimated Change in Persons Claiming Non-English Mother Tongue, 1970 and 1979

Language	1970	Est. 1979	Est. percent change
African	15,783	18,465	17
Albanian	17,382	22,597	30
Amerindian	268,205	348,667	30
Arabic	193,520	226,418	17
Armenian	100,495	117,579	17
Chinese	345,431	645,963	87[a]
Czech	452,812	522,771	15[a]
Danish	194,462	175,016	−10
Dutch	412,637	387,879	−6
English	160,717,113	170,636,000	6[a]
Finnish	214,168	192,751	−10
French	2,598,408	2,780,550	7[a]
German	6,093,054	5,486,186	−10[a]
Greek	458,699	574,612	25[a]
Hebrew	101,686	610,116	500
Hindi	26,253	45,943	75
Hungarian	447,497	523,571	17
Italian	4,144,315	4,351,530	5[a]
Japanese	408,504	531,055	30[a]
Korean	53,528	93,674	75
Lithuanian	312,568	331,322	6
Norwegian	612,862	601,892	−2[a]
Persian	23,923	27,990	17
Polish	2,437,938	2,562,273	5[a]

not dropped in the past twenty years, there are almost no German dailies now and most of the weeklies are organizational house organs that reach their readers as an automatic benefit of membership rather than as a result of independent subscriber interest. The average radio program has shrunk from 2.2 hours in length in 1960 to less than one hour today. Almost all of the schools maintained by mainstream Germans are held one day (actually one morning) a week, and those local religious units (three-quarters of them Protestant and one-quarter Catholic) that still make use of German tend to do so minimally and far less intensively than was formerly the case.

Thus the real issue seems not to be one of life or death, demise or

Table III. (continued)

Language	1970	Est. 1979	Est. percent change
Portuguese	365,300	474,890	30
Romanian	56,590	59,985	6
Russian	334,615	391,500	17
Serbo-Croatian	239,455	280,162	17
Slovak	510,366	597,128	17
Slovenian	82,321	87,260	6
Spanish	7,823,583	11,400,525	46[a]
Swedish	626,102	556,104	−11[a]
Turkish	39,314	45,997	17
Ukrainian	249,351	264,312	6
Yiddish	1,593,993	1,214,942	−24[a]
All other	1,320,052	1,691,022	25[a]
Not reported	9,317,873	8,386,086	−10[a]
Total ethnic mother tongue	33,175,172	38,242,647	15
Total (ethnic mother tongue, English, not reported)	203,210,158	217,264,733	7
Percent ethnic mother tongue	16.3	17.6	1.4
Percent ethnic mother tongue without Spanish	12.5	12.4	−.1

[a] Exact percent increase/decrease for persons ages fourteen and over derived from table 4, Special Studies Series, United States Census Reports, p. 23, No. 116, 1982, used in calculating 1979 figure (total for all ages).

continuity, but the very meager level at which German language life or continuity is maintained. German meant enough to main-line German-Americans, at least at a symbolic level, to snap back, as did all main-line, immigrationally distant mother tongues, during the ethnic revival of the mid-1960s. Indeed, the revival had important main-line institutional (rather than merely individual) manifestations. Main-line ethnic community publications, radio and TV programs, schools, and churches also reintroduced or retained a little bit of German in their total institutional efforts. Nevertheless, the mystery of the ethnic revival, the brunt of which is now past, is why a little German should be worth maintaining, as it obviously seems to be. Thus, although un-

Table IV. Ethnic Mother Tongue Publications by Language and Frequency of Publication

Language	Daily	Weekly	Monthly	Other[a]	No data	Total	Percent
Albanian	0	1	3	5	1	10	0.9
Amerindian	0	1	2	2	10	15	1.5
Arabic	0	4	5	0	8	17	1.6
Armenian	5	7	7	9	6	34	3.3
Chinese	15	8	1	2	16	42	4.1
Croatian	0	2	4	4	2	12	1.2
Czech	1	4	10	8	4	27	2.6
Danish	0	1	4	0	1	6	0.6
Dutch	0	2	1	0	2	5	0.5
Finnish	0	6	1	1	5	13	1.3
French	0	4	5	5	7	21	2.0
German	2	23	15	4	8	52	5.0
Greek	2	8	8	1	3	22	2.1
Hebrew	0	2	1	3	1	7	0.7
Hungarian	1	15	7	5	14	42	4.1
Irish	0	2	0	1	14	17	1.6
Italian	1	15	13	4	12	45	4.4
Japanese	7	4	1	1	9	22	2.1
Korean	10	1	1	0	10	22	2.1
Lithuanian	2	5	12	11	8	38	3.7
Norwegian	0	1	6	3	2	12	1.2
Pennsylvania German	0	0	4	1	4	9	0.9

diluted pessimism with respect to the future of the German language within main-line circles in the United States would seem to be unwarranted, the puzzle remains worthy of consideration: how and why is a little bit of German maintained?

The amount of German maintained by mainstream German-Americans beyond the third generation is insufficient to index German-American culture today. One must constantly use referrants for which the majority of German-Americans simply have no German term and for which they normatively use English terms. Indeed, for most German-Americans, there is no way back in this connection. They will never learn enough German to use it as an adquate index of their culture. In the area of cultural enactment, matters are only slightly better.

Table IV. (continued)

Language	Daily	Weekly	Monthly	Other[a]	No data	Total	Percent
Persian	0	0	0	0	2	2	0.2
Polish	4	11	14	13	23	65	6.3
Portuguese	0	9	3	0	12	24	2.3
Romanian	0	0	3	3	2	8	0.8
Russian	2	2	6	4	5	19	1.8
Serbian[b]	0	2	1	2	0	5	0.5
Slovak	1	6	12	4	4	27	2.6
Slovenian	0	3	6	0	0	9	0.9
Spanish	10	36	40	16	72	174	16.9
Swedish	0	4	5	0	4	13	1.3
Turkish	0	0	2	0	0	2	0.2
Ukrainian	2	5	10	7	8	32	3.1
Vietnamese	0	1	8	3	33	45	4.4
Welsh	0	0	1	1	0	2	0.2
Yiddish	1	8	10	17	0	36	3.5
Total	66	203	232	140	312	953	
Percent	6.9	21.3	24.4	14.7	32.7		100.0

SOURCE: Joshua A. Fishman et al., *The Rise and Fall of the Ethnic Revival* (Berlin: Mouton, 1985). In this table and those that follow, languages with very meager representations on the American scene have been omitted. Readers interested in the figures for these languages can find the data in the original source.
[a] Other = quarterly, semiannually, annually, irregularly.
[b] Includes Serbo-Croatian.

Certain ritualized aspects of German-American culture are still widely rendered in German, primarily songs, certain prayers, and particular formulaic acts and expressions. But the number of such enactments is small, whereas the number of their English counterparts is large. Thus it is at the symbolic level alone that German comes into its own. The German language still frequently stands for German-American ethnicity, even though most mainstream members who acknowledge this heritage can no longer use the language to index or enact the culture to which it pertains. As a symbolic vehicle, a modicum of it is all that is needed to discharge the role it plays. Indeed, it can continue to play this role at its current minimal level of intensity indefinitely provided it is institutionalized on an intergenerational basis.

Table V. Radio Stations Broadcasting in Non-English Languages, by Language and Hours per Week of Broadcasting (1980)

Language	Less than ½ hour		½–1 hour		1–3 hours		3–19 hours		20–83 hours		84–168 hours		No data		Total
	n	%	n	%	n	%	n	%	n	%	n	%	n	%	
Albanian	3	50.0			2	33.3							1	16.7	6
Amerindian	6	8.6	15	21.4	8	11.4	12	17.1	5	7.1	2	2.9	22	31.4	70
Arabic	1	4.3	9	39.0	4	17.3							9	39.0	23
Armenian			9	50.0	4	22.0							5	27.7	18
Chinese	2	8.0	5	20.0	5	20.0	5	20.0			2	8.0	6	24.0	25
Croatian	2	10.0	7	35.0	3	15.0							8	40.0	20
Czech	1	5.6	2	11.1	5	27.8	5	27.8					5	27.8	18
Danish													2	100.0	2
Dutch			3	27.2	2	18.1							6	54.6	11
Finnish			10	71.4	1	7.1							3	21.4	14
French	4	3.5	45	39.5	28	24.5	21	18.4	2	1.8			14	12.3	114
German	7	4.1	60	35.5	42	24.9	15	8.9	1	.6			44	26.0	169
Greek	3	3.4	30	33.7	19	21.3	9	10.1	3	3.4			25	28.0	89
Hebrew	2	13.3	2	13.3	4	26.7	2	13.3					5	33.3	15
Hindi[a]	5	25.0	6	30.0	6	30.0	1	5.0					2	10.0	20
Hungarian	3	8.1	11	29.7	3	8.1	2	5.4					18	48.6	37
Irish	1	2.0	18	36.7	11	22.5	5	10.2					14	28.6	49
Italian	6	3.9	59	37.8	35	22.4	23	14.7	5	3.2			28	17.9	156
Japanese	4	12.5	8	25.0	6	18.8	7	21.9	1	3.1	2	6.2	4	12.9	32

Korean	2	11.8	4	23.5	4	23.5	2	11.8					5	29.4	17
Latin					1	100.0									1
Lithuanian	4	14.3	6	21.4	4	14.3	2	7.1					12	42.9	28
Norwegian	2	50.0	2	50.0											4
Pennsylvania German	2	50.0	2	50.0											4
Persian	1	14.3	3	42.9	1	14.3							2	28.6	7
Polish	11	4.7	49	20.9	90	38.5	47	20.0	1	.4			36	15.4	234
Portuguese	2	3.1	6	9.4	25	39.0	10	15.6	4	6.3	1	1.6	16	25.0	64
Romanian	3	30.0	2	20.0									5	50.0	10
Russian	7	41.2	3	17.7	2	11.8	3	17.7					2	11.8	17
Serbian[b]	2	15.4	5	38.5	4	30.8							2	15.4	13
Slovak	2	10.5	7	36.9	1	5.3							9	47.4	19
Slovenian	3	27.3	1	9.1	2	18.2	1	9.1					4	36.4	11
Spanish	29	3.4	174	20.6	162	19.2	190	22.5	61	7.2	67	7.9	162	19.2	845
Swedish	2	13.3	6	40.0									7	46.7	15
Turkish			1	50.0									1	50.0	2
Ukrainian	6	16.7	8	22.2	6	16.7	3	8.3					13	36.1	36
Vietnamese	6	37.5	3	18.8	2	12.5							5	31.3	16
Yiddish	3	18.8	5	31.3	2	12.5	1	6.3					5	31.3	16
Totals	137		586		494		366		83		74		507		2247

SOURCE: Joshua A. Fishman et al., *The Rise and Fall of the Ethnic Revival* (Berlin: Mouton, 1985).

[a] Includes Hindustani.
[b] Includes Serbo-Croatian.

Table VI. Ethnic Mother Tongue Schools by Language and Frequency of Attendance

Language	Daily n	Daily %	Weekday after-noons[a] n	Weekday after-noons[a] %	Saturday Sunday[b] n	Saturday Sunday[b] %	No data n	No data %	Total
Albanian							1	100.0	1
Amerindian	37	25.7					107	74.3	144
Arabic					2	28.6	5	71.4	7
Armenian	12	13.8	3	3.5	43	49.4	29	33.3	87
Chinese	5	2.9	15	8.7	18	10.5	134	77.9	172
Croatian			1	6.7	6	40.0	8	53.3	15
Czech			1	7.7	6	46.1	6	46.1	13
Danish							3	100.0	3
Dutch							1	100.0	1
Finnish							3	100.0	3
French	23	19.5					95	80.5	118
German	6	3.3	3	1.7	39	21.3	135	73.7	183
Greek	20	4.5	31	7.0	22	5.0	369	83.5	442
Hebrew	501	19.4	1,659	64.1	406	15.7	23	.8	2,589
Hindi					4	80.0	1	20.0	5
Hungarian	2	2.4	1	1.2	14	16.9	66	79.5	83
Hutterite	61	100.0							61
Italian	2	2.7	4	5.3	7	9.3	62	82.7	75
Japanese	10	5.9	8	4.7	29	17.2	122	72.2	169
Korean					5	4.1	116	95.9	121
Lithuanian	1	1.1	2	2.4	18	21.2	64	75.3	85
Norwegian							5	100.0	5

Barring the reappearance of political and ideological problems between either West or East Germany and the United States, the problem of intergenerational continuity for German among mainline German-Americans is no different than the problem of intergenerational continuity for other immigrationally removed languages such as French, Polish, or Yiddish. These are all primarily second languages in their appropriate ethnolinguistic circles, regardless of what they may be historically or emotionally. As such, they must be handed on by primary ethnic community institutions such as schools and churches as much as and even more than they are handed on by families. It is a weakness of German among main-line Germans that it is overly dependent on

Table VI. (continued)

Language	Daily n	%	Weekday afternoons^a n	%	Saturday Sunday^b n	%	No data n	%	Total
Pennsylvania German	584	99.8					1	.2	585
Persian							1	100.0	1
Polish	9	7.1	3	2.4	14	11.1	100	79.4	126
Portuguese	1	2.3	7	15.9	1	2.3	35	79.5	44
Romanian							2	100.0	2
Russian					1	14.0	6	86.0	7
Serbian					1	25.0	3	75.0	4
Slovak	2	10.0	1	5.0	1	5.0	16	80.0	20
Slovenian					6	50.0	6	50.0	12
Spanish	54	7.4	2	.3	3	.4	672	91.9	731
Swedish					2	17.0	10	83.0	12
Ukrainian	6	6.8			40	45.5	42	47.7	88
Vietnamese					1	11.0	8	89.0	9
Yiddish	108	25.6	284	67.3	30	7.1			422
Totals	1,444	22.4	2,025	31.4	719	11.2	2,257	35.0	6,445

Source: Joshua A. Fishman et al., *The Rise and Fall of the Ethnic Revival* (Berlin: Mouton, 1985).
[a]Classes meeting two or more times per week including a Saturday or Sunday.
[b]Classes meeting one time per week or less.

secondary social institutions (periodicals, radio and TV) and drastically underrepresented in connection with primary institutions such as schools and churches (Table VIII). The situation for sidestream German is just the reverse, being primarily dependent on schools and churches. The intergenerational continuity of sidestream German would, therefore, seem to be more assured, even were it also to become increasingly a second language rather than a first.

The major anomaly characterizing German in the United States today is that it has such a major, vibrant sidestream alongside its mainstream. Indeed, in connection with schools and churches, those of the former clearly outnumber those of the latter. When considered alone,

Table VII. Local Religious Units (places of worship) by Language and Denomination

Language	Protestant	Catholic	Orthodox[a]	Other Christian	Asian	Jewish	Totals
Albanian		1	18				19
Amerindian	1,014	143	81	34			1,272
Arabic		66	10		4		80
Armenian	21	4	89				114
Chinese	343	8		2	22		375
Croatian		37					37
Czech	1	34					35
Danish	6						6
Finnish	71						71
French	5	169					174
German	196	65					261
Greek	1	34	443				478
Hebrew						3,209	3,209
Hindi					2		2
Hungarian	17	56					73
Irish		1					1
Italian		267					267
Japanese	50	4			93		147
Korean	12	14					26
Latin		10					10

							Total
Lithuanian		56					56
Norwegian	12						12
Old Church Slavonic		131	127				258
Pennsylvania German	1,705						1,705
Polish		462					462
Portuguese	3	55		1			59
Romanian	3	11	11				25
Russian	2	1	97			1	101
Serbian			2				2
Slovak	53	75					128
Slovenian		11					11
Spanish [b]	1,075	1,414		2			2,491
Swedish	13						13
Ukrainian	1	124	89				214
Vietnamese		44			1		45
Welsh	2						2
Yiddish						1,168	1,168
Totals	4,606	3,297	967	39	122	4,378	13,409

SOURCE: Joshua A. Fishman et al., *The Rise and Fall of the Ethnic Revival* (Berlin: Mouton, 1985).

[a] Includes other Eastern churches.

[b] Spanish entries include Puerto Rico and Virgin Islands. Corresponding figures for the fifty states alone are Protestant 1,059, Catholic 1,166, Other Christian 2, Total 2,227.

Table VIII. Ratios of Non-English-Using Institutions (1982) to Total Non-English Mother Tongue Claiming (1979), Both Taken as Ratios of Their Own Nationwide Totals, by Language

Language	Broad-casting	Local religious units	Periodicals	Schools
Albanian	3.83	2.33	16.17	.33
(Amerindian)	3.05	10.25	1.60	2.42
Arabic	1.76	1.00	2.80	.19
Armenian	2.48	2.71	10.65	4.29
Chinese	.83	1.63	2.41	1.55
Croatian	d	d	d	d
Czech	.51	.70	1.91	.15
Danish	.17	.09	1.26	.11
Dutch	.42	a	.48	.02
Finnish	1.16	1.04	2.52	.10
French	.65	.18	.28	.25
German	.48	.13	.35	.26
Greek	2.42	2.33	1.42	4.49
Hebrew	.46	14.71	.42	24.69
Norwegian	.10	.06	.74	.05
Old Church Slavonic	c	b	c	c
Pennsylvania German	b	b	b	b
Persian	3.56	a	2.71	.39
Polish	1.37	.50	.94	.39
Portugese	2.34	.35	1.88	.54
Romanian	2.88	1.12	4.87	.18
Russian	.69	.73	1.80	.11
Serbian[d]	1.85	.40	2.26	.40
Slovak	.47	.60	1.68	.19
Slovenian	1.83	.35	3.78	.78
Spanish	1.39	.61	.57	.37

in its own right, however, the mainstream has been fully normalized on the American minority ethnolinguistic scene. It responded to the ethnic revival although it had previously received very severe blows. It supports a goodly number (and a stable number) of community institutions that use the German language to a minimal but symbolically significant degree. Overall, it is still a numerically huge presence on the American scene. Given its unusual sidestream and barring fur-

Table VIII. (continued)

Language	Broad-casting	Local religious units	Periodicals	Schools
Swedish	.40	.07	.87	.12
Hindi	7.08	.17	a	.67
Hungarian	1.07	.39	2.97	.93
Irish	e	e	e	e
Italian	.65	.17	.38	.10
Japanese	1.14	.78	1.53	1.56
Korean	3.54	3.00	8.55	7.71
Latin	b	b	c	c
Lithuanian	1.34	.47	.47	1.49
Turkish	1.00	a	1.58	a
Ukrainian	2.13	2.38	4.49	1.94
Vietnamese	b	b	b	b
Welsh e	9.00	.10	8.76	a
Yiddish f	.20	2.69	1.09	2.02

SOURCE: Joshua A. Fishman et al., *The Rise and Fall of the Ethnic Revival* (Berlin: Mouton, 1985).

[a] No ratio can be computed because no units in this category in this language have been located. If mother tongue claimants of this language were reported by the Bureau of the Census, they are underrepresented for these units.

[b] No ratio can be computed because the Bureau of the Census does not report the number of mother tongue claimants for this language, subsuming them under some language-family cluster name or under "all others."

[c] Both [a] and [b], above.

[d] Census figures combine Croatian and Serbian; see Serbian.

[e] Census figures combine Irish and Welsh; see Welsh.

[f] Since most Yiddish-using schools and all Yiddish-using local religious units use Hebrew as well, the combined values for Yiddish and Hebrew are 9.63 and 6.72.

ther political and ideological antagonism between the United States and Germany (East or West), the likelihood that the German language will still play a role here when the quatricentennial of German immigration to the United States is being celebrated is excellent indeed (Table IX).

The ethnic revival heightened the saliency and the acceptability of minority ethnic identity not only in the United States but through-

Table IX. Rank Order of Survival Potential of Languages as of 1980 according to Criterion 3ª

1. Spanish	18. Korean	35. Persian
2. Hebrew	19. Slovak	36. Turkish
3. German	20. Czech	37. Tagalog
4. Polish	21. Welsh/Irish	
5. Yiddish	22. Serbo-Croatian	
6. Greek	23. Russian	
7. Amerindian	24. Arabic	
8. Italian	25. Dutch	
9. Chinese	26. Finnish	
10. French	27. Swedish	
11. Ukrainian	28. Slovenian	
12. Hungarian	29. Norwegian	
13. Cambodian/Vietnamese	30. Romanian	
14. Japanese	31. Thai/Lao	
15. Lithuanian	32. Albanian	
16. Portuguese	33. Hindi	
17. Armenian	34. Danish	

SOURCE: Joshua A. Fishman et al., *The Rise and Fall of the Ethnic Revival* (Berlin: Mouton, 1985).

ªCriterion 3 is a compromise criterion that recognizes both number of claimants and total institutional ratios.

out the Western world. This revival, indicative though it is of a distancing of middle-class populations from the integrative ethos and institutions of their respective countries, has also revealed a greater ability of both sides to compromise than was true before. Ethnic minorities eschewed separatism and opted for cultural pluralism instead. National mainstreams eschewed complete conformism (note the prevalence of bilingual education, bilingual ballots, bilingual services in hospitals, police, and other government areas) and opted for the recognition of minimal minority needs instead. Particularly in the American context, ethnicity has become a publicly recognized and permitted way of identifying and behaving. Indeed, being ethnic is as much a way of being American as being American is a way of being ethnic. Accordingly, German-Americans have found an acceptable way back to parts of their heritage and, in this process, to parts of their language heritage as well. Since World War I, German-Americans have contributed primarily to the American mainstream. For the rest of this century, at least, they may come once more to contribute increasingly to German-American culture as well.

Notes

1. Joshua A. Fishman et al., *The Rise and Fall of the Ethnic Revival: Sociolinguistic Perspectives on Language and Ethnicity* (Berlin: Mouton, 1985).

2. Joshua A. Fishman et al., eds., *Language Loyalty in the United States: The Maintenance and Perpetuation of Non-English Mother Tongues by American Ethnic and Religious Groups* (The Hague: Mouton, 1966; rpr. New York: Arno Press, 1978).

3. Fishman, *Rise and Fall of the Ethnic Revival.*

4. Calvin Veltman, *Language Shift in the United States* (Berlin: Mouton, 1983).

18.
The German Language in America: An Open Forum

JOHN A. MCCARTHY

WHEN THE FIRST GERMAN SETTLERS LANDED on the shores of North America they naturally brought their language with them. So many of their countrymen followed in the ensuing centuries that the English-speaking majority occasionally felt it was being inundated by the German language and customs. In the eighteenth and again in the nineteenth century the English component of American society feared it would become Germanicized rather than the Germans becoming Anglicized. The existence of German presses as early as 1738, when the first German-language books were printed in Germantown, and of German-language newspapers dating back to 1739 and peaking around 1900 were two of the most tangible signs of a considerable German presence in America. Given the dimensions of the German presence (250,000 immigrants prior to the War of Independence and more than 6 million more from 1820 to 1920), it is no wonder that laws were passed in state legislatures prohibiting the teaching of classes in any language other than English (for example, 1854 in Wisconsin).[1]

Young George Washington went too far, of course, when he diagnosed the German immigrants as being too ignorant as to be able to master the English language.[2] The Germans proved capable of accommodating to their new linguistic environment to the point of endangering the survival of their mother tongue in North America. The process of cultural assimilation, which was by no means linear and without idiosyncratic twists, is chronicled by Jürgen Eichhoff, Joshua Fishman, and Marion Huffines in contributions to this volume. Eichhoff and Huffines focus on the historical developments in the eighteenth and nineteenth centuries, especially in Pennsylvania and Wisconsin, while Fishman turns his attention to more recent trends and to the significance of a reawakened ethnicity since the 1960s. The conclusion reached by Eichhoff and Huffines coincides with the general view dominant in the research field that the prospects for the survival of the German language in America are poor.[3] Recent studies by Wolfgang Moelleken and Joseph C. Salmons on the state of German language maintenance among Pennsylvania and Texas Germans respectively corroborate Huffines's conclusion.[4] Nevertheless, Fishman is unabashedly optimistic about the prospects of survival: his demographic and statistical analyses lead him to claim that "the likelihood that the German language will still play a role here when the quatricentennial of German immigration to the United States is being celebrated is excellent indeed."[5] Fishman's optimism is fueled by such facts as a phenomenal increase of 93.7 percent in the number of claimants of German as mother tongue from 1960 to 1970. In raw figures, that percentage represents a rise from 3,145,770 to 6,093,050 persons. Moreover, the German-language press and its subscribers have remained stable since the radical decrease pursuant to World War II. Additionally, German-language radio and television programming increased by some 60 percent since 1960. These overt indicators of language use tend to show that the radical decline in German ethnic identification following the fascist era has leveled off and stabilized.

Survival means one thing to the cultural scientist or the ethnolinguist; it means something else to the embattled German teacher. The historian can trace the deterioration of Texas German or Pennsylvania "Dutch" in a dispassionate manner because his eye is mostly on the past, which cannot be changed. The language teacher, however, cannot afford detachment. It is often a matter of personal survival. The teacher's focus is on the present and future, which can be altered. Nevertheless, the studies by Eichhoff, Fishman, and Huffines are extremely relevant to the language teacher's concerns. Precisely because they do illuminate the historical conditions and culturalization pressures affecting German immigrant groups over the past three hundred years, these studies are applicable to the present. The same pressures broadly determine the current state of language study in America. An awareness of the past will—or perhaps should—provide the basis for future ventures to enhance German language use on these shores.

For this reason an open forum titled "The German Language in America: Present and Future" followed the scholarly session on the historical perspectives. The panelists took heart especially at Fishman's encouraging words: "There is more German language maintenance in the United States today than meets the eye and far more than meets the mood of many German-American scholars, who are still intellectually focused on better days in former years. . . . Careful examination of recent American ethnolinguistic phenomena reveals far more life on the German language scene in the United States than many had expected." At the same time, the panel felt it must come to grips with the perception that German comes into its own only at the symbolic level; that is, in certain ritualized enactments (songs, prayers, formulized expressions). It was felt that German language instruction, if it is to go beyond mere survival, must assume more than a symbolic role. To accomplish this task, it was argued, we must design an environment—or at least create a consciousness—conducive to vigorous language programs which appreciate the seminal role of language in a culturally diverse United States and world. The German immigrant experience should not be unrelated to this task.

The three speakers from the earlier session joined with language teachers from area institutions to address themselves to these and more practical problems facing the classroom teacher. The other members of the panel included William Durden, director of the Center for the Advancement of Academically Talented Youth (CTY) and assistant professor of German, the Johns Hopkins University; Delbert C. Hausman, chairman, Foreign Language Department, Lower Moreland High School; Marcy Hessinger, German teacher, Downingtown High School; Irmgard S. Langacker, German teacher, Wallingford-Swarthmore School District; and Herta Stephenson, coordinator of German studies, St. Joseph's University.

These panelists addressed themselves to current efforts in the field of German pedagogy to raise the general consciousness of the value of foreign language learning and use. Durden reported briefly on the unusual successes achieved by the CTY since 1978, when the first program in German was introduced. Intensive summer institutes on German language and culture have proved very popular with gifted students between the ages of eleven and sixteen. Upon completion of the summer program, participants regularly place in a high school level IV language course. The CTY is rapidly expanding its activities both here and abroad. Hessinger's special interest is in greater coordination of high school and college German programs. She is convinced that success depends upon the greater personal involvement of the language teacher and upon real discourse among educators at all levels of education. Langacker drew attention to the importance of recent emphasis at the university level on proficiency-based teaching and testing for the Foreign Language in Elementary School (FLES) and high school programs. As a textbook author, she is also keenly aware of the need to incorporate this communicative approach into curricular materials for use in the schools. Hausman was concerned with the role of foreign languages in the schools as seen from the administrator's point of view. As chairman of a nationally recognized high school language department, he recognizes the various pressures which affect course offerings and made suggestions about action which could be taken. Stephenson, as a current vice-president of the national American Association of Teachers of German (AATG), reported on the several options available for widening the sphere of influence of local German programs. Among these options are implementation of the Zertifikat Deutsch and Mittelstufenprüfung administered by the Goethe Institute, summer stipends for high school students from the American Association of Teachers of German and the Deutscher Akademischer Austauschdienst (DAAD), an Austrian summer tour, and a nationwide essay contest sponsored by AATG and Lufthansa Airlines. Such joint ventures are important motivators for instructors and students alike.

The composition of the panel thus ensured a relatively broad spectrum of institutions, programs, and interests involved in the furtherance of German language and culture in the United States. The open forum on the German language was viewed not just as an extension of the earlier session on the German language in America but as an outgrowth of the recent recognition of the need for cooperative efforts at all levels of education.

Laws and requirements governing the incidence of German instruction in the schools have been a factor in teaching ever since Ohio approved legislation in 1839 calling for German to be taught in the public elementary schools. Since then, requirements have changed frequently. Two of the most famous instances adversely affecting the use of German were the ban against the teaching of German in many public and private schools in 1917 and the move on the part of many colleges and universities in the late 1960s and early 1970s to drop or reduce the foreign language entrance requirement. The latter development precipitated a renewed crisis in language teaching at the college and high school levels. The crisis, which peaked in the mid-1970s, led to a critical reassessment of German language instruction at all institutional levels. In 1976 a special volume of the *Monatshefte* appeared entitled *German Studies in the United States: Assessment and Outlook*. The volume contained numerous articles purporting to focus on "the German-teaching profession in the United States in its full

context—from primary to graduate school."[6] Despite some incisive
comments and sound suggestions in individual essays, the volume
was disappointing. The focus was too much on survival tactics; there
were too many quick solutions; there was little awareness of the immigrant experience. Moreover, there were too many university professors
addressing other university professors. There was, in brief, no dialogue with colleagues in community colleges, high schools, or elementary school programs.

This lacuna was quickly detected by others. For example, Reinhard Kuhn wrote in his 1977 essay "German Studies Today: Some
Signs of Sanity in Bedlam" that "one of the areas in which our profession has been woefully remiss is in cooperation among university
faculty members, professors in teachers colleges, and high school
teachers."[7] In the same inaugural issue of *Profession*, Leon I. Twarog
made an even more forceful case for interinstitutional cooperation,
concluding his argument with the statement: "If we want foreign languages to advance beyond 'survival' levels in higher education, it is
clear that more attention must be given to developing foreign language
instruction in the two-year colleges and the high schools."[8]

The year 1980 saw a slew of publications which made similar
points while proffering other suggestions as well. Here I need mention
only Paul Simon's influential *The Tongue-Tied American: Confronting
the Foreign Language Crisis* and Richard I. Brod's volume *Language
Study for the 1980s: Report of the Modern Language Association—
American Council of Learned Societies Language Task Forces.*[9] These
and similar studies were instrumental in creating a sense of national
crisis, which ultimately led to the founding of the National Commission on Excellence in Education. That commission released its report
in April 1983 under the title *A Nation at Risk: The Imperative for Educational Reform*. The national importance of foreign language study as
a basic skill is noted: "Study of a foreign language introduces the students to non-English speaking cultures, heightens awareness and
comprehension of one's native tongue, and serves the Nation's needs
in commerce, diplomacy and education."[10] The commission's emphasis
on the liberating impact of foreign language study echoes views on the
communicative uses of foreign languages that have predominated in
discussions since the late 1970s, as evidenced by such commentators
as Richard Lambert (language use: 1982), Humphrey Tonkin (act of
liberation from cultural myopia: 1982), and Clifford Adelman (expanding the niche of language study: 1982).[11] The forum on the German
language in America repeatedly touched upon these issues raised by

observers over the past few years, applying them to the specific situation in German language instruction. Those deliberations are paraphrased and summarized in the following seven general areas.

1. First and foremost, the language community must make a concerted effort to capitalize upon the momentum acquired in recent years to broaden public awareness of the value of foreign language study. Above all, German instructors must educate policy makers, such as the members of Congress, school district supervisors, school board directors, principals, and guidance counselors, most of whom suffer from cultural provincialism, which restricts the effectiveness of language instruction in America. If the policy makers can be won over, the language teacher's battle is half won.

2. In connection with this first point, the language community must engage upon a new and separate citizen education program designed to improve the general public's awareness of America's global relations and cultural/linguistic diversity. Adult education classes in language and literature, an annual Foreign Language Week, and greater involvement of foreign language speakers in Parent-Teacher Association (PTA) activities are some of the actions that could be taken. Programs for the intellectually gifted, greater visibility of "Saturday" schools, and inclusion of the various *Vereine* in educational projects would fall under this category as well.

3. To achieve the first and second goals, German (and the other foreign languages) must move out of the "ghetto." That is what Lambert means when he argues that foreign languages must cease to be the sole responsibility of the language departments, that foreign languages must be used in other departments at colleges and universities as well.[12] That is what Adelman means when he speaks of foreign language study as a basic skill because it teaches the student a different form of thinking, thus enhancing his ability to perceive the broad ramifications of a question.[13] And, finally, that is what Tonkin means when he cites "the assimilation of language learning to all the disciplines."[14]

4. Without improved teacher education and language instruction at all levels, none of the above programs would be of lasting value. Tonkin makes the very important point that teaching language is not the same as teaching literature: "The gap is not between elementary and advanced knowledge within a single discipline but between disparate disciplines" (p. 41). College and university language teachers are normally trained to teach literature and are largely unprepared for meeting the challenge of the language classroom. Thomas P. Saine has pointed out the inadequacies of the teaching assistant system

whereby novice teachers are engaged to teach the German language while being indoctrinated in their graduate courses to value only literature.[15] That is not to say that improvements to the system are not possible. Special orientation sessions and ongoing pedagogical seminars at Pennsylvania, University of California-Los Angeles, Texas-Austin, Iowa, and elsewhere have shown that improvements can be made in the teaching assistant's preparation as a language teacher. For elementary and high school teachers, workshops, senior apprenticeships, and refresher courses (in both language and pedagogy) are extremely valuable. The *Fortbildungsseminare* offered by the Goethe House and Goethe Institute both here and in the Federal Republic of Germany are a step in the right direction. Another important step would be an exchange between high schools and colleges, a sharing of information, approaches, and cultural enrichment programs. In Twarog's words: "Foreign language departments need to reach out to the community and to other colleges and universities in close geographical proximity in order to create joint or cooperative programs of outreach that will be of benefit to all. . . . What is required first of all is a change of attitude on the part of college and university teachers and administrators, who must recognize the need to reach out to other segments of their own institutions, to the two-year institutions, and to the secondary schools in particular."[16] College German teachers could be invited to spend an in-service day with their counterparts in the local schools; those secondary teachers could also be invited to observe language classes at the college or university or to participate in the ongoing pedagogical seminars. The experience could only be enriching. In recognition of these benefits NEH and private foundations have helped create the Academic Alliances: School/College Faculty Collaborative, which is devoted to furthering closer cooperation among all levels of education.

5. A coordinator of foreign language instruction should be appointed by universities to oversee these cooperative efforts. School districts should make a similar appointment to coordinate districtwide activities in foreign languages with vice-coordinators for the individual languages. Moreover, faculty committees drawing members from various departments within a university could serve as clearing houses for ideas relating to secondary school relations. The University of Pennsylvania, for example, recently established a committee on school relations and has had, for some time, a coordinator of language study in the dean's office.

6. Hand in hand with improved teacher education must go the development of appropriate curricular materials reflecting the ideal of

language use and communication. Proficiency-based teaching and testing mirror these goals in particularly felicitous fashion. Language teachers should be trained in the concept of language proficiency or competence as a feasible goal for foreign language study in the United States. To facilitate these efforts at developing proficiency-based skills in the teacher and in devising appropriate curricular materials, regional centers could be established along the lines of the Proficiency Testing Center recently instituted at Pennsylvania by the American Council of Teachers of Foreign Languages. Using input from language teachers at all levels, these centers would establish proficiency criteria and examine means of implementing programs. The Texas decision to require language competence of its foreign language teachers by the year 1986 is a sign of things to come. We cannot afford to be caught unprepared.

7. Finally, incentives for excellence in language teaching and learning should be provided. These could take the form of monetary compensation, trips to the Federal Republic of Germany, Austria, or Switzerland, or collegial recognition. At the very least, funds and free time should be made available by school districts and colleges to the language teachers to enable them to attend workshops and seminars designed to hone their teaching skills while developing new instructional materials.

The implementation of the foregoing suggestions resultant of the open forum on the German language in America would go a long way toward establishing the "linguistic utopia" envisioned by recent critics of the state of language study in the United States. That ideal as seen from the university tower was described by Twarog in the following manner: "The college and university foreign language departments must communicate with the high schools, and must help to develop in the general citizenry an awareness of the need and the importance of foreign language study. Not only must there be someone in every language department who has a special coordinating or liaison function for the high schools in the immediate area, but this work must also have the active support of the departmental chairman. The ideal person for such a position would be someone with a Ph.D. or D.A. [Doctor of Arts] in foreign language education, a person who has actually had teaching experience both at the college and high school levels."[17] This ideal person would operate in an ideal situation, one marked by an altered attitude within the universities. Chief among the characteristics of this new attitude would be the higher estimation of linguistic scholarship, broadly defined, in relation to literary scholarship. That greater esteem would go hand in glove with the assimilation of language learning to various other disciplines.[18] But we cannot afford to wait for the "ideal person" or the enlightened administrator to happen along to help us break out of the "ghetto." We can begin by reaching out, by learning to work together more effectively, by communicating with those outside the discipline. Furthermore, each of us must be committed. As Hessinger noted at the open forum: "Success depends upon extra effort on the part of the language teacher; it takes personal involvement."

Without this personal commitment and a sincere desire to pursue some of the issues raised at the open forum, we would be engaged in mere survival tactics. The German language might indeed survive to the quatricentennial celebration; but would it serve anything more than a symbolic function? Can language teachers be satisfied with the prospects of such a limited role for language? The participants in the open forum on the German language in America think not.

Notes

1. Thomas Piltz, ed., *Die Deutschen und die Amerikaner* (Gräfelfing [Munich]: Heinz Moos, 1977), 19–53; *300 Jahre Deutsche in Amerika* (Gräfelfing [Munich]: Moos, 1982), 4–6.

2. *300 Jahre Deutsche in Amerika*, 5.

3. See the contributions of Marion Lois Huffines ("Language-Maintenance Efforts Among German Immigrants and Their Descendants in the United States") and Jürgen Eichhoff ("The German Language in America") in this volume.

4. Wolfgang Moelleken, "Language Maintenance and Language Shift in Pennsylvania German: A Comparative Investigation," *Monatshefte* 75 (1983): 172–86; Joseph C. Salmons, "Issues in Texas German Language Maintenance and Shift," *Monatshefte* 75 (1983): 187–96.

5. See the contribution of Joshua A. Fishman in this volume ("Demographic and Institutional Indicators of German Language Maintenance in the United States, 1960–1980").

6. Walter F. W. Lohnes and Valters Nollendorfs, eds., *German Studies in the United States: Assessment and Outlook. Monatshefte*, Occasional Volume, no. 1 (1976): 4.

7. Reinhard Kuhn, "German Studies Today: Some Signs of Sanity in Bedlam," *Profession* 77 (1977): 44–48, quotation, 46.

8. Leon I. Twarog, "Beyond Survival: The Role of Foreign Language Programs in the High School and the Two-Year Colleges," *Profession* 77 (1977): 49–53, quotation, 52.

9. Richard I. Brod, ed., *Language Study for the 1980s: Report of the Modern Language Association–American Council of Learned Societies Language Task Forces* (New York: Modern Language Association, 1980).

10. As cited by the *Northeast Conference Newsletter* 14 (1983):28.

11. Richard D. Lambert, "Language Learning and Language Utilization," *Profession* 82 (1982):47–51; Humphrey Tonkin, "Language and International Studies: Closing the Gap," *Profession* 82 (1982):39–46; Clifford Adelman, "Saving the Baby: Language Study and the New Reforms in General Education," *Profession* 82 (1982): 32–38.

12. Lambert, "Language Learning," 48.

13. Adelman, "Saving the Baby," 33, 37.

14. Tonkin, "Language and International Studies," 42.

15. Thomas P. Saine, "The Evaluation of Teaching and the State of the University," *Profession* 79 (1979):39–45.

16. Twarog, "Beyond Survival," 50.

17. Ibid., 52.

18. Tonkin, "Language and International Studies," 42–43.

Part V:

German-American Literature

19.

German-American Literature: Some Further Perspectives

HAROLD JANTZ

MUCH OF WHAT WE KNOW about German-American literature and literary relations, early and late, exists in isolated compartments to which meaningful connections have not always been made. If we start at the present day and move backward in time, we shall behold a repeated phenomenon with regard to the German *Amerikabild*: each generation is convinced that it has its own, modern, realistic transatlantic image, and it does not realize how much of that image is traditional, fictional, even mythical, with only surface changes in dress and hairdo. Every informed American traveling in Europe can gather much incidental amusement from current pronouncements about America by removing their wrappers and dating them back to their points of origin. The amusement grew to hearty laughter in 1966, when the literary *Gruppe 47* descended upon the United States. Siegfried Mandel in his book on the group has given us some choice specimens of its published nonsense about America,[1] and for years afterward those among the American Germanists who had observed the grotesque antics and dim-witted words of certain members of the group during their American travels could regale their colleagues at convivial meetings with anecdote after choice anecdote. Only a few of the group, of course, rose to this level of unwitting comedy, these simply the same silly European pseudosophisticates of the past 150 years who knew all about America in advance and were merely spouting forth with preprogrammed minds the traditional compulsive clichés. Carl Zuckmayer had produced a hilarious persiflage of this *Literatenamerika* a bit earlier after his years of living in the real world of the United States, when he recalled his and Franz Werfel's pre-exile visions of America.

The 1966 literati might have avoided some of their worst blunders if they had at least read Zuckmayer's "Amerika ist anders."

Actually, the complex of compulsive clichés goes back much farther; a few details of it are even endowed with the gray whiskers of the conquistadores, as I tried to show years ago in "The Myths about America."[2] My more contemporaneous analysis of the past 150 years came in "The View from Chesapeake Bay: An Experiment with the Image of America."[3] One of the German literati actually did read the latter and wrote me in thanks for the destultifying perspectives it provided. But my greatest reward came from Samuel Eliot Morison, who had enjoyed the paper when I read it at the meeting of the American Antiquarian Society. My reference to a Goethe anecdote that Robert Wesselhöft had told to Henry Wadsworth Longfellow stimulated him at the luncheon afterward to tell me about another Goethe conversation, this with a Harvard man, that had been passed down by word of mouth and had never been recorded. He subsequently wrote it down for me, and I intend to publish it along with another.

Several decades before 1966 there was, and still is, the B. Traven mystery with its multiple obfuscations, which, after a long line of predecessors, Will Wyatt finally penetrated in 1980.[4] Or did he? I think not. The B. Traven/Hal Croves who died in Mexico City in 1969 was almost certainly not the Otto Feige who had been born in Schwiebus in 1882. Indubitably, one further crucial critical task still needs to be undertaken before the real surprise ending will become manifest. Let me add a different instance of a lack of perspective in our century. Shortly after 1900 a Brooklyn furrier, Hugo Bertsch, won European-German critical acclaim for his novels. He continues to be known in German-American bibliography, but no one in recent decades has been curious enough to find out whether that critical acclaim continues to be justified in the 1980s. Up to his time, but chiefly in the preceding decades, there was another novelist, worlds apart from him, Rudolf Lindau, the cosmopolitan brother of Paul Lindau. He was fascinated by the lives and characters of the American expatriates whom he encountered and observed in Europe, China, Japan, and elsewhere. Theodor Fontane esteemed him highly, but there is never a word about him in any survey of German-American literary relations. And in German literature itself he vanishes under the shadow of his more famous and less distinguished brother (who also had more than a few words to say about America and the Americans).

I pass over the strange compulsiveness with which critics in the field continue to come back again and again to Ferdinand Kürnberger's

Der Amerika-Müde (1855) as the exemplary anti-American novel, even though Guy T. Hollyday in 1977 provided us with better perspectives.[5] No one will know how silly, witless, and derivative Kürnberger's novel is until he has read three or four such brilliant, firsthand, keenly observed anti-American novels as Albert von Halfern's *Der Squire* (1857) or Adelbert von Baudissin's *Zustände in Amerika (Peter Tütt)* (1862). For proper perspectives on the anti-American novel one would also need to pay attention to the better-balanced novel of mid- and late nineteenth century, not the romantic, idealizing kind or the mere adventure novel, but the kind that is built upon the alert observation of actual American phenomena and people. Most such novels, nearly all of them, are still resting silently on the library shelves waiting to be opened up by the inquiring student of German Americana.

In 1982 in a Festschrift for William H. McClain, I finally did away with an old, persistent, unquestioned assumption that the younger Goethe showed little interest in America and that only around 1807 and 1808 did he become interested in what was happening on this side of the Atlantic.[6] One can hold such a position only if one's knowledge of things American is so scanty that one overlooks them when they turn up in Goethe's works, letters, and diaries. A fractional knowledge of Goethe also helps preserve the illusion. In sum, past studies of America and the younger Goethe are based on less than a 20 percent knowledge of the pertinent facts and phenomena, and so the conclusions are more than 80 percent wrong.

Much the same can be said about large areas of other eighteenth-century German-American relations. The travel literature is reasonably well known, as is the rest of the expository literature with an openly American content. But when one turns to the novels, dramas, and poems of the century, it is only the obvious ones and a few others that have been recorded and critically regarded. This means again an approximately 20 to 30 percent knowledge of what is actually there, for most of the Americana in the creative, imaginative field is hidden Americana and can be found only if one reads beyond the title into the work itself. As I have shown on previous occasions, whole areas of German-American contact have escaped attention, for instance the motif of the veteran returning to Germany after the conclusion of the Revolutionary War, a motif central to several dramas and one that also fascinated Goethe, once negatively, twice positively. The actual veterans themselves occasionally produced writings of real literary merit. The most witty and perspicacious of them, an anonymous Brunswick officer, is known to a few American historians because of his colorful evocation of the Massachusetts countryside and people, but he still awaits the critical assessment of the literarily engaged. As for the German writers who came to America and stayed here, there are a number in the late eighteenth and early nineteenth centuries whose careers still remain to be explored. The industrious Johann Georg Meusel in *Das gelehrte Teutschland* (1796–), through his geographical index, made it easy to locate a few of these German-Americans, but no one bothered to do so until 1977, when in a few paragraphs of a contribution to the Karl Arndt Festschrift, entitled "German Men of Letters in the Early United States,"[7] I traced the careers of two dramatists, Gottlob Timotheus Michael Kühl and Anton Christian Hunnius, who in 1787 and 1794 came to Philadelphia, where their further American traces are still waiting to be uncovered.

It is in the mid- and early eighteenth century, however also in the late seventeenth, that it is especially important to increase and enrich our perspectives with a better and fuller understanding of the German and general European backgrounds. Central here is the contact that took place between the German-American and the Anglo-American writers, this not a one-sided matter, for the English writers repeatedly show the effect their German neighbors had on them, an effect that was reinforced by several influential Germans living in England and interested in American developments. For these English backgrounds a good introduction is Garold N. Davis's pioneer study of 1969, *German Thought and Culture in England, 1700–1770*. Looming large in this period is Pietism, a factor that had an abiding influence on the poetic literature of Germany, England, and America deep into the Romantic period and beyond. According to the *Oxford English Dictionary* the word *Pietism* entered the English language in 1697, and the examples given show that it was a German import. At least a year earlier the word came into Anglo-American usage, and the English over here also knew about the German origins. Indeed, a citizen of Newport, Rhode Island, Stephen Mumford (1639–1701), wrote to Johann Kelpius, the hermit of the Wissahickon, seeking to be "a little further informed of the Principles and Practices of those People that go under the Name of Pietists." Kelpius's letterbook contains the draft of his reply to Mumford, dated December 11, 1699. The reply differs widely and wildly from any reply that Philipp Jacob Spener or August Hermann Francke might have written, and it makes clear that there were two kinds of Pietism, that of the moderates in the Protestant church and that of the radical separatists. Even stranger than Kelpius's reply is the fact that an Englishman in Rhode Island would write

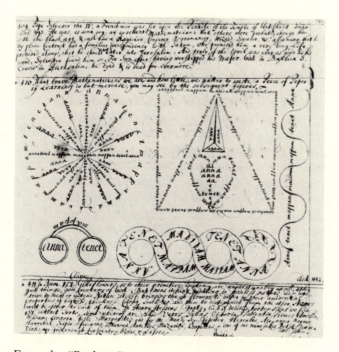

From the "Beehive," an extensive compendium of knowledge from many diverse areas by Francis Daniel Pastorius (1651–1719). The founder of Germantown began work on this manuscript in 1696 as a kind of private encyclopedia. While its breadth and form represent a typical Baroque inclination to display the author's erudition, the work itself is nonetheless the product of an original, open, and keenly observant mind. In the above passage from the year 1700, Pastorius injects a bit of playfulness between his more sober reflections on Pope Sylvester and on man's incursions into the world of nature in a fashion not unlike that of the modern Dadaist writer Kurt Schwitters. He interweaves the name of his wife Anna and the Latin words *tenet mappam madidam* into a palindrome which reads the same forwards and backwards ("Anna is holding a moist napkin"). While Pastorius used much German as well as Baroque literature in his more readily available manuscript "Deliciae Hortenses," the "Beehive" is written almost exclusively in English. (Special Collections, Van Pelt Library, University of Pennsylvania).

such a query to a German in Pennsylvania only a few years after the latter had arrived there. And this was not the only Anglo-American from another colony who turned to Kelpius for advice, since requests came also from Connecticut and Long Island. How can one account for a solitary hermit becoming so widely known so quickly? One possible answer might be Jacob Telner, a Krefeld merchant and mystic, who had made business trips to New York as early as 1678 and 1681, settled in Germantown in 1685 for thirteen years, and at least once traveled as a Quaker missionary to New England.[8]

Part of the answer may also be indicated by the strange story of the transmission of Kelpius's poetic works with their musical compositions. This was taken care of not by a fellow German but by a remarkable Englishman, Dr. Christopher Witt, who first joined the hermits of the Wissahickon, then became a friend and neighbor of Pastorius, was a talented mechanic and an esteemed botanist in collaboration with his famous friends, Peter Collinson and John Bartram. Christopher Witt's manuscript not only preserves the German mystical poems of Johann Kelpius together with their musical setting, it also transmits Witt's own English verse translation. To my knowledge, this is the first English translation of the "gesammelte Werke" of a German Baroque poet. Nicolaus Ludwig von Zinzendorf, with his large and faithful English and American following, did not have to wait long to have much of his verse and prose translated, but then there was a long interval before a third Baroque poet, Paul Gerhardt (1867), and a fourth, Angelus Silesius (1909), had a larger body of verse translated into English. Probably the first English translation of any single poem of Angelus Silesius was made by another Wissahickon hermit, Johann Gottfried Seelig.

We do know something, indeed a great deal, about the Anglo-Americans through the centuries who furthered the knowledge of German literature and even of German-American literature. Occasionally one or the other of them actually became a part of the German-American community. Just one little instance: in our young years when we lived on a wonderful farm on a ridge extending from Mount Wachusett, we had a jolly landlord and neighbor who had grown up in a Connecticut town with a large German population. He and his pals joined the German social clubs, *Turnverein* and so on, because, as he put it, the Germans were the only ones who had any fun. This is a trivial point to make here, but multiplied by the thousands all over the country, it becomes anything but trivial. When, after the United States entered World War II, the English sent over a contingent of aviators to be trained in the use of the new planes, each was given a handbook with advice on how to get along in the United States. One warning it contained was not to assume that because the Americans spoke English they were temperamentally and habitually just like Englishmen. Indeed, the handbook advised, the Americans are quite different in their reaction patterns, and one of the primary causes was that the large proportion of Germans, long a part of the populace, had helped mold the American character. Beyond the practical areas of daily life this influence carried over, of course, into the arts and literature, even in regions where the proportion of Germans was at first relatively small, as in New England. In that region, for instance, Novalis's *Heinrich von Ofterdingen* was first translated in 1842, then republished in New York eleven years later, even though in England there was no translation of the work for a long time. Likewise that other very German German, Jean Paul, received his first English biography from Eliza Buckminster Lee, also in 1842, this followed by the first English translation of four of his novels by her and by Charles Timothy Brooks. In the Boston literary circle of her older brother, Joseph Stevens Buckminster, German literature was being cultivated years before the first American students enrolled at Göttingen.

In a few of my youthful works I traced the German affinities of these Anglo-New Englanders back deep into the seventeenth century and showed how many of them had close German connections, including the poet Johann Rist and several other men of letters. In a recent article for the *Yearbook of German-American Studies* that looks more deeply into the earliest presence of Germans in the American colonies, I try to do something about that very puzzling statement by John White in *The Planters Plea* that a group of Germans crossed the Atlantic with the Winthrop fleet of 1630 and that more Germans were to follow. What happened to these early Germans in Massachusetts? The few historians who from time to time came upon John White's statement of 1630 could take it no further and dropped it back into oblivion. Some minute research in English as well as American sources can carry matters a few steps farther, for example the still unpublished diary of John Whiteway of old Dorchester that recorded the events, local and European, during the crucial years before the Great Migration. But then it is the comparative method that will show the way: common sense combined with the careful observation of what happened to the early Germans in the other colonies. I have heard rumors from northeast of here that evidence has been found that another shipload of Germans came to America some years before Pastorius and the Krefelders founded Germantown. But the fact remains that the Germans of Germantown and environs retained their identity and proliferated into the larger community of the Pennsylvania Germans and the still larger one of the American Germans. One chief reason why they did so was that there were from the beginning great minds and great personalities among them, and they left a literature that remained alive through the centuries and can still speak to us. The other region with an equally great, probably even greater intellectual endowment, was New England. In my early years I was able to write a book on *The First Century of New England Verse, 1620–1720.* Neither I nor anyone else could write a whole book on the first century of English verse in the Middle Atlantic colonies or in the South because apparently there just is not enough of it for more than a thin article. It is entirely possible, however, to write an unpadded, undiluted book on the Pennsylvania verse, English and German, of the decades just before and after 1700. By contrast, the ample Dutch verse of the Hudson region has only a thin trickle of English verse to accompany it. Perhaps one reason why there were more Anglo-Americans in Pennsylvania who wrote verse was that they had the example of so many of their German neighbors, who indulged themselves in the same addictive habit.

There is no need here to review again the dozen or two earliest Pennsylvania-German poets beyond the well-known Pastorius, Kelpius, and Beissel. Some good beginnings have been made here, but much more needs to be done, especially on those who returned to Germany or whose works were sent back there, as in the case of Heinrich Bernhard Köster or Johann Adam Gruber. Indeed, among the Americans who returned to Germany in the early and mid-eighteenth century there may have been a novelist or two. Among the various *Amerikaromane* of the time nearly all bear internal as well as external evidence of being based on travel narratives, foreign sources, and a sometimes overheated imagination, but a few do have a more authentic ring and call for closer scrutiny. The American who came (or returned) to Europe was a popular figure in European fiction and reality, and as a result a number of pseudo-Americans also appeared on the scene. Goethe's encounters with two pseudo-Americans during the 1790s and with one genuine but mysterious American in 1777 are characteristic of what was happening more widely at the time.

Even when we turn to the best known among the early German-American writers, it is astonishing what a new picture emerges when we set about widening the perspectives on them. Let us see what happens to Francis Daniel Pastorius, to Johann Kelpius, and to Conrad

Beissel. That Pastorius's father, Melchior Adam, was also a devoted versifier is generally well known. His relationship with the members of the Nuremberg literary society, the so-called Pegnitzschäfer, especially with Sigmund von Birken, has long been established albeit never adequately explored. Once one knows this, the son's affinity with the literary traditions of this society is manifest. But whence comes the rollicking good humor of so much of his verse? No doubt out of himself and many an outside source. But one source we now know definitely. It came during the period of his youthful sojourn in Regensburg, in very merry company that included the budding musician and novelist Johann Beer, who left a fictional record of these lively Regensburg times. The aftermath was that Pastorius, Beer, and another friend, Christopher Donauer, matriculated together at the University of Altdorf in 1675. Since Pastorius had been here before, he was probably the main motivating force in this direction.

The Altdorf-Nuremberg connections of Johann Kelpius are also known, but only insofar as they involve his relationship with his distinguished teacher, Johann Fabricius, who went on to Helmstedt, wrote to Kelpius from there, and probably received the reply the latter wrote on July 23, 1705. None of this touches on his poetic career and its possible Nuremberg affinities, however. Nuremberg poetry is most compendiously chronicled in Johann Herdegen's historical biographical collections entitled *Historische Nachricht von dess löblichen Hirten- und Blumen-Ordens an der Pegnitz Anfang und Fortgang* of 1744. Here we learn that Kelpius, not yet twenty, was a lecturer at the university and that a future head of the literary society, Joachim Negelein, was, through the good offices of a mutual patron, able to attend his academic classes. What the poetic consequences may have been we do not know. His occasional affinities to the older poet Johann Klaj are obvious, once they are pointed out. There are clear literary affinities to the mystic poetic circle at the nearby court of Sulzbach, but there is no evidence that these were also personal. Indeed, Christian Knorr von Rosenroth died in 1689 when Kelpius was only sixteen years old, and the tutor in the Knorr family, Christian Ludwig (Lodowick), had left Sulzbach for Newport and Boston by 1684. So here too there are no direct connecting links to the like-minded southern New Englanders with whom Kelpius associated.

In the case of Conrad Beissel the most vital of the relationships, even more vital than those with Berleburg and environs, is so tenuous as well as complex that no justice can be done to it here. A plain statement of the facts and relations sounds improbable enough to arouse disbelief, but here it is, in a few lines, without the pages of documentary evidence. Thomas Tillam, well known as the author of the beautiful lyric "Uppon the first sight of New England June 29, 1638" as well as of other poems, was later known as the fervent, charismatic leader of a group of mystic, millennarian, sabbatarian pilgrims and exiles from England who established their monastic community in the Palatinate about two-thirds of the way (some twenty kilometers) from Conrad Beissel's hometown Eberbach toward Heidelberg. Both English and German descriptions indicate clearly that this monastic establishment was remarkably close in principles, intent, and organization to the one that Beissel was later to develop at Ephrata. The few marked differences to be seen at the beginning grew ever greater as the genius of Beissel developed the life at Ephrata into a *Gesamtkunstwerk* of poetry, music, and painting that was without parallel.

Kelpius, after his strange life and enigmatic relationships, suffered an even stranger posthumous fame. The superimaginative George Lippard in 1848 transformed him into the sensational hero of his novel *Paul Ardenheim, or the Monk of Wissahikon*. Here, fictionally, he was first incorporated into the Rosicrucian fiction. The Neorosicrucians (Neurosenkreutzer) enthusiastically added corroborative detail to this unconvincing narrative until the all-too-uncritical Julius Friedrich Sachse sanctified it into a historic verity that even some serious recent historians are half inclined to believe. On the basis of the Sachse *Nachlass*, George Allen long ago gave me specific details on the way this author occasionally bent the evidence to bolster a favorite theory of his. And back in my Princeton days, another remarkable Philadelphia antiquarian bookseller told me of the time in his youth when he observed how the old gentleman would advance within a few weeks (or even days) from a merely speculative "What if . . ." to an utterly convinced "Certainly so." Nevertheless, Sachse's volumes are valuable despite these marginals and peripheries of hyperimagination and gullibility, and these can be forgiven him with a smile of gratitude for the indispensable good work he has done in the field of German Americana. His Rosicrucian volumes and speculations have migrated to California, and when this state once more becomes an island, as it was on many an early map, and the manuscripts are mysteriously transported to a monastery in the Himalayas long since prepared for them, we shall, I hope, be able to carry on our German-American studies no less imaginatively and creatively, though perhaps with a bit more critical common sense.

Notes

1. Siegfried Mandel, *Group 47: The Reflected Intellect* (Carbondale: Southern Illinois University Press, 1973), esp. 212ff.

2. Harold Jantz, "The Myths about America," *Jahrbuch für Amerikastudien* 7 (1962):6–18.

3. Harold Jantz, "The View from Chesapeake Bay: An Experiment with the Image of America," *Publications of the American Antiquarian Society* 79 (1969):151–71.

4. Will Wyatt, *The Secret of the Sierra Madre: The Man who Was B. Traven* (Garden City, N.Y.: Doubleday, 1980).

5. Guy T. Hollyday, *Anti-Americanism in the German Novel, 1841–1862*, German Studies in America, 27 (Bern: P. Lang, 1977).

6. Harold Jantz, "America and the Younger Goethe," *Modern Language Notes* 97 (1982):515–45.

7. Gerhard K. Friesen and Walter Schatzberg, eds., *The German Contribution to the Building of the Americas* (Hanover, N.H.: Clark University Press, 1977), 75–95.

8. On Telner see Friedrich Nieper, *Die ersten deutschen Auswanderer von Krefeld nach Pennsylvanien* (Neukirchen, Kreis Moers: Buchhandlung des Erziehungsvereins, 1940), 86–88.

20.
The Challenge of Early
German-American Literature

CHRISTOPH E. SCHWEITZER

I REFER TO EARLY GERMAN-AMERICAN LITERATURE as a challenge because I believe that although that literature is fairly unknown, it is of sufficient importance to deserve more attention from the American Germanist. In this essay I will try to explain why such relative ignorance prevails and then point out some of the highlights of the first period of German-American writing, that is, roughly from 1683 to the first quarter of the nineteenth century; finally, I will indicate steps I feel should be taken to make early German-American literature more accessible.

My training in Germanistics in this country was traditional, with courses in historical linguistics as well as in literature. For a dissertation topic or first publications even the most obscure manuscript at a German library or archive or a little-known Continental author was acceptable. Except for the works of the so-called exile authors of World War II, we were prejudiced against anything written by earlier Germans in this country. When selecting readers for our classes, we might have glanced at such titles as *Sutter* or *Carl Schurz*,[1] but they only confirmed our prejudices. Very few of us had contacts with German-American organizations. Those few who did knew that their members had other interests than we had as graduate students: the organizations were not the place to go to hear lectures on aspect in Old High German or on Franz Kafka. Only much later did some of us realize the invaluable work these organizations have performed and are performing, including the preservation of precious books and manuscripts. All of us owe the German-American organizations a great deal of respect and gratitude.

Nevertheless, the physical presence of German-Americana impressed itself even on someone with my preconceived ideas. Conrad Beissel and his Ephrata community turned me around and provided a first focus for research. Coming to grips with him and the Ephrata community proved to be more difficult than, for example, working out a new interpretation of Gotthold Ephraim Lessing's *Nathan der Weise*. For *Nathan* we have an authentic text, excellent notes, and a complete bibliography of secondary literature. For German-American literature the situation is much less clear. There is no comprehensive bibliography of the older material, and the current work is buried in a huge mass of the many different topics encompassed by the subject.

There are other problems. Many German-American entries in bibliographies deal with religious issues. As is well known, many of the Germans came to the colonies, especially to William Penn's tolerant Pennsylvania, because they did not belong to one of the major religious groups, that is, they were neither Catholics, Lutherans, nor Reformed but were members of one of the radical sectarian denominations. Literary historians need to look at some of the religious material, too. It can, for instance, explain the vocabulary and ideas of the hymns of a given group. Since we are dealing with an era of radical interpretations of the Bible, some going back to the mystic tradition in general and specifically to Jakob Böhme and other equally obscure authors, matters become truly difficult, not just for the literary historian but for theologians.

The literary historian is in for other surprises. In our ignorance we had assumed that nonreligious early German-American writing was in dialect or a folksy style, similar in language and subject matter to the *Heimatdichtung* of the Continent. Nothing could be further from the truth. Up to the early nineteenth century there is no printed dialect literature. The early German-American authors bring to their writings a great amount of learning. Francis Daniel Pastorius was trained as a lawyer at various European universities, knew Greek, Latin, Dutch, French, Italian, and after 1683, English, went on a grand tour through parts of Europe, had interests in and knew something about almost every subject, including languages and literatures, emblematics, history, theology, legal studies, horticulture, agriculture, and medicine. I needed the help of several colleagues in other departments to try to cope with the editing of just one short manuscript by Pastorius.[2] The difficulties become staggering when one tries to deal with the more than eight hundred pages of the "Beehive" manuscript, the encyclopedic book of knowledge from diverse disciplines which he collected for his children, and which is a prize possession of the Rare Book Collection of the Van Pelt Library at the University of Pennsylvania. Harold Jantz, who was the key person negotiating with the family to give the manuscript to the Rare Book Collection, is trying to make at least the most important parts of the "Beehive" generally accessible.

Other authors of the period received superb theological training as Lutheran ministers before converting to one of the frowned-upon denominations and emigrating to America. Even the self-taught Conrad Beissel wrote religious treatises and hymns that betray that he was steeped in theological issues. In a word, much of the writing of the early German-Americans is difficult both to approach and to evaluate.

There is one more point I want to mention. Several of those who studied the literary products of the early German-American authors expected to find *Erlebnisdichtung* and were disappointed when the *Erlebnis* turned out to be a thought, an image, a symbol, or a phrase handed down from earlier literature, including the Bible. We now have a better understanding of such literary products, of the Renaissance/ Baroque poetics, and thus can approach these writings with fewer preconceived ideas than did some previous scholars.

I firmly believe that American Germanists need to know more about the German-American material, printed or in manuscript form, that is in our libraries and archives. The receptive scholar will be fascinated to discover truly unusual personalities and their literary products and to know the joy that goes with the discovery of an unknown or almost unknown literary text.

Among the authors who have impressed me as unusual and whose literary products I learned to appreciate is Francis Daniel Pastorius. He was able both to add the English language to his poetic output and to include his new environment as subject matter of his writings. I find him most successful as an author of epigrams, short verses with a pithy and sometimes humorous twist. One example of a clever combination of his native German and his acquired English is the following maccaronic verse:

> Hanns has his hands and tongue at his Command;
> He keeps most fast what he did promise, and
> Verspricht, und lieferts nicht; Das ist ein Schand.[3]

The early German-speaking immigrants often came in groups as members of radical pietistic sects. Such was the case with another Germantown inhabitant, Johannes Kelp or Kelpius, who was the spiritual center of a small and loose-knit community that has been called

Der Neue Hoch Deutsche Americanische Calender, Auf das Jahr Christi, 1791.
This title page from Samuel Saur's almanac for 1791 may represent the first
illustration of an American printing shop. The woodcut (by an unknown
hand) shows two printers at the press on the right; one is inking the type while
the other is arranging paper on a frame which swings down over the type before it is rolled under the press. The printer on the left is receiving the copy
from Mercury, who says: "What I do not reveal now, I will bring to you
next year."

Calendars and almanacs played a large role in maintaining the cultural, religious, and linguistic traditions of the Germans. They were printed very artis-
tically—in fraktur—in printing shops constructed by German immigrants of
the eighteenth century. The fine reputation of these presses continued well
into the nineteenth century. (The Library Company of Philadelphia)

"The Woman in the Wilderness" or "The Hermits on the Ridge." Extremely well trained in theology, Kelpius left several manuscripts of hymns in the style of Christian Knorr von Rosenroth. Kelpius was also the author of an essay on the use of inward prayer that was translated into English as *A Short, Easy and Comprehensive Method of Prayer* (Philadelphia: Henry Miller, 1761) and was reissued by E. Gordon Alderfer in 1951 (New York: Harper). Kelpius's ecstatic anticipation of life after death is expressed best in the first stanza of a hymn he wrote on his sickbed:

> Hier lieg ich geschmieget
> > erkräncket im Schrein
> Fast gäntzlich besieget
> > Von süssester pein
> Ich dencke des blühenden Maÿn
> Allwo mich der schönste wird Ewig erfreu'n
> und diese zerbrechliche Hütte verneu'n.

> (Here lye I submissive
> > And weak in a shrine,
> O'ercome and made passive
> > With the sweetest pain:
> I think on the Blooming of that lovely May,
> Where I my Beloved shall ever enjoy;
> And this brittle Hut for a New do away.)

His quietism is demonstrated in stanza 23 of the same hymn:

> Zwar leide ich billig:
> > Ich hab es verschuldt!
> du machest mich willig,
> > und giebest gedult!
> Dein Wille dan über mich völlig ergeh'
> biss meiner in deinem gantz stille besteh',
> dass nichts ihn absencke noch weiter erhöh'.[4]

> (With Reason I suffer,
> > I have it deserv'd!
> Thou makst my will offer,
> > With Patience prefer'd!
> Thy will then within me, be ever most nigh,
> Untill mine upon thine does fully rely,
> That nothing may sink it, or raise it more High.)

With his unassuming and caring manner Kelpius is clearly one of the most admirable early German-American religious leaders.

The next important visionary, Conrad Beissel, is much more controversial. In contrast to Pastorius and Kelpius, Beissel was self-taught, the son of an impoverished baker in Eberbach near Heidelberg. Beissel, though, was able to do something that neither Pastorius nor Kelpius accomplished: he attracted a community of faithful around him at Ephrata, Pennsylvania—now a state historical site and well worth visiting—where sufficient funds were raised not only to finance the printing of his own works but also those of other members of the community and of other authors of whose views Beissel approved. Here the promised land and the freedom to express oneself resulted in an astonishing creative outburst. Many members of the Ephrata community wrote hymns, others religious treatises. Beissel became an accomplished and innovative composer, and the Ephrata services, known for their highly trained female voices, attracted the attention of many. Ephrata also produced the most beautiful Fraktur in the colonies.

In the course of the eighteenth century the religious issue was to become less important among the reasons for coming to the colonies and, later on, to the young independent nation. Sectarians, who felt a need to express their own way of relating to God and the world, were replaced by members of one of the established churches. Neither the sentimental and moral poetry of Justus Helmuth, a Lutheran minister in Philadelphia, nor that of Johann Christoph Kunze, another Lutheran minister who was active in the German Society of Pennsylvania and as a trustee of the University of Pennsylvania and then became professor of Oriental languages at Columbia University, are of special interest. Their poetry derives from Friedrich Klopstock and his imitators. Kunze even began to write a *Messias* epic but never completed it.

Among the publications by German-American authors in the latter half of the eighteenth century books in the areas of medicine, horticulture, laws and taxes became prominent. Some interesting personal accounts were also published, one of an escape from Indian imprisonment, another of a woman pursued by a "Poltergeist," who was finally exorcised at Ephrata, and the confessions of a man who made a pact with the devil.[5] Future studies should fill in the gaps of our knowledge regarding these marginal areas of the literary productivity of the early German-Americans. It is clear, though, that the earlier monopoly of religious writing had given way to a variety of interests that included the religious as well as the worldly sides of life. It is also clear that during this period the issue of *Sehnsucht nach der alten Heimat* (longing for the old homeland) did not come up as an important theme.

Vorspiel der Neuen-Welt, 1732, and *Zionitischer Weyrauchs Hügel Oder: Myrrhen Berg*, 1739. Early hymnals from the presses of Benjamin Franklin and Christoph Saur. Left: the rare *Vorspiel der Neuen-Welt* contains early hymns by Johann Conrad Beissel (1690–1768). Right: the *Zionitischer Weyrauchs Hügel Oder: Myrrhen Berg* is a hymnal of the brothers of Ephrata. Beissel's printing press, established in his monastery at Ephrata in 1742, produced from 1745 on the numerous hymnals and song books of his mystic-pietistic brotherhood.

Christoph Saur and Benjamin Franklin were competitors not only in the German-language book market but also in the political arena. While Franklin's German-language *Philadelphische Zeitung* (1732) failed after two editions, Christoph Saur's *Hoch-Deutscher Pensylvanischer Geschicht-Schreiber*, established in 1739, enjoyed considerable success. Saur's newspaper, like the *Zionitischer Weyrauchs Hügel*, was printed in fraktur and appealed much more readily in its form and content to the tastes and feelings of the Germans. Christoph Saur first became famous with his printing of the "Germantown Bible" in 1743, the first bible printed in America in a European language. (Library Company of Philadelphia)

The longing for the old *Vaterland* was to become a favorite topic in nineteenth-century German-American poetry, which was clearly derivative of Romantic poets of the Continent. The longing *nach Hause* of the early German-American poets meant the return to God.

One document, however, has not received the attention it clearly deserves. The War of Independence produced some writing by German-Americans, as would be expected. One interesting example is the pamphlet entitled *Wahrheit und guter Rath, an die Einwohner Deutschlands, besonders in Hessen,*[6] which was printed in 1783 in Philadelphia. The only extended reference to it I have found is by Oswald Seidensticker, who correctly describes it as "an appeal to the Hessians and other Germans in the service of England, not to return under the despotic sway of their respective sovereigns, who had basely sold them, but to become American citizens and settle in South Carolina where land is offered them on easy terms. The book closes with a spirited German poem of an American Grenadier addressed to Hessians and others in 1777."[7] Indeed, in terms that go back to a long anticourtly tradition, the anonymous author condemns the life of luxury indulged in by the German princes, who keep their subjects ignorant of the truth and are supported in this endeavor by the established church. Clearly, the language and themes are similar to those found a generation later in Georg Büchner's *Hessischer Landbote*. A passage from the 1783 pamphlet shows the eloquence of the anonymous author:

Hessians! You should be ashamed of your disgraceful, abject and most inhuman condition. Do not be the willing slaves of your fellow men any longer; break the chains of slavery; break free of the darkness and slavery to which your ancestors condemned you through cowardliness and fear. Come to the land of freedom where—should you even come naked—you will soon become free and happy men again. Here you can be pious, honest, humane and industrious and thus a man as God created him, according to His image: free and a servant to no one. You are the masters of the earth and all creation, happy here and for eternity with God. [P. 29]

The end of the appeal consists, as Seidensticker observed, of a poem in which an American grenadier addresses the Hessian and other German mercenaries. It is dated 1777 and thus is part of the attempts by the revolutionaries to persuade these soldiers, many of whom had been pressed into service, to defect. A closer look at the vocabulary of the poem makes it clear that the same author wrote the prose part of the pamphlet. Another look at some of the stanzas establishes the poem's literary progeny. The poet first addresses an individual Hessian soldier, then all of them:

17. Säh' von Wahlhalla, Siegmar dich,
      Säh' Hermann sein Geschlecht,
  Sie schämten warlich deiner sich,
      Und schämten sich mit Recht.
23. O kommt, lasst Deutschland Deutschland seyn,
      Und gebt uns eure Hand,
  Schmied't euer Schwerdt zu Sicheln ein,
      Und baut mit uns das Land.
24. Kommt zu uns frey von Groll und Trug,
      Und esst das Freundschaffts-Mahl,
  Wir haben hier der Hütten gnug,
      Und Länder ohne Zahl. (pp. 34 f.)

(If Siegmar saw you from Valhalla,
    If Hermann saw his people,
They would surely be ashamed of you
    And justly so.
O come, let Germany be Germany,
    And give us your hand,
Beat your swords to scythes
    And build this land with us.
Come to use without rancor or deceit
    And join our banquet of friendship,
We have ample shelter here,
    And immeasurable land.)

For "Säh' Hermann sein Geschlecht" there is a note to the effect that the author means the courageous ancestors of the Germans and Hessians, but there is no explanation for Siegmar, who is, according to Klopstock, Hermann's father (see his "Hermann und Thusnelda," lines 21ff.). The anonymous poet derived his references and language from Pietism, from Klopstock, or from his admirers of the Göttinger Hain. A fascinating combination of circumstances made the poet of this *Lied* put the cult of fatherland, freedom, Germanic mythology, Christianity, and friendship found in Klopstock and his followers to use as an appeal to his Hessian compatriots to defect and join the revolutionaries.

More such gems might be hidden among the various early German-American publications. I am especially unsure about the literary material that might be contained in the many almanacs of the period. Studies have been done of some aspects of the literary contents of nineteenth-century almanacs—Don Yoder of the University of Pennsylvania is a leading scholar here—but I have not found anything about the eighteenth-century almanac.

My last point concerns what needs to be done to make the writings of the early German-Americans more accessible. Again and again it seems to me that the contributions of German-Americans to the music of the colonies and the young republic have been dealt with competently and that various compositions have been published in scholarly editions. The same is true of the interest in and the research on the arts of the German-Americans. One need mention here only Henry S. Borneman's and Donald A. Shelley's work on Fraktur or the beautiful and well-documented recent catalog of the Philadelphia Museum of Art. The literary endeavors of the German-Americans, however, have fared less well, clearly because music, design, color, and craftsmanship transcend language barriers. For poetry we have the two anthologies referred to in note 4 and for publications in general Oswald Seidensticker's invaluable 1893 bibliography, *The First Century of German-American Printing, 1728–1830*, which was mentioned in note 7. That work is being redone; the revision was started by the late Wilbur H. Oda, then taken up by Karl Friedrich Arndt, and is now in the hands of Werner Tannhof, a research librarian at the Niedersächsische Staats- und Universitätsbibliothek Göttingen. Werner Tannhof's stay at the Library Company of Philadelphia and at Worcester, with the American Antiquarian Society, is funded by the Deutsche Forschungsgemeinschaft. One must be most grateful for such support.

There are also all-inclusive bibliographies of every book, pamphlet, and broadside printed in the United States before 1830. Items that appeared before 1819 are available under the title *Early American Imprints* by the Readex Microprint Corporation, a tool that is indispensable to any research in early German-Americana.

These sources seem to indicate that the necessary information to form a better idea of early German-American literature in all of its aspects is available. But the number of items in the *Early American Imprints* is so enormous that great efforts would be required to sort out those belonging to German-American authors. The augmented and revised Seidensticker bibliography will help because it follows the American version of the format used in the current *Eighteenth Century Short Title Catalogue* project. But it will still be necessary to establish the authorship and origin of many items in the bibliography because a good number of the German-language entries are reissues of Continental publications or are translations.

I have not mentioned the rich manuscript material that is spread all over the United States in well-known and not so well-known libraries and archives. Klaus W. Jonas of the University of Pittsburgh submitted a proposal to the National Endowment for the Humanities to catalog the German manuscripts in this country, but that proposal was not funded. Much of the archival material of the various denominations with German backgrounds is so substantial that, even if funds were available, the cataloging will have to be done by establishing larger groups of manuscripts rather than by trying to list each item separately. But such a catalog must be established. At this point we do not even have exact knowledge of what manuscripts by Pastorius, Kelpius, or Beissel exist.

Let me return to the desirability of making the texts of early German-American authors more easily accessible. Once we have a good idea of what material there is, an anthology with authentic texts and ample notes would be the next and very desirable step.

The late John Joseph Stoudt, who did much to further the cause of early Pennsylvania German literature and thought, had a plan to issue in English a series of documents that would bring Penn's holy experiment and the early German immigrants' contributions to that experiment to the attention of the American educated public. The title of the book was to have been "Friends and Brethren in the Holy Experiment."[8] It would have been a valuable addition to the field of early German-Americana. My interests are more literary than those of the late John Stoudt, and thus I would select different material. But I agree with him that the contributions of the early German-Americans to the intellectual climate of the colonies and the young republic and their idea of brotherly love and of a democratic community are known only to specialists and have not been given their due in American scholarship.

Notes

1. Both books: C. R. Goedsche and W. E. Glaettli, eds. (New York: American Book Co., 1953).

2. See Francis Daniel Pastorius, *Deliciæ Hortenses or Garden-Recreations and Voluptates Apianæ*, ed. Christoph E. Schweitzer (Columbia, S.C.: Camden House, 1982).

3. "Beehive," p. 148. Quoted with the kind permission of Harold Jantz.

4. The manuscript has been reproduced in *Church Music and Musical Life in Pennsylvania in the Eighteenth Century*, 2 vols. (Philadelphia: Pennsylvania Society

of the Colonial Dames of America, 1926), 1:138–49. The English translation is by Dr. Christoph Witt, a friend of Kelpius, and appeared in the manuscript next to the German originals. The hymn is also found in Heinrich Arnim Rattermann, ed., *Deutsch-Amerikanische Dichter und Dichtungen des 17ten und 18ten Jahrhunderts* (N.p.: German-American Historical Society of Illinois, 1915), 24–27, and in John Joseph Stoudt, ed., *Pennsylvania German Poetry, 1685–1830* (Allentown: Schlechter's, 1956), 7–12. The best account of Kelpius and the group he belonged to as well as of his hymns is in Willard Martin, "Johann Kelpius and Johann Gottfried Seelig: Mystics and Hymnists on the Wissahickon" (Ph.D. dissertation, Pennsylvania State University, 1973).

5. The simplest and most useful way of referring to these publications is by giving their numbers in Charles Evans, *American Bibliography* (Chicago: Privately printed for the author, 1903–55): 8347, 8778, and 22877. These items are available in the Readex Microprint edition of *Early American Imprints* published by the American Antiquarian Society.

6. Evans, *American Bibliography*, 18291.

7. Oswald Seidensticker, *The First Century of German Printing in America, 1728–1830* (Philadelphia: Schaefer & Koradi, 1893), 111; translated by the editors. Horst Dippel in *Germany and the American Revolution, 1770–1800* (Chapel Hill: University of North Carolina Press, 1977), refers briefly to the booklet on page 125 and devotes several pages to the various issues connected with the employment of German auxiliary troops by Great Britain (pp. 117–30).

8. I was told by Mrs. John Stoudt that her late husband's manuscripts have been deposited at the Schwenkfelder Library, Pennsburg, Pennsylvania.

21.
Radicalism and the "Great Cause": The German-American Serial Novel in the Antebellum Era

PATRICIA HERMINGHOUSE

MOST READERS WHO VENTURE into German-American literature, whether they approach it primarily as students of German-Americana or of literature, are all too quickly—and justifiably—disappointed in its lack of serious artistic merit. Highly derivative, maudlin, stylistically flawed, and often inordinately long, most works are likely to be set aside before the reader's interest is awakened by their unique value as social documents. Such is certainly the case with the novels to be considered here, works that not only constitute some of the earliest prose fiction published by Germans in the United States,[1] but whose authors are some of the most fascinating and politically significant German emigrants of the mid-nineteenth century. In most cases, their works were also published in a form new to the United States: in serialized installments in German-American newspapers of the 1850s, which the authors often edited. Although the novels were also circulated and even attained best-seller status in traditional book form, the book was merely a by-product of the journalistic endeavor. Indeed, it is the nonliterary aspect of these novels, their sociohistorical context, that constitutes their interest for us today.

To understand these works, one must begin not in Germany but in Paris of the 1840s, a city that had become home to growing numbers of exiles from the repressive regimes in Germany. Among them were figures such as Heinrich Heine and Ludwig Börne, Karl Marx and Arnold Ruge, and a seemingly insignificant Austrian entrepreneur named Heinrich Börnstein.

Börnstein had come to Paris in 1842 because his theatrical and journalistic enterprises in Austria were increasingly menaced by the censorship and repression of Metternich's regime. His entrepreneurial sense may have told him that Paris, with its colony of some sixty thousand German émigrés, would offer him more artistic and commercial opportunities than any other city inside or outside troubled Germany. Having secured himself a contract as Paris theater correspondent for the *Augsburger Allgemeine Zeitung*, he quickly made the arrangement even more lucrative by establishing a "translation factory," cranking out translations of some fifty French plays he was reviewing for the German theaters, to the chagrin of German authors. He opened a German news agency and secured a position as Paris correspondent for the *Deutsche Schnellpost* of New York, a liberal newspaper that reported events in Europe to its New World readers. As director of the German and Italian opera in Paris, he was in a position to obtain financial support from the composer Giacomo Meyerbeer for a new venture, which he announced at the end of 1843: the establishment of the first German-language newspaper in Paris, a biweekly entitled *Vorwärts! Pariser Signale aus Kunst, Wissenschaft, Theater, Musik und geselligem Leben*. The new paper was commercial rather than political in intent, conceived primarily as a vehicle to support his activities as producer and translator. Because he declared it to be a cultural journal, Börnstein did not have to post the surety required by French law of the editors of newspapers, who were likely to run afoul of political censors and be liable for financial penalties. For Germans, however, this system was an improvement over that which prevailed in their homeland, where various systems of pre- and post-censorship effectively precluded the publication of offensive material. The French system at least offered a modicum of "freedom" to those who were able to afford the attendant financial risk, and some French editors became very clever at increasing their circulation revenues so that the censor's fines were not likely to destroy them. Although Börnstein was well aware of these practices in the French press, he claimed to model his new journal on the German-language press in the United States, mentioning particularly the *Deutsche Schnellpost*, for which he was already a correspondent. Although hardly a model of journalistic excellence, the American press was indeed free of the problems of censorship that plagued its European counterpart. Börnstein introduced a *Zeitungsschau* into his paper, a feature column of excerpts from the German-American press, including some of his own dispatches to the *Deutsche*

Facing page. A representative anthology of German-American poetry from 1856. Although much of this poetry is an imitation of various styles and authors current in Germany in the early nineteenth century, it nevertheless served as a confirmation of cultural identity for emigrant poets in a new environment. A smaller proportion of these poets conveyed the political message of the Forty-eighters in their lyrics and took an active role in the Civil War on the side of Lincoln in the struggle against slavery. After 1848, in particular, there is considerable reflection on the dual existence of the emigrant, which is represented in the later part of this anthology by a number of poems inspired by Heinrich Heine and also dedicated to him.

Poetry and song played an increasingly central role in the social structures and celebrations of the German-Americans at the end of the nineteenth century. The songs of the Turner organizations and choral societies, which were regularly performed at mass festivals, originated in large part in Germany. However, the reproduction of foreign printed materials (such as sheet music from Germany) was permitted without regulation until 1911, with the result that individual literary production by German-Americans was an unprofitable venture, since their literary market was dependent on Germany. (German Society of Pennsylvania)

Schnellpost and amusing or sensational reports from other papers, such as the *Anzeiger des Westens* of St. Louis, to which his fate and fortune were to be closely tied in a few years.

Börnstein and his somewhat dubious associate Adalbert von Bornstedt began publication of *Vorwärts* in January 1844. In late February, two leaders of the more radical German faction in Paris published the first issue of their *Deutsch-Französische Jahrbücher*. Edited by Karl Marx and Arnold Ruge, ably assisted by Karl Bernays, the new venture was to be very short-lived, as the radicals themselves seem to have understood much more quickly than Börnstein and Bornstedt, who used the pages of *Vorwärts* to thunder away at them, Heinrich Heine, and the Young German movement. Bornstedt's political double-dealing finally led to his departure from *Vorwärts* in May and, by means that are not entirely clear, his replacement by the capable Bernays. We can speculate that Börnstein's anger with the German powers who refused to let his paper cross their borders may have led him to a somewhat more radical stance. At the same time, the imminent demise of the *Jahrbücher* probably led Marx and Ruge to consider how they might obtain a voice in *Vorwärts*, the only German newspaper in Paris. The key to the takeover, if it can be termed such, seems to lie in Bernays' securing an editorial position in June; by July, the subtitle of the paper had changed to *Pariser Deutsche Zeitschrift*, and the very persons who only a few months earlier had been attacked in its pages were now

Deutſch=amerikaniſcher

Dichterwald.

Eine Sammlung von Original=Gedichten

Deutſch=amerikaniſcher Verfaſſer.

Herausgegeben von E. Marrhauſen.

Detroit, Mich., 1856.
Druck und Verlag von A. & C. Marrhauſen.

publishing in *Vorwärts*. Whatever his original motives for joining the paper might have been, Bernays became a close friend of Börnstein. Rather than take sides when the Marxists split, Bernays followed Börnstein to the United States, where he became his key associate in the *Anzeiger des Westens.*

Because *Vorwärts* had become overtly political, its editors were prosecuted in December 1844 for publishing without having posted surety. Bernays was jailed and, at the behest of the Prussian government, other associates of the journal were ordered to leave Paris.[2] Börnstein seems to have bought the right to stay in Paris by promising not to carry through on a plan to publish *Vorwärts* as a monthly. After Bernays' release from jail, both he and Börnstein continued to work in Paris until their dismay at developments in 1848 led them to depart for the United States. There Börnstein drew on his experience as a medical student in Austria, practicing medicine in a small Illinois town until he was invited to edit the *Anzeiger des Westens* in St. Louis in 1850. He soon bought out the publisher of that paper and proved himself a formidable competitor to the sleepy German-language press of St. Louis. But before examining some of Börnstein's activities in St. Louis, it is important to look more closely at an aspect of Paris literary life that seems to have particularly fascinated him.

Börnstein's arrival in Paris coincided with the publication of a novel that took not only Paris but much of Europe and even North America by storm. Eugène Sue's *Les Mystères de Paris* ran in serial form for two years in the *Journal des Débats*, beginning in 1842, and was released in book form in ten volumes during the same period. A subsequent "roman feuilleton," *Le Juif errant*, was serialized in 1844–45 in *Le Constitutionnel*; public demand for the next installment increased the paper's circulation sevenfold. Naturally, the attention surrounding Sue's novel did not escape Börnstein's notice; in the fourth issue of *Vorwärts* he reported on the inability of lending libraries in Paris to meet the demand for the "mysteries" and on the number of German authors preparing their own "mysteries" of Vienna, Berlin, Leipzig, and the like. All told, some three dozen imitations were announced and, long before Germans began producing serialized novels, Sue's novel was carried simultaneously in a dozen German papers as well as in numerous legal and illegal book editions.[3] Börnstein's attitude toward this new rage was critical; he remarked that Germany was unfortunately far more vulnerable to being overpowered by the mystery literature of France than by the much more significant concept of "Öffentlichkeit," which also grew on French soil. It does not appear, however, that he saw the underlying current of social criticism which more perceptive readers of the novel discerned. Nor do his remarks indicate that he recognized that a revolution in novel writing was under way, that the poor and outcast of the cities rather than the rich and noble of the countryside had become the subject of literature for the masses. But although he may have scorned Sue's work, there is little doubt that he learned lessons from it that would later stand him in good stead in St. Louis. First, the example of the vastly increased circulation enjoyed by *Le Constitutionnel* was not lost upon him. A large and growing circulation provides an editorial base of power on which a newspaper can extend its influence throughout the political and economic arenas. Second, as many authors on German soil were already proving, the narrative techniques, figures, and motifs of Sue's novel provided a model that could be easily adapted and transplanted to other settings than his native Paris. Sue claims in his preface to have drawn the inspiration for his novel of urban barbarianism from the popular tales of the American wilderness written by James Fenimore Cooper, who spent the years 1826–33 in Europe, most of it in Paris.

Slang, sex and aggression, colorful names, subterranean passages, windy and rainy nights in shadowy side streets were the elements that every author borrowed from Sue. But most important was the local color represented in the title "The Mysteries (or Secrets) of (whatever city the author chose to portray)." This approach sold well because the inhabitants of that city recognized their own environment in the lurid tale that was being spun. Such a mixture of verifiable, realistic detail and fantastic "revelations" proved irresistible, even to readers who might normally have thought themselves above prurience in their reading tastes.

The New World to which Börnstein and Bernays came was likewise not untouched by Sue's success. George Lippard's *The Quaker City or the Monks of Monk Hall, A Romance of Philadelphia Life, Mystery and Crime* sold sixty thousand copies when it appeared in 1844 and was still going strong at thirty thousand copies a year a decade later,[4] as the genre blossomed in the German-American press. Lippard's novel was discovered by Friedrich Gerstäcker in his wanderings through the United States and translated by him as *Die Quäkerstadt und ihre Geheimnisse;*[5] it is still sometimes mistakenly attributed to Gerstäcker's authorship. Combining the exotic appeal of the American setting with the prevailing popularity of big-city novels, it was as much a success as Gerstäcker's other America novels. Despite its title, *The Monks of Monk Hall* does not deal with monks but with a sinister underworld group whose members call themselves "monks" and carouse in cowled black robes in their hideout, an old mansion named Monk Hall. But in addition to picking up all of Sue's tricks, Lippard's title was clearly capitalizing on another current in American life and literature: the waves of paranoia and virulent anti-Catholic propaganda that rippled across the still young nation as the tides of foreign immigration began to swell in the 1820s and 1830s.

Book upon book depicted Catholicism as a moral and political threat to pure American democracy and convents and monasteries as "dens of vice and iniquity in which nuns and monks wallowed in a slough of ignorance and corruption."[6] Unlike their Continental European counterparts, these American works were not serialized in newspapers, although they were sold in inexpensive installments on newsprint as so-called "penny dreadfuls," a genre Leslie Fiedler calls subpornography, "exposing, revealing . . . providing the 'inside dope' on those in power."[7]

No doubt the sudden growth of the Catholic church, to which many immigrants of these decades belonged, fed American Protestant fears of a "Popish" plot to take over the vast unsettled territories of the United States, particularly the Mississippi Valley, to which colonizing companies in Germany were turning their attention. It did not matter if the immigrants, such as members of the Giessen Society, who set their sights on Missouri, were not Catholics—or even conventional Protestants—there was still fear that they could be "Jesuits in disguise" and thus part of Rome's designs on the West. The Protestant press teemed with tales of lust, blood, and murder,[8] some of it contributed by such notable Americans as Samuel F. B. Morse[9] and Lyman Beecher, the father of Harriet Beecher Stowe.[10] Finding inadequate support for their ideas among the two major American political parties—the Democrats, who sought the foreign vote, and the Whigs, who were preoccupied with the problems of economic expansionism and the growing sectional conflict—the nativists reached for political power by organizing themselves into a party. As their base of support widened, their tactics grew more ruthless and extended to rioting and burning churches and convents. The revulsion these acts aroused among the American population occasioned the decline of the party until around 1850, when immigration from troubled Europe once again fed fears that foreign turbulence and ignorance were being imported by shiploads.[11] The nativists, now known as the Order of the Star-spangled Banner or "Know-Nothings," were helped immensely in their bid for power by the growing inability of the Whigs and Democrats to deal with the rifts within their own parties caused by the sharpening sectional conflict. The Jacksonian Democratic party, traditionally the political home of the immigrants, aroused their antipathies because of its ties to the southern slaveholders; the increasingly decadent Whig party had never had the sympathy of the immigrants because of its ties to the nativist element. In this political morass the new immigrants, such as Börnstein and Bernays, had to find their way. Many sought only the way to homestead lands, now endangered by the vexing question of the extension of slavery. Others, steeped in radical European political traditions that were very different from the rough and tumble of frontier democracy, attempted to gain or regain political and cultural influence among their fellow Germans. In a society pervaded by land speculation, slavery, and religious paranoia, it was only natural that they should turn to the press, either establishing their own papers or taking over existing ones. In the decade between 1850 and 1860, when the German population of the United States swelled from slightly more than half a million to over 1.3 million and the nascent Republican party sought support among those disillusioned with the Whigs and Democrats, this press became a serious political force, concerned with different questions than those on which it had built its readership.[12]

When Börnstein was called to take over the editorship of the respected *Anzeiger des Westens* from Wilhelm Weber in 1850, he immediately implemented a strategy to make it into the most important German newspaper in the West. In part, this plan involved developing political alliances with the leaders of the liberal, antislavery faction of the Democratic party in Missouri; in part, developing a base of support among the pro-labor, anti-clerical element of the German population in St. Louis. But with the example of Sue in Paris still clearly in mind, Börnstein set out to build the circulation of the paper—which he was soon able to buy from its publisher. Using all of the devices if not the plot of Sue's *Mysteries of Paris*, Börnstein introduced a journalistic first: a serialized novel, *Die Geheimnisse von St. Louis*, which was to bring the *Anzeiger* more than a thousand new subscribers in just a few months.[13] One must be careful not to give Börnstein too much credit for this innovation, however. In his memoirs, he indicates that, although the plan for the serial novel was his own, he changed the original title, *Die Raben des Westens* (under which the last edition of the book appeared in Germany in 1871) to the more appealing *Geheimnisse von St. Louis* when he heard that a rival newspaper was planning a serial under that title.

It is very difficult to determine whether Börnstein's *Geheimnisse* was actually the first of the numerous representatives of that genre in the United States. In 1850, the first installment of the anonymous *Die Geheimnisse von Philadelphia*, published by August Gläser, J. M. Reichard, and Nikolaus Schmitt, appeared in inexpensive newsprint format. Beyond various newspaper ventures that they attempted independently, these three men engaged briefly in the publication of a daily paper, *Der Volksvertreter*, in 1850.[14] The paper, no copies of which are extant, seems to have had ties to the radical circle around Wilhelm Weitling in New York, and it is conceivable that the fragment of the *Geheimnisse* that has survived was part of a serializing scheme similar to Börnstein's. In this work, the influence of Sue, in both form and content, is even clearer than in Börnstein's work. Probably the only one of the many "Mysteries of . . ." not to have been influenced by the St. Louis model, it reveals more of the social conscience evident in Sue's novel than do any of its other American derivatives. As the introduction states, the novel was to "reveal the terrible corruption which undermines certain aspects of our social relationships, so that either reform must be quickly undertaken or a terrible upheaval must be feared." Life will be shown in all its sordid reality, the author(s) assert, from the luxurious estates of the rich to the filthy huts of the poor. The novel is laced with comments on American society, including the position of women, business practices, and social customs. That Sue's work was the direct model is also suggested by the use of footnotes and parenthetical comments to explain American terminology and slang expressions included to provide local flavor. The atmosphere in which the underworld element is introduced, a cold, rainy, windy night, is so typical that it could have come from any other novel of the genre: "It was a stormy cold November night. Rain poured in streams from the skies and the wind howled, so that the old tin signs hanging in front of the houses creaked."[15]

For comparison, let us look at Börnstein's introduction of his underworld milieu: "Raw and wild, the wind howled in the black night, which enveloped the streets of St. Louis in an eerie darkness, the rain poured down in streams . . . here and there a few gas lanterns were flickering faintly."[16] But despite the obvious borrowings of motives and characters from Sue, Börnstein, like other authors of the genre, does not merely transfer the Paris plot to an American setting. He tells instead the story of a hardworking, upright immigrant family whose attempts to become established in farming in the Missouri valley are repeatedly frustrated by two evil forces: a heartless American land speculator with ties to a ruthless underworld gang of killers and counterfeiters, known as the Ravens, and the ubiquitous Jesuits, who stop at nothing, even alliances with the criminal element, in their quest for power and wealth. In an incredibly complicated story, which—like those of all the other "Mystery . . ." novels—would be impossible to relate here, Börnstein weaves strand upon strand of plot in and out of action-packed episodes that kept his readers coming back for more. Subterranean passages, buried treasure, grave robbing, leaps over convent walls, the California gold rush, death in the desert, fights with Indians, old lechers who prey upon virtuous maidens, mad hermits in the wilderness: all embellish the basic story of the virtuous immigrants versus a corrupt society, which is portrayed in such exact and realistic detail that anyone familiar with the city can easily recognize his daily environment. There is no doubt, as Alfred Vagts aptly perceives, that "the work satiated a craving on the immigrant reader's part, strongest in his first, often enough agonizing years after arrival in the new country, for an explanation of the dark forces that stood in the way of a just reward for his honest labors, and which seemed all too often to favor the triumph of the wicked."[17]

In considering the success of the novel against the background of rising nativistic sentiment and the struggle over the slavery issue within the Democratic party, it becomes apparent that Börnstein had other motives more noble than taking advantage of human needs to build circulation. To begin with, his German immigrant family is a refutation of the nativists' stereotype of the urban immigrant, taking away American jobs, given to drink, and lacking in the virtues of good citizenship. In Börnstein's version, the virtuous immigrants are beset by the likes of Mr. Smartborn, a ruthless speculator and counterfeiter, and the conspiratorial Jesuits, no less ruthless in their pursuit of buried treasure that rightfully belongs to the immigrant family—who, incidentally, decline to pursue it.

Börnstein's vehement anti-Jesuitism puts him in a peculiar position vis-à-vis the American nativists, whom he strongly opposed, because his depiction of members of this order is indistinguishable from the anti-Catholic texts that enjoyed great popularity among American readers. One could explain this choice of subject by referring to Börnstein's certain familiarity with Sue's second best-seller, *Le Juif errant* (1844), in which anti-Jesuitism figured prominently, but a much more likely explanation is found in another, otherwise puzzling scene of the novel in which—almost a decade before it really happened—Börnstein predicts the American Civil War. In the still of the night, on a Mississippi River island, the Jesuits rally in anticipation of the day when they will take over the entire United States. They interpret the sectional dispute surrounding slavery as a punishment visited by an angry God upon a nation that strayed from its Roman Catholic origins as a colony of Spain. When, finally, the bloody war comes, the South, lacking strength to win the battle on its own, will have to seek an alliance with Mexico, which by then will be firmly in the arms of Mother Church under a Hapsburg ruler. The North, unequal to this alliance, will turn to England for support; there, the specter of revolution and mass uprisings worldwide will have driven the nobility and the Anglican clergy back to the one true faith that prevails in Continental Europe. Thus whichever side "wins" in the Civil War, America loses because it will be reintegrated back into the worldwide Catholic empire.

This absurd speculation, which does not seem to have had any currency among either the American or the German population of the United States, makes sense only in the context of local politics, with which Börnstein was then deeply involved. German immigrants became increasingly disillusioned with the Democrats' closeness to the southern slaveholders and the urban Catholics. The development of a radical faction within the party, which protested this tendency, caused it to lose the 1850 city election to the Whigs, who had a strong nativist element. Börnstein's false depiction of the Catholic church as being in league with American-born citizens who would exploit the immigrant thus can be read as an attempt to win German support for the newly developing radical Democratic faction. This group eventually allied itself with the Republican party that emerged in the mid-1850s, a party in which the Germans ultimately gained considerable influence. Börnstein's novel won readers for his paper away from both his major competitors, the Whig *Deutsche Tribüne* and the Catholic *St. Louis Tageschronik*, thereby helping him build a financial as well as a political base in local affairs. It is difficult to arrive at exact figures, but Börnstein noted with satisfaction at the conclusion of the 1851 book edition of the novel that it had already sold four thousand regular and fifteen hundred extra editions of the *Anzeiger des Westens*. In his later memoirs, he reported that the book went through six American editions in a decade and was reprinted in numerous German-American newspapers—including the *Anzeiger* itself a decade later—three German editions, and translations into English, French, and Czech. With a German population of somewhat more than twenty-two thousand (out of a total of seventy-seven thousand) in 1850, a circulation increase of the magnitude Börnstein reports is indeed impressive. In the early 1850s he had built the *Anzeiger* into the largest of the twenty German-language dailies in the United States, and he reported with satisfaction that he was able to give the liberal Democrats enough support to assure a stunning victory in the 1852 congressional elections.[18]

Given the astonishing success of Börnstein's imitation of Sue, it is not surprising that Börnstein himself should have had numerous imitators. When Emil Klauprecht, who belonged to the earlier German immigration of the 1830s, decided to write a *Geheimnis* novel for his paper, *Der Deutsche Republikaner* of Cincinnati, he prefaced it with a foreword anticipating the reader's reaction to one more hackneyed, charlatan variant of the genre. Claiming that the horrors he would be writing about were no longer any secret to those who lived in America's cities, he indicated that he conceived his book instead as an anti-

PROGRAMM.

Dienſtag, 27. und Mittwoch, 28. Nov. '94:

Grünhörner,

(Greenhorns.)

Amerik. Lebensbild mit Geſang in 5 Bildern v. Hans Dobers, (Mitglied des Germania-Theaters). Muſik von Max Gabriel.

Neu bearbeitet. Neue Geſangs-Einlagen. Weitere neue Scenerien: Der Hafen von New York mit Hudſon River; die New Yorker Elevated Railroad; Bowery bei Nacht, etc.

Erſtes Auftreten der mehrfach preisgekrönten kleinen Ballet-, Serpentin-Tänzerin und Akrobatin:

"LITTLE VENUS."

Perſonen:

Paul Schädlich aus Leipzig	Heinr. Schefsky
Betty Nagel aus Wien	Juſtine Wegener
von Abelsfeld, Lieutenant a. D.	Hans Dobers
Jakob Knöpfle aus Ulm	Alex. Roſſi
Bärbele, deſſen Frau	Johanna Clauſſen-Koch
Hannele, deren Tochter	Carola Hammer
Michel,)	(Max Telle
Käthele,) Knöpfle's Verwandte,	Sidonie Schefsky
Chriſtel,)	(Fanny Cartell
Billy Klein,)	(J. Stein
George Müller,) Eingewanderte,	Max Roſſi
Amos, Neger	Jules van Cool
Kittie, Irländerin	Emma Roſt
Adolph Brüller, Conzertſänger	W. Klumb
Mary Thomas, Conzertſängerin	Emma Roſt
Meſi Taller,) Tyroler	Th. Störk-Vellmann
Mathi Brafl,) Conzertſängerinnen,	Tina Dobers
Smith,)	(Ad. Vellmann
Taylor,) Polizisten	(Ferd. Har
Honeſt, Zollbeamter	Herr Helfer
Blackwell, Polizeirichter	Kurt Ebenſtein
Schröder, Advofat	Ad. Koch
Billion, Gerichtsdiener	Herr Harm
Stiefelputzer	Hans Peters
Gepäckträger; Matroſen; Herren und Damen.	
Ort der Handlung:	Hoboken — New York.

Regie: Hans Dobers.

Program of the Germania Theater in New York for the performance of a musical comedy, 1894. The play by the German-American Hans Dobers, entitled *Greenhorns*, brings together various stereotypes from among German immigrants in a New York setting. Comedies and farces of this type, modeled after the successful plays of August von Kotzebue, Roderich Benedix, and the Schönthan brothers, soon became an integral part of German-American culture. In contrast with the area of prose literature, where authors such as Charles Sealsfield, Friedrich Gerstäcker, or Otto Ruppius achieved considerable prominence, the theater poduced few well-known authors. Serious dramas, which were imported from Germany, were also performed successfully in such cities as New York, Philadelphia, Chicago, Cincinnati, St. Louis, Milwaukee, New Orleans, and Baltimore. (Special Collections, Van Pelt Library, University of Pennsylvania)

dote to the Continental German's fascination with the romantic tales of James Fenimore Cooper, Charles Sealsfield, and other pioneers of the literary forest primeval. Because, alas, the America to which they would come did not match this ideal, readers in Germany were sorely in need of a more realistic presentation. Because few copies of the book, printed in Cincinnati, much less its serialized version in his paper, were likely to reach readers in the Old World, Klauprecht's explanation does not ring true, particularly when one compares it with the conclusion of the novel. What it was possible only to surmise about Börnstein's attempts to condemn the Democratic party's ties to the slaveholders and the Catholics is stated openly here: "Jesuitism always recognized its truest friend and ally in European absolutism. . . . In America, cotton is king, the absolute ruler in political affairs. United with it, as it is, the black band [Catholicism] can withstand all storms which might beset them in the political arena. Only the fall of the slaveholders' party, only the victory of freedom and enlightenment with the legal weapon of the vote will wrest the victory, too often boasted of, from Jesuitism. But to achieve this, all patriotic and intelligent people of the republic will have to work together. The ancient enemy of human welfare has made good use of its time to gain hold of the means of making the land of Washington and Jefferson into the site for the kinds of calamitous wars it has waged for centuries against domestic peace in Europe."[19]

In evaluating these novels, it is difficult to temper our usual scorn for their production and marketing with an eye to the difficult political situations in which their editor-authors found themselves. No doubt they had to subordinate some of their own values and goals to the themes they recognized would sell papers. No doubt, too, that in attempting to walk the line between variously unacceptable alternatives on the existing political scene, they unwittingly fell into alliance with causes to which they could hardly have been sympathetic. Such is obviously the case with the position in which their vehement anti-Catholicism put them vis-à-vis the nativists, whom they opposed on every other issue.

For authors such as Börnstein and Klauprecht, literature was not a social weapon in itself but a means subordinate to the higher end of their journalistic enterprise. Although it did not directly contradict what they advocated in their press, it seldom was as unmistakable in its social intent as was the work of Sue. Certainly no one has ever suggested that the novels had any effect on outlawry and crime in nineteenth-century American cities. But they are interesting as documents of the process of political and cultural assimilation of this group of immigrant leaders.

The mystery novels, with their peculiar combination of American and European elements, reflect fairly accurately the concerns of their authors in the early 1850s: the problems of would-be homesteaders, land speculation and money-grubbing, nativism, the power of the church, and the lack of high culture in America were among the issues that concerned them most. Significantly, their experiences in attempting a unification of the German states led them to be initially more concerned about the danger of a split in the Union over slavery than about the slavery question itself. As they established themselves in the tumultuous political life of antebellum America, they became more and more involved in these issues. Whereas the "great causes" around which they rallied in the early years were ethnic issues, particularly nativism and homesteading, the great cause around which most of them ultimately rallied and found unity was the slavery question, which had been conspicuously absent from their early works. We need not recount here their involvement in the Civil War era, either as soldiers and officers in the Union army or in diplomatic positions abroad—often sinecures which they obtained as a reward for their services to the Republican party, particularly in supporting the nomination of Lincoln in 1860.[20] Having established a firm base in their ethnic communities, they learned to play the American political game by American rules for American prizes: financial security, local influence, and political, military, and diplomatic offices.

Notes

1. See George Condoyannis, "German-American Prose Fiction from 1850 to 1914" (Ph.D. diss., Catholic University of America, 1953), 6; and Oswald Seidensticker, *The First Century of German Printing in America, 1737–1830* (Philadelphia: Schaefer and Koradi, 1893).

2. Walter Schmidt, "Einleitung," *Vorwärts. Pariser Signale aus Kunst, Wissenschaft, Theater, Musik und geselligem Leben,* ed. by Heinrich Börnstein (1844–45; repr. Leipzig: Zentralantiquariat der DDR, 1975), xxxviii.

3. Norbert Miller and Karl Riha, "Nachwort," *Die Geheimnisse von Paris,* by Eugène Sue, new ed. (Munich: Deutscher Taschenbuchverlag, 1970), 682, 665.

4. Leslie Fiedler, "Preface," *The Monks of Monks Hall,* by George Lippard (1844; new ed. New York: Odyssey Press, 1970), vii.

5. George Lippard, *Die Quäkerstadt und ihre Geheimnisse,* trans. Friedrich Gerstäcker (Leipzig: Otto Wigand, 1846).

6. Ray Allen Billington, *The Protestant Crusade, 1800–1860: A Study of the Origins of American Nativism* (New York: Macmillan, 1938), 67. Billington cites especially the infamous novel published in 1836 under the pseudonym of Maria Monk: *Awful Disclosures of the Hotel Dieu Nunnery of Montreal,* which sold three hundred thousand copies before the Civil War.

7. Fiedler, "Preface," xx.

8. Billington, *Protestant Crusade,* 119, 243.

9. See Samuel F. B. Morse, *Imminent Dangers to the Free Institutions of the United States through Foreign Immigration* (New York: E. B. Clayton, 1835); *The Proscribed German Student; Being a Sketch of Some Interesting Incidents in the Life and Death of Lewis Clausing; to Which is Added; a Treatise on the Jesuits, a Posthumous Work of Lewis Clausing* (New York: Van Nostrand and Dwight, 1836); *The Confessions of a French Catholic Priest, to Which Are Added Warnings to the People of the United States* (New York: D. Van Nostrand, 1837); *Foreign Conspiracy against the Liberties of the United States* (New York: Leavitt, Lord and Co., 1835).

10. Lyman Beecher, *A Plea for the West* (Cincinnati: Truman and Smith, 1835).

11. Billington, *Protestant Crusade,* 127.

12. See Carl Wittke, *The German Language Press in America* (Lexington: University of Kentucky Press, 1957).

13. Heinrich Börnstein, *Fünfundsiebzig Jahre in der alten und neuen Welt. Memoiren eines Unbedeutenden*, 2 vols. (Leipzig: Otto Wigand, 1881), 2:99.

14. See Karl R. J. Arndt and May E. Olson, *The German Language Press in the Americas*, 3d ed., vol. 1 (Pullach: Verlag Dokumentation, 1976).

15. *Die Geheimnisse von Philadelphia. Eine Tendenznovelle* (Philadelphia: A. Gläser, 1850), 3, 4, 18; my translation.

16. Heinrich Börnstein, *Die Geheimnisse von St. Louis* (St. Louis: Druck und Verlag des "Anzeiger des Westens," 1851; 2d ed., St. Louis: C. Witters Buchhandlung, 1874), quote from 2d ed., p. 3; my translation.

17. Alfred Vagts, "Heinrich Börnstein, Ex- and Repatriate," *Missouri Historical Society Bulletin* 12 (October 1955):115.

18. Börnstein, *Fünfundsiebzig Jahre*, 2:99, 161–69.

19. Emil Klauprecht, *Cincinnati oder die Geheimnisse des Westens*, 3 vols. in one (Cincinnati: C. F. Schmidt, 1854–55), 3:182; my translation.

20. See Frederick C. Luebke, *Ethnic Voters and the Election of Lincoln* (Lincoln: University of Nebraska Press, 1971).

22.

The Representation of America in German Newspapers Before and During the Civil War

MARIA WAGNER

IN THE GERMAN PRESS of the nineteenth century, the *Augsburger Allgemeine Zeitung* played a comparable role to the London *Times* in the English-speaking world and the *New York Times* in our contemporary period. Contributors to the paper included the most important figures in German cultural life: historians, geographers, economists, poets. Heinrich Heine's Parisian reports first appeared in its pages and were subsequently published in his *Französische Zustände.* In the preface to this work, Heine states that the *Augsburger Allgemeine Zeitung* had "earned its renowned worldwide authority to such a degree that one could well call it the common—the 'allgemeine'—newspaper of Europe."[1] In conjunction with its associated papers such as the *Ausland* and the *Morgenblatt*, the *Augsburger Allgemeine Zeitung* thus is ideal for an examination of the representation of America in the German press of the nineteenth century.

The aims and objectives established by Johann Friedrich Cotta at the founding of the publication in 1798 subsequently were pursued by Georg Cotta and his editor-in-chief, Gustav Kolb: "Comprehensiveness . . . impartiality . . . truth . . . reporting which attempts to place every event in the context in which it can be most clearly and correctly understood, expressed in language appropriate to its subject matter and objectiveness."[2]

Until the early 1830s, journalistic reports from the United States played only a minor role in the *Augsburger Allgemeine Zeitung.* The AZ, as the paper's name was abbreviated, until this period published all news pertaining to Canada, the United States, and South America in one column entitled "America." In a letter to Johann Friedrich Cotta of July 29, 1827, Barthold G. Niebuhr criticized with justification the scantiness of American news reports consisting largely of secondhand accounts "which were of no use whatsoever."[3] Finally in the 1830s the separate column "United States" was introduced with permanent news reports provided primarily by German-American correspondents.

This new focus, formulated during the period when Georg Cotta became publisher in 1832 and Gustav Kolb was appointed editor-in-chief in 1837, was primarily the result of two factors. First, the German reading public had a heightened interest in developments in North America because it was the new home for thousands of friends and relatives. From 1820 to 1830, only 5,753 Germans emigrated to the United States, but in the following decade 124,726 German immigrants arrived. In the 1850s, their number soared to 976,072.[4] Second, in contrast to German immigration in the seventeenth and eighteenth centuries, a much greater percentage of intellectuals emigrated to the United States, and they had the interest and ability to write for the *Augsburger Allgemeine Zeitung.* The contributions of these correspondents are investigated here.

To their contemporaries, Georg Cotta's correspondents remained largely unknown. Cotta believed that he owed his journalists the safeguard of anonymity.[5] Only by specific request of the journalist was his name indicated in print. Nevertheless, because of Cotta's careful administrative management, it is possible today to determine the authors of certain articles (and even the honoraria paid) through marked editorial copies, account books, and correspondence located in the Cotta Archive. Extant letters indicate the working relationship between Georg Cotta and his contributors. Personal circumstances are often mentioned, such as the simultaneous employment of almost all of Cotta's permanent correspondents by other German newspapers. This duplication suggests a certain uniformity in American news reporting and further substantiates the representativeness of the *AZ* within the German press.

A survey of this news reporting from 1828 to 1865 reveals a distinct division in the journalistic writing that requires separating these four decades into earlier and later periods. The dividing line occurs approximately at midcentury following the Revolution of 1848–49, when a new wave of German immigrants began to become established in the United States and to engage in political and journalistic activity. The image of America presented to Continental Germans from 1828 to 1865 varied in many respects, but it was consistently benevolent. Examples from the two periods will illustrate the particular perspective of German-American journalists before and after 1850.

Much has been said and written about the later immigrants, the so called "Greens," and the conflict that developed between them and the "Grays," those who had emigrated to the United States before 1848. This opposition has been portrayed primarily as an internal conflict among German-Americans, caused by the different political outlook and historical experience of the "Greens" in Germany. The Forty-eighters are referred to as radicals, revolutionaries, and world reformers on the basis of their political beliefs and activities in Germany. As we shall see, however, the impressions and experiences they gained in America were of at least equal importance for their tone and conduct in the American political arena.

An examination of the image of America as reflected in the *Augsburger Allgemeine Zeitung* sheds light on the forces at work that simultaneously united and separated the two groups. As the articles in the *AZ* demonstrate, the decisive factor uniting the German immigrants was a general process of assimilation; a major factor in separating them was American political conflicts. It becomes clear that the conflict between Green and Gray is symptomatic of the general evolution of American politics in the middle of the nineteenth century.

Let us now examine in greater detail the two periods of American news reporting in the *AZ*. In both, articles appeared initially on a great variety of subjects of interest to the German reader: travel reports, personal experiences of immigrants, descriptions of topographical peculiarities, and observations on national holidays, religious sects, Indians, and the position of women in American society. Many reports dealt with the problems of immigration and offered advice on the most hospitable regions for settlement, good and bad news regarding the situation of Germans in the United States, and descriptions of German communities in America. Once immigrant correspondents became accustomed to their new environment and began to consider themselves part of American society, these largely ethnographic descriptions were replaced by analytical accounts of American political, economic, and social problems and issues.

In the earlier period, the great majority of correspondents revealed a sympathy for the Democratic party. Though written in German for Germans, these articles express an American point of view and an identification with the United States, exemplified, for example, by the use of the pronouns "we" and "us." In foreign affairs, the authors defend the interests of the United States against German tariff laws, seek an improvement in American foreign trade, and debate the precarious diplomatic relations with Great Britain. In domestic politics, the *AZ* correspondents address all the issues of concern to Americans at that time, including presidential elections, the banking system, western expansion, the Texas and Oregon questions, and the colonization of Liberia. In all these articles, the authors regard themselves as American citizens with a positive attitude toward their new country. One already senses an awareness of an American "mission," an anticipation of the philosophy later known as "manifest destiny." The journalists reveal the deep impression which the scope and grandeur of the American continent has made on them and predict a great future for the United States. An early report in the *Ausland* in 1828 written by Charles Sidon (that is, Karl Postl under the pseudonym Charles Sealsfield) shows the sentiment of this generation of journalists for their new country. The article is a travel report describing a visit to Jefferson's tomb: "As I gazed down on the endless hills and valleys covered with primeval forests or luxuriant fields, I dimly felt the divine pride which once might have moved Jefferson. In the distance, like a fairy castle, the University Monticello rose with its dome, colonades and halls. Charlottesville lay at my feet. America, I exclaimed, what are you and what will you yet become! A grand future rose in my mind's eye."[6] American achievements in culture, the field in which Germans considered themselves superior, were also acknowledged with a positive attitude. A detailed report in 1845 entitled "On Literature and Art in the United States" thoroughly examines a series of American writers and their works. The author of this essay, Francis Grund, addressed the perceived inferiority of American to English literature by indicating that

our national consciousness, that great fountain of every national literature, is of course still in its infancy. But considering its youth, it has truly been exploited sufficiently, and every year increases its treasure. We have by far not passed through the many human conditions which historically, and through vivid recollection poetically develop a people. . . . This explains in part why America has not yet produced a Shakespeare or a Byron. As far as the remaining English authors are concerned, the discrepancy is not so infinite as that we may not remain in the modest expectation of equaling them in time.[7]

In general, articles of this period reveal admiration for the country, which was shared by most correspondents. When writers were critical, they were so *en famille* and considered themselves partly responsible for grievances mentioned.

The debate over slavery, that bondage Germans always found abhorrent, is a case in point. It illustrates the changing political perspective that developed after midcentury. In the 1830s and 1840s, attempts were being made to find a peaceful solution to the problem. Correspondents of that earlier period sided with the then prevailing opinion of the day, regarding abolitionists as a radical minority who would only bring mischief. Wilhelm von Eichthal expressed this point of view in the *Augsburger Allgemeine* of 1842:

The influence of this party generally appears to increase. Unfortunately, this is not cause for congratulations, for a great narrow-mindedness reigns among these people. . . . This results in an empty, worthless fanaticism demanding of the constitutionally protected slave states tremendous material sacrifices, virtually destroying their existence without wishing to offer the slightest compensation. Such a policy must evoke the most bitter hate and determined resistance. As long as the abolitionists persist in this vein, the only peaceful emancipation—that is a gradual one in the interest of blacks as well as the plantation owners—becomes virtually impossible. Were the abolitionists to secure decisive influence, we would be face to face with the bloody monster of a slave war, or the dissolution of the Union.[8]

One possibility considered for the peaceful solution of the slavery question was the colonization of Liberia with freed American slaves. Franz Lieber, certainly no friend of slavery, wrote in 1829 that "this project could contribute significantly to the suppression of the slave trade at its source."[9] In 1840, Franz Grund believed that "trade with Central Africa will surpass that of the northern European powers in less than twenty years, and once this is the case the slave trade will cease by itself."[10] Ottilie Assing, a niece of Karl Varnhagen von Ense, reported on African colonization in 1859 but displayed a completely different opinion:

It would be a great error to believe that the execution of this project would contribute in the least toward the abolition of slavery. On the contrary, it would only weaken the abolitionist movement by causing the loss of individuals whose strength and abilities could contribute much more effectively toward the cause of emancipation and the progress of the black race in the United States. . . . But this is precisely the intent of the colonization society . . . whose very origin derives from the self-preservation drive of the slaveowners.[11]

Ottilie Assing was writing in the late 1850s, the decade during which a transformation occurred in the point of view of the column on America in the *Augsburger Allgemeine Zeitung*. Gradually, the correspondents of the earlier period were replaced by a new generation of journalists composed of the immigrants from the Revolution of 1848.

Although a critical and even aggressive voice now surfaced in the AZ, the underlying sentiment of benevolence toward the United States remained evident. The following report by Ottilie Assing on female emancipation is an example. She was at first skeptical of the movement and criticized its extreme manifestations. Assing soon became acquainted with its more central issues, however, such as the limited scope of female education, lower salaries, lack of professional opportunities, and denial of franchise for women. But Assing compared the movement for emancipation on both sides of the Atlantic:

Imagine what would happen if the women of some German state were to address a ministry or assembly with such a petition! What clamor about Bluestockings and rationalizations about the transgressions of the natural sphere of woman would arise! Here, in contrast, tolerance is the first requirement of social intercourse and is in fact largely practiced. One is rather inclined to allow room for every agitation which is not in complete violation of all social norms rather than brutally suppress everything one does not entirely approve of.[12]

Even on a purely formal level, a new aspect in the manner of news reporting became apparent at midcentury. Journalism was transformed from factual reporting to the marshaling of public opinion, and criticism was used to serve a higher ideal. This criticism, which made the "Greens" so unpopular with the "Grays," was closely related to political developments in the United States as a whole. To come to this conclusion, one needs to remember that the arrival of the Forty-eighters coincided with a turning point in American domestic politics.

In the first half of the nineteenth century, Americans looked with pride on the achievements of the past, the development of the nation and its unique Constitution, the expansion to the West and the South, and the consolidation of national boundaries. But by midcentury differences between North and South, between the industrial and agrarian sectors on social, political, and economic levels had become extreme. A reorientation in public opinion occurred at midcentury in which conflict became more pronounced and public debate more acrimonious. Party affiliations began to waver, and the abolitionists substantially increased their influence. Slavery was being more and more urgently debated and condemned without equivocation. Characterized by the founding and rapid growth of the Republican party, the new era attained its zenith with the election of Abraham Lincoln as president. News reports in the *AZ* from New York refer to this shift in public opinion and to "the greatest division of viewpoints amongst the population that has ever existed."[13] As the Republican party finally emerged victorious on the national level, the "Greens" succeeded in bringing a great number of the "Grays" into the Republican camp. Among Germans, intellectuals who had emigrated in the 1830s were the first to be convinced to join the antislavery party, as the Republican party came to be known. By 1860, the strife between the Democratic and Republican parties had run its course on the political level, and the war between the North and South began. As foreseen by the *AZ* correspondent in 1842, the "bloody monster" of civil war had become reality.

The hardening political conflict between North and South is depicted in the *Augsburger Allgemeine*. The sympathy of the reading public in Germany, reflected in the editorial position of the newspaper, lay with the Union. This bias is evident in the tone of articles accepted for publication and in the correspondence between editors and journalists. To Europeans, slavery appeared as the most urgent problem the United States had to eliminate. The constitutional, territorial, and economic conflicts between North and South were of limited interest to the general readership of the *AZ*, whereas slavery increasingly aroused the indignation of German readers. Cotta and his editors were initially neutral on the question of the American Civil War, publishing both conservative and radical points of view. But as the war progressed, the *Augsburger Allgemeine* openly supported the cause of the North. Articles by reporters from the southern United States, such as Maximilian Schele de Vere, eminent professor at the University of Virginia and supporter of the Confederates, no longer appeared. Cotta's and his editor's leanings are also underscored by the appointment of a special war correspondent, Colonel Otto Corvin-Wiersbitzki, who had been a prominent military leader of the revolutionary forces in 1848–49. He was to report directly from the battlefields of the American conflict; most of the permanent reporters, in contrast, covered the Civil War from the northern states. Ironically, however, Corvin's were the only reports to express skepticism about the motives of the North and Yankee principles. If Corvin had objectively clarified the position of the South, he would have implemented the *AZ*'s original ideals of truth and impartiality. But he wrote in a sarcastic and malicious tone in an effort to entertain his readers. In one of his articles one reads for example: "Whether a Yankee with a heart exists as we know it, I have not yet determined from my own experience. I doubt that one could find such an individual in the United States, except perhaps in some poor

house or in an asylum for the insane. I have heard that nature grows
tired of producing things which are perpetually exterminated."[14] Hermann Raster, another Cotta correspondent and editor of the *Illinois
Staatszeitung*, regarded by his contemporaries as an ingenious editor
and journalist,[15] protested Corvin's skepticism and sarcasm. Inspired
by the same patriotism that had characterized the articles of the earlier
period, Raster objected to Corvin's cynical views of the North. He designated Corvin as a "foreigner whose brief residence in this country
has not permitted him to properly interpret the masses of factual details produced by a free press." Raster wrote further: "When your correspondent remarks . . . with facile levity that the abolitionists were
only motivated by crudest egotism, by a mentality of hagglers and
sharpies, and by petty greed in the struggle for the abolition of slavery, he commits an injustice against hundreds, even thousands of the
noblest, most courageous and, above all, self-sacrificing and altruis-
tic men and women."[16] We can see from Raster's objection that the
"Greens" were as much motivated by patriotism and were no less pro-
American than the "Grays." Corvin cannot be regarded as a "Green"
because he arrived in the United States in 1861 and not as an immigrant but as a European war correspondent, attempting to satisfy his
thirst for adventure. Although hired by Cotta himself as a special correspondent, Cotta dismissed him in 1863 because his views "differ so
blatantly from those of the editors."[17] Kolb wrote of Corvin's "more and
more pronounced sympathy for the South while the sympathies of the
European continent lie with the North and against slavery, and there
can be no doubt that the North must eventually emerge victorious."[18]
Inexplicably, Corvin at this point obtained a commission as lieutenant-
colonel in the Union army. At the conclusion of the war, he returned to
Germany.

   Ottilie Assing, writing in the *Morgenblatt*, shared Hermann
Raster's political viewpoint. Her ecstatic description of the end of the
Civil War reveals her own political convictions and prophesies future
problems:

Slavery has received its mortal blow and can never again assume the force of
sovereign power. The equality of all citizens is the logically necessary consequence of that first great accomplishment and will sooner or later become the
law of the land despite all opposition. Progress, civilization, and the spirit of
the century command it and it is the condition for the greatness, strength, and
permanence of the republic. Now the question is whether a just and wise government can soon lead the people toward this great goal to ensure the blessings of a permanent, prosperous peace or whether such equality must be the
result of future struggle and conflict.[19]

The critical analysis of American news reports in the *AZ* and its allied papers reveals the assimilation process experienced by correspondents and the effect of the underlying American political developments on the two groups of journalists. In the earlier period German immigrants had been attracted by the Democratic party; later immigrants adopted the aims and rhetoric of the antislavery movement and the Republican party. To a degree, the conflict between the two immigrant groups parallels the confrontation between Democrats and Republicans until the outbreak of the Civil War.[20] The news reporting of the earlier period echoed the prevailing American mood of contentment, whereas the journalists in the second half of the century supported through their writings the increasingly active antislavery movement and the newly emerging Republican party. The new immigrants adopted the partisan strife and combativeness they found upon their arrival, just as the immigrants of the earlier period had adopted the sentiment of admiration and American national pride. Common to both groups was a political assimilation process that resulted in different and even contradictory conduct and attitudes in the two groups: admiration in the first case, criticism and aggressiveness in the second. In their own manner, both groups demonstrated their allegiance to their new country and its ideals.

The general characteristics of American news reporting in the German press from 1828 to 1865 can be summarized by noting three main points. First, news reports were presented from an American point of view and were, even in their criticism, favorably disposed toward the United States. Second, journalism evolved from a factual and analytic style to a reporting style in the later period that was intended to shape public opinion in the service of the American nation. Finally, the antagonism between the two generations of journalists can be traced to the political assimilation process both groups experienced. During the earlier period, assimilation occurred at a time of national pride and contentment; later it occurred in a mood of political upheaval and unrest.

Notes

1. Heinrich Heine, *Werke und Briefe*, ed. Hans Kaufmann, 10 vols. (Berlin: Aufbau Verlag, 1961), 4:368.

2. Liselotte Lohrer, *Cotta. Geschichte eines Verlags, 1659–1959* (Stuttgart: Cotta, 1959), 78–79.

3. Eduard Heyck, *Die Allgemeine Zeitung 1798–1898* (Munich: Verlag der Allgemeinen Zeitung, 1898), 73.

4. Kathleen Neils Conzen, "Germans," in Stephan Thernstrom et al., eds., *Harvard Encyclopedia of American Ethnic Groups* (Cambridge, Mass.: Harvard University Press, 1980), 410.

5. Georg Cotta to Eduard Pelz, February 3, 1859, Kopierbuch, Cotta Archiv, Stiftung der Stuttgarter Zeitung.

6. Carl Sidons, "Jefferson's Grab," *Ausland* 1, no. 78 (1828): 309–10. Excerpts from *Ausland, Augsburger Allgemeine Zeitung, Monatsblätter,* and *Morgenblatt* are being reprinted with kind permission of Schiller Nationalmuseum, Marbach a.N., Cotta Archiv (Stiftung der Stuttgarter Zeitung).

7. Franz Grund, "Über Literatur und Kunst in den Vereinigten Staaten," *Monatsblätter,* June 1845, p. 231.

8. Wilhelm von Eichthal, *Augsburger Allgemeine Zeitung,* no. 332 (1842): p. 2653.

9. Franz Lieber, "Über die Fellatah's und Liberia," *Augsburger Allgemeine Zeitung,* no. 355, 356 (1829): pp. 1421, 1426.

10. Franz Grund, "Die Colonisation von Liberia," *Augsburger Allgemeine Zeitung,* no. 126 (1840): p. 1002.

11. Ottilie Assing, "Neue Bestrebungen für die Colonisation der Neger," *Morgenblatt,* no. 5 (1859): p. 116.

12. Ottilie Assing, "Frauenrechte," *Morgenblatt,* no. 16 (1858): p. 383.

13. Hermann Raster, [no title] *Augsburger Allgemeine Zeitung,* no. 119 (1862): p. 1962.

14. Otto Corvin-Wiersbitzki, "Briefe aus Washington," *Augsburger Allgemeine Zeitung,* no. 41 (1862): p. 670.

15. "The Hermann Raster Papers," *Newberry Library Bulletin* 3 (December 1945): 26.

16. Hermann Raster, [no title] *Augsburger Allgemeine Zeitung,* no. 108 (1862): p. 1773.

17. Georg Cotta to Otto von Corvin-Wiersbitzki, September 7, 1863, Kopierbuch, Cotta Archiv, Stiftung der Stuttgarter Zeitung.

18. Gustav Kolb to Otto von Corvin-Wiersbitzki, February 22, 1863, Handschriftensammlung, Cotta Archiv, Stiftung der Stuttgarter Zeitung.

19. Ottilie Assing, "Der Prozess. Trauerfeierlichkeiten," *Morgenblatt,* no. 27 (1865), 645–46.

20. I am tempted to postulate that lingering memories of this conflict and of the "Donkey Grays" (die Eselsgrauen), as they were called, might have inspired Thomas Nast, the German-American artist of the next generation, to choose the donkey as a symbol for the Democratic party.

23.

Women of German-American Fiction: Therese Robinson, Mathilde Anneke, and Fernande Richter

MARTHA KAARSBERG WALLACH

THE MAJORITY OF GERMAN WOMEN who looked at America in the nineteenth century did so from the vantage point of Ellis Island or a kitchen window. Few of them recorded their impressions and, if they did, they usually wrote about their husbands and children and about such topics as the monotonous work of cutting shingles or the number of eggs the chickens were laying. Some exceptions, however, were a few privileged, educated German women who saw America from their study windows and who wielded a pen rather than a broom. They wrote works of fiction with American settings in which the lives and values of women play a large role. During the second half of the nineteenth century, they included such relatively well-known authors as Therese Robinson, Mathilde Anneke, and Fernande Richter.[1] To explore the picture of nineteenth-century America they presented, I will examine the female characters, the role of women, and social interaction in Robinson's *Die Auswanderer* (translated as *The Exiles*), in Anneke's serial stories "Die Sclaven-Auction" and "Die gebrochenen Ketten," and in Richter's "Ein Farm Idyll in Süd Missouri."[2]

Therese Albertine Luise Robinson (née von Jacob) wrote under the pseudonym TALVJ, which she derived from the acronym of her full birth name. She was well known for her works on Slavic folk songs, North American Indian languages, and the colonization of New England and for her literary criticism. She published her first novel, *Heloise or the Unrevealed Secret*, in English in 1850 and in German in

1852.³ *Die Auswanderer* on the other hand, first appeared in German and a year later in English translation as *The Exiles*. The latter version, which the author called "A Tale" despite its four hundred pages, is the basis of the discussion to follow.

The main characters are Clothilde Osten, who, like the author, is the well-to-do daughter of a German professor, and her fiancé Franz Hubert, her father's former student, who has spent six years in jail for his liberal political views. After his release, he and Clothilde are reunited but have to leave Germany immediately as exiles. As they sail toward New Orleans they are shipwrecked; Clothilde loses all of her wealth and believes Franz has been drowned. There follows a lively description of life among her rescuers, wealthy southern plantation owners in Florida and South Carolina. After the lovers are reunited, the scene shifts to New England, where Franz Hubert has recovered from his shipwreck injuries and where they make their new home. A love triangle involving Virginia, Clothilde's former student of German, brings death to both protagonists, and they are buried on their Vermont farm, Woodhill, which provided the title for the novel's second English edition.

The two female characters who represent the South in this novel are Clothilde's charges, Virginia and Sara. A more unequal pair of sisters is difficult to imagine: one a stereotyped southern belle, a literary ancestor of Scarlett O'Hara, and the other her opposite in every way and pious in the extreme. Kind, gentle, devout, demure, and self-effacing Sara shares her bed with her German teacher Clothilde (the latter is surprised that no private room is made available to her in this wealthy household). Sara can find a biblical quotation to explain every possible situation and asks her new teacher and roommate how many hours daily she spends in prayer. She justifies slavery because it has brought Christianity to the slaves, and she prays with them and the entire household daily. The lack of devotion among the other members of the family causes her to suffer. The author, despite her own obvious commitment to Christianity, satirizes this exaggerated religious fervor and contrasts it with Clothilde's deeply felt but not overstated faith.

A stark contrast to pale and pious Sara is the colorful, willful, and beautiful Virginia, who, with her charm and wiles, tyrannizes her father, her sister, her slaves, and the young men who court her. She lives only for pleasure and rushes from one amusement to another. She suddenly develops a great predilection for German literature and is the only member of her family to adopt the abolitionist position; both interests result from the influence of a German political refugee she has met. Her abolitionism is superficial, however. The author skillfully shows the reader that in her heart Virginia still accepts slavery, as is demonstrated in her relationship with her personal maid Phyllis, whom she punishes cruelly one moment and bribes with gifts the next. Virginia is portrayed as an irresponsible, childish, and self-indulgent creature, who flirts with all the men who admire her and plays most cruelly with her cousin Alonzo, whom their common grandfather had chosen as her future husband to bring the family fortune together again. Although we are encouraged to pity poor Alonzo from the start, we are not at first urged to condemn Virginia. Her beauty and charm are obviously intended to dazzle us as she dazzles all the characters in the novel. But when she is consumed by jealousy and rage at being rejected and makes Alonzo the instrument of her revenge, she becomes the novel's evil genius.

The sisters are the two American characters with whom we become most intimately acquainted. The author takes us into their boudoirs (modest and white in Sara's case, opulent and colorful in Virginia's) and gives us insight into their daily lives. The sisters have in common excessively planned days, leaving little or no time for German lessons. Sara goes to church daily and is constantly involved in church-related activities such as sewing for charity; Virginia beautifies herself, receives a steady stream of callers, and goes out to dance. The author seems to enjoy dwelling on the American custom of "calling" and of doing volunteer physical work such as sewing, while one's own work is done by slaves.

The role of American women is discussed at length in the novel. Hubert tells Clothilde how surprised he is at the respect with which women, especially young women and girls, are treated in America. He cites the example of his hosts in Maine, where the little boys in the family were taught to be polite and considerate toward their sisters, were sent on errands, and had to give up their seats at the main table when company arrived, whereas in Germany little girls would have to play those roles and wait on their brothers besides. He concludes that some girls become spoiled as a result of this deferential treatment and characterizes them as "mostly bold, noisy, greedy of admiration, often presumptuous in the consciousness of their charms" (*E* 228–29). Although he feels that the esteem in which they are held gives women beauty and grace, we are also told that "European travellers have often objected to the excessive politeness of the Americans toward their women, but particularly to the arrogance with which it is demanded by the latter as their right" (*E* 231). As an example, men are expected to give up their seats in public conveyances to women with "smiling indulgence." According to Hubert, a similar attitude toward the emancipation of women exists in America, where it has "never excited any sensation but good-natured ridicule" (*E* 232). He sees the origin of the form male-female relationships have taken in America "in the protecting forbearance of the strong for the weak; it has," he adds, "with all its civility, something of condescension" (*E* 232). He traces the protective deference toward women, present among all classes in America, to colonial times, when there was always "danger of being attacked by the Indians," and concludes: "The dependence in which the female sex was thereby kept, was . . . very unfavourable to its rightful position" (*E* 233). As an example, he cites the prohibition against women earning income and holding property in most states of the United States. The privileges of the American woman are only apparent because "in reality custom allows her much less liberty in acting for herself, than for instance, in Germany and England" (*E* 234). He does not want such a relationship with his wife because it is not in keeping "with the dignity of woman" (*E* 235). He does not want her to be a "petted plaything" but a companion in "joy and sorrow, in misery and death" (*E* 235). The relationship between Clothilde and Franz might appear to be traditionally German, however, in that she is usually shown listening to him, agreeing with him, urging him to continue, and echoing what he says; only twice does she mildly disagree with him. When her objections are ignored as he continues his diatribe, she does not insist on being heard. Her dedication to being his companion in sorrow, misery, and death is so complete that, although young, healthy, and pregnant, she dies of a broken heart after he is killed. It is clear that he is the author's mouthpiece when she tells us that he judges conditions in America with "freedom and clarity" (*E* 300). The analysis of the position of women in the United States is indeed perceptive; it has since been borne out by sociological and historical studies such as Ronald Hogeland's *Woman and Womanhood in America*.[4] The position taken in *The Exiles* differs appreciably from most German-American commentary of the time, which saw only the privileges of American women but not the resulting dependent role.[5]

One picture of America, in the second part of the novel, which does not take the form of such lecturelike pronouncements, is the difference in class consciousness between the main characters, especially Clothilde, and the Americans with whom they come into contact in the northern states. Although when theorizing about American values, the Huberts laud the proud bearing of Americans, they find this pride cumbersome when it keeps them from living their upper-class waited-on existence in a country where people consider it degrading to serve others (*E* 237). The most telling example is the vain effort to find a servant girl for Mrs. Hubert in New England, which lacks a "serving class" (*E* 333). The neighbor woman who initially helps with the housework insists on being treated as an equal and reminds Clothilde that she is only doing her a temporary favor (*E* 333). As they drive around in their newly acquired carriage (which they are very glad to have because in America "no one walks, who can ride in any way"— *E* 334), trying to find "help" (they have given up trying to find a maid), they are asked time and again: "Can't the young woman do the work herself?" (*E* 335). When the daughter of a neighbor is finally willing to try the job, Mr. Hubert is asked to pick her up in the carriage, but Mrs. Hubert declines for him and informs the family with a smile that the black boy who works for them will pick up the newly hired household helper instead. The Americans seem to miss the fine point that it is not below Mr. Hubert's dignity to serve as coachman to Mrs. Hubert but that it is out of the question that he be one for a mere servant! The new maid erroneously assumes that she will eat at the same table with the Huberts but is told as a pretext that she is not dressed properly; she tries to remedy the situation by cleaning up and, to Mrs. Hubert's consternation, uses her mistress's hairbrushes to do so. The final break comes when the Huberts fail to introduce her to a visiting neighbor while she is serving tea to both the visitor and the Huberts. Mrs. Hubert decides that she will do without a maid (she does have a charwoman for the "coarser work") rather than put up with a New England woman who wants to be a companion rather than a maid (*E* 293).

There are other indications of the Huberts' class consciousness: Mrs. Hubert keeps a posture of distant superiority toward her neighbors in rural Vermont. She accepts rides after church whenever Franz Hubert keeps her waiting; she skillfully questions the man who gives her a ride but gives him no information about herself (*E* 345). The author seems to approve of this tactic. We are disdainfully told about the "brood of insolent beggar children" in New York, and immigrants are spoken of condescendingly (*E* 304–5). The Irish are a "thoroughly raw, uneducated people," and the Germans on the streets of New York always wear hideous clothes because they are saving their Sunday best for Sunday and to pass on to their grandchildren (*E* 304). The familiarity of people who serve guests in the hotels of New York is remarked upon critically (*E* 306). In Vermont, Mrs. Hubert's "dignified manner" excluded all familiarity (*E* 343). The Huberts are *exiles*, not *emigrants*; we are told that Clothilde "clings to Europe" (*E* 298) and that Franz does not want to become naturalized (*E* 301). This feeling is underscored in the title of the first English edition: by calling the work *The Exiles*, rather than "The Emigrants," which would have been a closer rendition of the original German title, the author emphasizes that the main characters left Germany under pressure and are not necessarily happy to be in America.[6]

It is interesting to compare Therese Robinson's class-conscious, servantless exiles with the descriptions of a family with a similar background but an entirely different attitude toward America in "Ein Farm Idyll in Süd Missouri" by the popular St. Louis author Fernande Anna Therese Franziska Auguste Richter (née Osthaus, pseudonym Edna Fern).[7] This humorous account of farm life in southern Missouri is told in first-person narrative form by the daughter of an intellectual German family who had experienced so much evil (Böses) in the Old World that they decided to leave their country estate, the university, and the art academy and to try farming in America. The narrator informs us that a German university education is not very helpful in clearing the forest and milking the cows but is very helpful in appreciating the humorous aspects of such a venture (*G* 78). And they do need a sense of humor because the farming efforts of our German greenhorn family are not crowned by success: their well dries up, their pigs break out of the pens and run wild in the woods, they have crop failures, and in the end they discover that they were only squatters on a farm that belongs to a rich widow from the East who now wants it back. They give up farming to try their luck in the city.

The narrator seems to enjoy the experience nevertheless. She is neither spoiled nor particularly protected. Like her mother, she sleeps in a hammock in the open doorway of their one-room cabin so as to help keep out the animals while allowing in the fresh air on hot summer nights. The men sleep upstairs in the loft. She has to fend off an unwelcome suitor—the local blacksmith, who is tall, skinny, narrow-shouldered, and seems to have a vertebra too many. He comes to call and irritates her by wanting to learn German words and then asking how they are spelled. To confound him, she answers his request to spell her first name by rapidly spelling all of them without stopping; like the author, she has five given names: Anna Maria Therese Franziska Auguste! After this, the discouraged suitor gives up. She is alone in the house when a horse thief comes to visit and, after eyeing the rifles on the wall, makes off with the neighbors' horses and the doctor's mule.

Of the narrator's mother, we learn little more than about her shock at seeing a female neighbor smoking a corncob pipe. The neighbor women, Mrs. Nimmocks and Mrs. Yaeger, are both comical figures. Mrs. Nimmocks is tall, skinny, and stern, and her English is fast and unintelligible. She often goes to prayer meetings and neglects her husband and daughters. Like Sara in *The Exiles*, she is the only one in her family who is excessively religious. Mrs. Yaeger, whose husband anglicized his name after he became rich, is too intimidated to speak in his presence and often comes to call alone. Smoking her corncob pipe and rocking ceaselessly in the rocking chair, she tells the story of the Yaegers' squatter existence during the Civil War, using a German heavily laced with English words to which German endings have been attached. Except for smoking and keeping out the animals at night, the women in this story play fairly traditional roles and are not shown doing the heavy physical work that German farmers in America were often accused of allowing their womenfolk to do.[8] Threshing is done by the four men in the narrator's family together with the other male neighbors as a community enterprise. The narrator's brothers also milk the cows, which is often done by women in Germany.

The author takes pains to show the intellectual family taking this adventure in stride and being willing to do unaccustomed physical work. They have a good relationship with their neighbors, whose advice and boundless hospitality they accept; we are told that they will put up any stranger and feed him as well, as long as the stranger does not mind sleeping on the floor. Unlike the main characters in *The Exiles*, they show no direct condescension toward the uneducated farmers of the surrounding countryside. There is, of course, some implied superiority on the part of the author in the satirical presentation of the local "types," but it does not overstep the boundaries of good fun, and the greenhorn family is made fun of as well.

An entirely different world is portrayed in the stories of Mathilde Franziska Anneke. A Forty-eighter, feminist, abolitionist, and journalist, she was well known for her work in the women's movement of her time, for her essays, her fiction, and her poetry and, in Wisconsin, for her boarding school in Milwaukee. She has recently been made accessible to modern readers through Maria Wagner's sensitive analysis of her life and work and the publication of her letters.[9] Wagner's work also contains a full examination of "Gebrochene Ketten" and "Sclaven-Auction," which are here treated only as they deal with the role of black women.[10]

Anneke's strong abolitionist stand is evident in both stories. They were obviously written for the purposes of shocking the reader (whom she assumes to be female and addresses as "Leserin") by exposing the evils of slavery and of justifying the Civil War as a war of liberation for these unfortunate people. As a feminist, she was particularly interested in making known the outrages to which female slaves were subjected. The female main characters in Anneke's short stories "Die Sclaven-Auction," and "Die gebrochenen Ketten" are black slaves. In both stories they are the potential victims of the lust of their white would-be masters and at the last minute are saved from this dreaded fate through the intervention of a *deus ex machina*. This role is played by an abolitionist, who buys one endangered woman in "Die Sclaven-Auction" and by the Emancipation Proclamation, which frees the other in "Die gebrochenen Ketten." Both women are portrayed sympathetically: they are kind, gentle, devout, beautiful, and well loved. The indignities to which they are subjected and the further indignities with which they are threatened arouse the ire of the reader. In both stories, a desperate black mother kills her child to spare it a fate that she considers worse than death.

Isabella, the heroine of "Sclaven-Auction," who is described as "dark, but beautiful," cuts her long hair so she will appear less beautiful on the auction block. We first hear her voice, the lovely, insistent voice of a "tender being." The auctioneer praises her as a lively firebrand with looks that spell trouble. The daughter of a white man killed in a duel, she is on the auction block only because her master's entire property had to be sold. Her childless white mistress saw to it that she received singing, piano, and guitar lessons. When she is asked to play the guitar and sing, she chooses a religious song with a melancholy German melody, which touches the hearts of those sympathetic to her plight but increases the lust of those who would have her as a mistress. After she is bought by an abolitionist, she is free to leave for the northern states with her lover, Alfonso. From Alfonso we hear the story of his sister Lili, who was drowned by their mother when it became apparent that she was to be sold as a mistress. As a boy of eight, he witnessed the heart-rending scene of his mother taking his poor sister to the woods to the steep bank of a brook and pushing her to her death. Like Isabella, Lili also has hair down to her waist and is the beautiful daughter of a white master.

Sixteen-year-old Lelia, in "Die gebrochenen Ketten," has been treated like a daughter by her kind white mistress, Lady Kingsbury, who lies dead as the story opens. Her haughty and envious daughter and her decadent son are fighting over the inheritance, especially the possession of Lelia, whom the latter wants as his mistress and whom the former wants to put in her proper place by treating her as a slave. Lelia prefers the hard work and mistreatment of slavery to being kept "like a queen" by Alan Kingsbury, whose embraces she dreads. On her knees, she begs his sister to take her and keep her as her slave. Since the siblings cannot agree who is to get Lelia, all slaves are to be sold at auction. They are stunned by the prospect of being sold to someone in the dreaded deep South, when suddenly the act freeing all slaves in the District of Columbia "breaks their chains." They are ecstatic, except for Nancy, who has killed her baby so it will not be sold and separated from her as her other five children were. When she hears of the new freedom and realizes that her sacrifice was in vain, she also dies.

There is a hierarchy among the female slaves that seems to be determined by the treatment they have received and by their looks. Nancy, who has been very badly treated, has almost ceased to be human. Her looks are described as "mürrisch und abstossend" (ill-humored and repulsive), and her heart is said to have turned to stone; no one loves her, and she loves no one except her child. When it is dead, there is no reason for her to live. Nancy is also very black. Unlike Nancy, the two women in the middle range of the hierarchy both have someone who loves them. Jane, the maid, is said to be "flink" (quick), has been given a beautiful dress by her mistress, and is engaged to the butler. She is envious of Lelia and is not unhappy that the latter is in danger of losing her privileges. Juno, the cook, who is described as "a quite pretty mulatto woman," is married to the coachman and has an intelligent, lively European-looking son. At the top of the hierarchy is Lelia with her full, cherry-red mouth, her pearly white teeth, her starry eyes, her beautiful long hair that covers her body like a veil, and her olive-colored, transparent skin. Among the slaves, she alone is able to read. Like the cook's European-looking son, she is transformed by the news of their freedom and suddenly speaks to her would-be mistress with proud self-assurance. Anneke seems to have established her hierarchy to demonstrate how slavery affects people. Those who have been treated worst in the past and are not loved by anyone cannot enjoy freedom when it finally comes. Those who have been well treated and well loved are able to change when they are given freedom. They are also the most European-looking and those for whom we are encouraged to feel more than pity. The author tells us that to see ugly people as slaves provokes pity, but the sight of beautiful ones in this position cries to the heavens for redemption. In this case the whiter, the more beautiful.[11]

Black women in *The Exiles* do not fare as well as Anneke's characters do. Clothilde displays gratitude toward the black women who nurse her during her illness, but she considers others childish, willful, and without pride. She is dismayed, for example, to see Virginia's maid forgetting a cruel lashing as soon as she is given a colorful dress. Others are described as ugly and even compared to monkeys. The author seems to be annoyed to see on the streets of New York a black face that seems to her "to resemble a monkey more than a member of the human race" (*E* 304). There is criticism of the institution of slavery, and the description of the blacks, who have been captured after a futile attempt at flight, is genuinely sympathetic, especially the portrayal of a mother who hoped to lead her children to freedom and who is now stunned by her recapture. But when the Huberts go to live in the servantless North, they "make do" with a black boy and his charwoman mother for want of more suitable servants. The house of their black servants is symbolically located at the foot of the hill on which they themselves live. Although the author disapproves of slavery and seems to feel pity for black slaves, she also betrays a certain revulsion in the pictures she shows of them. The situation of female slaves does not arouse her indignation as it does Anneke's.

Robinson also shows a traditional view of women in the female main characters she portrays. Clothilde is a devoted German wife who cannot conceive of life on her own. Sara is subservient to God and to her father. Virginia, who has an independent fortune, defies her father when she runs away from home; she is not a positive character, however, but rather an example of the arrogance and greed for attention which the author believed resulted from too much deference toward women in America. The depiction of these traditional women exists side by side with an enlightened analysis of the position of women in America which is not as hostile to the emancipation of women as Irma Voigt suggests.[12] Their class consciousness keeps Robinson's exiles from a greater appreciation of America's egalitarian aspects and the evils of slavery.

Richter's egalitarian world knows neither masters nor slaves; there are differences in wealth but not in status. Her female characters are comical, sturdy farm women, well integrated into rural life. They are described with a sense of humor, and although they generally conform to traditional views of female roles, they are neither pampered nor protected.

Anneke's black women are all shown in an extreme situation: about to be sold, about to become the mistresses of white men against their will, killing their own daughters to spare them such a fate. The author's antislavery position is obvious and strongly stated. To demonstrate how slavery affects people, she has established a hierarchy based on past treatment and looks. She focuses on the lives of women more than do the other two authors and assumes her readers to be female.

All three authors have given women an important role in the works discussed here: there are many female characters, and most main characters are women; issues concerning women are emphasized, such as the daily lives of white women and their social status in Robinson's and Richter's work and the insitution of slavery as it affects black women in Anneke's work. Another common element is an analysis of social interaction, in the case of Robinson's and Richter's work chiefly between newly arrived Germans and more established Americans and in Anneke's both among black slaves and between white slaveholders and their slaves. These writers see conditions in America with a critical eye: Richter's vision is tempered by a sense of humor, Robinson's is affected by European cultural disdain, and Anneke's is politically charged and filled with missionary zeal to abolish slavery, which to her was an uncharacteristic blemish on this otherwise free country. Although all three authors were German women who lived similarly privileged urban lives in the New World, their views of women and life in America are anything but uniform.

Notes

For editorial assistance, I would like to thank my colleagues Kenneth Fleurant and Patricia Johnson.

1. Robinson and Anneke are the first women writers mentioned—and the only ones discussed at length—in Albert Bernhardt Faust, *The German Element in the United States* (Boston: Houghton Mifflin, 1909), 448–65. Robert E. Ward also lists them first in his discussion of women writers, adding Fernande Richter, who "was acclaimed as one of America's outstanding German writers in 1908" ("The Case for German-American Literature," in Gerhard Friesen and Walter Schatzberg, eds., *The German Contribution to the Building of the Americas: Studies in Honor of Karl J. R. Arndt* [Worcester, Mass.: Clark University Press, 1977], 383).

2. Therese Robinson, *Die Auswanderer* (Leipzig: F. A. Brockhaus, 1852), translated as *The Exiles* (New York: Putnam, 1853) (hereafter cited in the text as *E* and the page number); Mathilde Anneke, "Die Sclaven-Auction," *Didaskalia*, June 25–29, 1862; Mathilde Anneke, "Die gebrochenen Ketten," *Der Bund*, November 17, 1864 (both of Anneke's stories appear in the anthology Maria Wagner, ed., *Mathilde Franziska Anneke, Die gebrochenen Ketten: Erzählungen, Reportagen und Reden (1861–1873)* (Stuttgart: Hans Dieter Heinz Akademischer Verlag, 1983); Fernande Richter, *Gentleman Gordon und andere Geschichten* (Zurich: T. Schröter, 1901) (hereafter cited in the text as *G* and the page number).

3. Therese Robinson, *Heloise or the Unrevealed Secret* (New York: D. Appleton, 1850); *Heloise* (Leipzig: F. A. Brockhaus, 1852).

4. Ronald W. Hogeland, *Woman and Womanhood in America* (Lexington, Mass.: D. C. Heath, 1974).

5. See Martha Kaarsberg Wallach, "German Immigrant Women," *Journal of German-American Studies* 13 (Winter 1978): 99–104.

6. For a discussion of the author's general attitude toward America, see Guy Hollyday, *Anti-Americanism in the German Novel, 1841–1862* (Bern: P. Lang, 1977), and for a treatment of the European perspective, based largely on literary sources, J. Martin Evans, *America: The View from Europe* (San Francisco: San Francisco Book Co., 1976); Evans shows that much European criticism of America was motivated by utopian expectations, firmly rooted in the European mind.

7. Condoyanis lists her as having been born in 1861 and having immigrated to the United States in 1881, where she lived in St. Louis as the wife of a physician. George Condoyanis, "German-American Prose Fiction from 1850 to 1914" (Ph.D. diss., Columbia University, 1954), 399.

8. See Wallach, "German Immigrant Women."

9. Maria Wagner, *Mathilde Franziska Anneke in Bildzeugnissen und Dokumenten* (Frankfurt: Fischer, 1980).

10. See also Maria Wagner, "Zerbrochene Ketten: Ein Beitrag zum literarischen Feminismus," in Ralph Ley, Maria Wagner, Joanna Ratych, and Kenneth Hughes, eds., *Perspectives and Personalities; Studies in Modern German Literature Honoring Claude Hill* (Heidelberg: Winter, 1978), 344ff.

11. Anneke's general view of blacks is not free of what George M. Fredrickson calls "romantic racialism": the belief that there are innate differences between the races, coupled with a comparatively "benign view of black 'peculiarities'" (*The Black Image in the White Mind* [New York: Harper & Row, 1971], 101).

12. Irma Elizabeth Voigt, "The Life and Works of Mrs. Therese Robinson (Talvj)" (Ph.D. dissertation, University of Illinois, 1913), 133.

24.
German-American Literature: Critical Comments on the Current State of Ethnic Writing in German and Its Philological Description

ALEXANDER RITTER

GERD MÜLLER WRITES in the Swedish periodical *Moderna Språk* (1982) that a critical assessment of contemporary German literature written abroad represents something of a "sensation"; in fact, he considers this topic of literary criticism to be "extremely dubious" and the author's enterprise in undertaking such a study "rather daring."[1] The obvious dilemma in judgment which the professor of German must confront when he examines this thematic area is the same one that has confronted critical and historical evaluations of literature and the development of German philology since 1945.[2]

German-American literature is a part of this context. Those assessing it must take into consideration skeptical comments such as Müller's and come to terms with the complexity and sociohistorical conditions of minority literature. The word "dubious" used by Müller aims much too generally, however, at the historical burden of *Germanistik*, *Volkstumskunde*, and *auslanddeutsche Literatur* for the German writer. The Swiss professor of German Max Wehrli maintains that for ideological reasons "those terms and methods which remain suspicious to this day" have been suppressed.[3] This is still particularly true for the term *auslanddeutsche Literatur* (German ethnic literature outside Germany) and for German ethnic literature in general, which is therefore often viewed in the wrong context.

Such a taboo, which has resulted in a relatively widespread ignorance of our subject, prevents the necessary theoretical considerations. The assumption of inferior literary quality—J. Frank Dobie warns the ambitious literary scientist that "nobody should specialize in provincial writing,"[4]—results most often in personal and scientific caution when dealing with this field of literature. The comparative approach, which is methodologically necessary here, presents further barriers. Only with a considerable knowledge of the history of international migrations and the individual national culture with its internal interactions, for example in language or literature, can the reception of literature in ethnically divided landscapes be treated with the necessary care.

From the point of view of the German germanist, various factors taken together hinder the private, journalistic, and scholarly reception of this literature in its place of origin as well as in other German-speaking lands. These factors include ideological prejudices related to the subject, insufficient subject material or knowledge of the subject area, and a lack of necessary reflection on this area as a whole.

Let us ask ourselves first what we understand by the term "German-American literature." All efforts to define this term in secondary literature or by the authors of the literature meet with uncertainty and contradictions.[5] Let us consider the first part of the double attribute, "German-." Hugo von Hofmannsthal maintained in 1927 that these writers belong to the category of "roaming lost sons who carry their national colors with them."[6] Does this statement accurately reflect the situation or, rather, does the public refusal of the West German politician Carlo Schmid in 1963 to pursue *Bindestrich-Politik* (hyphenated politics) for *Bindestrich-Amerikaner* (hyphenated Americans)?[7] Both opinions are responsible to a certain extent for the almost complete exclusion of German ethnic literature from literary criticism and literary histories as well as its rejection by prominent contemporary German authors.[8]

As to the second part of the attribute, "-American," in 1972 the Ethnic Heritage Studies Programs Act (Title IX: Ethnic Heritage Program/Statement of Policy) was officially declared an important part of federal cultural policy in the United States. In 1978 Wolodymyr T. Zyla in the preface to the documentation *Ethnic Literatures since 1776* pleaded for "the many voices of America" generally "to recognize the value of every ethnic group's contribution to the society."[9] In 1981 the Chicano author Rudolfo Anaya complained at the American Writers' Congress that minority literature was "a victim of the ugliest censureship imaginable: the censureship of being completely ignored."[10]

Even these few hints point out some implications of research that can complicate critical viewpoints on ethnic literature and leave the author and the critical reader in doubt as to whether they are taking part in a sectarian grouping of German or American literature. I shall attempt to examine this issue from the point of view of some basic facts.

German-American literature is an immigrant's literature. Its outstanding feature is the German language, which claims various national origins (Germany, Austria, Switzerland, and other nations). In both the quantity and quality of its authors and readers this literature is dependent on immigration, which is determined historically by varying circumstances. Its development appears to have been limited by the German-speaking immigrants' economically motivated readiness to assimilate as well as by the extreme scattering of settlements and the mobility of these individuals in a very large country. These negative conditions prevented regional awareness and concomitantly a unified minority awareness. Such conditions were, for instance, responsible for the erosion of a widespread landscape of newspapers down to a few remnants. Generally, these conditions do not offer a sufficient basis for the existence of an effective system of publishing houses, radio, television, and education as in Romania or the Soviet Union. Furthermore, they hinder the production of literature and its reception to a great extent by complicating effective journalistic and scientific reactions.

If this situation does exist, the contemporary German-American author is more or less left alone with his talent, his language competence, and the linguistic, thematic, formal, and general artistic effects of the interaction between the German language and his American experiences. He is dependent on the distribution of his work by the publisher and its critical reception, both of which are essential for his existence. The consequences of such an existential situation could be a personal or artistic retreat, but it might result as well in an intentional demonstration of exaggerated ethnic writing when factors such as language, place of origin, and minority consciousness combine to lead the writer to the ideological assertion of some vague concept of "German-America."

If we simplify to a very great degree by grouping German-American and other minority literatures together—insofar as they are dependent on immigration—it seems evident that the elementary danger for minority literature is, as Lion Feuchtwanger wrote in 1943 concerning the "problems of writing in exile," "the bitter taste of being separated from the flow of one's mother tongue,"[11] that is, linguistic and formal erosion, the provincialism connected with it, or, finally, silence. Such a bitter evaluation of linguistic isolation does not necessarily lead to literary failure. These negative circumstances also include the chance for the writer to escape from this minority situation, providing of course that "he is in the possession of a visionary talent and the ability to dream." If that is the case, it is possible to produce literary works of universal validity because the author "has geographically drifted away from Germany . . . drifted away from the German language," and in so doing "becomes capable of forming a new style."[12] Let us keep these two evaluations in mind when we examine present-day German-American literature.

The limitations of space force me to narrow my report and reflections. All of the following observations and remarks concentrate on the present-day situation as it is revealed in three anthologies: *Deutsche Lyrik aus Amerika* (New York, 1969) edited by Robert E. Ward; *In Her Mother's Tongue* (Denver, 1983; first edition *Reisegepäck Sprache*, Munich, 1979), edited by Lisa Kahn; and *Nachrichten aus den Staaten— Deutsche Literatur in den USA* (Hildesheim and New York, 1983), edited by Gerhard Friesen. Three hundred years of literature as well as the literary, historical, and communicative circumstances of German-language literature in the United States can be only marginally dealt with here. In spite of these necessary limitations the two latter text collections enable us to recognize that which is symptomatic of German-American writing in the United States.

Why do German-American writers write at all, and why do they use the German language for fiction in a society in which English is the official language? Lisa Kahn's inquiry into the question "why I still write in German"[13] helps us to identify characteristic poetological assumptions. With a careful assessment of statements from individuals, three positions can be distinguished. First, German is a literary language because it is the "mother tongue,"[14] because one "was brought up in this language," and as a result it is "more efficient for poetry," because one's own language and poetology are influenced by education in one's mother tongue, academic achievement, and occupation with German literature.[15] To put it in a word, the German language is "Heimat."[16] "Landscape and characters originate here," writes Ilse Pracht-Fitzell. "I do not achieve what some people imagine to be their aim in German-American literature. I do not write nostalgic poetry. I am more concerned with the soul and its unfolding."[17] Second, German competes with English as the language of literature. Lielo A. Pretzer emphasizes the literary advantages of bilingualism because she "lives in two languages," looking at language functions as a possible form of existence like a "continent to be lived on." As in the process of the literary transformation of the world, both languages are effective through each other.[18] Third, German literary language—and thus literature in the German language—becomes a literary existential problem because of the neglected position of the German language in daily life. The scope of this relationship to the mother tongue continually ranges from "complicated and tormenting"[19] to a painfully experienced loss of writing ability. This is the result of one's own position between the languages and one's recognition of a change of language as a consequence of the identity change, as noted by Marianne Ultmann, who sees herself "physically and mentally miles away from the living German language, in order to be able to write as a contemporary. . . . I live and write in the same language, English."[20]

Individual circumstances such as favorable professional conditions for university germanists belonging to the first generation of immigrants, the type of German language they brought with them, and its literature are all important conditions for the preservation of the language. Nevertheless, the problematic existence of a minority author writing in German is even more obvious than is described by a literary critic from Bucharest, Gerhardt Csejka, commenting on Romanian-German authors:

Anyone who realizes just how much art—and in particular literature as language art—continues to live to this day from the reality of its national character, will grasp the essential difficulty of any literature which has been taken out of this organizational context. The problematic position of this literature arises from its language (with all its inherent characteristics and consciousness) which is indebted to a previous reality to which it is no longer tied except through language. Likewise, it confronts a new reality which cannot be completely overcome by means of this language.[21]

How do these authors come to terms with this artistic predicament in their literary works? Listings of writers and their publications point to a typical minority preference for the short form in German-American literature, above all lyrics rather than the short story, novel, or drama—the latter two genres playing a very small role. The literary short form corresponds directly to conditions of a linguistic and cultural diaspora as well as a greatly reduced mechanism of critical reception in comparison with German-speaking lands. These circumstances direct poetical impulses, artistic evaluation, and literary identity in such a way that even authors of average or minor talent are considered significant. Thus a comparatively wide range of authors seeks public recognition. This situation exists, for example, in contemporary German-Canadian and Soviet-German literature.

Since a specific tradition of native German-American literature hardly exists because of a lack of group feeling and rapid assimilation, its thematic limits tend to be rather narrow. They are confined, first, to the experience of emigration from Europe, bound to aspects of origin, "Heimat," National Socialism, anti-Semitism, European memories in general, and the trauma of the return to Europe; second, to the experience of migration to the United States, in particular the arrival, "Heimat," loneliness and isolation, imminent loss of the German language, life in America, the trauma of reality, and the inclination to project this reality into the subjective mystical world of a more secure inner emigration; and third, to the experience of bilingualism in the double role of citizen and poet and how it determines these identities in the broadest sense.

These thematic accents parallel but few themes of contemporary American literature with regard to literary historical development (and one's own position within this development), ethnic-historical interrelationships, sociopolitical proceedings, and so on. With the gangway still close behind them after the transatlantic crossing, German-American authors tend to describe and reflect primarily their uneasy existence.

These topics and motifs as well as the personal and linguistic aspects of this literature can be demonstrated with the help of a few texts. Luise Bronner's poem "Neuer Anfang"[22] and Alfred Gong's "USA"[23] reveal a characteristic pattern of present-day German-American lyrics in the United States. Luise Bronner powerfully describes the emigrants' optimism by means of the letters "Z" and "A," which mark the extremes of the alphabet. Here their sound reminds one correspondingly of Omega and Alpha, the end and the beginning. Alfred Gong presents, on the other hand, a kaleidoscope of the New World in his hymnlike poem celebrating the destination of the immigrants. Gong spreads out a panorama of images by means of long syntactical sequences and captures the complex structure of this big country through nouns, participles, and genitive metaphors, mystically conjuring the condition of this new society: "First draft of past gods, / laboratory of future gods."[24]

Let us examine individual thematic elements and their literary realization one by one. Even Rita Terras's use of the title "Auswanderer—

Einwanderer" (emigrant—immigrant) signals the tenseness and conflict in the double existence of the poet.[25] The compressed language of this text supports the reduction of the author's experience to the polarity of two languages and two homelands. This reality, which the author cannot escape, is convincingly represented through variations of the ambivalent meaning of the verb "setzen." The autobiographical retreat to the Old World and the present connection to the New World remain the integral components of the individual's experience. They can therefore be an enriching condition for the writer, as Hertha Nathorff mentions in "Drei Städte:" "When I dream: LAUPHEIM . . . when I think: BERLIN . . . and then when I feel: NEW YORK."[26] Memories of Europe can also be a traumatic spiritual burden. In this context the American reality can and—in my opinion—will prevail through the erosion of the German language which the authors brought over with them because the divergence of semantic possibilities from a social reality not dependent on them leads to problems in the reception of this literature, unless of course the German language tradition develops a viable autonomy—if that is possible. Burghild Holzer refers to this problem of reception in her poem "translating the milky way" with various gestures of helplessness: "If only I could tell you— . . . and if only you could understand."[27] Lisa Kahn directly points out the time limitation that confronts the language competence of German-speaking immigrants by means of the metaphor "Reisegepäck Sprache." The lyrical speaker in this work feels "Angst," sees "Gefahr," and signals "fear of the impoverishment of becoming monolingual," that is, of losing one's identity with the language, thus experiencing extreme loneliness.[28] The fear of loneliness is a widely used motif, as for example in Kurt Fickert's poem "Beim Alban-Berg-Konzert": "Suddenly the concert hall lost its roof / . . . I sensed an emptiness, like a thistle which stabbed / like the loneliness in the paintings of van Gogh."[29]

Present-day German-American literature thus proves to be literature in the German language by immigrants of the first generation. It is closely tied to the temporary social situation of the writer, and it has a limited duration of existence, caught between two cultures, not born of a new culture. The authors, although "residing in the Garden State of New Jersey / but not arrived there yet," as Gert Niers writes, will become silent at the moment of integration.[30] The sad "Traum eines deutsch-amerikanischen Dichters"[31] by Don Heinrich Tolzmann and the resigning memories of Gert Niers's "Das Haus A. Rattermanns (deutsch-amerikanischer Dichter)" are longing gestures, which hardly attempt to conceal the literary and linguistic capitulation in the "thicket of foreign tongues."[32] Lisa Kahn demands: "Stop carrying poems around with you over a thousand miles and more. It would be better if no one heard them read."[33]

The observed variations in this thematic context which appear in the poems cited above as well as in other works of German-American authors require a summation. The works of this literature seldom use simple traditional rhyme conventions or conjure up a false harmony in the world with sentimental phrases. They are, as Günter Kunert demands of poetry, "Gedichte gegen den Strich" (poems against the grain).[34] They are poems that erase the hyphen between German and American; their dividing and coupling function is hardly overcome in this ambivalence. These poems are not haughty literary constructs burdened with metaphors. But they are also not meaningless or laborious gestures of literary preservation for the well-being of a minority culture that does not truly exist. German-American poetry is nourished by the concurrence of world experience, literary transformation, and the intention of credible authenticity.

Several features characterize this literature as one of immigration in the narrowest sense of the word: the aforementioned predominance of topics closely connected to the immigrants' experience, a one-sided sociological structure attributed to this loosely connected group of writers by academics such as germanists, university professors, and journalists, and the well-known process of assimilation in the second generation. In these respects it differs from traditional Romanian-German literature. These assumptions and their interdependence on one another limit the artistic freedom of the individual writer. Although not independent of place of origin, mother tongue, and European communication system, they nonetheless seek to create a literature of universal validity within a new culture. That the authors have retreated from a cultural-political projection of German-American culture or German culture in America is not only to be seen as an ideological unburdening on their part but also as a symptom of the lack of a minority culture. Thus the authors keep "their distance from any question of this kind," as Franzi Ascher-Nash says, and keep free of trivial folklore, writing because they themselves want to write and write for the sake of a good poem in the German language.[35]

How can we evaluate present-day German-American literature in comparison with other literatures in non-German-speaking countries? If we ask whether there is such a thing as *the* German literature, we must admit that this question is superfluous with regard to German ethnic literature. *The* German ethnic literature does not exist. An assumed affinity and clear relationship to German literature were artificially exaggerated for sociopolitical and ideological reasons as a result of the *Volkstumideologie* and National Socialist view of culture.[36] The controversial efforts of the germanist Josef Nadler are well known for their false orientation on this point.

All literature in the German language that originated outside the national boundaries of German-speaking lands must be viewed in the context of its own particular individuality. This individuality is a result of the varying distance to the central European German language and literature, of special historical, linguistic, literary, and sociological circumstances and domestic and foreign politics, and in general of conditions pertaining to individual production and reception. These factors influence all literature but are of particular relevance here because minority literatures are also shaped by linguistic and literary influences that require a comparative perspective. Only under these assumptions can German literature written abroad be put into the necessary value context. Thus a comparison can be made with German-language literature in France (Alsace), Romania (Siebenbürgen, Banat), and the Soviet Union. In these three countries characteristic conditions for the existence of present-day German literature are present and provide the basis for a relatively autonomous tradition of ethnic literature. In this essay, however, I can only point to the information available in the sources cited in the notes.[37]

This discussion requires a certain amount of healthy skepticism. Can one talk about an independent German-American minority literature or should we rather say literature in the German language written in the United States? The quantity and quality of the production and reception of a minority literature that claims to have a literary independence and uniqueness based in a minority culture is dependent on the degree of regional identity and the standard of relative cultural autonomy associated with this identity. It is determined by the cultural place of origin as well as the place of immigration (immigrant minority) or by its own regional cultural history and the quality of cultural contact with neighboring German-language areas (border minority). It is dependent on the degree to which the minority tends toward assimilation and the mobility of the group in general. Furthermore, it is supported by the intensity, level, and effectiveness of the respective systems of education and communication. It is preserved and stimulated by the structure, extent, and quality of language competence, by existing conditions that aid preservation and propagation, and by the reciprocal effects of contact with another language. Minority literature exists in the area of cultural exchange between regional and minority culture, the native culture, and the culture of its place of origin. It develops within three literary-historical traditions and three areas of critical reaction: the minority group itself, the present homeland, and the country of origin. Minority literatures draw their themes, language, and forms—in other words, their literary and artistic orientation—from these factors.

If all these points pertaining to the existence of a minority and its literature could be answered positively, the literature of a minority could reach a sufficient level of literary achievement and could be competitive in quality. That very few of these conditions apply to German-American literature would appear to confirm the evaluation presented earlier.

The present study of minority literature in the German language and the discussion of examples from German-American literature cannot hide the fact that there are still more questions than answers on this topic. In view of the unsatisfactory situation of research on this topic, as well as its reception, I shall summarize the preceding thoughts in six points.

1. Present-day German-American literature is written in the German language in the United States. It cannot be termed genuine ethnic literature of a German-American cultural tradition because of the objective circumstances. The circumstances discussed earlier point only to a limited degree to a specific German-American literary tradition within the context of German and American literature. The loss of publishing opportunities in Europe and the reinforcement of European criticism would mean at present that the supporting basis of this literature will all but disappear.

2. The relatively few critical writings dealing with this literature are in general more strongly characterized by rhetorical claims of an autonomous minority literature than is the case in philological analyses, which better correspond to the literary reality and approach it from methodologically differentiated standpoints. Every essay that claims to offer results without sufficient methodological reflection and uses questionable literary-historical references as well as inflated estimations of the German heritage of the American population lends the wrong accents and does not treat the actual facts of the literary achievements and the situation of scholarship in the necessary way.

3. The well-known criticism by German-American writers of the reserved reaction of publishers, literary critics, and private individuals to their writing in the United States points out the significance of

German-American literature. This situation, however, is an expression of the widespread ignorance and uncertainty in evaluation that came about in part because of the insufficiency of philological reception. In this context it remains regrettable and hard to grasp why German philology has not learned from the reflections and methods of English and Romance philology in the discussion of literatures outside the country of linguistic origin.[38] The same holds true for the almost nonexistent recognition of scholarship in countries with German and other minorities as well as for the necessary exchange of information on this topic from one minority to another.

4. The primary conditions for the literary development or erosion of minority literatures have not been identified or sufficiently discussed in terms of German-American literature and minority literature in general. One reason is an aversion to such an undertaking on the part of German philology as a result of its own historical past in the context of *Volkstumideologie* and National Socialist cultural ideas, with which it has not yet fully come to terms. In addition, one must take into account the cultural foreign policy of the Federal Republic of Germany, which has been consistently pursued since the nation's founding in 1949. This policy includes a lack of cultural support for German-speaking minorities, which is carried so far beyond clear political or moral needs that one is hard-pressed to understand its rationale.

5. On the basis of these points there remains for literary scholars, linguists, historians, sociologists, ethnographers, and cultural politicians on both sides of the Atlantic an immense field of potential interdisciplinary activity which must bring together a variety of individual scientific achievements. There must be stronger systematic research and documentation of German-American literature in its cultural and historical context in conjunction with the multilingual situation in the United States, research on migration and exile and on the cultural, historical, and political interrelations between Europe and America. So, too, a discussion of literary and historical categories and critical scholarship should be included.

6. The most important prerequisite for implementing these suggestions seems to me to be a renewed willingness on the part of German philology to deal with this thematic area. Similarly important are the establishment of a financially and organizationally sufficient center for documentation in the Federal Republic of Germany as well as the stimulation of public interest by means of the media and government cultural policies.

Let us ignore the arrogant smiles that conceal the belief that anyone dealing with German literature from abroad and its related themes
is somehow imitating the folly of the American detective Bobby Dodd.
He too chased a phantom around the world, a certain fellow from
Hamburg, and later the German-American bookkeeper Peter Voss,
who attempted to save his firm by means of a pretended embezzle-
ment.[39] Ewald Seeleger's comical American novel *Peter Voss, der Millionendieb* is entertaining fiction, with a grain of salt, of course, but the
seriousness of our appeal remains unchanged, and we can say with
the Luxembourg writer Roger Manderscheid:

Burst the provincial bubble with the sharpness of our words. Create sentences
from ideas and conclusions from beginnings. No more aphorisms; concentrate. No more fragments; be serious—regionalism itself is not the problem
but rather how little we are able to make of it. This is not intended as a plea for
a kind of collective literary introspection. But if we want our writing to be authentic, then this regional consciousness is essential; we can't get around it or
pretend it doesn't exist.[40]

Notes

1. Gerd Müller, Review of Manfred Durzak, ed., *Deutsche Gegenwartsliteratur:
Ausgangspositionen und aktuelle Entwicklung* (Stuttgart: Reclam, 1981) in *Moderna
Språk* 76 (1982): 390–92.

2. For information see the following essays by the author: Alexander Ritter,
"Deutschsprachige Literatur des Auslands: Perspektiven germanistischer Analyse,
Beurteilung und Aufgabenstellung," in Reingard Nethersole, ed., *Literatur als Dialog*
(Johannesburg: Ravan Press, 1979), 109–27; "Zwischen literarkritischem Vorbehalt
und kulturpolitischer Empfindlichkeit: Die deutschsprachige Literatur des Auslands,"
Recherches Germaniques, no. 11 (1981): 229–45; "Deutschsprachige Literatur der Gegenwart im Ausland," in Durzak, ed., *Deutsche Gegenwartsliteratur*, 632–61; "Deutsche
Lyrik aus der sprachlichen Diaspora: Kritische Anmerkungen zu einem ungeschrie-
benen Kapitel der deutschen Literaturgeschichte," *Zeitschrift für Kulturaustausch* 33
(1983): 200–215; "Germanistik ohne schlechtes Gewissen. Die deutschsprachige
Literatur des Auslands und ihre wissenschaftliche Rezeption," in Alexander Ritter,
ed. *Deutschsprachige Literatur im Ausland* (Göttingen: Vandenhoeck & Ruprecht,
1985), 10–34.

3. Max Wehrli, "Deutsche Literaturwissenschaft," in Felix Philipp Ingold, ed., *Literaturwissenschaft und Literaturkritik im 20. Jahrhundert* (Bern: Kandelaber, 1970),
15. See also Eberhard Lämmert et al., *Germanistik: Eine deutsche Wissenschaft* (Frankfurt: Suhrkamp, 1967; 5th ed., 1971); Jürgen Kolbe, ed., *Ansichten einer künftigen Germanistik* (Munich: Hanser, 1969).

4. J. Frank Dobie, *Guide to Life and Literature of the Southwest*, 6th ed. (Dallas:
Southern Methodist University Press, 1969), 1.

5. Linus Spuler, *Deutsches Schrifttum in den Vereinigten Staaten von Amerika* (Lucerne: Lehranstalten, 1960); Robert Spiller and William Thorp, "German-American Literature," in Robert Spiller, William Thorp, et al., *Literary History of the United States* (New York: Macmillan, 1974), 678–84; Erika A. Metzger, "Deutsche Lyrik in Amerika," *German-American Studies* 9 (1975):2–20; Robert E. Ward, "The Case for German-American Literature," in Gerhard K. Friesen and Walter Schatzberg, eds., *The German Contribution to the Building of the Americas* (Worcester, Mass.: Clark University Press, 1977), 373–89; Carl Hammer, Jr., "A Glance at Three Centuries of German-American Writing," in Wolodymyr T. Zyla and Wendell M. Aycock, eds., *Ethnic Literatures since 1776: The Many Voices of America* (Lubbock: Texas Tech Press, 1978), pt. 1, 217–32.

6. Hugo von Hofmannsthal, "Das Schrifttum als geistiger Raum der Nation" (1927), in Hans Mayer, ed., *Deutsche Literaturkritik*, 4 vols. (Frankfurt: Fischer, 1978), 3:491–92.

7. Carlo Schmid, "Zur auswärtigen Kulturpolitik," in Walter Hinderer, ed., *Deutsche Reden* (Stuttgart: Reclam, 1973), pt. 2, 1115.

8. Günter Kunert, "Hört endlich auf, uns ständig neue Paradiese zu versprechen: Überlegungen zur ungeteilten deutschen Literatur," *Die Welt*, August 14, 1982.

9. Wolodymyr T. Zyla, "Preface," in Zyla and Aycock, eds., *Ethnic Literature since 1776*, pt. 1, 5–7.

10. Teru Kanazawa, "Der American Writers' Congress 1981," *Dollars und Träume*, no. 5 (1982):131.

11. Lion Feuchtwanger, "Arbeitsprobleme des Schriftstellers im Exil" (1943) in Mayer, ed., *Deutsche Literaturkritik*, 4:200.

12. Marie Luise Kaschnitz, "Rede an den Preisträger" (1960) in Dietlind Meinecke, ed., *Über Paul Celan* (Frankfurt: Suhrkamp, 1970), 69–76.

13. See both anthologies: Lisa Kahn, ed., *Reisegepäck Sprache: Deutschschreibende Schriftstellerinnen in den USA 1938–1978* (Munich: Fink, 1979); and Lisa Kahn and Jerry Glenn, eds., *In Her Mother's Tongue: Bilingual Updated Edition of Reisegepäck Sprache* (Denver: Emerson Press, 1983).

14. Kahn, ed., *Reisegepäck*, 120; Kahn and Glenn, eds., *Mother's Tongue*, 253.

15. Kahn and Glenn, eds., *Mother's Tongue*, 229.

16. Kahn, ed., *Reisegepäck*, 75.

17. Ibid., 97.

18. Ibid., 103–4.

19. Kahn and Glenn, eds., *Mother's Tongue*, 139.

20. Ibid., 363.

21. Gerhardt Csejka, "Bedingtheiten der rumäniendeutschen Literatur," in Emmerich Reichrath, ed., *Reflexe: Kritische Anmerkungen zur rumäniendeutschen Gegenwartsliteratur* (Bucharest: Kriterion, 1977), 45.

22. Kahn and Glenn, eds., *Mother's Tongue*, 103.

23. Gerhard Friesen, ed., *Nachrichten aus den Staaten: Deutsche Literatur in den USA* (Hildesheim: Olms, 1983), 55.

24. Ibid., 55.

25. Ibid., 123.

26. Ibid., 93.

27. Kahn and Glenn, eds., *Mother's Tongue*, 141.

28. Friesen, ed., *Nachrichten*, 69.

29. Ibid., 51.

30. Ibid., 94.

31. Ibid., 125.

32. Ibid., 94–95.

33. Kahn and Glenn, eds., *Mother's Tongue*, 175.

34. Günter Kunert, "Kontroverses Schreiben," in his *Warum schreiben?* (Munich: Hanser, 1976), 255–56.

35. Franzi Ascher-Nash, ". . . rika-Deutsch-Amerika-Deutsch-Amerika-Deutsch-Ame. . . ," in Friesen, ed., *Nachrichten*, 130–33.

36. See Hugo Grothe, ed., *Grothes Kleines Handwörterbuch des Grenz- und Auslanddeutschtums* (Munich: Oldenbourg, 1932); Adolf Meschendörfer, "Die Stimme der Auslandsdeutschen," in Heinz Kindermann, ed., *Des deutschen Dichters Sendung in der Gegenwart* (Leipzig: Reclam, 1933), 138–45; Heinz Kindermann, "Wesen und Entfaltungsraum der grenz- und auslanddeutschen Dichtung," in Kindermann, ed., *Rufe über Grenzen: Antlitz und Lebensraum der Grenz- und Auslanddeutschen in ihrer Dichtung* (Berlin: Junge Generation, 1938), 11–31.

37. See "Bibliographie zur deutschen Sprache und deutschsprachigen Literatur im Ausland (1945–1978)," in Karl Kurt Klein, *Literaturgeschichte des Deutschtums im Ausland*, ed. Alexander Ritter (Hildesheim: Olms, 1979), 475–555. See also Adrien Finck, "La Poésie d'expression allemande en Alsace depuis 1945," *Recherches germaniques*, no. 6 (1976):205–49, and "Mundart und Protest: Zur neuen Mundartliteratur im Elsass," *Recherches germaniques*, no. 7 (1977):197–221; Heinrich Stiehler, "Deutschsprachige Dichtung in Rumänien: Zwischen Utopie und Idylle," *Akzente* 21 (1974):21–52; Heinrich Stiehler, *Paul Celan, Oscar Walter Cisek und die deutschsprachige Gegenwartsliteratur Rumäniens* (Frankfurt: Lang, 1979); Peter Motzan, *Die rumäniendeutsche Lyrik nach 1944: Problemaufriss und historischer Rückblick* (Cluj-Napoca: Dacia, 1980); Alexander Ritter, "Sowjetdeutsche Literatur: Patriotische Akklamation und nationale Existenzbeschreibung," *Akzente* 22 (1975):46–74; Herold Belger, ed., *Zweig eines grossen Baumes: Werdegang der sowjetdeutschen Literatur* (Zelinograd: Kasachstan, 1974).

38. See Heinz Kosok and Horst Priessnitz, eds., *Literaturen in englischer Sprache* (Bonn: Bouvier, 1977).

39. Ewald Gerhard Seeliger, *Peter Voss, der Millionendieb* (Berlin: Ullstein, n.d.).

40. Roger Manderscheid, *Leerläufe* (Esch-Alzette: Kramer-Muller, 1978), 10.

Contributors

WILLI PAUL ADAMS is Professor of North American History at the John F. Kennedy Institute for North American Studies of the Freie Universität Berlin. He is the author of *Republikanische Verfassung und bürgerliche Freiheit: Die Verfassungen und politischen Ideen der amerikanischen Revolution* (1973), has recently edited *Die deutschsprachige Auswanderung in die Vereinigten Staaten: Berichte über Forschungsstand und Quellenbestände* (1980), and published "Die Assimilationsfrage in der amerikanischen Einwanderungsdiskussion, 1890–1930" in *Amerikastudien/American Studies* 27 (1982). He is presently directing a research project, sponsored by the Stiftung Volkswagenwerk, on the assimilation of German-Americans between 1830 and 1930.

AGNES BRETTING is a contributing scholar of the research project "Edition und Dokumentation zur deutschen Amerika-Auswanderung im 19. und 20. Jahrhundert" being carried out by the History Department of the University of Hamburg. She is the author of *Soziale Probleme deutscher Einwanderer in New York City, 1800–1860* (1981) and has written on the Little Germanies of the United States and the Americanization of German immigrants. Her study *Die Funktion und Organisation der Auswanderungsagenturen in Deutschland im 19. Jahrhundert* is to appear soon.

KATHLEEN NEILS CONZEN is Associate Professor of History at the University of Chicago. She is the author of *Immigrant Milwaukee, 1836–1860: Accommodation and Community in a Frontier City* (1976) and of the "Germans" entry in the *Harvard Encyclopedia of American Ethnic Groups* (1980). She is currently working on a study of German immigrant farmers in Minnesota and on an overall interpretation of German-American ethnicity.

JÜRGEN EICHHOFF is Professor of German at the University of Wisconsin-Madison. He is a linguistic geographer with the two-volume *Wortatlas der deutschen Umgangssprachen* (1977, 1978) to his credit. His areas of professional interest are the present-day German language and German-English cultural contacts in North America. His publications on the German language in America include "Deutsch als Siedlersprache in den Vereinigten Staaten" in *Festschrift für Gerhard Cordes*, vol. 2 (1976) and "Niederdeutsche Mundarten in Nordamerika: Geschichte und Bibliographie" in *Niederdeutsches Jahrbuch* 104 (1981).

JOSHUA A. FISHMAN is Distinguished University Research Professor of Social Sciences at Yeshiva University in New York. He is the author (or coauthor) of *Language Loyalty in the United States* (1966), *Bilingualism in the Barrio* (1971), *Language in Sociocultural Change* (1972), *The Spread of English* (1977), *Bilingual Education: An International Sociological Perspective* (1976), and *The Rise and Fall of the Ethnic Revival* (1985). He is also the founder and general editor of the *International Journal of the Sociology of Language* and of the book series *Contributions to the Sociology of Language* and *Contributions to the Sociology of Jewish Languages*.

PATRICIA HERMINGHOUSE is Professor of German at the University of Rochester. She is editor of the series *Crosscurrents: Writings of German Political Emigrés in Nineteenth-Century America* (48 vols., 1984–). In addition to articles on women as writers, East German literature, and nineteenth-century literature, she has edited *Literatur und Literaturtheorie in der DDR* (1976) and *Literatur der DDR in den siebziger Jahren* (1983) with Peter Uwe Hohendahl and an anthology of contemporary women writers for American students, *Frauen im Mittelpunkt* (1984).

JOHN A. HOSTETLER is Professor of Sociology and Anthropology at Temple University in Philadelphia. His interests lie in both traditional and modern communitarian societies and their socialization practices. His publications include *Hutterite Society* (1974), *Amish Society* (1968), *Children in Amish Society* (1971), and *The Hutterites in North America* (1967). He has served as expert witness in a number of legal cases involving education and environmental problems of minorities in the United States and Canada.

MARION L. HUFFINES is Associate Professor of German and Linguistics at Bucknell University in Lewisburg, Pennsylvania. Her research has recently focused on the English of the Pennsylvania Germans and her publications include "English in Contact with Pennsylvania German" in *German Quarterly* 53 (1980); "The English of the Pennsylvania Germans: A Reflection of Ethnic Affiliation" in *German Quarterly* 57 (1984); and "Pennsylvania German Stereotype: Particles, Prepositions, and Adverbs" in *Yearbook of German-American Studies* 19 (1984).

HAROLD JANTZ is Professor Emeritus of German at Duke University where his famous collection of German Americana and early editions from the Renaissance through the age of Goethe is now housed. The collection of German Americana printed before 1801 is the largest in the United States, and his collection of nineteenth-century German Americana is equally comprehensive. He is the author of *The Form of Faust: The Work of Art and Its Intrinsic Structures* (1978) as well as numerous publications on American-German literary relations and early American literature.

HARTMUT KEIL is the Director of the Chicago Projekt at the Amerika Institut of the University of Munich and a scholar in modern American history, immigration, and labor history. He has recently published *German Workers in Industrial Chicago, 1850–1910* (with John Jentz, 1983) and "Chicago-Projekt: Arbeitswelt und Lebensweise deutscher Arbeiter in Chicago, 1850–1915" in *Amerikastudien/American Studies* 29 (1984) and has edited *Sind oder waren Sie Mitglied? Verhörprotokolle über unamerikanische Aktivitäten* (1979); and *Deutsche Arbeiterkultur in Chicago von 1850 bis zum Ersten Weltkrieg. Eine Anthologie* (1984).

FREDERICK C. LUEBKE is Professor of History and Director of the Center for Great Plains Studies at the University of Nebraska-Lincoln. Among his publications are *Immigrants and Politics: The Germans of Nebraska, 1880–1900* (1968), *Bonds of Loyalty: German Americans and World War I* (1974), and several edited books including *Ethnicity on the Great Plains* (1980).

JOHN A. McCARTHY is Associate Professor of German at the University of Pennsylvania and has written on eighteenth-century German and European literature. His publications include *Fantasy and Reality: An Epistemological Approach to Wieland* (1974) as well as essays on Wieland, Schiller, and the reading public. He is also actively involved in the current reforms of German language teaching in the United States.

JOSEPH G. McVEIGH is Assistant Professor of German at Smith College. He is the author of *Kontinuität und Vergangenheitsbewältigung in der österreichischen Nachkriegsliteratur* (1986) and essays on modern German and Austrian literature.

GÜNTER MOLTMANN is Professor of Medieval and Modern History (with special reference to Overseas History) at the University of Hamburg. Since 1978 he has directed several research projects on German immigration to North America which were funded by the Stiftung Volkswagenwerk. The volume *Germans to America: 300 Years of Immigration, 1683–1983* (1982) is based on some of the results. His publications include *Amerikas Deutschlandpolitik im Zweiten Weltkrieg* (1958), *Atlantische Blockpolitik im 19. Jahrhundert* (1973), *Aufbruch nach Amerika: Friedrich List und die Auswanderung aus Baden und Württemberg 1816/1817* (1979), and the edition *Deutsche Amerikaauswanderung im 19. Jahrhundert* (1978).

STEVEN MULLER, President of the Johns Hopkins University, was born in Hamburg and came to the United States at the age of thirteen. He received his Ph.D. from the Department of Government at Cornell University, where he later taught. He is the author of a textbook in comparative government and a number of articles in this field. He was the founding chairman of the National Association of Independent Colleges and Universities and served as a member of presidential commissions on White House fellowships and on world hunger.

CAROL POORE is Assistant Professor of German at Brown University. Her publications in the area of German-American relations include *German-American Socialist Literature, 1865–1900* (1982). She is currently collaborating with Patricia Herminghouse on the reprint series *Crosscurrents: Writings of German Political Emigrés in Nineteenth-Century America.*

ALEXANDER RITTER has written on Sealsfield, J. G. Müller, Raabe, and the field of German-American literary relations. The publications of his Arbeitsstelle Steinberger Studien, Itzehoe, have raised new scholarly interest in German literature outside German-speaking countries. He is the editor of *Auslandsdeutsche Literatur der Gegenwart* (13 vols. since 1974); *Deutschlands literarisches Amerikabild* (1977); Karl Kurt Klein's *Literaturgeschichte des Deutschtums im Ausland* (1979, with a bibliography for the years 1945–78); and *Deutschsprachige Literatur im Ausland* (1985).

LEO SCHELBERT is Professor of History at the University of Illinois at Chicago. He is the author of *Einführung in die schweizerische Auswanderungsgeschichte der Neuzeit* (1976) among other books and has published a series of articles relating to immigration to North America, especially by Swiss and South German groups.

CHRISTOPH E. SCHWEITZER is Professor of German at the University of North Carolina and has published on topics from the seventeenth to the nineteenth centuries. Special areas have been seventeenth-century Spanish-German relations, early German-American authors, German literary manuscripts in American collections, and the function of works of art in fiction. He is the editor of Albrecht

Goes's *Das Löffelchen* (1968), Lessing's *Nathan der Weise* (1970 and 1984), and Francis Daniel Pastorius's *Deliciæ Hortenses or Garden-Recreations* (1982).

HANS L. TREFOUSSE, Professor of History, teaches at Brooklyn College and the Graduate Center of the City University of New York. He is the author of *Germany and American Neutrality, 1939–41* (1951), *Ben Butler* (1957), *Benjamin Franklin Wade* (1964), *The Radical Republicans: Lincoln's Vanguard for Radical Justice* (1969), and *Impeachment of a President: Andrew Johnson, the Blacks, and Reconstruction* (1975). His most recent venture in German-American history is a biography of Carl Schurz, published in 1982.

FRANK TROMMLER is Professor of German at the University of Pennsylvania. He has written on modern German literary, cultural, and social history. Among his works are *Roman und Wirklichkeit* (1966), *Sozialistische Literatur in Deutschland* (1976), *Die Kultur der Weimarer Republik* (with Jost Hermand, 1978), *Jahrhundertwende* (coed., 1982), and *Der Mythos Jugend "Mit uns zieht die neue Zeit"* (coed., 1985).

MARIA WAGNER is Professor of German at Rutgers University and has published in the fields of modern German literature, German-American literary relations, and feminism. She is the editor of *Basic Concepts in the Humanities* (with J. Ainsworth) and *Perspectives and Personalities* (with R. Ley et al.) and has broken new ground with her works on Mathilde Anneke: *Mathilde Franziska Anneke. Eine deutsche Dichterin des Vormärz und amerikanische Feministin* (1980), and *Die gebrochenen Ketten. Erzählungen, Reportagen, Reden von Mathilde Anneke* (ed., 1983).

MARTHA KAARSBERG WALLACH is Associate Professor of Humanistic Studies and German at the University of Wisconsin-Green Bay. She has published on the topics of German immigrant women and women writers, German literature of the eighteenth and nineteenth centuries, and the German film and is the author of *Heinrich Heine: Elitism and Social Concern* (1972).

HERMANN WELLENREUTHER is Professor of History at the University of Göttingen. He has published numerous articles on Pennsylvania history and colonial history in general as well as on eighteenth-century English history. He is the author of *Glaube und Politik in Pennsylvania, 1681–1776* (1972) and *Repräsentation und Grundbesitz in England, 1730–1770* (1979).

MARIANNE WOKECK is Associate Editor of *The Papers of William Penn* (The Historical Society of Pennsylvania). She is the author of *A*

Tide of Alien Tongues: The Flow and Ebb of the German Immigration to Pennsylvania, 1683–1776 (1983) as well as various publications dealing with German immigration to America and German immigrant culture in Pennsylvania.

STEPHANIE GRAUMAN WOLF is Associate Professor of History and Director of the Program in Early American Culture at the University of Delaware. Her research concentrates on social history of the colonial period, the development of ethnic cultures in America, and Pennsylvania German history. She has published *The Sound of Time: A History of Western Man and His Music* (with N. W. Hess, 1968) and *Urban Village: Population, Community, and Family Structure in Germantown, Pennsylvania, 1683–1800* (1976).

DON YODER is Professor of Folklife Studies and Adjunct Professor of Religious Studies at the University of Pennsylvania, where he teaches courses in Pennsylvania German history and ethnography. He has written widely in the field of Pennsylvania German studies. His books include *Songs along the Mahantongo* (1951, 1964), *Pennsylvania Spirituals* (1961), *Symposium on Folk Religion* (1974), *American Folklife* (1976), *Pennsylvania German Immigrants, 1709–1786* (1981), and *Rhineland Emigrants* (1982). He was the cofounder and editor (1961–78) of *Pennsylvania Folklife*. His Roughwood Collection (with William Woys Weaver) is the largest personal collection of objects and texts documenting Pennsylvania German cultural history.

Index

Emancipation movement (*continued*)
  German-American literature
  for women
    fiction writing on, 334, 340
    journalistic writing on, 326
Employment
  and German-American socialist move-
    ment, 176–87
  opportunities for, affecting immigra-
    tion, 4, 6, 11, 12, 18, 35
  and work habits of Pennsylvania Ger-
    mans, 111
  and working-class culture, 189–206.
    See also Working-class culture
England, in colonial America, 85–105
  and loyalty of Pennsylvania Germans
    to, 89, 91–92, 94
Englischer Sprachlehrer, 237
English language
  in assimilation process, 135, 138, 228,
    247, 249–50
  in church services, 247, 248
  German words in, 96, 238
  Pennsylvania Germans using, 45, 46,
    47, 54, 57, 90, 93–94, 236, 237
  in colonial America, 90, 93–94
  in Germantown, 71
  trend toward use of, 247–50
Essellen, Christian, 136
Ethnicity of German immigrants, 129–
  220
  American stereotypes concerning,
    208–12
  in Brazil, 207–20
  and Centennial celebrations of 1876,
    176–87
  in Chicago, 189–206
  Civil War affecting, 140
  definition of, 133, 140, 144
  invention of, 131–47
  and language used, 135, 138, 140, 141,
    228–30, 249–50, 258–59
  leadership functions in, 148–59
  literature on, 134–35
  in melting pot model, 133, 134, 137,
    138–40, 141, 143, 145
  and national loyalties, 90–91, 94, 141,
    156–57
  in nineteenth century, events in Ger-
    many affecting, 160–75

in Pennsylvania, 41–65
in pluralist model, 133, 134, 137, 140–
  43, 144
preserved in assimilation process,
  131–47
Puck cartoon on, 131, 132, 133
sense of superiority in, 136, 139, 140,
  209, 211–12
  in Brazil, 212–13, 215, 217
  in separatist model, 134, 137–38
  sociability in, 137, 139, 140, 154
  in socialist movement, 176–88
  unification of Germany affecting,
    160–75
  and working class culture, 189–206
  relationship of, 201
Ethnic writing, critical comments on,
  343–56
Exiles, The, 332–36, 337, 339–40

Fabricius, Johann, 291
Family immigration to America, in eigh-
  teenth century, 5, 8
Fersammlinge (Versammling), 54, 59
Fickert, Kurt, 349
Fiction written by German-Americans
  role of female characters in, 331–41
  serialized in newspapers, 306–20
  by women immigrants, 331–41
Folk model of Mennonite community,
  107
Fontane, Theodor, 284
Foreign languages. *See* Languages, non-
  English
Forty-eighters, 51, 131, 136, 141, 160,
  162, 308, 309, 326, 327
Fourth of July celebrations, of German-
  American socialists, 176–87
France
  German-language literature in, 351
  in war with Prussia (1870), 161, 162,
    163, 164, 168–71
Franklin, Benjamin, 86, 87, 227–28
  printing press of, 300
Frederick III of Prussia and Germany,
  167, 172
Fröbel, Julius, 135–36
Furly, Benjamin, 4
Furniture styles of Germantown crafts-
  men, 71–73

Germany (*continued*)
  ethnic leadership in defense of, 156–57
  financing travel costs of poor immi-
    grants, 17–18
  legislation concerning emigration,
    25–38
  nineteenth-century events in, affecting
    German-American ethnicity,
    160–75
Gerstäcker, Friedrich, 311, 317
Gong, Alfred, 348
Government
  of colonial America, attitude of Penn-
    sylvania Germans toward, 88,
    89–90
  election of German-Americans to, 151,
    155–56, 225
  of Germany. *See* Germany
  legislation of. *See* Legislation
Gruber, Johann Adam, 290
Grundsow Lodches, 54

Halfern, Albert von, 285
Harbaugh, Henry, 60
Haymarket Affair in Chicago, 184, 185,
  210
Hecker, Friedrich, 164–65
Heine, Heinrich, 306, 321
Helmuth, Justus, 50, 299
Herdegen, Johann, 291
Hermann's Monument, in New Ulm,
  Minnesota, 142
Heroes, cultural, 153
Hiester, William, 227
Holiday celebrations of German-
  American socialists, 176–87
Holzer, Burghild, 349
House of Representatives, German-
  Americans elected to, 151,
  155–56, 225
Houses in Germantown, architectural
  history of, 70–71, 75–81
Hughes, John, 89
Hunnius, Anton Christian, 286
Hutterites, German-speaking, 235, 236,
  242
Hymns of German-Americans, 295, 296,
  298, 300

Identity, ethnic. *See* Ethnicity of German
  immigrants
Immigration, 1–38
  and American stereotypes of immi-
    grants, 208–12
  areas of destination in
    Brazil, 207–20
    geographical distribution of, 223,
      224, 225
    New York City, 33, 34, 35
    Pennsylvania, 3–13. *See also* Penn-
      sylvania Germans
    Texas, 232
    Wisconsin, 233–34
  areas of origin in, 42–43, 223
    of Chicago's German population, 192
    as Dutch or German, 68–69
    of Pennsylvania immigrants, 42–43,
      68, 70, 77, 223, 230–31
    and regional dialects, 230–31
    of Texas immigrants, 232
    of Wisconsin immigrants, 233
  and assimilation, 131–45. *See also* As-
    similation of German immigrants
  and deportation of unwanted immi-
    grants, 35
  in eighteenth century, 3–13, 14, 61
    and English-German relations, 85–105
    expectations concerning, 87–88
    hazards of, 9–10
    legislation regulating, 28–29
    on recommendations of former
      migrants, 7, 11
    as traditional response to adversities,
      3–4, 5–6, 12
    transatlantic transportation in, 4,
      6–11, 12, 26
  experience of, affecting German-
    American literature, 345, 350
  and generational changes of children
    born in America
    in Chicago, 192, 195, 201, 203
    in German language use, 94, 228,
      230, 254, 258, 262–63
  and head tax collected on incoming
    passengers, 35, 36
  historical phases of, 14
  legislation regulating, 25–38

Nast, Thomas, 168
National Society for German Emigrants, 31
Nationalism
in Europe, xxx–xxxi
of German immigrants. *See* Loyalties of German immigrants
Negelein, Joachim, 291
Neighborhood analysis, of Chicago's German workers, 196–97
Neisser, Georg, 90
Newlanders, recruiting new immigrants, 7, 11, 26
antisolicitation laws on, 26–27, 29
Newspapers
in German language, 228, 246, 247–48
during World War I, 216, 217
in Germany, representation of America in, 321–30
serialized installments of mystery novels in, 306–20
New York City
immigration to, in nineteenth century, 33, 34, 35
socialist movement in, 183, 185
New-Yorker Staats-Zeitung, 164, 165
New York Volkszeitung, 183, 186
Niers, Gert, 349
Nineteenth century
Centennial celebration of 1876 in, reaction of German-American socialists to, 176–87
Civil War in. *See* Civil War
German-American ethnicity in, events in Germany affecting, 160–75
German-American literature in, 285, 286
journalistic writing, 321–30
serial novels, 306–20
immigration in, 14–24. *See also* Immigration, in nineteenth century
working-class culture in, 189–206
Norms, in assimilation process, 133, 134
Novels
anti-American, 285
serialized installments of, in antebellum era, 306–20

Pastorius, Francis Daniel, 3, 68, 77, 287, 290–91, 295–96

"Beehive" manuscript of, 287, 295–96
Pastorius, Melchior Adam, 291
Patriotism of German immigrants, 141. *See also* Loyalties of German immigrants
Paul, Jean, 289
Pemberton, Israel, 86
Penn, William, 3
Pennsylvania Dutch, 44–45, 68–69, 231
Pennsylvania German dialect, 45–47, 230–31, 238, 242–45
church services in, 57, 235–36, 243, 265
maintenance of, 242–45
radio programs in, 261
regional variations in, 231
in schools, 58, 263
sense of ethnicity in, 54
social evenings promoting, 54, 56
theater programs in, 58
in twentieth century, 54–57, 58, 234, 243–45, 271
Pennsylvania Germans, 39–127
areas of origin of, 42–43, 68, 70, 77, 223, 230–31
arriving before 1808, 61
assimilation of, 41–42, 43, 45–50, 93–94
in colonial America, 91, 93–94
German opposition to, 50–51
in language, 45–47
pressure for, 93–94
in religion, 47–50
in colonial America, 3–12, 61
assimilation of, 91, 93–94
attitudes toward government and authority of, 88, 89–90
communal life of, 90–91
in Germantown, 66–84
languages used by, 90, 93–94
loyalties of, 89, 91–92, 94
relations with English settlers, 85–105
English-speaking, 90, 93–94, 236, 237
ethnic identity of, 41–65
Germanizing movement among, 50–51
German-speaking. *See* German language use, in Pennsylvania
in Germantown, 66–84. *See also* Germantown, Pennsylvania